European Notebooks

European Notebooks

New Societies and Old Politics, 1954-1985

François Bondy

With an introduction by
Melvin J. Lasky

Routledge
Taylor & Francis Group

LONDON AND NEW YORK

First published 2005 by Transaction Publishers

Published 2017 by Routledge
2 Park Square, Milton Park, Abingdon, Oxon OX14 4RN
711 Third Avenue, New York, NY 10017, USA

First issued in paperback 2018

Routledge is an imprint of the Taylor & Francis Group, an informa business

Copyright © 2005 by Taylor & Francis

All rights reserved. No part of this book may be reprinted or reproduced or utilised in any form or by any electronic, mechanical, or other means, now known or hereafter invented, including photocopying and recording, or in any information storage or retrieval system, without permission in writing from the publishers.

Notice:
Product or corporate names may be trademarks or registered trademarks, and are used only for identification and explanation without intent to infringe.

Library of Congress Catalog Number: 2005043723

Library of Congress Cataloging-in-Publication Data
Bondy, François, 1915-
   European notebooks : new societies and old politics.
     p. cm.
   Includes index.
   ISBN 0-7658-0271-6 (acid-free paper)
    1. Europe—Civilization—20th century. 2. Europe—Intellectual life—20th century. I. Lasky, Melvin. II. Title.

CB205.B65   2005
940.55—dc22   2005043723

ISBN 13: 978-1-138-50980-1 (pbk)
ISBN 13: 978-0-7658-0271-2 (hbk)

Contents

Introduction: François Bondy: A Man of Letters Melvin J. Lasky	ix

The 1950s

A Moment in Budapest	3
"Asia": Does It Exist?	6
Paris on the Psychoanalyst's Couch	9
Young Spain and the Old Régime	13
The Sick Man of Europe is...Europe: Thoughts after Kennan	26

The 1960s

Letter from Jerusalem: On Misunderstanding Eichmann	35
Letter from Berlin: The Pilloried Pope	44
Letter from Paris: The New Puritans	50
The Struggle for Kafka and Joyce: A Conversation between Hans Mayer and François Bondy	55
Notes on a Lady Mandarin	68
Letter from Prague: The Empty Pedestal	78
Letter from Paris: The Forty Immortal Chairs	93
Letter from Paris: Decline of the French Left	103

The 1970s

Letter from Paris: The Idiot, or Sartre's Flaubert	113
D'Annunzio and Mussolini: New Letters	119
Letter from France: New Society, Old Politics	126
Letter from Rome: Italy's "Cultural Crisis"	129
Frantz Fanon: "Black Orpheus" of the Homeless Left	134

Letter from Paris: As Sartre Grows Old	141
Letter from Zurich: "What Thinketh Solzhenitsyn?"	144
The Quest for Serendip	146
"Where Have All the Flowers Gone?"—The New Left Today	148
Ignazio Silone at 75	152
European Notebook: What's Left	154
European Notebook: Arguing about Fascism	157
European Notebook: Giants on the French Left: Thorez and Aragon	162
European Notebook: Porno-O; A New Prince?; Régis Debray's Novel	167
European Notebook: On the Death of Pasolini	173
European Notebook: *Le Monde*; Italian Censorship; Solzhenitsyn and Spain	178
European Notebook: Telos	184
European Notebook: Heidegger; Amalrik	186
European Notebook: Doris Kearns and Lyndon Johnson; Polish Democracy; Andrey Amalrik	190
European Notebook: Miracle in Milan	195
European Notebook: Dictatorships and the EEC; Religion in America; French Elections	197
European Notebook: Budapest's October; The Two Cultures; Nathalie Sarraute	201
European Notebook: *Le Canard Enchaîné*; Murder in Rome	206
European Notebook: Alain Peyrefitte; Death of Prince de Broglie	209
European Notebook: Boris Souvarine; "Gambizzazzione"; "Execution" in Turin; On the French Left	212
Prize Winners	219
Between Frost and Thaw	221
Terror Targets	223

The 1980s

European Diary: The Line of Non-Alignment	227
European Diary: The Very Latest from Paris	229
European Diary: The Veterans	232
European Diary: How to Relax in the Cold War	236

European Diary: The Comeback of Drieu La Rochelle	239
European Diary: Of Passing Scandals	242
European Diary: "Russian" (Good), "Soviet" (Bad)...	245
Mauriac, between Province and Paris	248
European Diary: Milosz, the Unknown	252
J-J S-S Rides Again	255
European Diary: Incident in Vitry; "Terza Pagina"; Exit This Way	258
European Diary: French Ideology	265
European Diary: Sartre, a Year Later	267
European Diary: A Dividend for Marchais; Italian Miracle	271
European Diary: On the Death of a Friend: Romain Gary	275
A Man and His Double	279
European Diary: Where is Prussia?; In the Vienna Woods	281
European Diary: Ceremonial Farewell; The Lowenthal Paper	285
Thinking about Flaubert	292
European Diary: Mosques in the Factory; "1983"; News of the Day; Wajda's *Danton*	296
European Diary: Boomerangs?; The Trial Begins; Germans Among Themselves; Latin Learners	305
European Diary: More Sartriana; Kisielewski and Warsaw; Genet's Comeback; Bettino Craxi	315
Manès Sperber	326
European Diary: Words, Phrases, Conceits; Of the Once and Future Leader; German Illusions: Remembering Wroclaw	329
Sherlock Holmes and Socialist Realism	339
Kultura's Achievement	342
The Crown Jurist: The Death of Carl Schmitt	345
Raymond Aron	349
Index	357

Introduction

François Bondy: A Man of Letters

Melvin J. Lasky

To write about the passing of a close friend, with whom intellectual life and personal affairs have intimately bound one for half of a long lifetime, is necessarily to be involved in private reminiscence. One could try to offer a portrait in ideas to sketch the large outlines of important literary and political controversies, and to evaluate the contribution made to the cultural life of our contemporary world. But this would smack inappropriately of the finality of an ultimate reckoning rather than of the vibrant tribute to an admirable contemporary whose energy, wit, and knowledge enriched our lives. Too much objectivity would issue in "a ballet of abstract categories." And yet the subjective exercise cannot really remain merely that: it criss-crosses, hurtles and leaps (much like the man himself when he was crossing a city street or cannibalizing a foreign newspaper)...from one year to another, or one genre to another, from the private to the public, from the anecdotal to the intellectual, from little moments of sentiment to large images of reflection.

It was always so. When I first met François Bondy in the early years of the post-World War II era it was not simply—for me at least—an encounter of two young journalists, sharing certain common interests in literature and politics. As a New Yorker, youthfully impressed by the Henry Jamesian notions of the transatlantic relationship—American innocence *vs.* European experience; naïve Yankee optimism *vs.* chastened European weariness—I immediately cast my newfound friend in Zurich as a species of culture-hero. I had read an essay or two of Benedetto Croce; he had translated whole books from the Italian. I told him excitedly about my first impressions of passing through German cities; he told me he had actually been born in Berlin. I expressed my new concern about the political future of Eastern Europe; he told me of his old family connections with Prague (where his father was a prominent man of the theater) and Budapest (where his mother came from). I rehashed a few notions about "Existentialism" which I had gleaned from some badly translated pages of Jaspers and Heidegger in a handbook of philosophy I had read in the Bronx; he offered me his impressions of Sartre and Camus at the Café de Flore.

Of course, these were essentially colorful vignettes of a growing, ripening friendship. But somehow they then appeared—and were indeed—something more. Europeans in both World Wars were struck by (in Woodrow Wilson's phrase) the New World coming to redress the wrongs of the Old. Now, in a new era of transatlantic reconstruction, the culture of the Old World would perhaps be in a position of reciprocity, helping to redress the simplicities of the American mind. The historic process had already begun, with Einstein's scientists in Princeton and Fermi's in Chicago, with the Fritz Lang and Max Reinhardt and Thomas Mann in California, with Marc Chagall and André Masson in Greenwich Village. Translated into a small personal adventure I too was plunged into a historic process of "*Europeanization*." I still find the melodrama of the memory affecting, if somewhat embarrassing, my finding François Bondy in Zurich. What was I looking for? A cicerone to the splendors and miseries of the old-new world? A cosmopolitan intellectual in the spirit of Goethean world-awareness?

I can already see and hear François's quick mind moving towards quite an alternative explanation of those early days of intensity when we dreamt of establishing magazines which would change "the climate of opinion," when we longed to be great readers of a new great literature, when we wanted to play a role in adding critical clarities to simple commitments in a world still endangered by ideological fanaticism. Modesty was of his nature, and sometimes he was infuriatingly indifferent to his own mental uniqueness. No, he would often insist to me, you have it the wrong way around: not European complexity and pessimism would be instructive, but the American optimistic hope that Europe could be free and creative again. Not a Swiss-bound spirit, cut off from the tragic turbulence of twentieth-century disasters, would fructify that which had now to grow and flower; but rather the "stormy petrels" of the large disquiets raging in the world. And so he tried to turn the record of personal history around (in vain, I trust). Accordingly, not he but I was the enterprising Virgilian to the scenes of what was emerging: I had invited him back to Berlin; he had lived tremulously on the borders of the Third Reich but I had been in Dachau on that first day of liberation. He had studied *Sein und Zeit* but I had been in that Black Forest *Skihütte* talking to the philosopher as an existential un-person in disgrace. We had both been in Hungary during the October 1956 revolution but I had published a book on it; etc. No, it wasn't this way at all! This was autobiography through the opposite end of the glass, a curious example of the transformation of values, a case of "transposed heads." On his part it was, as I have suggested, a matter of modesty tempered perhaps by bouts of absent-mindedness. It was he, even if he sometimes seemed to forget it, who was the moving spirit, he who was blessed with the *élan vital*.

This curious pattern of mutual stimulation over forty and fifty years became almost a comic routine of high spiritedness. I remember innumerable meetings in Paris at the *Deux Magots*. We would sit at a street table for hours, indulging in short-hand gossip about Silone's circle in Rome (and Chiaromonte's aloofness); Torberg's troubles in Vienna (and the Hapsburg backbiting which afflicted an emigré's return); the tensions between that "odd couple" editing *Encounter* in London (Stephen Spender and Irving Kristol); the depressing transatlantic gap which still separated us from *Commentary* and *Partisan Review* in New York; the valiant if faltering efforts of our friends in Delhi, Tokyo, Buenos Aires and Lagos, to maintain those personal and spiritual contacts without which our shared dream of a truly cosmopolitan intelligentsia would only remain a Western figment, cut off from the global extension of the ideals of a free and creative culture. This had been our faith and commitment from the earliest days when he responded to my effort to establish *Der Monat* in Berlin, and I to his effort to launch *Preuves* in Paris. In a quarter-of-a-century hurling texts and quotations at each other, perhaps these two meant more to us than any other.

The first was from that brilliant Englishman, Cyril Connolly, who wrote of his editing *Horizon* magazine: "Editing a magazine is a form of the good life; it is creating when the world is destroying, helping where it is hindering."

The second was from T. S. Eliot who, when he made his famous pleas for "the unity of European culture" in 1946, explained why he had, as editor of *Criterion* in London, had sought out Max Rychner in Zurich and Croce in Naples (among others):

> The existence of a network of independent reviews, at least one in every capital of Europe, is necessary for the transmission of ideas—and to make possible the circulation of ideas while they are still fresh. The editors of such reviews, and if possible the more regular contributors, should be able to get to know each other personally, to visit each other to entertain each other, to exchange ideas in conversation....Their cooperation should continually stimulate...fertilize and renovate....And through such cooperation should merge into view [that which] is not only of local but of European significance.

This had been our original inspiration, but now with the new and additional range which is the urgency of our time: not merely international but intercontinental; not merely European but with a vital sense of the worldwide unities which embrace Europe, Africa, Asia, and America.

And so back at the café table in the *Deux Magots*, we thought it might be a good idea for Richard Wright, the Negro novelist (as he then was), to go to Bandung and report for all the journals, for me to travel in East and West Africa...for Bondy to visit Tokyo and Rio. The names of then still unknown writers came up: Marquez, Gombrowicz, Grass.

At the end of each such session we had a plan to fill a dozen exciting numbers of any periodical that were at our disposal. We would fold our little scribblings away into our notebooks, drink our last *café noir*, and François would—characteristically, generously, if always mistakenly—pay tribute to my editorial ingenuity. Hour after hour he had spoken freely, ranged widely, stimulated endlessly. I had only been careful and attentive enough to make notes. He was astonished that at the end of hundreds of such pleasurable *causeries* would emerge such an effective program of "editorial creativity" and "literary stimulation" as Connolly and Eliot had called for. He was the *spiritus rectus*; and he will be remembered as the editorial advisor of our time *par excellence*.

Perhaps it was his very quick-wittedness, combining the riches of a well-stocked mind, with a phenomenal memory and an astonishing reading speed, which made him move on from literature to politics, from image to idea, from author to movement, from history to philosophy to current politics, before taking time out to take full stock of the subject he had just illuminated and the perception he was about to formulate. I remember once taking a long airplane ride with him. It was an old propeller machine, and it was difficult in the loudness and noise to talk; we decided to read. From my shopping bag I took out a book, a magazine, and a few newspapers and tried to make as much progress as I could before arrival. But, by the time our plane had landed, François had completed the latest Goncourt Prize-winner, the current collection of Sartre's essays (*Situations IV*, as I recall), Saul Bellow's new novella, a pamphlet by Karl Jaspers (later to be interviewed by him, memorably, in Basle), as well as the series of *reportages* by Moravia from China in the *Corriere della Sera*. He might have mastered whole encyclopedias if one could keep him behind a fastened seatbelt long enough.

If immobility concentrated his mind wonderfully, on the move he was a breathtaking spectacle. I had known him to read and walk, to think and talk, all at once (and still be making mental notes for his next article). At international conferences he would gallop and lurch from plenum to working sessions and back, and we used to say that he was the only person alive who could leave a room before entering it. I remember once in Berlin—it was during the Big Four Conference of Molotov, Eden, Bidault, and Dulles (1954)—when he lost his way somewhere between the Kurfürstendamm and Dahlem, arrived late to the American briefing, threw a quick glance at the advance text of John Foster Dulles' speech, and before one could even hear the rustling of the pages he had inked an embarrassingly missing "NOT" where Dulles was supposed to be telling Molotov that "unlike the USSR the USA is an aggressive imperialist power...." (It was called quickly to the attention of the briefing officer, who red-facedly made the correction; and I once again got credit which was due elsewhere.) Bondy was the most eagle-eyed of proofreaders (and in four or five languages yet).

Early or late, seated or standing, awake or asleep, his incomparable spiritedness would always be darting from point to point, paying attention and idly wandering at once. I sat next to him one Sunday morning at a Werner Höfer TV-*Frühschoppen* in Cologne, which was the leading meet-the-press talk show of the day.

The conversation ambled on in desultory fashion, and I could see from my chair the "monitor" screen in the studio corner, and noted that François had closed his eyes. Had he dozed off? Höfer, as was his wont, suddenly turned from one side to the other and pointedly asked, "Und was meinen Sie dazu, Herr Bondy?..." Surely, having dozed off, M. Bondy could have no opinion on what had been said about the alienation of German intellectuals from the Bonn *Republik*; I was tempted to interrupt and venture some tentative opinion on behalf of both of us. But without further ado he opened his eyes in innocent surprise, and slyly smiling away traces of his slumber, quickly made a number of pertinent distinctions between the alienation of a Grass and Böll as against a Brecht and Hermlin, and the "existential" differences in France between a Sartre and an Aron or Camus.

This kind of *pointillisme* belonged to the painterly design of his mind. Taken all in all, he still continues to represent for me perhaps a Henry Jamesian "*New-man*," that strange and life-enhancing complex of political culture and literary sensibility that only the critical European spirit, with all its creativity and curiosity, has been able to produce. Alas, no single article among the thousands he has written (and there have been magnificent pieces in *Monat*, *Preuves*, and elsewhere) completely recaptures that flex of intellectual suppleness with which he confronts a book, a writer, an event. And no single book, not even the collection of his interviews with famous men, records that distinctive lilt of voice as he rushed to make a point, register a dissent, or round out (with wit or wisdom, sometimes both) an epigrammatic formulation. Somewhere, along the way, he should have found an Eckermann or a Boswell.

And yet no colorful bit of conversation recorded or stylish essay extracted from a yellowing scrap-book of clippings can compare with the remembrance of, and the gratitude for, the "essential Bondy": a liberal and humane democrat from the center of the Western heartland "free of every totalitarian temptation," sturdy and unfailing in his devotion to the liberties and civilities of a humane social order. I mention this last, but it is not least. He has been a splendid comrade (in the gentlest sense of the word); and surely everyone who has ever known him must be reminded by the pieces which I have collected in this anthology of the importance of being sound as well as brilliant.

This "European Journal" contains almost all of the articles, mostly in my quick and rather free translations (although he wrote and spoke English fluently), which he contributed to *Encounter* between its founding, under the Anglo-American editorship of Stephen Spender and Irving Kristol, and its closure in 1990 after thirty years of my editorship. They have, I think, lost nothing of their readability and relevance. Not unlike Orwell, Bondy was a master of the short journalistic report, mixing facts, analysis, and acuity. And as in Orwell's journalism, every little piece deserves to be saved and re-read. They still offer intellectual pleasure, and more than that: his whole work sets many of our current cultural issues in a proper and deeper context. As Karl Jaspers remarked in one of Bondy's wide-ranging interviews, "History didn't begin yesterday afternoon. One must, to catch up, read a lot of old books, to be able to remember the past...." Taken together, the variegated themes he raised in his work as a Zurich journalist, a Paris editor, and a European *homme des lettres* sketch the guidelines for an entrancing portrait of the Intellectual as a Cosmopolitan.[1] In a world of increasing cultural provincialism—a paradoxical side effect of a mindless economic globalization—this remains a worthy ideal; and François Bondy (1915-2003) was one of its most dazzling figures.

January 2004

Note

1. The *London Times* and the *New York Times* (for whom Bondy worked for many years as a roving cultural correspondent) simply couldn't find the space to report his death: in Zurich, on 27 May 2003 at the age of eighty-eight.

    All the other leading newspapers from Paris and Zurich to Vienna and Warsaw —including *Le Monde, Die Welt, Frankfurter Allgemeine Zeitung*, and the *Neue Zürcher Zeitung*—published fitting appreciations.

The 1950s

A Moment in Budapest

On the day I left Budapest—the second of November—most of the foreign journalists crowding the lobby of the Hotel Duna were keenly aware of impending tragedy and disaster. The spokesman for the revolutionary military committee had already forecast, the evening before, the eventuality of "a fight to the death." But on that Friday morning the atmosphere at the office of the Hungarian Writers' Association, next door to the Soviet Embassy, had been entirely different. There, everything was intense and hopeful: a moving and strange air of exhilaration pervaded the rooms. Most of Hungary's distinguished writers were there, working and conferring, for their literary centre was functioning as a kind of brains-trust for Prime Minister Nagy. I listened to the discussions of new plans for reconstruction and education, for various publishing projects, and for a new issue of the literary journal, *Irodalmi Ujság*, which was due to come off the presses in a few hours.

Through an interpreter (for he does not speak any foreign languages) I talked with Peter Veres, chairman of the Writers' Association, a famous peasant writer and political leader, who stood there with his old-fashioned heavy boots and handlebar moustache like some Hungarian Gorki. "We have learned that an author must have the right to keep his silence on political issues, as well as the freedom to speak out on behalf of his community...." As he spoke to me, a peasant from the region of Győr was announced. He tramped in with mud on his boots. He came to ask Veres to get him a publisher for a long manuscript on which he had spent "many, many nights." Veres told him that this, under the circumstances, would have to wait. There was a brief argument. The farmer went into a corner, sulking and muttering. Veres went on to ask me not to publish any complete verbatim accounts of his remarks because "I am, after all, a writer and it is so rare that the spoken word can have style...."

On this last morning, I met again the playwright Julius Hay, in whose house I had spent the previous afternoon. Madame Hay, who is a member of one of the Budapest theater groups, told me how happy she was that her husband's new play, which had been suppressed by the censorship, would be produced as soon as "the patriotic strike of the actors" was over. I asked Hay how it was that he and other "old Bolsheviks" were now openly fighting the Party leadership. He replied: "There were many reasons for the break. The first, I confess, was my instinctive disgust with Stalinism's utter lack of taste and its insensibility in every field of art and letters. As writers, we were all sharply aware of that. Secondly, there was the experience of deep social injustice in our society. A third motive was the glaring failure, even bankruptcy, of our type of economic system. There was finally—and it may have been the most important element—the pressure of our youth...."

"We writers," Hay explained to me, "have always thought of ourselves as the *avant-garde* in the struggle for freedom. This is a Hungarian tradition of which we are very proud.... I was supposed to be a guide for our youth, but in reality, the youth had become a guide for me. For years I had been lecturing them. I gave interminable ideological answers to every question. I could feel that my young listeners found it all very shallow and boring. At first I thought: how strange and incomprehensible it is that we, the older generation, should work so selflessly to build the future of a happier Hungary for our young people, and that these very young people should not care at all! Why were they so blind, so unfeeling, so cold? Gradually I began to wonder. Were they all, every last boy and girl in Hungary, hopeless reactionaries? Or could it be that we, the old men, were wrong, and that they were right? I began to talk with more frankness. I looked at their problems with more openness. In my public meetings, which were attended by eager thousands, I forced myself to answer every question directly. Some weeks ago, they asked me at a meeting in Györ, 'What is happening in our uranium mines?' I knew the Russians were there, but could only answer: 'I just don't know.... But as a Hungarian citizen, I ought to know! And you ought to know! Keep asking!' And so they did."

He went on: "And as for me, I keep on asking too. Have we been building in this country a socialist society, marred only by some ugly distortions, or was this not a horrible regime for which I have no name and which was all distortions and no socialism? Even now, I long for the Party which once had our love and loyalty. But its leadership has destroyed it. It is difficult to love a thing which does not exist. I would still support a new and pure Marxist movement. But I would not want to become a Party member ever again.... Was I courageous in speaking for truth, even under Rakosi? The pressure of the young on us all was so great that I can only say, in the words of one of our poets, 'I was too much of a coward to remain dishonest!' ..."

I talked, too, with Tibor Dery, an inspirer of the Petöfi circle of Hungarian intellectual dissidents, and a Communist of long standing. I was surprised when he asked me to pass on greetings to one of his closest Viennese friends— a well-known Stalinist functionary who has never deviated from the Party line. Yet Tibor Dery told me, in his halting but perfect French, "Cette révolution est la plus grande, la plus pure, que nous ayons connate. Peutt être sera-t-elle la première révolution victoreuse dans toute notre histoire!"

Many of the talks I had with Hungarian writers were recorded on tape by a Swiss radio reporter who traveled with me. In the safety of Vienna, while

Budapest is still burning and armored violence has taken command, while thousands of refugees are pouring across the Western frontier into Austria, I have listened again to these calm, cultured voices, speaking to me in Hungarian, French, German, and Italian. And I am trying helplessly to relate these talks, held in a mood of revolutionary confidence, with the final SOS broadcast three days later from Radio Kossuth in Budapest, that desperate and pathetic appeal for help by the same Hungarian Writers' Association.

ATTENTION ATTENTION DEAR LISTENERS! YOU WILL HEAR NOW THE APPEAL OF THE FEDERATION OF HUNGARIAN WRITERS. THIS IS THE APPEAL OF THE FEDERATION OF HUNGARIAN WRITERS TO EVERY WRITER IN THE WORLD, TO ALL SCIENTISTS, TO ALL WRITERS' FEDERATIONS, TO ALL SCIENTIFIC ASSOCIATIONS, TO THE INTELLECTUAL ELITE OF THE WORLD. WE ASK YOU ALL FOR HELP AND SUPPORT. THERE IS BUT LITTLE TIME. YOU KNOW THE FACTS. THERE IS NO NEED TO GIVE YOU A SPECIAL REPORT. HELP HUNGARY. HELP THE HUNGARIAN PEOPLE. HELP THE HUNGARIAN WRITERS. HELP! HELP! HELP!

They had had the first and the last word in the brief, agonizing moment of Hungarian freedom.

December 1956

"Asia": Does It Exist?

In the course of a recent journey through Southern and Eastern Asia, one fact insistently pressed itself upon my attention: that part of the world which goes by the name o f Asia has no real coherent existence—it is a geographical but not a cultural unit. The villages of Japan have far more in common with those of Denmark than with those of India. The Mohammedan of Karachi is much closer to his co-worshipper in Egypt than to his Hindu neighbor in Bombay. The concept "Asia" is a figment of the Western mind, which has little connection with reality—even when used by Asian statesmen.

This statement may perhaps be challenged on the ground that "Europe" is also no more than a geographical concept. But there is a fundamental difference. Europe retains its essential unity in spite of national divisions and local contrasts. It does so by virtue of the cultural heritage that is shared by all European peoples: the longing for European union has deep-rooted origins in the rearm of ideas, as well as in that of practical problems. An educated European is a man whose cultural background embraces the whole European tradition, and who feels himself a part of a European community of ideas that commands his loyalty and affection. And this is so, irrespective of whether he belongs to the Middle Ages, to the Renaissance, to the period of Voltaire, or to that of Goethe, Croce, Toynbee, or Ortega.

In contrast, it can fairly be said that not one of the leading personalities of the Asian world can claim to possess a viewpoint that would embrace all the Asian civilizations. One evening in Bombay, I met the outstanding Japanese writer, Kyo Komatsu, in the company of a group of Indian writers. With the exception of Gandhi's autobiography, Komatsu had not read a single book by an Indian author. And even his appreciation of Gandhi—a fellow "activist"—was not exactly intimate He talked first about recent developments in Japanese literature and then about Malraux, Camus, Orwell, and Hemingway. It was soon evident that the only common topic of conversation between Japanese and Indian was the work of Western writers. I spent most of the evening acting as interpreter between the Japanese (who spoke French) and the Indians (who spoke English).

On another occasion, I spent an afternoon at Madras in the company of the leading writers in the Telugu and Tamil languages. I later discovered that these writers, who were of outstanding caliber, were almost unknown among Maharati, Bengali, Hindu, Urdu, or Gujarati literary circles. In fact, the educated Indian only knows of the work of writers outside his own community in so far as it has been translated into English—the common language of independent India. For the most part, he is far better versed in English than in Indian literature.

In Siam and Burma there is even clearer evidence of these two parallel tendencies in the outlook of educated Asians; on the one hand, the return to the narrow—if deep—cultural traditions of their own community, and on the other, the urge towards the acceptance of Western literature. Sometimes these two movements combine in a strange fashion. In Siam there is a literary cult of the writing of legends, fables, and epic poems, based on the national folklore; one of the leading exponents of this school, Prince Prem Burachatra, prefers to write his country's folklore in the English or French language, because he feels more at home in the Western tongue. Again, it is a remarkable fact that the centre of literary life in Burma is the "Translation Society" where works by foreign authors, and in particular those from the Western countries, are translated into the Burmese language; it is the activity of these translators that has played a major part in transforming the Burmese language into a modern literary medium.

In Ceylon, I was present at an animated discussion in the seminary at Colombo on the subject of the reestablishment of the Singhalese and Tamil languages in place of English. The return to the mother tongue as the language of literature offers enormous advantages, particularly because it gives scope for the creation of new forms of expression, which are not likely to take root in a foreign language, even if it is perfectly known. But in Ceylon this return has the grave disadvantage that it brings to the fore the profound differences which exist between the indigenous languages: it creates a risk of mutual isolation, and consequently of the collapse of cultural life among the Singhalese and Tamil populations.

The tendency of each of the Asian peoples to return to its native heritage of religion, customs, and literature, together with a general readiness to accept the standards of literary accomplishment embodied in the work of the great Western authors, seems *to* leave no room for the development of a genuine cultural community in Asia. Interest in world literature, which is extremely strong in Asia, is almost exclusively limited to the literature of the European countries. In this respect, literature occupies a unique position, for European music arouses no interest, except in Japan, and European painting only interests the Asian artists living in Paris.

Contemporary Western authors provide the cultural background of the educated classes in Asia. In Japan, more than fifty thousand copies of Camus's novel, *The Plague*, were sold in a few months. In Tokyo, the students cried in the streets when they heard that André Gide had died. In Pakistan, T. S. Eliot is just as famous as in England. In Calcutta, the director of a theatre asked me whether it would be possible to obtain the rights for a performance of the latest play by Sartre. Russian literature is accepted as part of the common fund of Western culture. The great Russian storytellers, from Gogol to Gorki, are read everywhere, and their influence is as strong as it is widespread. Even contemporary Russian literature, which is, on the whole, not in the first rank of contemporary writing, is regarded by educated Asians as part of Western literature. The only breach in this universal preference for Western culture has been made by the impact of contemporary Chinese writing on Japan; but the Eastern part of Asia has in any case a degree of cultural unity absent from the rest of this vast continent.

Even the revolt against the West and against the hegemony of Western countries is itself linked to the assimilation of Western ideas. Their modernity is valued as an instrument of progress. A local judge at Lahore told me, with a wealth of detail, of his studies of the writings of Russell, Dewey, and Sartre. His view was: "I concentrate on studying Western authors because they are useful in our work of social progress. As for our own writers, I read them for pleasure, but with no sense of purpose."

In the last resort it is the power of local tradition that is the determining cause of the absence of any unifying "Asian" consciousness. For seven hundred years, Indians and Mohammedans have lived together side by side. But as soon as external compulsion was removed, two new and different countries inexorably took shape. Even the existence of a common bond among the inhabitants of continental India is a remote prospect, and the possibility of a common basis of life between continental India and Ceylon is absolutely inconceivable—in spite of their membership in 'the Commonwealth, that sole supra-national link which is still a living force in Asia.

The strongest common cultural bond in Asia is Buddhism. A large part of Asia, which is dominated by Buddhism, could form a truly united cultural community. But in the new states that have grown up in Asia, the religious element has been hardly more significant than it was in the case of the national states that were formed in nineteenth-century Europe. It is possible that devotion to Buddhism may succeed in limiting nationalist passions more effectively than did Christianity in Europe. In any case, one may hope that Asia will be able to assimilate Western influences and experiences without repeating all Western mistakes, and especially without taking as their model a Balkanized Europe. The breakup of the British Empire has about the same significance for contemporary Asia as did the break up of the Hapsburg Monarchy for Europe. The disappearance of this overriding unifying power has created a void, and communalism, Communism, and petty fanaticisms of all kinds are rushing in to fill the gap.

January 1954

Paris on the Psychoanalyst's Couch

Can a great city be shown, like a patient, into the consulting room of a psychoanalyst, placed upon a couch, and asked to let her subconscious speak? Frédéric Hoffet, a Protestant minister from Alsace who has been converted to psychoanalysis and who had already created a stir with his previous book *Psychoanalysis of Alsace,* has bent over Paris in his role of psychiatrist and has come up with a *Psychanalyse de Paris,* in which he so thoroughly analyses the spirit and magic of the city that nothing remains of her but an enormous scandal.

Diatribes against great cities have existed at lease from Old Testament times (Babylon, the great whore), and, though the style may have altered from prophetic ardor to scientific pedantry, the content remains similar: the great city is a parasite on the country, a hothouse of decadence and of every perversion, the seat of spiritual disease and moral decomposition. In the course of centuries, much has been written about Paris—the favoritism of her salons, the capricious, centralized authority of her bureaucracy, the immorality of her intelligentsia. Even such an ardent admirer of Paris as Balzac sketches, in *The Girl with the Golden Eyes* and many other books, the vision of a city spectral and perverted, feverishly living and rapidly exhausted. Hoffet's tirade against Paris divers from its many predecessors by reason of its prosaic and humorless presumption. But why has it provoked the entire literary world of Paris into so violent a reaction? Why, from among the dozens of books about Paris which appear in Paris every month, has this one in particular created such a stir?

The provinces of France live for and by themselves and stand on firm foundations. But Paris, in part at least, lives by her "aura," by the image that the world has of her. Nowadays especially, Paris embodies, far more than does the French state, France's claim to be a world power. Paris remains—incomparably more than London, New York, Washington, or Moscow—the place that provides a measure for ideas and fashions. Throughout the fields of intellect and taste, Paris asserts her authority; whoever touches this, endangers the nation's prestige. And because today this authority is no longer so self-evident as it has been for three centuries, she has become more sensitive to attack.

The collective Parisian with whom Hoffet is concerned is admittedly not representative of the millions of inhabitants of Paris and her environs, but only of the few hundred personalities who belong to the "inner circle" of *le tout Paris,* and who, it is alleged, hold in their hands every decision in politics, society, and literature, as successors to the Court of the past. But, explains Hoffet, in these circles charm and not merit, influence and not ability are decisive; and because all who wish to succeed are compelled to make themselves as pleasant and as popular as possible, since Paris is not an objective but an affective society, feminine, courtesan-like, and narcissistic trades develop at the expense of the really masculine qualities. Hence homosexuality becomes for him the true symbol, and the most important symptom, of the Parisian intelligentsia and so of Parisian decadence; at this point, of course, the names of Proust, Gide, Cocteau, and Genet must appear.

Every feminine group—including, therefore, Paris—loves to be subjugated by the masculine, conquering, imperious type. *Cherchez l'homme*: Hoffet does not need to look far, for he has already found him—it is the foreigner. Moreover, this former Protestant pastor has what in his terminology one would have to call a masochistic complex: he is particularly suspicious of Protestants. Even the Jews of Eastern Europe, he writes, are capable of being assimilated into Paris. But the Protestants, and especially Swiss Protestants, whose dominant influence in present-day Paris is Hoffet's particular discovery, not to say invention, remain foreign bodies, and, precisely because they are so completely different in kind—methodical, farsighted, efficient, and masculine—they subjugate the native Parisian. However little Hoffet admires the feminine Parisian, he has even less love for the masculine conqueror who seizes power over Paris by virtue of being different. The two are complementary, the ruler and the ruled, in that they live a free life. The Parisian is freed from the ancient obligations, inhibitions, and taboos of life in the provinces, free from the pressure of that "superego" which sets bounds to the individual ego, taming its lusts and curbing its desires. But this very freedom, we are told, is a weakness, for it expresses itself in the irresponsibility of an infantile dream world. In place of moral obligations and conventions, the individual is forced to seek refuge under the protection of a clique, a *chapelle,* in order to obtain a certain feeling of safety and security; and in this feeling, of course, the psychoanalyst at once recognizes a yearning for the maternal womb. The same yearning drove the youth of Paris, after the war, into the cellars of the *Rive Gauche,* the famous *caves* of St. Germain des Prés, which with their narrowness and darkness symbolize the flight downwards and the return to the Mother. (The fact that from 1940 onwards, during air-raid warnings, Parisians had become accustomed to sit about in cellars a good deal, and to chat and drink there, would naturally be far too simple an explanation to take in the deep-sea investigator of the psyche.) The Parisian, then, is by constitution not only a woman but also a child; and to his childishness belongs the dreamworld of Parisian luxury—but also the much larger world of Parisian filth and misery: a world due to the indifference of dreamers—who can certainly transfigure reality or cast a spell over it, but cannot transform it in their everyday life.

It has been easy—perhaps too easy—to reject Hoffet's thesis. His own publisher, Bernard Grasset—who during the German Occupation idolized the conqueror in what Monsieur Hoffet would perhaps call a "feminine" way— amuses himself by taking Hoffet to task in a preface to the book. Hoffet's other critics in the Paris papers, too, have not found their task very difficult. But when one has read these critics, one really begins to wonder whether Frédéric Hoffet's prosaic and presumptuous book can really be dismissed so lightly, and whether this collection of half-truths might not contain some whole truths, too. Hoffet does not claim to describe the whole of Paris, and he knows that the majority of Parisians are just as solid, sober, and provincial as any group in the French provinces. He concentrates on that small circle in which for some years the Marquis de Sade has been feted as a great thinker, and Jean Genet as a saint; and, although he confuses many issues—the intellectuals of the Left Bank, the salons, and politics— yet he has not invented the "cult of perversity" and more particularly the egocentricity of the Parisian intelligentsia.

Paris is not only an interpreter, at times unreliable, of France to the world and to herself; she has also been for centuries the center and the meltingpoint of the modern world, the Rome of modern times; and the Parisian has long been accustomed to the idea of his worldwide significance and radiance. Yet once the real meaning of Paris, and the Parisian's view of that meaning, no longer coincide, there must arise a feeling of uneasiness about Parisian culture—a feeling of which the Parisian is only partly conscious in actual fact, but one which is an integral part of his present-day experience.

No big city accepts without a struggle the twilight of its greatness. Even Vienna lives still in the glow of its past. For Paris the situation is different, because, though she no longer stands at the center of the world, no other city has been able to replace her in this position. Therefore the illusion of standing at the centre can be easily retained by the Parisian: the intellectual of Tokyo and of Rio de Janeiro, not to mention Rome and Copenhagen, still listens attentively to everything that comes from Paris, even when it is badly translated German metaphysics.

Formerly an idea was provincial until Paris had weighed and accepted it. Today, it is Paris that feels herself provincial if she fails to seize and advertise new thoughts and tendencies immediately. What was once a matter of course for Paris has now become a problematic task; and, in his clumsy way, Frédéric Hoffet has stumbled on this problem, which most Frenchmen step over elegantly without even noticing its existence. His treatment of the problem is not a loving one and, what is more serious (for there have been plenty of declarations of love for Paris), not a particularly intelligent one. But the Parisian is too close to his city to see her as a problem, and for this reason his unanimous and violent rejection of Hoffet's curious "psychoanalysis" leaves behind in its turn a sense of ambiguity.

April 1954

Young Spain and the Old Régime

> "Los laberintos que crea el tiempo se desvanecen."
> —"poema del Canto jondo,"
> Federico Garcia Lorca

"Franco's Spain is a country living under a totalitarian regime, with its single-party rule, its monolithic press, its regimentation and censorship...."

"The Franco government has suspended the publication of the two liberal literary reviews, *Insula* and *Indice*...."

During the past few months, statements such as these have frequently appeared side by side, and this juxtaposition suggests—to me at any rate—a certain contradiction. A totalitarian regime in power for seventeen years does not kill liberal journals, for the simple reason that it does not tolerate their existence in the first place. On the other hand, would a non-totalitarian regime be able to suppress, by simple decree, periodicals that do not even concern themselves with politics?

Spain unquestionably is "the land of paradox" described by Julian Marias, one of its leading contemporary thinkers. May not, however, some of the paradoxes we encounter be due to our own superficiality and vagueness, our lack of precise information, our preconceptions? What exactly is this regime that appears so eccentric in relation to Europe? Instead of starting out with the usual confident assertions and exclamation marks, it may be wise to adopt the Spanish punctuation system, which calls for a question mark to be placed at the very beginning of an enquiry. One may then consider the uncertainties of the regime—so much more interesting than our own certainties.

The Dissidence of the Intellectuals

To begin with an impression that I formed in Madrid, and which was subsequently confirmed in other cities: the mood of the intellectual world as a whole, ranging from the aged celebrities of literature to the student youth, is openly one of indifference. In no intellectual milieu is there the faintest trace of enthusiasm for the Caudillo and his state.

This state of mind can assume different forms: refusal to concern oneself with public affairs; a very marked taste for erudite research; multiplication of small literary circles (*tertulias*) and "little magazines" devoted to poetry; fascination with the intellectual life of freer countries—France above all; immense curiosity about everything coming from abroad, including the work of Spanish refugee scholars; etc. This attitude can reach the point of almost open defiance of all political dogmas, as in the case of the Congress of Young University Writers, laboriously arranged by the authorities of Madrid's University City a year in advance, with the active support of the rector, Don Pedro Lain Entralgo, and with the aid of subsidies from the Ministry of Education. This Congress, so long prepared and finally prohibited, published several issues of a printed bulletin that express a genuine "revolt of the younger generation." (Both the rector and the minister were subsequently dismissed.)

Speaking generally, one has the feeling that there is among the young—beyond the purely intellectual ferment—a widespread impatience and disgust with an ageing, ossified, and sometimes corrupt "ideological" bureaucracy that has a hold on all the available jobs and blocks the horizon in the name of Falangism: itself nominally a youthful, dynamic, and revolutionary movement. Thus the students, weary of having to pay compulsory membership fees to the Falangist students' union, the SEU, whose leaders were imposed from above, started to elect their own "compromisarios" (delegates) at the Madrid law faculty; they also gathered, within a few hours, thousands of signatures for the convocation of a students' congress to overhaul the existing union and elect new leaders. Numerous youthful Falangists took part in this democratic movement, and the organ of the SEU, supposedly the authentic voice of Falangism, was itself suppressed in consequence of this incident and the clashes between students and militiamen which followed.

Evasion, indifference, revolt, frank aspirations towards greater intellectual and political freedom, allied to the need for a practical recompense after years of study—these are among the motivations behind the "rebellion of the young." To a large section of Spain's over sixty thousand students, all pathways appear closed and all hopes doomed to disappointment. Circumstances have induced a curiously mixed state of mind among this generation of intellectuals, hope mingling with despair, disappointed idealism with dissatisfied ambition. There is an estrangement between this youth and an ageing regime that incarnates the past and represents the defense of vested interests. In relation to the living forces of the present, Spain carries on under an *ancien régime* which symbolizes neither hope nor the future, but which has a remarkable capacity for endurance.

Now an *ancien régime*—with all that goes with it, in the way of oppression and vexation—is something quite different from a modern totalitarianism, and indeed very nearly its opposite. One must not allow oneself to be taken in by the similarities present in all antidemocratic regimes, or even by the unbelievable monotony of a daily press as rigidly and totally regimented as that of a "people's democracy," and equally remote from the real problems of the country. The factor that is lacking in this regime is a pervasive dynamism, the burning conviction of representing or prefiguring the future. There are totalitarian countries where the opposition clings to stirring memories, to a consciousness of imperishable human values, but where it none the less suffers from a sense of being left behind, and ends by asking itself whether after all the future—however detestable it may be—is not on the side of the regime. Such an opposition may question its own ability to communicate with a youth organized by the regime from early infancy, a youth molded in the image of an oppression that has been "internalized" psychologically. We are indeed becoming aware that the achievements of the "dynamic" totalitarianism in this sphere fall short of their own hopes and of the apprehensions of their critics. Our retrospective knowledge of Hitler's Third Reich, as well as our incipient understanding of the intellectuals and the younger generation in the USSR, suggests that even the most up-to-date totalitarianism is not as total as all that. But with the Franco regime, this question does not even arise.

What are We Celebrating?

I was in Barcelona last summer on the anniversary of the "liberation," that is, the military *pronunciamento* which gave the signal for the civil war and which has consequently become the official holiday of present-day Spain. A great Barcelona daily, whose editor is a convinced Falangist, ran an editorial that day which said inter alia: "Numerous young people ask us: 'What exactly are you celebrating today? What is the content of this celebration and what does it signify?'" To this unorthodox enquiry the editor did not reply, as one might have expected, that the day marked the renaissance and the upsurge of a movement that had refashioned a greater Spain. Instead, he wrote: "We shall never forget that this day marks the success of a movement thanks to which Spain was able to remain outside the war, and Hiroshima was not named Madrid."

A truly realistic justification, and perhaps the best and most convincing that the writer could have found. But it is the justification of a Vichy regime—one that studiously avoids adventures and busies itself with keeping dangerous draughts away from the body politic.

That particular day was marked by official receptions and some military parades, but I gathered this only from the newspapers, not from anything that went on in the streets of the Catalan capital. The papers had likewise informed me that the day was going to be enlivened by an outburst of popular joy and gratitude taking the form of a great display of flags and bunting, but the only flags I saw were displayed by some buildings and shops in the center of the town, while the suburbs were totally bare of decorations. Does Catalonia continue to be the least pro-Franco province of Spain because of its national and linguistic resistance to Castilian centralism? One thing is certain: the regime is not sustained by any wave of enthusiasm, on the part of anyone. It does not identify itself with the people, in the manner of the Fascist, National Socialist, and Communist regimes. It is frankly hierarchical and con-servative. Falangist "radical" demagogy is no more than an empty facade, and the fiction is barely kept up. Thus in March 1956 the newspapers in Madrid (and possibly all over Spain) gave the greatest prominence to a ceremony which concerned the nobility: in the presence of the German ambassador, Prince Adalbert of Bavaria, the "*hijosdalgo*" had renewed an oath in a form long ago discontinued, and this event took precedence over almost all the news from Spain or abroad. What could be more characteristic of a hierarchy-conscious *ancien régime* than this emphasis upon aristocratic tradition, caste distinction, and the importance of noble birth?

This regime reconciles itself fairly easily to the existence of a wide fringe of illiterates, unlike others that know no rest until all citizens have spelled out the same verses in honor of a leader or an infallible committee. Franco Spain does not number among its writers an Ehrenburg or a Simonov. It is a country where the opposition—or at least the independence and reserve, of the leading thinkers and writers is tacitly or openly recognized. This alienation, or non-cooperation, corresponds to what Ortega y Gasset had on pre-Republican days already described as the "secession of the best." But it is also the mark of a regime that, for all its oppressiveness, is too remote from the educated class—and perhaps from the mass of the people as well—to refashion it, affect its mind, enter into living communion with it.

On the morrow of Ortega's burial, over a thousand students assembled at his grave in San Isidro cemetery, and it was one of them who spoke these words: "This homage is being rendered by the youth of Spain, by students without universities who have to learn almost everything outside the lecture hall, from books not prescribed for study and written in languages other than Spanish—students without teachers. Between Ortega and ourselves there is an abyss which cannot be crossed. Every day we become conscious that something has been lost. No one tells us what to study and how. No one tells us what purpose the university is supposed to serve. But we are certain that it serves us little, and that it ought to be changed root and branch."

These tolerated outbursts, or manifestations of free thought, as well as the official reactions and reprisals, culminating in arrests and trials, are not as self-contradictory as might seem. They belong to one and the same situation: that of an ancient regime thrown upon the defensive.

The Dangers of Reading

In January 1954, on the occasion of the eightieth birthday of that great old man of letters, Pio Baroja, the review *Indice* took the occasion to render public homage to his career. Foreign subscribers obtained their copy of this issue, for the censorship authorities had first allowed it to appear; but they then stopped its sale in Spain. Why? A bishop had complained that the growing number of homages rendered to impious authors like Ortega and Baroja constituted a scandal, and the censorship bureau, frightened by its own liberalism, had had second thoughts. For the rest, the pressure exercised by the Church in the direction of stricter censorship is undeniable. Its official organ, *Ecclesia*, itself exempt from censorship by virtue of the Concordat, none the less demands an even more rigorous control of other publications, and on January gist, 1956, expressed itself as follows: "Ortega was throughout his life the chief idol of laicism in Spain, and continues to hold this position since his death, although there are reasons to believe that in his final hour he withdrew his apostasy. We fervently hope that he was able during his last moments to reconcile himself personally to the Supreme Judge before whose tribunal he appeared shortly thereafter. But his destructive work remains.... His apostasy began, like that of many others, with the unauthorized study of impious works, such as those of Renan, which shook his Catholic faith, despite the foundations laid by the priest Don Ramon Miguela and the Jesuit Fathers of the college at Malaga. But in fact the impious Renan was himself the victim of certain writings by German rationalists which he had read without the necessary precautions end without an ade-quate theological grounding."

In another recent issue, *Ecclesia* published an article by Mgr. Zucarro de Viscarra, a bishop attached to Catholic Action, explain-ing that love and charity are due to unorthodox writers (of whom Spain counts not a few, from Cervantes to Unamuno), but only as love and charity are due to lepers and other carriers of infectious diseases, who must be isolated and not allowed to come in contact with persons other than those qualified to treat them.

It is worth noting that, for all this clerical zeal, the regime on the whole takes a less rigorous view of the benefits of quarantine. Some prohibited works are subsequently published in Latin America, and manage to reach Spain. It is also worth observing that while the censorship is intolerant, it is not always intelligent. The censorship of foreign films eliminates allusions to adultery and replaces the relevant passages of dialogue by others: there are at least two cases of husband and wife having been transformed into brother and sister by the censor—thus unwittingly substituting incest for adultery.

A Stable Regime

The most remarkable thing about the Franco regime is its capacity for survival. How many oppositionists in Spain—or in exile–have been awaiting its fall almost weekly for at least eleven years! A strike of transport workers in Barcelona and Madrid, of factory workers in Bilbao, and already the regime is thought to have been left stranded by a resurgent working class. A clash between students and militiamen, and promptly there are those who believe Spain to be heading towards a new revolutionary cycle marking the end of a regime "which nobody wants any more." It would be invidious to adopt an ironical tone towards the disappointed hopes of an emigration that naturally reads its own impatience into the future. But if one fails to understand the reasons for the durability of Franco's government, one makes it impossible to discriminate between passing tremors and an eventual decisive crisis.

What is it that enables Franco to stay in power? Clearly he could not have won the civil war without Italian and German intervention, but one must not underrate the traditionalist forces he was able to mobilize in his fight. Had he not been the representative of indigenous forces, how could he have resisted Hitler's pressure in the midst of war and marked out for himself an independence comparable to that of Tito in relation to Moscow?[1] And if today it is argued that he has been saved by the American alliance, and that he would have been overthrown by the democratic forces if the United States had not provided economic aid, arms, prestige, and protection, one must bear in mind the Tenor six years after the war during which Franco Spain lived in the most complete isolation: ostracized by the democracies and the Communist states (who today also pay it flattering attention), subjected to serious pressure, and yet able to survive without significant foreign aid. The regime has endured notwithstanding the hopes of large numbers of Spaniards, notably Catalans and Basques. It has done so thanks to an apparatus of coercion of which the army rather than the Falange remains the core, but also thanks to the terrible memories of the civil war. There is in this phenomenon of survival an element of sheer fatigue, a yearning for quiet and stability at almost any price, which must not be underrated.

The first essential was to regain a "normal" life and to reorganize the country. True, Spain under Franco has not resolved its principal economic problems. The economic balance sheet is unfavorable, in conformity with a system marked by corruption, nepotism, a multiplicity of contradictory regulations, autarchist tendencies, and a general discouragement of initiative.[2] But the balance sheet is not entirely negative. The *"viviendas,"* or low cost workers' dwellings, are not of a high standard, but it is a fact that total house construction this year will for the first time keep abreast of population growth. Again, Falangist syndicalism clearly bears an unpleasantly paternalist character, but its achievements must not be ignored. It appears that the Falangist system of syndicalism (i.e., compulsory pseudo-unionism) has not resulted in anything beyond a certain redistribution of incomes within the salaried class. But, at the local level, the minor functionaries who are supposed to embody the authority of the State in relation to the workers, often end up by voicing the latter's demands upon the State. Last summer a syndicalist congress witnessed the spectacle of delegates chosen by indirect election going much further in their demands than was pleasing to the government; since then, certain benefits, such as family allowances, have been extended to agricultural workers.

But to return to the question: what is it that has enabled Franco to hold out? In discussing this topic with Spaniards I was reminded of a visit to Poland in 1947, in the course of which I met civil servants clearly hostile to Russia and Communism, but who did not withhold their cooperation from an unpopular regime when it was a question of reconstructing a ruined country. Post-civil war Spain, like postwar Poland, appears to me to be marked by the priority given to work and the daily round of living over all questions of principle. Lastly, let us not forget that any regime which has endured for some time can count on the support, not just of a few vested interests, but of a whole host of petty functionaries who have cause to fear any change. There is in Spain a vast and proliferating bureaucracy at the syndicalist and quasigovernmental levels. I was told in Madrid that the director of Social Insurance had proudly informed a foreign visitor: "I have forty thousand functionaries working under my direction, and do you know how many I would need if the work were properly organized? At most three hundred." I don't guarantee the truth of the story, but it accords with the prevailing atmosphere. And there is at any rate no doubt that the unfinished buildings intended to house new Ministries in Madrid, which greet the eye of the departing visitor on the northern route, are the biggest in Europe, if not in the entire world.

A Fragile Regime

Franco is sustained by the past, and there is something precarious about this dependence on established interests on the one hand, and traumatic memories on the other. The overpowering impression carried away by the traveler in Spain is one of mingled boredom, oppression, and corruption. A whole new generation has grown up for whom the civil war is only a shadow in the background, while daily vexations are ever present. Thus it is not by accident that, seventeen years after the close of the civil war, a malaise begins to kind more open expression, and a new opposition element is added to the older ones.

This element consists of the sons of Falangist leaders and other "profiteers of the regime." It is typical of this cleavage between the generations that the son of Spain's foreign minister, Martin Artajo—a former Christian-Democrat who became a Franco supporter—has become a Protestant convert (and consequently ineligible for the more attractive careers); the son of the air minister declined a chance to obtain a law professorship, on the grounds that he did not wish to teach law under a regime contemptuous of legality. Among those arrested last February there was the young scientist Miguel Sanchez Mazas, the son of the Falangist writer and leader Rafael Sanchez Mazas. This judgment pronounced upon the status quo by the privileged student elite marks the Franco government as an *ancien régime*, and its Falangist decor as a facade that no longer deceives the Falangists themselves.

Every conflict of generations, every youth movement, proceeds from a twofold motivation: a spirit of adventurous revolt against stagnation and oppression, allied to the legitimate ambition to find a field of action, an opportunity for useful work, and for asserting oneself against those who have monopolized all places and preferments. A nondemocratic regime that finds an outlet for such practical ambitions, while frustrating the desire for liberty, can no doubt hold out very long. A regime that satisfies neither moral aspirations nor practical ambitions, lays the groundwork for an irremediable crisis. And this is precisely the position of the ageing Franco regime in its relationship to the new generation. It is futile to speculate on the number of years it may still be able to hold out, but it is just as futile to suppose that the fundamental trouble can be dealt with by imprisoning a few hundred "agitators."

The War of the Spanish Succession

The fact of the matter is that no one in Spain is concerned with the future prospects of the regime; the sole topic of discussion is the eventual succession.

Is it to be the Monarchy? The "pure" Falangists, that is, the hard core ones, as well as some of the more "impure" who have managed to hold on to their jobs, detest this solution. Arrese, the new Falangist secretary, has demanded that the Falangist succession itself be legally guaranteed. Falangism may be only a matter of decor for the mass of Spaniards, but for the Falangist "cadres" and the militia it remains a means of existence; to a good many sons of the impoverished lower-middle class, the Falangist militia offers material advantages, an illusion of power, and the chance to "be someone." Hence the mélange of traditionalism and Evolutionism in the makeup of this "radical" movement that would like to preserve its status, and which still has a good deal more influence in the provinces than in the great cities, where it is discredited and where no one bothers to sport its insignia.

Some Falangists likewise fear that a monarchical restoration would make nonsense of their syndicalism and their social-revolutionary rhetoric. Significantly, Franco has repeatedly tried to reassure the Falange on this point. In an interview granted to Arrese on January 23, 1955, he had to deal with some questions which were as remarkable as the answers he gave: "Can you reassure our readers that an eventual restoration of the Monarchy would in no way affect the ideals of our national revolution, or the achievements and the institutions of the Movement?" Answer: "You can give your readers the most categorical assurance on this point. I have already said that the National Movement itself will assure its continuity. There can be no doubt on this subject." Yet uneasiness continued to persist, and three months later, on April 8, a talk given by the Italian monarchist Cantalupo in the exclusive Ateneo club was interrupted by Falangist cries of "Down with the king."

The anti-Franco liberals, and even some of the socialists and anarchists, are prepared to accept a Monarchical restoration, on condition that it brings with it the return of certain liberties. The royal family has, however, taken no occasion to appear as an independent political factor, and the acceptance by certain of its members of a pension paid to them by Franco has hurt their standing even among traditional Monarchists. The Monarchy as a simple continuation of the Franco government has no appeal for anyone. At present Franco's regime bears a marked resemblance to the dull oppression of Ferdinand VII at the time of the Holy Alliance, and Spain does not wish to live permanently under Ferdinand VII.

Communism—A Danger or a Pretext?

Can one conceive a Communist succession passing through various transitional stages, including a Popular Front? This specter constantly is evoked by the official press, notably in the articles written or inspired by Luis Apparicio, the propaganda chief; it is employed to discredit liberal tendencies, or to justify the saving mission of Franco—that last bulwark of a Christendom imperiled by the liberal road to Bolshevism and perdition.

There is today in Spain no significant organized Communist movement. True, the Communists are actively trying to infiltrate the underground opposition movements and the official Falangist unions, and are willing to espouse liberal or Falangist demands with-out any trace of "sectarianism." There was at least one Communist in the liberal group which organized the Congress of Young University Writers. But that movement was not due to Communist influence, nor did the Communists infiltrate it. They simply attach themselves to anything that offers them and opportunity to gain a hearing. One must not underrate the effect of the prolonged political "diseducation" of the young under a regime that bars any discussion of political ideas. The effect is not confined to the large proportion of the student youth who conform to the image of Italy's *vitelloni*—bored and apathetic young people who take no interest in anything beyond the sports page of the daily paper. It also makes itself felt in they liberal movements, with their frequently utopian demands (e.g., the proposal that "unsatisfactory" university teachers be dismissed after two years). How should this youth, which has never experienced any form of democracy, display a sudden maturity and make its first halting steps towards liberty in a wise and prudent manner? If there is a danger of Communist infiltration—and I believe it will grow—the fault lies not with the regime's eternal scapegoat, "liberalism," but with the Franco government itself. Communism is in fact opposed to the liberty to which the youth of

Spain aspires, but what they are told by the spokesmen of the regime is calculated to give them a very different impression.

There has recently appeared a bulky pamphlet signed by one Mauricio Carllaville and bearing the title—in flaming letters on a black cover *Sodomites*. The author sets out to demonstrate that Communism is synonymous with pederasty, and to this end investigates the "sexual perversions" of Robespierre, Azaña, and Martinez Barrios—an eighteenth-century Jacobin, and two modern Presidents of the Spanish Republic! Pornography of this sort is not hampered by an otherwise rigorous censorship. Or consider a recent series of articles in *El Español*, denouncing Communist influence among the students, wherein the author warms to his theme by listing the following forbidden works found in the homes of some young people: Arthur Koestler's *Spanish Testament*, poems by Rafael Alberti and Pablo Neruda, some pamphlets issued by the European Youth Movement and the liberal youth supporters of the European Community, and finally a brochure published by the Council of Europe and "printed in Strasbourg" (an aggravating circumstance this?). To confront young people avid for serious information with such a tissue of nonsensical rubbish is to make them feel that anti-Communism is synonymous with mediocrity and stupidity, and that Communism must consequently stand for the opposite qualities. Communism is thus rendered interesting and attractive—no small achievement considering the experiences of the civil war period!

The Church

If Franco were to yield his power, and if some kind of appeal were made to the voters, it is improbable that the new intellectual elite would find itself backed by the electorate. During the early stage at any rate, the conservative forces would stand the best chance of preserving their cohesion and gaining support. The best organized of these forces under the present regime is clearly the Catholic Church.

But does this Church, which has so much influence under and over the regime, really hold the key to the soul of the Spanish people? No clear-cut reply is possible. For a large section of the opposition, notably in Catalonia, the Church has ceased to count. It is said to have missed every opportunity of rising above the battle and dissociating itself from the regime. And one may also note the opinion of the Archbishop of Valencia who estimates that "three-quarters of the workers have no religion whatever."

If there are indications of a process of de-Christianization among the masses, there is even clearer evidence of a certain aversion felt by the intellectual elite for the Church, and more particularly for the confusion of the temporal and spiritual powers. Where is one to look for a leading Spanish thinker or writer who can be described as orthodox? In the seminaries, theses on Ortega and Unamuno are not accepted, and may even constitute ground for expulsion. Then, too, the thousands of conversions to Protestantism among the young—the precise figure is unknown, but it is rumored to be around thirty thousand—is an interesting symptom, recalling as it does the attraction which "heresy" had for Italian intellectuals at the time of the Counter-Reformation. Reference has been made to the son of that ultra-Catholic pillar of the regime, Martin Artajo. One must bear in mind that, in Spain, Protestantism is barely tolerated, and that conversion may be tantamount to virtual exclusion from any sort of career, and even to termination of one's studies. Yet there have been cases of conversion even in the villages where—in the absence of any understanding of what Protestantism signifies—the bare idea of "protest" evokes a response. These conversions represent an extraordinary phenomenon, and the Church not surprisingly is worried.

What of the Church itself? The Spanish anticlericals tend to regard it as a monolithic bloc, a rigidly organized political force within which, moreover, a carefully elaborated strategy allots different roles to various tendencies. Yet Spanish Catholicism, like Spanish society as a whole, exhibits a certain spiritual ferment, signs of renewal, a new way of looking at modern problems. The former rector of Madrid University himself belonged to this more open-minded school of Catholicism, as does the philosopher Julian Marias, and that remarkable writer J. L. Aranguren who—despite the covert opposition of the Opus Dei—has been appointed professor of ethics at Madrid University. (Opus Dei may be described as "freemasonry" of the radically "integrist" Spanish Catholics; it stands in opposition to Pax Romana, the international movement which, after the war, did so much to help Spain get out of her isolation.)

There is always something unsatisfactory about "structural" analyses that make no allowance for personalities, circumstantial details, and other imponderables. In Spain at any rate, personalities and temperaments count for something. Cardinal Segura, for example, owed his rise to the part he played in the divorce of Alfonso XIII, which no other bishop was at that time prepared to accept. His quarrel with Franco probably goes back to a dinner at which the prelate objected to the precedence given to the Caudillo's wife. There are ardently Falangist bishops, and some who think the regime too liberal. There are others who are shocked by the prevalent social conditions and inclined to take up a mildly reformist attitude, for example, the bishop of Malaga. Lastly, there are those like the bishop of Pamplona, Mgr. Delgado, who wrote the preface to a book issued under his auspices—a book that is difficult to obtain: I searched Madrid in vain for a copy, and finally located one by accident in a stationer's shop in Cordoba. It is called *Why Are We Poor?* and its author is a woman teacher, Manuela Gallardo y Gomez. Having presented this study to a symposium organized by the Ministry of Education on the causes of illiteracy, she saw it rejected as "being without any interest." The book is a meticulous comparison of the educational systems of Spain, Holland, Norway, and Germany, and arrives at the conclusion that the cause of the widespread illiteracy in Spain is the failure of the authorities to combat it. It also maintains that the atrocities committed during the civil war were the responsibility of a privileged class that did nothing to free the people from their ignorance and barbarism. "The ignorant masses represented a charge of dynamite which we had all accumulated."

Army and Falange

The succession to Franco is a matter that depends on the outcome of a tug-of-war between forces more or less openly organized under a regime that is not the sole fount of authority. In the current idiom, the regime represents "the four S's"—saber, soutane, syndicates, and *sinverguenza* (shamelessness, i.e., corruption). Of the four, the saber is now the most important. For the past eleven years, there has been a quiet shift from revolutionary Falangism to conservative militarism, a shift not affected by the recent appointment of "radical" Falangists like Arrese to certain leading positions. The current unrest may even precipitate a movement in the direction of military dictatorship pure and simple.

A witness of the recent clashes between students and Falangist militiamen described to me how he took shelter, with his fiancée, in a nearby cafe, where every one was greatly excited by what was happening—save for a group of officers who did not pay the slightest attention: Falangists or liberals, these distinctions evidently mattered little to them. They were clearly conscious of being the true possessors of authority. The Falangists are aware of it, too. The not very numerous blueshirted militiamen who move about with the air of an army of occupation amidst a hostile population are not the masters of the State, and Franco does not depend on them to anything like the extent to which he depends on the Army—with which indeed he identifies himself. He appears in his general's uniform, and not in Falangist dress, even on the occasion of an anniversary reception arranged by the Falange. By now he seems to regard the Falange as nothing more than an auxiliary bureaucracy. When at a recent meeting of the Falangist Council some of those present tried to bring up political topics, the Caudillo cut them short, told them to present a report on their activities, briefly outlined their tasks for the coming year, and promptly left the meeting. Franco is himself a military man before everything else, and his *pronunciamento* in 1936 was something different from— and a great deal more traditional than —the Falangist idea, now represented symbolically by a man long dead: Jose Antonio Primo de Rivera.

But will the Army not be shaken and demoralized by the inevitable loss of Spanish Morocco? One knows what Morocco has meant to the tradition of this Army, to Franco's own career, and finally in the civil war: a military colony inhabited by at least 25,000 officers; final vestige of Spain's once worldwide empire; a bastion unshaken by movements of opinion on the mainland Morocco by a thousand threads is closely linked to the prestige of the regime and for the Army its loss is especially painful.

How will this affect its political attitude? Most of the higher grades are fairly well content with their military privileges. They cannot envisage a regime more favorable to them and have no interest whatever in political adventures. Yet the Army may wish to compensate itself for the loss of prestige inherent in the retreat from Morocco by a visible and sensible reinforcement of its official position in the State. Thus both the intellectual ferment which does not touch it, and the Moroccan negotiations, which touch it very closely, seem to conspire to emphasize the military character of the Franco regime.

July 1956

Notes

1. For proof of this relative independence one may consider the efforts made by the Spanish Government to have Jews of Sephardi origin exempted from the German and Vichyite racial laws, and the "repatriation" to Spain of several hundred Jews of Sephardi Spanish origin specially released from the concentration camps. (Cf. E. van Kuchnelt Leddin, "L'Espagne et les Juifs," *Etudes*, April 1956.)
2. Anyone who wants to start a new branch of industry has to insert a declaration to this effect in the official journal, and wait for possible objections emanating from other firms that may fear competition. Such objections are generally sustained by the authorities if the sponsors are well entrenched and able to secure official support. Cases could be cited of industrialists being prevented in this fashion from manufacturing goods of which there is a real shortage.

The Sick Man of Europe is...Europe: Thoughts after Kennan

The word "disengagement" is not to be found in the text of George Kennan's Reith lectures. Indeed, the term has, in its protean ambiguity, been linked with political tendencies and sentiments for which Kennan and such systematic D-planners as Hugh Gaitskell and Denis Healey have a scant regard. None of these men, for instance, believes that Western policy towards the Soviet Union should be based on "trust," as so many who agitate for "disengagement" do. For Kennan and his true supporters, the problem of "trust" or "confidence" is real enough: it pertains, however, not to Russia, but to Germany and, implicitly, to Europe.

To the question whether a united Germany should be allowed full freedom of action, Kennan replies:

> If Germany cannot be accorded reasonable confidence in these coming years then I would know of no promising solution to the entire problem of Europe. To assume that such confidence cannot be given is to cut ourselves off in advance from possibilities that may be vital to our very survival. If we are going to make so negative and so hopeless an assumption, let us be terribly, terribly sure that our judgment is drawn not from the memories and emotions of the past but from the soberest sort of attention to present realities.

And in an article in *Western World* (April), examining the arguments around the question of "disengagement," John Midgley, former *Times* correspondent in Bonn and now foreign editor of the *Economist*, wrote:

> In the end, these arguments will be determined by the degree of faith which the leaders of opinion in Europe have in the peoples of their own continent. Do they believe that Europe—not merely its western extremity but the whole continent west of Russia—has become incapable, if 'abandoned to its own devices,' of establishing a stable political life and pacific internal relationships of its own? If this is so, then the obvious answer is to keep the Russians in Central Europe in order to prevent the Americans from leaving.

It will be noticed that Kennan's and Midgley's framing of the question pretty much anticipates their answer: no one likes to disclose himself as having a suspicious nature, lacking in faith. But might not a European be allowed to enquire in what Europe the Europeans themselves and the great powers are supposed to have confidence? In view of the fact that national and political conflicts in Europe gave rise to two world wars, it is not exactly reassuring to be told now: "We will restore the Europe we had before, and hope that this time things will work out better."

When Don Quixote set forth to accomplish his heroic deeds, he made a helmet of cardboard and tested it with his sword. The helmet was cut in two. Whereupon he made a second helmet of cardboard, but refrained from testing it. That is one way of learning from history; but perhaps it is not the best way.

German nationalists of the Right, as of the Left, have often hurled at Chancellor Adenauer the reproach that he is reluctant to trust the German nation as such, that he wants to tie the Germans so firmly to the West that they will no longer have the opportunity of pursuing a foreign policy of their own. And such "European" statesmen as Robert Schuman in France and the late de Gasperi in Italy were subject to sharp criticism in their own countries, for the very same reasons. But is it not significant that these three statesmen refused to trust their own peoples, and their own historical and political traditions? Meanwhile, the larger Europe to which the three chancellors looked has failed to emerge; European national sovereignties are now held in check only by the relations among the world powers. But the question remains: how shall Europe organize itself after the eventual withdrawal of the non-European world powers?

Only yesterday it seemed that nothing but Hitler and his mania for power stood between Europe and a peaceful future. Today, the argument runs, only the Soviet occupation forces, and the satellite regimes they maintain, stand between Europe and a peaceful future. But the position of a united Germany in a more or less neutralized Europe, consisting of the traditional national states, would be one Of tremendous superiority; and so long as there was no supreme body for Europe, no common European policy it would be unreasonable to rule out in advance the possibility of France's seeking once more an ally in the East to counterbalance the weight of Germany, however wisely Germany was ruled. The Western bloc and the Eastern bloc would then be replaced by alliances cutting across both. What, precisely, would have been gained?

Moreover: the tradition of East European nationalism, when directed against alien rule and dictatorship, appears primarily as a movement for freedom. But is it a movement for freedom in every respect? Would the reestablishment of these nations, as so many sovereign states, guarantee a peaceful settlement of all those national quarrels that so marked the East and Central European scene of yesterday?

Europe still bears within itself the seeds of disruption, for itself and for the world. The idea of restoring a Europe cleared of Russian and American troops, and to trust this Europe because "we have no other choice," simply cannot be accepted without further scrutiny. Indeed, examined more closely, this "confidence" so passionately appealed to is not so confident. The Europe that is to emerge from "disengagement" would not be distinguished from the Europe it supersedes by a new and better order. It is to differ from the Europe of the past *by being of power* in world politics. Kennan envisages a future wherein the United States and the Soviet Union will still dispose of the full range of deterrent weapons, while the countries of continental Europe (and perhaps also Britain) will have only militias to maintain internal security and order. Europe strikes the world, and George Kennan too, for all his confidence, as an explosive continent that it would be wiser not to trust with highly explosive weapons.

Thus, the contemplated "liberation" of Europe is to be accompanied by a declaration of Europe's incompetence to play a role in world affairs. Kennan's warning against the atomic arming of the Bundeswehr as an irreversible and hence tragic decisions[1] must be seen in the light of his broader conception—not so drastically formulated but unmistakable nevertheless—of a disarmed and neutralized Europe as in effect a ward of the Great Powers, this being the only kind of Europe from which Russia and America could afford to withdraw.

In the background of "disengagement"—and a not very distant background—the outline is beginning to take shape of a comprehensive, large-scale American-Russian agreement, starting from those implicit rules and restrictions which, in the Cold War (and even in the "hot war" in Korea), determined Russo-American relations and set limits to the danger of a world conflict. But one implication of this agreement seems to pass unnoticed; it nullifies all hopes for the establishment of a genuine "Atlantic community" as the potential nucleus of an eventual world government. In its stead, there would be a more or less permanent, uneasy stalemate between the two great atomic powers, with only fear and weakness in between.[2]

Western community or Russo-American atomic hegemony with all its tensions and conflicts? Have we Europeans, or some of us, still the power to make a choice between these two groping beginnings of two so different world orders?

At the very least, those who advocate "disengagement" ought to make it clear that there is a choice involved, whether Europe makes it or whether it is made for Europe. The policy of "disengagement" is credited with the ability to overcome the crisis in NATO. ("Disengagement is not an alternative to N.A.T.O., it is an alternative policy for N.A.T.O."—Denis Healey) and also to liberate the peoples of Central and Eastern Europe from the most oppressive features of Communist dictatorship. What Western policy could not achieve in its moment of confidence and strength (when America had an atomic monopoly) is now to be achieved by a gesture of weakness. And what Russia could not be made to yield in its moment of weakness, it is now expected to surrender in its moment of strength. As the French say: "the bride is too beautiful."

It is now generally forgotten that, in his Reith lectures, Kennan uttered a specific warning against a summit conference, as conflicting with the principles of sound, "old-fashioned," secret diplomacy. But the compound of interest in Kennan's ideas with pressure for a summit conference is precisely a part of that muddled "Kennanism" which is a peculiar political climate—the climate of European demobilization. There is of course a great difference, and even a contradiction, between the real possibilities of a Russo-American agreement and the hysterical pressure for a summit conference, which is expected to work miracles—as though the Geneva Summit conference in the summer of 1955 were not enough to destroy one's belief in such miracles once and for all. But the very mood in Europe is in itself a proof that, at any sober summit, there is really only room for two. Looking ahead, therefore, one can say that the chances of the European and American halves of the Atlantic community growing together seem fewer than the chances for an American-Russian agreement about some kind of neutralized Europe. And it is disturbingly possible that this neutralized Europe will bear little or no resemblance to what at least some eloquent European spokesmen for "disengagement" have in mind.

In the last eight years European passivity and European activity alike have in the queerest fashion converged to weaken the Western community.

As to passivity: Paul Henri Spaak, as secretary general of NATO has actually said that "There has probably never been an alliance which has realized its principal objective so completely." What he meant was that, at the decisive moment after the putsch in Prague, it saved Europe from a "Korean" fate. This is incontrovertible, and the great debate of those years between believers in the Atlantic pact and the neutralists, who were prepared to capitulate, was to the point. But the debate today between the "Atlanticists" and the: "disengagers" has a different meaning—although behind Kennan and the D-planners are hidden very many Europeans who, like the earlier neutralists, are moved by nationalist aspirations, pacifist illusions, and even a readiness to capitulate.

The question that has now come to the fore is: Was the Atlantic pact a full partnership or was it primarily an American shield for a part of Europe between the Atlantic and the Mediterranean? Was it a genuine alliance with mutual obligations or simply an American guarantee?

About a quarter of a million American troops are stationed in Europe. How many European soldiers stand beside them? It is enough to think of France, which today has only one division in West Germany under NATO command, and has actually dissolved its elite (and American-equipped!) divisions, built up in ten years of hard work—even trained air crews have been assigned to the infantry in Algeria. France, it is clear, has had sufficient confidence in the American shield to devote itself entirely to the war in Algeria, and to leave the defense of France itself to the United States. The truth is that, in essentials, the West Europeans have relied on the United States for their defense, and that NATO is the instrument, not of a partnership, but of a receivership. Nobody can maintain that America would not have preferred much stronger and self-reliant European allies—even if that would have meant less comfortable allies.

As to activity: France and Britain took an uncalculated risk in the Middle East at the moment of the Hungarian uprising. Ever since this event, one suspects that the ardent rhetoric about the Atlantic community as "a way of life" is premised on growing doubts of its value as a military agreement expressing a specific minimum of political and strategic unity among the partners.

The more the national states of Europe— especially those with an imperial past—turn their forces, whether in desperation or confidence, to pursuing their own national policies along traditional lines, the more they weaken Europe as a whole. And to the same degree, they weaken the European-American partnership, without which the United States remains a world power, but not one of the European nations does. Thus, a supranational Europe—even a Little Europe—as a clearinghouse in which the national policies of the member states were subordinated in advance to the common interest, offered the only possibility of sustaining and carrying forward a European-American partnership. Perhaps it was really the rejection of the European Defense Community by the French National Assembly on 30 August, 1954, which undermined the Atlantic community. There was a good deal of derision in France at the time about John Foster Dulles' warning of a possible "agonizing reappraisal" of American policy. The phrase was laughed off as a typical "Dulles bluff" and an empty threat. But the reappraisal was not a matter of one day or one year; it was a gradual and unavoidable shift of weight. And it has taken place—as Suez demonstrated. The United States may not have, ultimately, any real choice between Western Europe and Soviet Russia. But it does have freedom of action as between Western Europe and the non-European world. And it is gradually exercising that freedom more and more.

When the United States does now intervene in Europe, it is not as a senior partner, but as a power representing "the forces of order" which cannot tolerate local troubles in a part of the world which is of concern to it —not least because of its engagement in other parts of the world that might be affected. One need only mention Algeria to see the point. Today Europeans have begun to notice that NATO is becoming a kind of Spanish inn, where you eat and drink what you carry with you.

Meanwhile the Soviets have caught up with the American lead in armaments, and the American umbrella over Europe has sprung a leak. If, in the interval granted by history, no foundations were laid under its shelter, no house built, then—at least in this respect, and in the eyes of this European—America is not to blame.

Few signs point at present to the emergence of a deeper and more comprehensive Atlantic community; but there are more and more indications that some agreement on a neutralized Europe is on its way. It may be worthwhile, then, to speculate on the prospects for Europe outside present political engagements, that is, in "disengagement." The dispute between those who lay the blame on American leadership, and those who lay the blame on American failure to lead, is beside the point. So is the longing, particularly marked in Dean Acheson's writings, for a return to the less ambiguous position before 1950. That particular phase of the recent European past no longer provides a guide to the future.

The trend towards an American-Russian agreement over a more or less powerless and not wholly sovereign Europe, should make a special settlement for Germany, or rather a special status for Germany, superfluous. At least it is to be hoped that no distinction will be made between "engaged" and "disengaged" Europeans. A great and present danger would arise out of an unequal division of privileges, responsibilities, and burdens among the democratic European states; this inequality could generate new national hatreds and rivalries, and make of Europe simply a greater Balkans.

One of the few significant political achievements of postwar Europe has been Franco-German reconciliation and cooperation; perhaps even Socialists would admit that, in so far as it depended on him (and that was a good deal), Chancellor Adenauer acted in this respect like a statesman and that all Europe is indebted to him. For reconciliations and agreements of this kind there will still be opportunities in the relatively powerless Europe of the future. The first task will be to smooth out, as far as possible, the inequalities between France's imperial position and that of her European partners, which presupposes a settlement in Algeria. At the same time, one must be careful to avoid creating a new and more severe inequality between a France that belongs to the Western bloc and a Germany outside it. Cooperation between France and Germany, now functioning in so many fields, remains dependent on a basic equality of risks, of obligations, and of responsibilities, and it would not survive the destruction of this equality.

One should also consider the political and psychological conditions: so far as the readiness to engage in a Western coalition under American leadership is concerned, the citizens of the Federal Republic are decidedly more "Western" or "Atlantic" than the French. Even apart from the large Communist Party and the extreme nationalists, various forms of neutralism and of *attentisme* play a large role in French politics. To neutralize Germany and to burden France with correspondingly greater responsibilities in the Western community is a policy which may be deduced from geography but which runs directly counter to the psychological climate in both France and Germany.

Balkans or Switzerland? Perhaps neither goal is likely to arouse enthusiasm in the citizens of that Europe which discovered the modern world, established it, and ruled it for so long. But Balkanization will only be the fate of those who are themselves ready for it, and prefer to be a shrunken power rather than a small state. Switzerland—using the model in its broadest sense—implies the union of European cultures under a common democratic law, with adequate conventional military forces to deter aggression and the renunciation of those worldwide political ambitions which can only be satisfied by military power. Today, when the hopes for a democratic Western community born of the war have faded, and with the new balance of power whose outlines have become clearer since Budapest and Suez, that is still an idea, and even an ideal.

Wherever the Atlantic pact has replaced the will of nations to defend themselves, instead of strengthening it, its usefulness has become questionable. As an American, George Kennan defined Europe as a "vacuum," and so it must appear to an observer without illusions. But as the Swiss journalist, F. R. Allemann, has written: "The military disengagement of the world powers would be a reasonable formula for an eventual agreement between East and West, and for a settlement of Central Europe's political problems, only if the vacuum which resulted were to be filled by the political and military engagement of those living within it."

June 1958

Notes

1. In subsequent conversation with Kennan, I had the impression that he does not despair of the reversibility of new military, arrangements, even atomic ones.
2. But even such a compromise is not so sure a thing. Is a limitation of rivalry, and restrictions imposed by implicit or even explicitly formulated rules, compatible with the character of the Moscow regime? Does its vision of the world, and of the historical process is a whole, allow it to make such a compromises without subverting its own claim to legitimacy? This is not a question that anyone can answer dogmatically. But on the basis of past experience, it is a question one cannot dismiss as unreal.

The 1960s

Letter from Jerusalem

On Misunderstanding Eichmann

The Case *"GeneralAttorney of the State of Israel V. Adolf, son of Karl Adolf Eichmann"* in the District Court of Jerusalem is about to be closed. 1,500 documents, 120 statements from witnesses, and the "longest cross-examination of all time" constitute the material that the three judges are now working through before they come to the announcement and justification of sentence. A possible appeal and petition for leniency could postpone the final confirmation of the sentence for another year. According to the law of 1950, the part Eichmann played in the organization of mass murder, which has been demonstrated over and over again, makes anything other than a sentence of death unthinkable. Against the actual carrying out of such a sentence, men like Martin Buber have already protested, legitimately conscious of their position as representatives of a great humanistic Jewish tradition. Only by refusing to demand an execution (which would be the first ever in the young state of Israel) could the trial stand as the unquestionable and absolute opposite of the nightmare world of totalitarian bureaucracy that Adolf Eichmann has so convincingly embodied for those who have witnessed this trial.

One thing is certain: if a palpable demonstration was required of the real nature of this world of blood and paper devoted to the pedantic annihilation of human beings, with its mixture of ideology, stupidity, and official zeal, then a more suitable defendant could not have been found. This has come out in every sentence of the preliminary hearing, in the cross-examination, in everything the man says—in his choice of phrase perhaps even more than in the content of his utterance, and whether he is making admissions or excuses.

The German-language text of the Eichmann interview conducted by Captain Less, which was given to the press in Jerusalem in some six volumes, containing 3,564 pages, offered some of us an extra advantage, as unavoidable as it was unsolicited, over other colleagues. Firstly, these were transcriptions of an interview that lasted from 29 May 1960 to 7 January 1961, taken from tape and corrected and approved by Eichmann personally. Secondly, it was available in no translation, and I can understand why—for Eichmann's German cannot simply be translated without being transposed. In his case, der Stil ist der Unmensch.

Admittedly, we have to distinguish between the locutions of a bureaucrat who is concerned to present himself as an insignificant cog in the wheel ("A peaceful citizen," as his counsel Dr. Servatius said: after all, has he caused a single Jew to be transported or gassed since the collapse of the Third Reich?...) and the behavior of the same man at a time when his rank, although not particularly exalted, gave him powers over life and death. His language is both that of a fussy bureaucrat, as well as the rough speech of a trooper. In Argentina, he appeared to be a great connoisseur of the copious Eichmann literature, and wrote marginalia in books that earned his disapproval (these were of such expressive force that they caused the courtroom translators some embarrassment).

It is quite absurd to imagine Adolf Eichmann only recently acquiring his fluent administrative jargon, his *Amtssprache*. Not just now, when he is displayed to us like a specimen in a testtube, but even then, as he sat in his military H.Q., he must have seen blood in terms of paper. All the more strange, how his colorless, lifeless language, which turns horror into an official record, still gets its own back in the clichés that he thoughtlessly uses—phrases that evidently evoke no visual impression for Eichmann himself—and in the way reality, however repressed and "digested," rises up, unheard and unconsidered, to take the macabre and ludicrous forms of, say, Karl Kraus' *Letzte Tage der Menschheit*. At a point in the interview where the discussion is of death sentences, Eichmann can happily say, "*Zum Henker*" or "Hang it all!" On the deportation of children from France into extermination camps ("first we must clearly define the degree of legality at this level") he comments: "At this point there were the beginnings of a carveup (*Zerhacken*) in the administrative machinery" (by which he understands that the relative spheres of competence of the SS, the Security Police, the Foreign Office, and Vichy had to be clarified). And when he is telling how Himmler ordered mass killings, he remarks: "He must have got the order from Hitler; otherwise he would naturally have exploded sky high." The "naturally" is inserted by hand in the transcription, as a neat stylistic correction.

When questioned about the children of Lidice, all of whom (with the exception of seven "re-germanifiables," *Ruckeindeutschungsfähigen*) he arranged to be moved to the Litzmannstadt (Lodz) camp to be slaughtered, and confronted with the documents that allow no evasion, Eichmann explains that the affair was handled by his office "purely transportation-wise (*rein transportmässig*). And a little later in the same conversation, when asked about the fate of the inhabitants of the "evacuated ghetto" at Lodz, he comments rather testily: "Das sind mir alles böhmische Dörfer," or "They're just a lot of Czech villages to me." But Lidice, of all places was nothing of the sort to him. It was just a dim, vague memory: "I believe the place was actually demolished, I'm not sure, but I seem to remember something of the sort." But then Lidice "was: dealt with on a general instruction from above"; *von oben* is an expression that means for him a particular administrative procedure, rather than, say, bombs falling from above. The same expression is then used of Litzmannstadt: "Das Suede hen oben beartfeitet" (That was dealt with from above).

"Dealt with from above," "digested," "clearly defined," "sifted through," "special material," "administrative treatment," "child's play" (*eine Kindersache*, referring to child transports to death camps): the point of this smokescreen of officialese comes out particularly clearly in two places. The first is when Eichmann is "clarifying" *das Ich*, the "use of the first person" in a letter he signed, but for which he no longer wishes to accept responsibility:

> Every Official, every Departmental chief writes in the "first person," the *Ichform*, it doesn't matter who is the Central Authority. This wasn't only true of the Police, it was true of every Central Authority. And he writes in the first person on behalf of his authority, in this case the Chief of the Security Police and the Secret Service—and I've said several times before, Captain, I couldn't hand out any information on my own initiative. Obviously, that would have been disastrous, and produced nothing but confusion, and would have led eventually to none of the people concerned knowing where they stood any longer, and endless questions of precedence would have come up, producing nothing but unpleasantness and chaos.

Unpleasantness, chaos, disaster, all were happily avoided by the Eichmanns, but only just. And it is not difficult to imagine how the official, even now that it is all over, still breaks out in a cold sweat at this vision of an insoluble conflict between the appropriate ministries of mass murder as to their spheres of competence.

Even more revealing is this definition of "clearance" (*Abdecken*), a process with which Eichmann was constantly preoccupied, while in office and for years afterwards.

> From this point of view, everything was progressing; furiously, and only the administrative machinery camp in for abuse. But I've learnt from Muller how a careful processing of the documents was a perquisite for any police action. Nothing could happen without it. And this is where the popular expression "to clear" came from. It was often used. People understood by this "clearing" not only how a man personally cleared himself so that he could always produce evidence—see for yourself, I haven't gone beyond my authority, everything took place and was arranged like this or that, in accordance with this or that directive, but also how it could serve to clear the office as well, so that he could produce evidence that the office itself hadn't exceeded its powers. In this way, disputes about limits of competence with other Central Authorities, and clashes of this sort could be more or less ruled out.

For Eichmann there is all the difference in the world between "setting in motion" (*ueranlassen*) and "doing" (*tun*). The first is a matter for sensitive educated people, among whom he obviously still includes his chief at that time, the "taciturn" Heinrich Müller. The second is for the brutes, who found it amusing to drag their more delicately tuned colleagues down to their infernal depths. One example was Höss in Auschwitz:

> These people, when you went there, naturally got quite a kick out of making the whole thing as horrific as possible for a man straight from his desk, and making the whole thing as much of a shock for you as possible, and naturally they were always pleased when your nerves weren't up to their standards of behaviour, as they called them. Höss said to me once—I must have been. in Auschwitz three times, two or three times—Höss told me that Himmler had been there, and Höss said that he actually went weak at the knees. And he meant this disparagingly—he was quite brutalised, was Höss

Of himself Eichmann says—and it could stand as a motto over these 3,564 pages, or over the whole trial for that matter: "Ich sass am Schreibtisch And machte meine Sachen" (I sat at my desk and got on with my job).

But even Adolf Eichmann is human and fallible in the last resort, and he was not spared the experience of being swept into an act of "brutality," the memory of which still weighs heavily on his spirit, and which he confesses with frankness and a measure of manly severity:

> I must now interpolate something I had forgotten. Dr. Löwenherz, released at that time from arrest, was a bit excited, as often happens of course, and started off by saying something that wasn't true, and in my anger, I lost control of myself, a thing I'm not normally prone to, and slapped him. It couldn't have hurt, of course not, because I didn't possess enough physical strength, but I didn't hide the incident. Later, I—when I was SS Major or Lieut. Colonel—in front of my officers, officers under me, with Dr. Löwenherz present, I asked his pardon for having boxed his ears that time in the heat of the moment, and said I was sorry.
>
> I did this quite consciously, because—and you can check this easily enough if you want to—because in my subsequent administrative capacity I never permitted anyone in my department to be physically assaulted. That was my reason for apologising in uniform, and in front of my officers.

But apart from these exceptional cases, where his nerves gave way, he claims to be something quite different—the "typical Austrian" that everyone likes. In his dealings with the functionaries of the Jewish community in Vienna, he was, generally speaking, as polite as he was helpful. Consider this:

> When Dr. Rothenberg asked me early on whether I would let him emigrate to Palestine, not immediately, but after various things had been arranged and prepared, I said, when he first put it to me: "Let's wait a bit, until one or two things have cleared up, as long as it is really only a few months!" And then: "*Bitteschön*" (all right). And that's how it happened. When he came back, I said: "Certainly, Dr. Rothenberg, off you go, make all your preparations. You can go." And he went.

Someone else who did not go was the industrialist Storfer, former major in the Austrian Imperial Army, with whom Eichmann also had a lot of dealings.

("We worked together, from first to last, throughout: the whole period.") Storfer's behavior was "ill considered," and he finished up in Auschwitz. There Eichmann had a "normal human meeting" with him, which had the great disadvantage that only one of the two participants is still alive to report on it. This is how it went:

> He complained to me of his miserable position. I said: "Ja, main lieber guter Storfer, my dear fellow, there's a nice mess we've got ourselves into, eh?" and then I said: "Look, I really can't help you. Nobody can get you out, except by order of the Reichsführer. I can't get you out. Dr. Ebner can't get you out. I gather you've committed a Dummheit here, hidden yourself or tried to escape, which wasn't at all necessary, you know." And then Storfer said to me—I asked him how he was—and he said, he'd like to ask if he could be let off the work, it was heavy work. And then I said to Höss: "There's no need for Storfer to work." "Everyone works here," said Höss. So I said: "All right," I said, "I'll make out a chit to the effect that Storfer has to keep the gravel paths in order with a broom." They were only little gravel paths there, and he would have the right to sit down with his broom on one of the benches whenever he chose. "Is that all right, Herr Storfer?" I said. "Does that suit you?" And he was very pleased, and we shook hands and then he was given the broom and sat down on the bench. It was a great inner joy to me.... When I happened to come back from Hungary, I heard that Storfer had been shot."

Even after the most grisly experiences, Eichmann can be reawakened to humanity. He was once forced to witness a mass shooting in Minsk (a rare thing for him). "The trench was full of corpses?" "Yes, it was full, it was full." Afterwards, *ohne Befehl*, he drove in his car to Lemberg.

> And when I get to Lemberg, I see the first agreeable sight after the terrible things I had seen. It was the *Bahnhof*, which was put up to mark the occasion of Emperor Franz Josef's diamond jubilee; and since I personally have a great passion for this Franz Josef period, because I heard so many nice things about it in my parents' house and about the things that happened at that time—my stepmother's relations, you know, during that period were—as you might say—enjoyed a considerable social standing, spent a lot of money—that sight chased away for the first time—I've never forgotten it—otherwise I should certainly never have noticed the jubilee numbers carved on the *Bahnhof*—chased away those terrible thoughts of Minsk that I couldn't get rid of.

"*Mein lieber guter Storfer*" and "*bitteschön*," as well as the passion for the Monarchy, are understandable when we learn that Eichmann "never hated the Jews, was never an anti-Semite." Horrifying as it may seem, it is quite possible that he is speaking the truth here. He had chosen *das Judenreferat*, the "Jewish sector," because it offered a chance of quicker promotion, and he was just as zealous and untiring in expediting emigrations as he was later on with the organization of "transports." (In Jon Kimche's book, *Roads to Israel*, Eichmann does not come out badly.) It is at this point that we begin to suspect that this trial is about something quite different from the "great historical line of development" from Haman. to Eichmann that the prosecution has traced, and that perhaps fits into Prime Minister Ben Gurion's way of thinking.

The same man who had a "human meeting" with "dear old Storfer," later tells us, with the evidence in front of him, how he drew up a document in sober officialese, authorizing Globocnik, on Heydrich's instructions, to "conduct a further 150,000 Jews towards the final solution." They had already been killed. But the "clearance" was still not in order.

> At this time I received an order from Heydrich, to draw up the following letter for Globocnik: Heydrich dictated to me: I authorise you to conduct; a further 150,000 Jews towards the *Endlösung*.
> I can't remember now whether he ordered the letter to be headed "*Head of SS and Chief of German Police in the Reichs Ministry for Internal Affairs*" and signed p.p. Heydrich, or whether he wanted it headed. "*Chief of Security Police SD.*"L...
> —But did the letter contain the words "conduct a further 150,000 Jews towards the final solution"?
> E.:150 or 250, I think. I really don't know.
> —But that meant extermination and death!
> E.: Oh yes, oh yes. These Jews were already dead.
> —And Globocnik had them posthumously documented afterwards.
> E.: I think it must have been 250,000. I think so. Yes, Globocnik had it drawn up for a second time.
> —And this second posthumous order also passed through your Department, through your hands?
> E.: *Jawohl, jawohl.*

The linguistic Eichmann extends from "*bitteschön*" to this repeated "*jawohl, jawohl*," and so does the real man. The Israeli psychiatrist who had to examine him pronounced afterwards: "This man is quite normal." He then added, "More normal than I feel myself after this examination."

Adolf Eichmann—a man without inner compulsions, zealous, ambitious, worried, complete with documented clearances, the Managing Director of Extermination—reminds me of a line in Paul Celan's magnificent poem, *Todesfuge*: "Der Tod ist ein Meister aus Deutschland" (Death is: a master craftsman from Germany), and the horror is inexpressibly heightened by the undertone of traditional East-European respect for the great craftsman and experts from this industrious land. And for this reason I never felt that the man in the glass case here in Jerusalem was any kind of a "legal pretext" or figurehead: he stood at the very center of his trial, although not always in the sense that the prosecution saw him.

What was heard in the long sessions of the trial added, I feel, nothing essentially new to what was already known from the documents. Nevertheless, it was right and necessary that the trial should have taken place, for it has brought these monstrous happenings of which the new generation in all countries—even in Israel, even in Germany and Austria—has been only dimly aware, into the forefront of consciousness. I am sure that as far as the survivors of concentration camps, and the relatives and friends of victims are concerned, these reports have merely served to reopen old wounds; and in most cases, renewed suffering has overshadowed any satisfaction from seeing justice done.

The dark central fact about this past was that thousands of professionals were zealously and conscientiously employed in hunting, trapping, and killing human beings. Suitable *"Menschenmaterial"*—to use a popular Nazi expression correctly for once—was in abundant supply at that time in Germany and Austria; but I wonder if there is really anyone who would subscribe to the theory that it couldn't be found in sufficient quantities in every country in the world, given certain conditions....

Eichmann, the "filing cabinet on a pile of corpses," as one German correspondent called him, is now known to us in a way that very few of our contemporaries are. Is there any significant difference between his present and his past? Anyone who looked at him fussing about with documents in his glass box, making sketches, interpreting maps, questioning and instructing his counsel on his special telephone, could easily imagine him as the SS Colonel of the forties. When asked why he never expressed any feeling of guilt in all his written and dictated recollections, the "filing cabinet" admitted that this was so, but "that doesn't exclude the possibility of my endeavouring to deal with this question privately, in my own way." And no one is surprised to hear him say that his crony Sassan had been forced to liven up the reports he sold to *Life* magazine because "officialese (*die Amtssprache*) was my only language." And indeed, he can discuss torture, misery, and murder entirely in terms of pencilwork, paperwork, and in-and-out baskets. But the accused was, I think, still right to insist, as against the public prosecutor, that he was first and foremost a *Befahlsempfänger*, a "receiver of orders"; and right again when he says on one occasion, with unusual immediacy: "Now that I'm the only one left, everything goes wrong and I'm in it...."

It was in the nature of his activities that they were only one part of a collective crime on a national scale, carried out by large numbers of people in highly differentiated capacities. Clearly, his greatest incentive was always the cultivation of a career, with all its little rewards and opportunities for the exercise of power, rather than any particular driving passion or private obsession. By trying to establish the opposite, Dr. Gideon Hausner cast more darkness than light on the essence of the totalitarian state in question. For with the exception of Hitler himself, no one there really carried "full responsibility" for anything; they were all receivers of orders, and could always invoke their "military oath," their "subordinate position," or "pressure of circumstances." Eichmann himself says that he consulted Müller "wegen jedem Schmarren" (on the most trivial issues), and the Gestapochief Müller, "an official of the old sort, a punctilious bureaucrat all the way through," behaved in the same way.

But how was it that Gideon Hausner, who succeeded after all in fastening some massive contradictions on the accused, nevertheless managed to give the impression rather of a crisscross examination? Why did he get bogged down in details (e.g., the circumstances under which Eichmann was sacked from Vacuum Oil) merely in order to catch him out in a not very telling lie? Why did he get so worked up, even confused, and try to get the accused to admit that he was a "liar" and a "half-wit"? Why did he rave at him, saying he wasn't "worthy to mention the name of Theodor Herzl" (earning an immediate rebuke from Landau, the President of the Court)? These questions are, I think, important, because it was Dr. Hausner's fault that this long trial never turned into a "great trial." My own impression was that Gideon Hausner was determined, at any price, to find in the accused the greatest conceivable quantity of personal malice or fiendishness in order to match the enormity of the events. He was looking for a completely personal guilt and a completely personal sense of guilt, and because he hoped to find too much, he never came to grips with the true characteristics of this type of *DurchschnittsUnmensch*. He wanted a Pharaoh, a tyrant, a Shakespearean villain in the grand style, and found instead an official passionately guarding his little empire and trying to make it grow; a man with girlfriends in the towns where his official trips often took him, riding behind a motorpool chauffeur towards a requisitioned villa; a man who helped the Jews to emigrate as eagerly as he later hunted them down, and who was himself incapable of thinking up anything like "the Final Solution."

Dr. Hausner obstinately insisted on trying to prove, in spite of inadequate evidence and psychological improbability, that this junior executive of Death had personally killed a young Jew for stealing fruit from "his" garden, and he didn't realize that he was only weakening his case by all this. He evidently felt that Eichmann's bureaucratic activities were not really "murder" in the same full sense of the word as a purely personal act would have been. But if he believed that, he had all the more reason to show up Eichmann's criminal activities, which were the point at issue, in their peculiar uniqueness, and in this way to provide a completely different basis for the trial. Hausner's search for the daemonic, for the man acting on his own, driven by uncontrollable urges, is, I suspect, connected with the fact that the Jews of Eastern Europe have for centuries regarded Germany as the home of *Kultur und Humanität*, and that many of them were so completely unable to grasp, even remotely, the brute fact of what the Germans did, that it all could only be explained on the assumption that those involved were possessed by some unique and monstrous mania. In a way, Hausner is too fundamentally decent a man to be able to see into the soul of a mass-murdering mediocrity. He knows all the facts, and has never really understood them. We respected the man, but was he really the right prosecutor?

The three judges examined the accused in the sessions of 20, 21, and 24 July in his (and their own) *Muttersprache*, and more was gained from these three "talks" than from the long cross-examination. Judge Rasch thoughtfully asked what had happened to the Kantian Categorical Imperative, which Eichmann saw himself living out, and the answer was: "Sticking to the regulations was the categorical imperative for the household use of the little man." And it was clear from the next few answers that orders from the *Führer*, even without written confirmation and in literal conflict with the regulations, counted as regulations. Kant and Eichmann, der Denker für den Haugebrauch des Henkers....

Judge Halevi enjoined him: "You may rest assured that the Court has nothing against you personally...and that our only concern is to arrive at the truth. If you wish this as well, then our aims are identical." Recalling, perhaps unconsciously, the "confession" of Klaus Fuchs, Eichmann said that he had never known crises of conscience, but that he had experienced a "split in consciousness ('controlled schizophrenia') where you rush from one side to the other." In an answer to President of the Court Landau, he said: "I could always console myself with the thought that I had no part in all these things." But it was not really so much that he was "split," as that he had "switched off" reality to the best of his ability; and as soon as he was forced to confront several separate realities isolated from each other, he tangled himself up in the most glaring contradictions.

This utter conformist, who was unlucky enough to specialize in something that lost its market value when times changed, this mediocre careerist, should be much more disturbing for the "normal" rest of us than an Eichmann possessed by black passions could ever have been. There were countless decent people who just didn't "join in"; thousands of Germans who were executed; innumerable Italian "fascist" officials who proved their "civilized self-control" by their refusals to assist the deportations (all spontaneous, humane impulses without benefit of Kant). And yet, what the world has been shown under glass here for four months is no fiend in human shape, but a harrowingly familiar type of official specialist. In times of crisis, these *"total Brauchbaren,"* these "100 percent employables," are used for purposes that they themselves would never have suspected; and the discrepancy between their unemotional zeal, directed mostly towards being "in the clear" and "on the make," and the ensuing tragedies, is too immense to grasp. Nevertheless, that and perhaps no other is the truth that has come: out of this trial and out of the grisly proceedings that it exposed in retrospect.

November 1961

Letter from Berlin

The Pilloried Pope

The most passionately discussed cultural event in postwar Germany is a play called *Der Stellvertreter* (scheduled to open in London at the end of September as *The Representative*), produced in Berlin by Erwin Piscator — the man who can claim to have "invented" epic theatre together with Bertiolt Brecht, if not earlier. *Der Stellvertreter* does not possess great literary distinction, and even its dramatic merits, with the exception of a few scenes, are scarce. The performance in the Theater am Kurfurstendamm—ended because of previous commitments, for nobody had foreseen its sensational success, just as no director, except Piscator, wanted to stage this play—was hardly up to the level of productions in the fifty odd excellent theaters in Berlin and West Germany. Yet my file of cuttings on the play, and on debates originated by the play, collected at random, bulges with a hundred articles; and this can only be a small fraction of a discussion that is still raging.

Der Stellvertreter—this title may mean the "Vicar" of Christ or refer to a priest who acts "in the place of the Pope"—is the contribution of an angry and serious young German, Rolf Hochhuth, to the recurrent "Bewaltigung der Vergangenheit" a complicated phrase concerning the reexamination of the past which combines many meanings: the affirmation of the guilt incurred, the acknowledgment of that guilt in a way which creates solidarity with the victims, the wish for atonement, and the endeavor to create a moral climate in which nothing like this could happen again. To make of the past something present appears to such Germans as Hochhuth a duty, and the only hope of shaping a different future.

However, if *Der Stellvertreter* had concentrated on the guilt and complicity of many Germans, even of "respectable" German society, towards Nazism and its monstrosities, it would not have created a noticeable stir. Some would have accepted it, some shrugged it off. But Hochhuth has not focused his play on the guilt of the Germans. It is a "Christian tragedy"—although this definition is omitted from the book version, where the play is simply called "*ein Schauspiel*"—and the central character, although he appears only in one scene, is Pope Pius XII. The Pope is cast as the culprit, the man who remained silent when the Jews of Rome were rounded up under his eyes and deported to Auschwitz, although his appeal might have stopped the extermination just as the appeal of the churches against the so-called "euthanasia program," the extermination of mental defectives, did stop that particular "final solution."

The play, as it can be read in Rowohlt's paperback edition—although Hochhuth works for the biggest German publishing house, Bertelsmann, his own employer had not cared or dared to publish his play—and the drama as it could be seen on the Kurfurstendamm, are not quite the same. It would take eight hours to perform the play as it was written, and Piscator did the only thing possible, extracting from this unwieldy mass six "pictures," which make a play of normal length. Of an original cast of forty-two, barely sixteen characters remain. Eichmann has been left out, as is the infamous Professor Hirt, whose letters formed part of the Jerusalem trial—he had created for his University of Strasburg a collection of "judeo-bolshevik" skulls and was very much concerned that the killings should be done in such a way as not to impair the scientific value of his exhibits; gone as well is the director of Krupp (for a "committed" *régisseur* like Piscator this must have been a real sacrifice), gone too the representative of the armament industry and the chief of the German police in Rome.

With so many guilty Germans left out, and one rather un-typically "demonic" doctor in Auschwitz left in, the Pope and two other representatives of higher Vatican hierarchy, the Nuncio in Berlin and a Cardinal in Rome, move to the center of the indictment. Inasmuch as this play is, in fact, an accusation and a verdict, it might appear, quite wrongly, that Hochhuth is less worried by the moral corruption of Germans under Nazism, or even by the guilt of the German Church, than by that of the Roman hierarchy. Since his play is a work of indignation, and has to be judged in moral and not aesthetic terms, one can understand why many German Catholics have reproached the author for a thesis which allows the German people to escape their complicity or guilt by thinking: if the Pope, who ran no risk and who had a real chance of making his voice heard did not protest, why expect me to have acted, when my action would have been useless as well as suicidal? However, Hochhuth obviously has the right to feel strongly about the Pope; if a Christian like Dante could condemn a Pope, Celestin V, to Hell, why should not a modern playwright have the same privilege?

In a long postscript to the play, Hochhuth has given the sources from which he has drawn the opinion that the conduct of Pius was inexcusable. One may wonder whether this young Protestant has not overrated the importance of a gesture from the Pope in the last, maddest years of Hitler's reign; and this question arises out of what I consider the true weakness of the argument taken in its own terms as a "morality play." Hochhuth's question is not: what was the duty of the Vicar of Christ, the "*Stellvertreter Christi*" in those times, regardless of the consequences, either for himself, for the lives of many priests and other Catholics, for the fate of the Church in German-dominated countries, and even for the Jews? Rather, the author's question is: since the

Pope had the power to stop the deportation and extermination, why did he not do so?

Thus, he does not lead to a moral problem, but to a historical question and to endless debate over the likely outcome of a protest by the Pope. This debate by its very nature can hardly be conclusive. Hochhuth may cite the example of the Slovakian clergy, which at one point was able to stop the deportations; but others may reply—and have replied—with the instance of the Dutch clergy which protested against racialist persecution, only in consequence to have Dutch Catholics, of non-Aryan origin, singled out for deportation and extermination. If one has to contend with so many different and sometimes contradictory facts of recent history in order to judge whether the main thesis of a play is "correct"—it is here really a matter of being "correct" rather than "true" in the profound sense—then the play is not convincing in its own right. Leaving aside the matter of the "success" of any action by the Pope, it might have been much more persuasive.

The contradiction goes deeper than this, however. In the book the author indicates that he wants groups of two, three, or four characters to be played by the same actor—for instance a cardinal and Professor Hirt; an officer and a Jew in Auschwitz; the Pope and the director of the Reich armament organization. Hochhuth adds that only by such groupings can one show that at a time of total terror there are *no distinctions* of personal merit or choice, of the uniform one is wearing, or whether one is executioner or victim. Under a regime of terror, he is saying, people don't act as individuals seeking to make their own decisions, but as a faceless mass.

The play, however, belies this fatalist conception, which appears therefore as a cliché. The play is dedicated to the memory of two Catholic priests, Father Maximilian Kolbe, who died in Auschwitz in the "Hunger block" where he had taken the place of another tortured prisoner, and Dean Lichtenberg, who preached in Berlin against anti-Semitism and died en route to Dachau. The hero of the play is SS Sturmbannführer Kurt Gerstein, a real person. Gerstein, a militant Christian anti-Nazi, managed as an engineer to get into the SS, after having been in concentration camps, where he learned of the "functioning" of extermination camps like Treblinka. He communicated his knowledge to the Allies—mainly through Dutch resistance groups—but disappeared mysteriously in a Paris prison in 1944, probably killed as an "SS Bloodhound" by French patriots (many who conducted such executions after victory were not those who had borne the dangers of the fight) although this is not a certainty.

This man, who wears the SS uniform in Hochhuth's play, performs as he did in reality, acts of individual conscience and courage. He appeals in the very first scene to the Nuncio in Berlin to intervene against the deportations, and, not surprisingly, is suspected of being a "provocateur." In the second scene, he is shown hiding a young Jew in his apartment, and he asks the young

Roman priest and diplomat Fontana, who complies, to change clothes in order to allow this Jew to flee to Italy. (The Jew whom Gerstein saved, learning that his parents have been deported, bursts out that he will be unable ever to forgive any German—including his saviour Gerstein—and adds: "One day I will return and take revenge."

At every single major point Gerstein appears in a decisive way. Every word of his proves that one man may choose his destiny, that nobody is predetermined by nationality or uniform—just as the young Fontana who, in the presence of the unutterably shocked Pope, pins a yellow star on his cassock and ends in Auschwitz, has not been shaped by "anonymous forces." Significantly, Hochhuth has not placed Gerstein and Fontana in any "grouping," or lumped them with other persons to be played by the same actor.

The real lesson of the play is, therefore, the possibility of an individual moral act of decency, even of martyrdom. And since we see persons who have so chosen, the acts of others in refusing to choose, refusing to witness or to speak out, do not appear as the expected behavior of mediocre people under stress, but as unforgivable cowardice. The theory of the "interchangeability" of characters has thus not only been forgotten, but proved wrong.

Except for the Pope. His individual action could have been decisive, but he appears as a banal person, as are his whole milieu of high dignitaries. These are typified by a cardinal whose main concern is for good food, good cigars, and good talk. The scene in which the Pope—obsessed as he was in fact by the fear of microbic contagion—washes his hands while disclaiming any responsibility for the fate of the Roman Jews, has a dramatic quality despite the obviousness of the symbol. And it is a daring scene to be acted before a public of whom many are Catholics. We hear the Pope use the words *"mit brennender Sorge"*—words which begin the famous encyclical of his predecessor Pius XI denouncing anti-Christian measures in Nazi Germany—but this Pius applies them to his concern that the Italian factories in which the Vatican has some investments are being bombed. And we hear the Pope say that, considering the menace of the anti-Christian Russia, we need a "chastised" and more modest Hitler, but not Hitler's defeat. But such dramatic moments are rare. The last scene, set in Auschwitz, is in every sense unbearable—in part because it brings so close an unbearable, unrepresentable reality; in part because it centers on the demonic "doctor."

This sensational play—and wherever it is staged it will again create a sensation—is written in a blank verse, which is intended to show the banality of the Nazis; but which itself becomes a cliché because the author has no gift for style. The contrast between the "poesy" prose and the mediocrity of the style leads to effects that are involuntarily comical or painful. Further, because so many real persons and events are brought in, so much "documentation" put in the mouths of its characters, the play might be compared to a "collage," yet the contrast between the "plastered-on" elements of reality and imagination is not used in a fresh or even modernistic way: rather we are reminded of those overwritten reportages which appear in German (and probably other) illustrated papers, that pretend to show History in the making, to give the very words which people spoke at crucial moments and reveal what happened behind the scenes. The term "psychodrama," used by a French commentator, does fit the double aspect which is presented: of an obsession, and the acting out of an "exorcism"; and as a psychodrama this play differs from a dramatized reportage.

Apart from the many weaknesses and inconsistencies Hochhuth has written a play that belongs to a "hybrid," perhaps even an impossible, genre. But it also shows us the power of the theater. Nothing but a play could have created such a deep stir, could have been at the center of such prolonged and passionate attention. The audience's awareness that this is not imagination, but a record of real happenings, creates a sense of participation, of shared emotions, from which it is hard to detach oneself. One may not want the theater to achieve this kind of effect—but one cannot deny it.

Der Stellvertreter has shocked and offended many people, above all Catholics. And many have reacted strongly, sometimes in an unpleasant and unconvincing tone. Father Leiber, who was close to Pius XII, and whom Hochhuth never bothered to interview during his researches on the Pope, has answered quietly. He admits that the Pope never publicly protested against the extermination of tine Jews, and he compares his attitude with the conduct of the leaders of the International Red Cross in Geneva. They could help in individual cases, but only if they did not speak up about the gruesome fact of the systematic mass murder itself. And he cites the many cases in which lives were saved by congregations, by individual priests, and also by the Vatican. Survivors of the Jewish community in Rome have expressed to priests and to the Pope their deepest sense of gratitude. However one wonders whether for a Catholic it is quite enough to show that the Vicar of Christ acted under the same impulses and with the same reasoning as the distinguished Swiss gentlemen of the Red Cross.

A German writer, Rudolf Krämer-Badoni, has remarked that never in all history have popes protested against atrocities on general humanitarian grounds, but only when such issues concerned the right of Catholics to follow their faith. But it is difficult to compare the murder of millions of Jews by a government with whom the Church had concluded a Concordat (and of whose leaders many remained formally Catholics) with most other occasions for "protest." And many Catholics will not feel comfortable with an explanation that a pope does not feel impelled to speak as the Voice of Conscience. Be that as it may, Father Leiber does recognize that some other pope, not trained as a diplomat, might have acted differently, although a spokesman of militant German Catholicism, Prince Karl zu Löwenstein, argues that it ill behooves West Berlin to tolerate a play which may jeopardize some of the sympathies that this free city needs—an argument which ironically echoes Hochhuth's play, with its theme of the predominance of diplomatic and opportunistic considerations over everything else in the Roman hierarchy.

Hochhuth, if he can be judged by this first play, is not likely to become the new German writer whom dozens of richly endowed excellent theaters all over West Germany are eagerly hoping for. He fails, I believe, not only by literary standards, which in the theater are not necessarily the only valid standards, but he fails in his purpose: to make us feel the weight of the past over the present. Yet even if there remains a wide gap between Hochhuth's "success" and his "achievement," nobody would dream of denying that *Der Stellvertreter* is, as the Germans like to put it, an event, *ein Ereignis*. And to Berliners it is a cause for satisfaction that this event should have happened in Berlin which claims still to be the intellectual capital of Germany.

October 1963

Letter from Paris

The New Puritans

Freedom of expression has, in France, been threatened from various sides since the war—not, as might be thought, only by civilian and military representatives of the state, but also by their critics and enemies, as much under the Fourth as under the Fifth Republic as much from the Left as from the Right. My folder bulges with clippings about such scandals, confiscations, lawsuits, fines, and the like; yet I think it can be said that no significant work of literature, or opinion, or piece of information actually fell sacrifice to this censorship. Considering the long colonial wars, the dangers of civil strife, the *putsches*, acts of terrorism, and attempts to murder high state officials, the extent to which freedom of opinion was maintained throughout nearly two decades of crisis is striking.

This optimistic view is, at any rate, shared by M. Jerôme Lindon, publisher of Editions de Minuit—the publishing house, that is, which holds the record in confiscations, penalties, and lawsuits arising from its books on the Algerian war (especially the murders and acts of torture by the army and police). And I begin with this preamble in order to prevent giving a black total impression which any report of cases of censorship inevitably does.

Again and again there were borderline cases where one asked oneself, after the event, whether the government had overreached itself or had acted properly. Two examples, ten years apart. 1952: The high point of Stalinist communism, with agitprop calls to *la France* to violent demonstrations and political strikes. Associated with this are nasty campaigns of intimidation and incitement. A Paris theater puts into its repertoire a play by the then communist Roger Vaillant, *Colonel Foster Pleads Guilty*, a piece about the Korean War, in which the Americans are the aggressors, and confess as much. There is also much talk about "germ warfare" (around which the Communist Party at that time built a great deal of propaganda, only to retreat from it all later). The prefect of police in Paris did not dare to ban the piece for its political bias; but some one at the Prefecture discovered that the theater was not safe from fire, and delayed the performance. When the curtain finally went up, disturbances occurred which did not seem exactly spontaneous and which made a ban possible "for the protection of public order." The way in which the play "failed" was thus something less than elegant; clearly the government officials themselves acted with rather a bad conscience. In those same months, communist mayors had several times prohibited performances of the film based on Jean-Paul Sartre's *Les Mains Sales* (and also several other films) in their towns; what the C.P. was really demanding was not "freedom of opinion" but their own monopoly.

1962: the radical rightwing pamphleteer and essayist Alfred Fabre-Luce (whom first the Germans, then the French imprisoned at the end of the war because of his independent *Diaries*) publishes a new book, *Haute Cour*, a fictional indictment for high treason against General de Gaulle, the betrayer of *l'Algérie Française*. At a time when attempts were being made on the president's life and civil peace was endangered by OAS terrorism, such a book could conceivably have been considered a danger. Nevertheless, the left-of-center papers, too, protested against the ban, which was certainly inept, and gave the book more attention than it deserved. More than that, it was a confiscation without subsequent prosecution, that is, a purely administrative and arbitrary one.[1] The suppression of freedom of opinion has thus from time to time, been clumsily effected, with conspicuously bad conscience (even in cases in which it would seem to unprejudiced observers entirely possible to put forward some kind of reasonable justification).

From Vaillant to Fabre-Luce: the left-to-right reversal of the government's target was particularly obvious during the Algerian war. At first—and, on the whole, more during the last years of the Fourth Republic than under de Gaulle—leftwing papers like *l'Express* and *France-Observateur* (opponents of the Algerian war) were frequently confiscated; after the peace treaty of Evian, however, only papers of the extreme right, like *Rivarol*, were endangered.

As a whole, I don't think it can be said that political discussion in France seriously suffered as a result of such individual interventions of censorship. On the contrary. Each censorship scandal received the greatest publicity and the censors for the most part achieved the opposite of what they intended. Henri Alleg's book on his tortures, *La Question*, was confiscated, but the text then reappeared as "a document" and was reprinted several times. A second report on methods of torture in Paris jails, *La Gangrene*, was labeled "a vulgar tissue of lies" in the Senate by Michel Debré (at that time not yet prime minister); but the confiscation was cancelled, and it was later quietly admitted that *La Gangrene* had been a reasonably accurate report.

Should the publication of "everything" be allowed in times of national danger and emergency? In France the reply has been "almost everything." Thus, after the execution of Bastien Thiry (he had organized the attempt to murder de Gaulle), the periodical *Esprit Public*, which had been a firm supporter of the OAS, dedicated a special issue featuring many well-known rightwing authors in honor of this would-be assassin; and I saw it conspicuously exhibited at many Paris newspaper kiosks.

The threat to books and periodicals from the various laws concerning "morality" and "the protection of youth," is at present greater than that from partisan politics. Jerome Lindon told me how the printers had refused to set up a Samuel Beckett novel for fear of prosecution for "immorality." How curious it is that today France should be more puritanical than England and the USA. The Paris publishers Pauvert and Girodias especially have been prosecuted because of pornographic works. A celebrated case (it is still running through a series of appeals) concerned the book, *Eros*, by the little-read but nevertheless highly regarded and rather difficult thinker, Georges Bataille. The book dealer Maspero was prosecuted—because the book was visible behind a glass wall! Any suspicion of a "pornographic intention" here was decidedly farfetched.

But who is competent to judge? The Ministry of the Interior has the right to "confiscate and to destroy" books of every kind that might be "a danger to youth" (even if they are not specifically addressed to young readers); and there is also no independent group of experts who can be summoned to form an opinion (as in England's so-called Jenkins Law, which governed the Chatterley trial), no more than there is any appeal against purely administrative decisions. A law for the protection of youth of 1949 forbids that writings in which "banditry, lying, theft, sloth, cowardice, hate, depravity are shown in a favorable light" be made accessible to the young. This, as Maître Maurice Garçon (Pauvert's lawyer) said, would even enable the Arsène Lupin thrillers to be banned. This law was, however, made even more severe under de Gaulle in December 1958, by a supplementary decree; it now applies to publications of any nature whatever (in other words, also to those that are not meant especially for the young). How arbitrary can one get?

So at the moment literary freedom in France is really a matter of state tolerance—the authorities being, for one reason or another, afraid of ridicule—but it is not a matter of clear right. There are no qualified independent counsels, no appeal before a court of law. In principle, this can be traced back a century to the time when Flaubert's *Madame Bovary* was prosecuted for "lewdness," only then it was within the competence of the court for a lawsuit to be brought (which the prosecution lost). Could it be that our grandfathers were more liberal? Today the decree of 1958 legalizes almost every arbitrary whim. Publishers who have been sued three times because of their books must submit their further publications (not the manuscripts, but the printed volumes!) to the Ministry of the Interior. They then wait for approval, which can be withheld with no obligation on the part of the authorities to show cause and with no opportunity for appeal.

Curious that things should be so different in the cinema. Here, quite on the contrary, the attitude on moral questions is on the whole very generous, and the attitude towards politically inflammable issues very narrow, so that hardly one really pertinent and fundamental subject can be dealt with in the cinema.

Not even a social one: not about Algerian workers in France, nor about housing conditions, indeed as far back as the days of the Dreyfus affair and Maupassant's *Bel Ami* hardly a film on a controversial subject has ever been shot in France. Some recent films have been held back for years, for example, Claude Autant-Lara's *Thou Shalt Not Kill*, Jean-Luc Godard's *The Little Soldier*. Other films were mutilated, like Alain Resnais' *Statues Die Too*. Here the list would be very long. Quality films need subsidies and this exposes them to all kinds of pressure from above, of which censorship is only a part. I doubt whether the censors alone carry the blame for the frequently lamented lack of "boldness" on the part of the producers. At any rate, an unhappy situation.

In broadcasting and television, censorship again is only a small part of the great ensemble of instruments of influence and control by the government (and also by the UNR as the government party). The RTF (Radiodiffusion et Télévision Françaises) lacks a statute that effectively guarantees its independence. At times this, of course, can be disagreeable for the government itself, for, whatever happens to be broadcast, it is taken to be responsible. Thus a Syrian démarche to the Quai d'Orsay was enough to suppress, literally at the last minute, an eyewitness account of Nasserism; on other occasions, an interview with Khrushchev about Stalingrad and a television film called *Dying in Madrid* were withdrawn. Such direct intervention—combined with the disciplinary punishment of producers—has aroused widespread public attention, and the consequences have been negative for both the government and the reputation of the RTF.

Even worse, I think, are the cases of direct influence through television. I refer to sham interviews with ministers, with previously arranged questions, and answers that always completely satisfy the interviewer.... I feel sure the French viewer notices what is being staged for him, but it is a disagreeable piece of theater every time. In broadcasting, it has actually been established that the so-called "peripheral transmitters," like Europa I, Radio Luxembourg, Monte Carlo (which are not—or at least not so visibly—subject to governmental influence), have many more listeners, especially for their political news bulletins and commentaries.

The RTF is often, or at least sometimes, better than its reputation; but as long as there are important officials there like the chief television producer, André Gérard, who wrote recently in a newspaper: "Whoever is against the government stands outside the nation," as long as the promised statute making the RTF a public corporation is not concluded and its budget is not independent, there will be malaise. Is the government entitled to complain that France's broadcasting network and television system does not enjoy the reputation of "impartiality," and "objectivity"? The television journalists are not at all happy about this reputation and about this way of performing their duties—believe me, one can read it in their faces.

January 1964

Note

1. Arguments have just been heard in Paris' Criminal Court, the prosecutor having asked for the final suppression of the book and destruction of all copies. (An English translation was published by Methuen in London under the title *The Trial of Charles De Gaulle.*

The Struggle for Kafka and Joyce: A Conversation between Hans Mayer and François Bondy

—May I ask whether during your teaching career in Leipzig you ever took part in any of those conferences which seemed to us to be such harbingers of "cultural thaw"? For example, the Prague Conference on Franz Kafka which was so extensively discussed in the Czech press?

MAYER: This conference was held in late May 1963.... Earlier during May I had been lecturing at various Yugoslav universities. It is interesting to note that out of all the subjects I had proposed and sent to Sarajevo, Belgrade, Zagreb, Ljubljana, and Novisad, the Yugoslavs selected only Kafka and Brecht! So in Yugoslavia I spoke only on Kafka; and then I heard from Prague that they would like to have me at their forthcoming conference, which was to be largely under the direction of the German Institute of the Charles University of Prague, in fact of my colleague, Professor Eduard Goldstücker. [Goldstücker had been condemned to life imprisonment at the Slansky trial in 1952; he was freed in 1956, and "rehabilitated" in 1962.]

—Did he invite you personally?

MAYER: No, I heard from Goldstücker himself that I was going to be invited; but no invitation ever came. Which showed clearly enough that all was not well. Then, an East German delegation turned up in Prague, and although I was not invited, my chief assistant, Dr. Helmut Richter, was. Richter had worked with me for his doctorate—a thesis on Kafka—and I arranged for it to be published. Apparently there was no great keenness in East Berlin to see me there.

—How was it reported in East Berlin?

MAYER: It wasn't even mentioned. The Czechs wrote it up, so did the Austrians, the Hungarians, and the Poles—but there was not a single reference to it in East Berlin or Leipzig. Now, this was a very important conference. It wasn't just about Kafka the writer; the real subject was—"how is Kafka to be fitted into a socialist society," what is a socialist society to make of him? No one faced up to this question until several Western Marxist critics, e.g., Roger Garaudy in Paris and Ernst Fischer in Vienna, spoke on Kafka and were promptly rebuked from East Berlin by Alfred Kurella. The result was a rather silly sort of lineup of opposing forces. Ernst Fischer made a formidable impression and his lecture ended with the words: "Are you going to give Kafka a permit to stay?" The upshot was that people began to look upon Kafka (and the conference) as "swallows heralding a new spring." Whereupon the irate Herr Kurella leaps to his feet to announce that he for his part could see no swallows heralding spring—only bats coming out at nightfall.

—How is it that an author like Kafka, who belongs after all to our past, is still able to exert such a topical and disturbing influence?

MAYER: Do you know the address that Jean-Paul Sartre delivered in Moscow in 1962? He went very explicitly into the question of Kafka and put it this way: Kafka is a cartload of dynamite standing between East and West which each side tries to wheel into the other's camp so that it will explode there. The West tried to use Kafka as a Cold War weapon with a view to softening up Eastern ideology. Whereupon the East—to quote Sartre again—took up the challenge and declared they would have nothing to do with such a writer. The cartload of dynamite could stay just where it was. "We reject Kafka and we refuse to print him." And indeed to this very day, not one line of Kafka has been printed in the Soviet Union. In other words, Kafka has become a weapon in the Cold War.[1] Our job now is first of all to rescue a great writer from this ridiculous and perverse situation, and secondly to ask ourselves this question: how is it possible that a man who died in 1922 can figure so largely in the present split between East and West—so that one side can say, "Print Kafka and you are opening the door to revisionism!" while the others say, "Print Kafka if you want to show that you are really more liberal...."

—You know better than I do that there is no general agreement on this in the East. Poland, for example, chose to go her own way and quite a lot of Kafka was printed after 1956 and very favorably received; many Polish writers have explicitly acknowledged their indebtedness to this new and important force in their lines. Which is what Sartre really meant.... But should we limit our conversation to Kafka alone? It is remarkable how some writers who belong to the past still exercise this revolutionary power on us today.

MAYER: Joyce is one—and Faulkner is another.

—During the thaw in East Germany, you once said as much in a widely quoted essay.

MAYER: I wrote "On the Present Condition of Our Literature" in 1956, and they still haven't forgiven me! What I said was this: Let us stop behaving as though Kafka never lived, as though Joyce never wrote *Ulysses*. This, of course, involves the whole question of the Cold War, the theoretical basis of what is called "ideological coexistence" or its rejection. In Yugoslavia, Kafka is extremely popular; you can buy paperback editions of *The Castle* and *The Trial* in any bookshop in Belgrade or Zagreb—if they're not sold out. He is a very popular and much published author in Poland. In Hungary, too, more and more of him is being printed, especially in the excellent periodical *Nagy Világ*, devoted to world literature. Last year *Nagy Világ* printed a first Hungarian translation of the famous letter Kafka wrote to his father.

—I remember I was in Hungary in November 1956, when the rising took place. After the Russian intervention, people used to tell a story about Georg Lukács: how, when he was arrested, he was taken to Rumania and shut up in some sort of weird castle where he and his fellow prisoners were treated sometimes like felons and sometimes like guests of honor. After a few days of this, Lukács is supposed to have said, "So Kafka was a realist after all!"

MAYER: Yes, but that's something he wouldn't try to justify theoretically. When I was lecturing at Budapest University in 1962—again it was about Kafka, and the place was packed—I went to see Lukács who had just written the book which has appeared in West Germany under the title of *Against Mistaken Realism*. The book contains one major essay entitled "Thomas Mann or Franz Kafka?" and it shows us a Lukács far from convinced that Kafka is a "realist." For a moment he may have experienced Kafka as a realist but he stopped short of committing it to print. On the contrary— "Thomas Mann represents tradition, Kafka represents decadence." Lukács has not changed his mind on this score. I think he is mistaken, and I also think that Lukács' attitude has had much to do with the general mistrust of Kafka in the East. But let me be careful not to confuse cause and effect. Lukács rejected Kafka because of an ideological situation; I don't suggest that Kafka was rejected because Lukács rejected him.[2]

—Some of my Czech friends have told me that when the scene was being prepared for the Slánsky show trial, they knew people who found themselves accused and didn't even know what they were supposed to have done—such people felt themselves living in a world whose only literary counterpart was

Kafka's *Trial*. What he describes there—that was what was actually happening to them. How few so-called realistic writers would be able to give people in such a predicament this feeling! Am I reading too much into this?

MAYER: No, I don't think this is an artificial construction put on Kafka. On the other hand I don't think that it is only in countries of the Eastern bloc that one finds Kafkaesque reality— what the French now call "le Kafkaesque." I was in Vienna in spring 1963 when the Orson Welles film *The Trial* was first shown. A Vienna newspaper critic argued that the film made a great mistake in attempting to evoke the "Kafkaesque" from such a proliferation of Brobdingnagian halls and robot colonies. Walk into any Viennese office (wrote this paper) and you will find more genuine Kafka than in all these echoing halls put together. Clearly, Kafka is of significance to all of us in our modern situation; but some of us will recognize certain facets more readily than others. Many of those who know what reality is like in the Eastern countries will recognize each other in *The Trial*, in episodes of *The Castle*, in this anonymity. And yet it is probably not this but the problem of what is called "decadence" that is essential.

—I still think that if we look at moments and areas of greatest liberalization in the Eastern bloc—say, Poland in 1957 or present-day Hungary—we find in purely literary spheres an amazing degree of openness. But the moment that certain conceptual matters such as—"what is capitalism?" "what is socialism?" "what is a multiparty state?" etc., raise their heads, then expression is restricted. It is because of this that I suggest one might usefully distinguish between literary and ideological coexistence.

MAYER: The whole question of decadence and ideology and coexistence is also a question of theory, wherever Marxism is "theologically" applied and practiced—i.e., wherever it is held that every word that Marx or Engels or Lenin wrote, no matter whether a deliberate statement in print, a rough draft, or a quick scrawl in a diary, are all Holy Writ. When things come to this pass it is natural for a mentality to develop —a mentality which still holds its ground in Moscow, and, of course, East Berlin and Leipzig try to out-Herod Herod in this respect—which sees the revisionist devil, the reprobate infidel, in anybody who dares to question any of these sacred fiats. The whole problem of ideology and coexistence proceeds from a petrified and sterile theory which is ipso facto not really a theory; for a theory which assumes the right to call itself "dialectical materialism" and then proceeds to put petrification in the place of dialectic, can hardly claim to be living up to its own terms.

—Looking at the matter purely psychologically, where does this urge to keep out whatever is uncomfortable or disturbing come from? Marx has to be falsified in the process—for Marx was far from dogmatic vis-á-vis the writers of his time, and there is as little trace of this doctrinaire attitude in him as there is of the Inquisition in the Gospels. At some point this brand of purely dogmatic Marxism must have been infected into the Doctrine as it simply cannot be found in Marx himself. In other words, Marx has not only been canonized; in order to make him appear so and keep him so, he has also been distorted and even censored.

MAYER: Both. He has been falsified—that is to say, sentences he wrote have been taken from their historical context (which is in itself from the Marxist standpoint a deadly sin); he has also been censored, i.e., his earlier works on philosophy and economics (actually very important documents in the development of Marxism) have been omitted from the canon. Let me give you an example of two interpretations of one text—the official dogmatic and the revisionist interpretation—which will show you what I mean. One of the main texts of the Eastern dogmatic school—it is fortunately safe to call them the Stalinists—is Lenin's pamphlet on *Party Organization and Party Literature*. The most momentous and far-reaching misuse has been made of this little work (and this remains true whether we agree with Lenin's original argument or not). A ruling on the meaning of this pamphlet has actually cost many men their lives and many more their liberty! Lenin wrote the book in 1907 after the abortive revolution of 1905 and its thesis can be stated simply: writers who are members of the Bolshevik Party must toe the Party line in all their writings. That is to say, the Party must have the right of supervision over whatever writers belonging to this small conspiratorial party of 1907 produce. There is, as a matter of fact, no agreement even on the relatively minor point whether the ruling applied to dramas and novels—not that there were very many of those forthcoming from Lenin's little party—or whether it meant that a writer who was also a Party member could only publish political pamphlets. But what happened under Stalin? This scrap of Holy Writ according to Lenin was inflated into the general dogma that the Party—no longer Lenin's handful of conspirators but the Communist Party of the Soviet Union—and the State have the right to decree that nothing be written or published that is not in line with Party doctrine. This interpretation of this Leninist text sealed the fate of many important writers and artists, censored and hounded to death like Isaac Babel, Boris Pilnyak, Mandelstam, and Meyerhold. These writers had expressed opinions that ran counter to the current Stalinist party line, and judgment was accordingly pronounced: it is written in Lenin that you are wrong, therefore your books must be censored.

—What is it that makes such people—you yourself must have met and been well acquainted with many of them, especially in East Germany—delight in sniffing about for subversive passages in books, setting themselves up as censors? There seems to be a special type of person who enjoys doing it. I have often wandered how it is that men of education and culture like Josef Revai in Hungary, or—I suppose—Kurella in East Germany take such a delight in depriving the younger generation of the chance of reading what they must hare read themselves in their younger days. From a purely human standpoint I find this very difficult to understand.

MAYER: We won't get very far if we look at this from a purely psychological standpoint. But we can throw a lot of political light on the matter. Writers who follow the party line in East Germany always trot out the same old argument, which I, for my own part, do not regard as valid. In Germany, divided as it is, we have a very special situation, and if we are to meet the demands presented by our special road to socialism then we must make certain conditions binding for culture and literature as well. In Prague, in Hungary, in Poland, things may be quite different (though this bit sticks in their gullets because, in 1956, they were all trumpeting how horribly wrong things were going in Poland and Hungary). Thus, special East German measures are alleged to be necessary, and these have led naturally to tension, crises, and finally to the erection of the Wall. So it is that special measures are always begetting special situations, very special situations which in their turn engender a fresh round of restrictions and more very special measures. It is a vicious circle. But the individual case is quite different. As for Alfred Kurella—now, there is a portentous figure for the whole cultural life of Eastern Germany. He comes of a bourgeois family and was a member of the *Jugendbewegung*. In October, 1913, he climbed the Hohen Meissner and a friend of his who knows him very well and even likes him, once said to me. "The trouble with Kurella is that he's never come down—he's still on the top of that mountain." The man has never really outgrown the *bündische* ideals of the German youth movement. This man who rejects Kafka and Joyce and the whole of modern literature and who regards Expressionism as drivel to be banned from German universities—this same man comes up suddenly with a brilliant brainwave: he is going to create a cultured nation, with everybody in Bitterfeld and Erfurt reading Hesiod and Homer and reciting the *Nibelungenlied*. A curious mésalliance between the Youth Movement of 1913 and Marxism of the twenties, plus, in Kurella's case, the experiences of an emigré German in Stalin's Russia. Of course, there are psychological factors as well. It was not enough for Kurella to fail as a painter; he had to fail as a novelist as well. Even Aufbau, his publishers, who had perforce to print his novel, *Gronauer Akten*, and other products of his pen, used to split their sides over the stuff. So that's Kurella for you—a human catastrophe who sees himself in the role of State preceptor for the younger generation. There are no doubt psychoanalysts who can explain this sort of thing; but all that really matters is that a man like this, fundamentally lacking in the requisite spiritual, philosophical, and literary essentials, has it in his power to censor and to silence. When, a few years ago, the East German poet Peter Huchel was offered the West Berlin Fontane prize, Kurella threatened him and warned him not to accept. Huchel refused. And Kurella said to him: "Huchel, in the Soviet Union I have seen proud men going to their death...." When such things happen, then what we are faced with is something very much bigger than Herr Kurella's complexes. Here is one of the contemporary masters of the language faced with brute force from this specimen of human failure.

—So that's Kurella! In recent weeks people hare been asking what sort of man Wilhelm Girnus is. If we may stay on this personal note for a little longer—I think you worked with him.

MAYER: I'm not at all sure that my personal reminiscences are of any value, but I'm very willing to say something about Wilhelm Girnus. He was a pupil of mine and wrote an excellent thesis on Goethe's conception of art and literature. Ernst Bloch was coexaminer with me and we had no hesitation at all about accepting the very scholarly work that Girnus submitted. His drawback, I suppose, is that really he knows nothing about modern art or literature; he is only interested in the German classics. He is a great Goethe fan. Well, so am I. But it seems to me that using Goethe to stifle modern creative writing is not being exactly true to Goethe; rather the reverse; to me it seems a denial. To Girnus modern literature is a closed book and he did a great deal of harm up to 1953 when he was an "ideological consultant" to the so-called State Arts Commission. Brecht was always at loggerheads with him, and Girnus hated Brecht. When Girnus wrote his articles in Neues Deutschland attacking Ernst Barlach, Brecht was moved to answer with his fine essay in defense of Barlach that appeared in *Sinn und Form*. Girnus has always rejected and reviled everything that smacked of modernism in literature, mainly, I should say, because of inherent inability to think himself into it, to grasp it. He is a man of considerable culture, no doubt of it, but he is mainly interested in the party line. And sometimes he's not too particular. Let me mention my own experience of him. First of all, he pursues me to Hamburg urging me to return my Chair in Leipzig—needless to say, I turned a deaf ear. Failing in Hamburg, he sends a registered letter to my address in Tübingen full of typical Girnus arguments, hoping to bring off what he failed to achieve in Hamburg. Again he draws a blank. Whereupon he breaks out in a spirited parody of my recent essays which appeared in *Sonntag*. That still doesn't satisfy him. So off he goes to my old flat in Leipzig and has fifty cases of my books carted away, presumably in the interests of State security.

—Perhaps he wanted something decent to read.

MAYER: Maybe possibly for his own library but quite certainly for the Humboldt University Library and for his own Institute. Be that as it may, a pupil who purloins fifty cases of books belonging to his old teacher is a curious fellow.

—You mentioned Brecht. It has always seemed strange to us that it was precisely in East Germany, in cultural matters the most inflexible of the satellites, that this man worked, whose influence on the whole world has been and still is so very lively and infectious. How much persists of his spirit in the country which he himself chose to live in?

MAYER: It seems to me that first we have to take stock of the situation as it was in 1948/49 when Brecht elected to come to East Berlin. The Eastern Republic was not set up until 1949. At the time the spirit of hope was vigorous; one could discern enormous possibilities.

—Were you there yourself?

MAYER: I myself moved there at about the same time, and people have often asked me what on earth possessed me to move in October 1948, from Frankfurt-am-Main to Leipzig. Let me give you a few facts. At the same time Ernst Bloch was coming from America to Leipzig; also from the States came the distinguished anthropologist Julius Lips (whose premature death was such a great loss to us); in November 1948, Arnold Zweig turned up from Israel, and Bertolt Brecht came via Switzerland and Prague to East Berlin. Early in 1949 the periodical *Sinn and Form* was founded and at the same time the "Berlin Ensemble" was founded by Brecht, Hans Eisler, Ernst Busch, Erich Engel, and others. A few months before I moved to Leipzig, Walther Felsenstein had re opened the Comic Opera. All of which goes to show that much was happening here, that things looked very promising. The first DEFA films were remarkably good. It was only later that things began to petrify. This tendency increased until we arrive at the present day situation in East Germany—and find not one of the creative spirits behind that tremendous intellectual and cultural upsurge still there or still working in the manner envisaged in 1949. Bloch and I are in the West; Peter Huchel has had to abandon *Sinn und Form*; Brecht is dead. But nothing is left of the spirit that drew us all together in those days of common hope and endeavor.[3]

—Of course these years saw a literary renaissance in other countries too, e.g., in Poland. There, too, great hopes were cherished which were soon to be nipped. This frost was more widespread than one sometimes thinks. What is of interest is the fact that "the Thaw," when it came, took specific national forms. Which brings us back to what you call ideological coexistence. Do you think that what we are suffering from is the aftermath of the epoch that died with Stalin and out of which something new can yet emerge—or is it the onset of a new ice age?

MAYER: I think it is both. Stalinism is not yet a spent force; but on the other hand something different is emerging. I remain convinced that we must distinguish the East German situation very sharply from that of the other states in the Eastern bloc. There has never been a West Prague or a West Warsaw or a West Budapest. In these countries the bourgeois intelligentsia is actively at work, especially in the universities, which they run on admirably rational lines (in striking contradistinction to much that was laid down as education policy in East Berlin by Secretary of State Girnus). The result is that if we go to the German seminars in Budapest, or Prague, or Warsaw, we shall find curricula embracing the *whole* of German literature— while in East Germany, Old and Middle High German Literature, and the whole of the sixteenth and seventeenth centuries, have been dropped in toto.

—Why is that?

MAYER: Because they think it is not ideologically necessary—because it doesn't matter. Instead, the students have to read the latest stories about tractors and the partition of Germany. The classical period still figures in German literature courses but in a very abbreviated form—for in-stance, one single scene from *Kabale und Liebe* does duty for the whole of Schiller! Thus the fact that Warsaw and Prague have never been divided cities like Berlin, the fact that the teaching staffs at these universities stayed put, means that they enjoy two advantages: first, there is an unbroken intellectual and cultural tradition, and secondly, all the forces are there present whose task it is to oppose any new freeze-up of creative talent, any fresh plague of dogmatic scholasticism.

—One usually speaks of coexistence as though it were a problem arising only between East and West. The fact is, of course, that there is today quite a considerable degree of coexistence, cultural relationships, exchanges, and information services between the West (especially Western Germany) and the countries of the Eastern bloc. What about coexistence between East and East?

MAYER: Well, my impression is that cultural relations between East Germany and the other satellites, so far as they exist, are far cooler than they are, for example, between Polish writers and artists and the West. Of course there are also cross-connections. For example, the Leipzig Theater Company has made a practice of exchanging with their opposite numbers in Brno. Theatre companies in university towns are also under the patronage of the universities, all this, of course, State-organized. The fact it that while there are plenty of cultural agreements among the East European countries, there is precious little sign of any genuine living cultural exchange. I certainly have never gained the impression that anyone in Moscow or Leningrad is particularly keen on finding out what the latest artistic or literary trends are in Warsaw.

—Still, Tibor Dery—after years of prison, from which he emerged as uncompromised as the day he went in—attended the Writers' Congress in Leningrad and he was listened to with great respect, and this at a time when no other East European country had as yet invited him. So Moscow is not the North Pole of this particular cold front.

MAYER: Most certainly not. On the contrary—in 1956, a few weeks before the events in Poland and Hungary, when I had the honor of being the first German professor to lecture at the Lomonosov University in Moscow, I was deeply struck by the extraordinary interest displayed by these Soviet students in every aspect of West German and West European art. I was present in the hall of the University when the Moscow students met the Paris Théatre National Populaire. The French actors (Gérard Philippe and Daniel Sorano were still alive then) asked what their audience would like to hear them do. And what did these Russian students want to hear? —Apollinaire, Rimbaud, and Baudelaire! That is to say, three writers who are, as far as Soviet officialdom is concerned, still labeled decadent. When it came to the French turn to listen to Russian poetry, a young student got up and recited Mayakovsky. Plenty of intellectual common ground there! And when one of my colleagues was in Leningrad in 1961 he was asked to lecture. He agreed. "But look here, you won't talk about Bredel and Marchwitza and Apitz, will you? We know all about that sort of thing. Do you think you could do something on a West German writer?" It so happened that he had been doing some work on Heinrich Böll, which he suggested might do for a lecture subject. "Böll?" came the answer. "Splendid! You talk about Böll."

I did not mean that opinion in Moscow is not open to influences from the West; what I meant was that there is not the same readiness in Moscow to welcome innovation from Poland or Hungary. Tibor Dery is, of course, a special case. You see: Dery—it is no accident that he is one of Georg Lukács' favorite authors—is a splendid writer, but he belongs to the realist school of nineteenth-century novelists, the Balzac-Tolstoy tradition. And that, I think, is how he is looked upon in Moscow and Leningrad. But whether they would accord the same reception in Moscow to Tadeusz Rózewicz or Slavomir Mrozek, that is, to young Polish dramatists strongly influenced by Ionesco and Beckett—that's another question.

—To leave purely literary matters for a moment. Consider the present situation in which Communist ideology, split in the quarrel between Russia and China, turns in upon itself to criticize itself almost to the point of dissolution—is this not a process which may profit literary freedom of expression?

MAYER: I believe that literature, modern, creative, honest literature can only profit from this dissension. This seems to me incontestable—all attempts to prevent this happening are bound to fait in the long run. I am not naively optimistic enough to say "The wind bloweth where it listeth" and leave it at that. That just won't do. Events in the Soviet Union have shown us how such an immensely gifted people as the Russian people can land themselves for thirty years in total collapse of their entire intellectual life. Throughout all the decades of Stalin's rule, in the whole of the mighty Soviet Union, there appeared not one single book on literature, on philosophy, or on history that could be described as a genuine act of literary creation. All the officially sponsored books to appear in the Stalin period had to be subsequently vetted. After Stalin's death, special commissions were appointed in the Soviet Union to vet all the theses submitted for higher degrees under the Stalin regime; and a large number of doctorates had to be annulled as the work turned out to be nothing but a farrago of catchphrases and "theological" quotations. Even today, consider the harm done to creative talent by Ilichev, aided and abetted by Khrushchev, in their bid to win better ground for their ideological squabble with Peking by sacrificing a few intellectuals to the Chinese. No tactical advantage was gained vis-á-vis Peking, and the whole camp was deeply embarrassed by the preposterous and anachronistic discussion on art and literature that ensued—so much so that several parties, e.g., the French and Italian Communists, fibbed at taking part in the farce. I believe that in the long run everyone will have to admit— and here we are back to Kafka and Joyce—that it is as impossible to ignore new manifestations in the literary world as it is to ignore new discoveries in the fields of cybernetics or nuclear physics It is impossible to lead a healthy literary life in Warsaw, Moscow, or Leipzig, without knowing about Joyce and Kafka, Beckett and Ionesco, Brecht and Duerrenmatt, et al.

—I'd like to come back to an expression you used a moment ago—"theology." As long as some states practice government by idea and ideology, so that a number of canonized texts enjoy a monopoly of public opinion, it may be that authors instead of being censored and silenced can be, more simply, interpreted and built into the system for use. Isn't every form of literary development in jeopardy as long as this sort of mental and physical closed shop exists for a particular doctrine?

MAYER: We are, of course, again experiencing the great sociological phenomenon of an idea becoming a material force. Marx says somewhere in a celebrated phrase that "an idea becomes a material force when the masses take it into their grasp." To what extent has the Marxist idea become a material force for the masses in the Eastern bloc?

—But can an idea remain an idea after officialdom has got hold of it?

MAYER: That's the decisive question. As it becomes a material force, the idea is transformed; often it takes on a reactionary character, as we know from the history of all ideas, especially all religions. There is a very remarkable essay by Anna Seghers (published in spring 1963) which is full of suggestive material in this connection—and I wonder indeed whether Anna Seghers herself was really aware of the implications of what she was writing. It is a study of several of Dostoevsky's characters as derivatives from Schiller; and when we examine it we find that it is really only one character that is analyzed in both Schiller and Dostoevsky—the Grand Inquisitor, the one in *Don Carlos* and the one in *The Brothers Karamazov*. I think it is significant that Anna Seghers has chosen this theme—just as significant as the fact that here she links up with something her one-time close friend and counselor Georg Lukács once wrote—*Theory of the Novel*—which Lukács has just had republished in West Germany. A theory of the novel, I must add, for which Lukács wrote a new foreword in which he says (much like André Gide in *Nourritures Terrestres*), "Nathanael, if you want to be a man, do not follow me." Lukács writes: "Whoever reads this theory of the novel must understand that he is reading a book which I —the author—deprecate..."

—Well, even if he does deprecate it, I'm glad he has given us the chance of coming to grips with it ourselves.

MAYER: I agree. But it shows rather clearly how difficult and complicated this whole question of literary and ideological co-existence has become. It is the psychological problem of individuals, e.g., Lukács, who is castigated by East Berlin as a revisionist, while in Budapest many of his own pupils regard him not as a revisionist but as a dogmatic Marxist; this same Lukács who at one moment does what we know he did in 1956 and at the next (and now we have come full circle and are back at the point of departure) champions Thomas Mann against Franz Kafka (and argues that Kafka should not be allowed into print). These are questions of tradition, of the individual, and at the same time of the whole international situation. There is no simple unified solution for the problems of the Eastern bloc. That in East Germany this development process has taken on the most negative, the most inflexible, and—I should say—the clumsiest form is obvious. But if we look at the overall process, I think we shall see signs of the dawning, realization—and the sooner it comes the better—that modern literature must be common property just as modern science is. We had better stop behaving as though Kafka had never lived and as though Joyce had never written *Ulysses...!*

May 1964

Notes

1. Two Kafka stories have now been published in the January 1964 number of *Foreign Literature* (Moscow)—The "Metamorphosis" and "In the Penal Colony."
    The pressure for this has been building up for years. Victor Nekrassov has related that when he and other Russian writers (Vera Panova, Daniel Granin) met Alberto Moravia in Leningrad in 1958, "he asked us something about Kafka. We looked at one another in silence, and could not reply. At that time we hadn't even heard of Kafka...." In view of the theme of Kafka's "In the Penal Colon"—the old cruel commandant is dead but is not allowed to lie in the churchyard, the new milder commandant has difficulties in changing the organization significantly —C. L. Sulzberger, in the *New York Times* (2 March) was "led to wonder whether some liberal Communist intellectual is not deliberately twitting both Moscow censorship authorities and the Party hierarchy...."
2. In Lukács' recently published study of *Aesthetics*, Kafka is compared favorably with Beckett, unfavorably with Chaplin.
3. In a recent number of *Sinn und Form*, an East Berlin scholar (Werner Mittenzwei) dares to suggest that Kafka was one of Brecht's favorite authors, that he had called him "prophetic" and even "a true Bolshevik writer." One of the poems by the young lyric poet Gunter Kunert, which put him into trouble with the Party, was subtitled "On the Work of Franz K."

Notes on a Lady Mandarin

"I have always secretly imagined that my life was being inscribed art the minutest detail on a giant tape recorder so that one day I should be able to play back the whole of my past life.... By my own hand and on paper I can only record my life in its rough outlines; l will make a book out of it. At thirty-five I hoped that one day my life would be read with deeply-felt curiosity, I unwanted to become 'a famous author.' The small girl whose future has become my past exists no more.... How am I to retrieve her from the void of nothingness?"
—La Force Des Choses

The three volumes of Simone de Beauvoir's *Memoirs* contain nearly a million words. The first volume—the story of the development of a "dutiful daughter" from a completely conventional home into an independent, spiritually free young woman who finds happiness and meaning in her work and in an intellectual marriage—has moved many readers (especially, I hear, many women). The emancipation of woman—a suppressed class hitherto bereft of its full power of development, and so described on the purely theoretical level in *The Second Sex*—is here expounded as a personal experience, as an example and a possibility. The death of her friend Zaza who was unable to master the tensions in her life that became too strong for her gave the story a tragic background against which success appeared not as a foregone conclusion but rather as a hard-won victory.

The second volume, *La Force de l'Age*, was a record of human relationships, experiences, and travels, leading straight into wartime occupied France, and also into the discovery of politics as well as, in an unforgettable passage, death (her friend Bourla's deportation by the Nazis). One or two unpleasant qualities began to intrude: notably the tendency to tittle-tattle and the didactic urge, the latter so humorless on the erotic that she won the nickname "the teaching body" (*le corps enseignant*). The book contains several detailed justifications of the interest that "we" (i.e., Sartre and the author herself) have taken in individual persons with their special problems: "The investigation of a particular case is more instructive than the general abstract answer." Curious, this emphatic insistence that they are both really interested in particular individuals!

These memoirs are curiously constructed rather along the lines of a *normalienne's* essay or academic thesis. After each major section the narrative is interrupted; the foregoing section is summarized, the conclusions drawn. In her introduction to the second volume the author declares that she has no use for gossip: "I hate *clabaudage*." But the revelations of the intimate concerns of her friends are hardly the soul of discretion. In the third volume where this feature of her writing is equally evident she herself remarks on it and argues, "I was not the one to start it." To whatever indiscretions of others this may refer, one has the impression that, once again, offense is considered the best self-defense.

Taken together, her books have achieved a huge circulation in many languages. I am saddened to think that all those people who have found their characters exposed or their views distorted in them have such limited opportunities of redress. In a hundred years' time, I am afraid that thesis writers will still be drawing on these massive memoirs and on the slightly disguised earlier version in her novel, *The Mandarins*, to guide them in their enquiries into life as it was lived on the left bank of the Seine. Will this not, alas, emerge as the authentic picture of the ideologists and utopians of our time?[1]

Mme De Beauvoir insists in *La Force des Choses* that *Les Mandarins* was not a roman á clef. Does she really expect us to believe that "*Espoir*" is not *Combat* and "Scriassine" not Koestler, even if she has successfully camouflaged Sartre and Camus? She does admit that the novel contains a description of her (by now) world famous love affair with the American writer Nelson Algren. One is therefore rather surprised to find a detailed account in the new installment of her life-story of this same affair which she had, after all, described as vividly and excitingly as one could wish in the novel. Here again, however, she has her didactic reasons. She writes:

> Although I have told this story very inexactly in *Les Mandarins* I have come back to it not out of any pleasure in the anecdotal, but in order to explore more closely a problem which in *La Force de l'Age* I had rashly presumed to have been solved: can there be a reconciliation between loyalty and freedom? And at what cost? Often preached, but seldom practiced, perfect loyalty is usually seen as a mutilation by those who abide by it: they console themselves by sublimation or with drink...Sartre and I wanted "contingent love." The question remains, how would the third persons involved reconcile themselves to our understanding.[2]

The clinical devotion to the accurate description of affairs is almost convincing. In the interest of the most thorough documentation one should mention Nelson Algren's recent book *Who Lost an American?* with his own portrait of a naive woman of good will. Of Mme. de Beauvoir's existentialism Algren remarks that it was "not a philosophy at all, but a means of living in freedom and happiness." It would seem that this is precisely what it was not.

The way in which this liaison and the affair with Jacques Lanzmann (and also, in the background, Sartre's relationship with women) are described is scarcely calculated to move the heart or quicken the imagination. Erotic pleasures are nothing if not momentary and immediate, and who can even preserve them in memory? How much more difficult to communicate them to others, except possibly through poetry, but least of all in a didactic chronicle full of politics, whisky, and even *fêtes du corps*. Was this all erotic bliss? One thinks of Byron's

> My days are in the yellow leaf
> The flowers and fruits of love are gone....

"*Malveillance*"—malevolence—is an expression that often recurs in the *Memoirs*. But what is malevolence on the part of others is reckoned only as critical justice from her. And in two cases her pen is so malevolent that the informed reader can only blush with shame. Oddly enough her victims are in both cases women whom this pioneer of feminine dignity doesn't hesitate to disparage (and one of the two is not in a position to defend herself).

First: Germaine Tillion. This well-known ethnologist, a member of the first Resistance group in Paris, was arrested and deported to Mauthausen. Still, despite her damaged health, she has traveled every year in her small car to Libya or Morocco, camping out in some village, and continuing her scholarly studies of North African language and customs. Her books on Algeria and its economic decline have been deservedly famous and her social work earned her the respect of both the French authorities and the FLN. She was able to save the lives of a number of Algerian nationalists who had been condemned to death, and, on one occasion, as the result of a mission which she conducted entirely on her own, she secured a long armistice during the "reign of mutual terror."[3]

If, apart from its use as a purely literary category, the term "engagement" suggests nobility or selflessness or usefulness, then Mme. Tillion is the very model of the "engaged" person. Once without her knowledge *L'Express* published a detailed account written by her of her negotiations with Algerian terrorists. On this Simone de Beauvoir writes as follows in *La Forces des Choses*:

> We all had supper at Marie-Claire's and tore to pieces the article by Germaine Tillion, which Bose, Lanzmann, and I consider a filthy piece of work....

From a woman whose contacts with the Resistance were of the most remote nature, who was completely un-political well into her maturity and whose knowledge of politics even now is confined to the black-and-white certainties of moral decisions, this seems a piece of polemical frivolity. No great damage has been done. Mme Tillion set it all right in an article in *Le Monde* (March 11, 1964). At the end she dryly remarks that, as compared with the "tearing to pieces" that took place at that dinner, the cards she gets every year from three members of the present Algerian government who, thanks to her, were saved from execution, do offer a certain comfort....

The case of the other victim is quite different: she is Olga Ivinskaya. Simone de Beauvoir thought *Doctor Zhivago* a very bad book; it had taught her "nothing at all" about the Soviet Union. She also thinks that the Swedish Academy's offer of the Nobel Prize to Pasternak was a "deliberate provocation" of the Soviet Union. Later on she praises the Russian authorities for their current acknowledgment of Pasternak. In spite of the fact that previously she has found nothing "bad" in the Soviet Union, she now points out that everything is "good again." She writes: "There is no longer any official attack on Pasternak and if his former friend was sent to a camp—incidentally, only common lawbreakers are sent to camps today—it was because she trafficked in foreign currency."

Pasternak had known that his friend would be in serious danger after his death and this fear darkened the last months of his life. Not a word about the daughter who was also condemned As for the currency transactions, Feltrinelli; Pasternak's first European publisher, has given an exact account of these; still to maintain that the sentence passed on Olga Ivinskaya was right and proper is more than a delusion. More than once the pressure of public opinion has helped to secure an amnesty for prisoners, and pressure, I am convinced, should never be relaxed. A "voice of France"—of a woman who is a famous author and who still approves of this sentence—carries weight. Surely an "engaged" writer must know that words are deeds.

An objection to the passage about Ivinskaya was made by Marie Craipeau, from Poland, in an article printed (December 12, 1963) in the weekly *France Observateur*. She asked where Simone de Beauvoir got her information. Sartre replied to this in a deplorable letter to *France Observateur* (December 12, 1963), which, some think, will always remain one of the strangest documents of his career. Using abusive language more violent than anything he has ever indulged in before, he writes:

> What right have you to question what Simone de Beauvoir has written about Pasternak's companion? Have you been in the Soviet Union? Have you carried out an enquiry, as we have? Nowadays it is quite naive to be possessed by a preconceived suspicion of the Soviet Union. Like the Pavlovian dog that slavers at the sound of a bell you slaver when you hear the name of the Soviet Union.

This is again the Sartre who, in an unfinished essay on "The Communists and Peace" (published in *Temps Modernes* on the occasion of an unsuccessful strike which the workers had boycotted and which was later repudiated by the

Party), established with the utmost clarity that the French proletariat is identical with the Communist Party, and the Communist Party with Stalin—so that anyone who criticizes Stalin is inevitably an enemy of the people. Then it was amusing, an abstract joke; but here the victim is specific and real. And was there ever an "enquiry"? Surely it never took place except along the lines of: "Surkov told me himself...." It is not worthwhile to quote what Mme. de Beauvoir has written about Ignazio Silone (who made a humorous reply in the January 1964 *Preuves*), about Arthur Koestler, Manes Sperber, David Rousset, and many others. In her second volume Simone de Beauvoir wrote that "I prefer passing judgment on people to trying to understand them," and we gladly credit her with a piece of accurate self-knowledge. All the same, it is worth mentioning in passing that she has falsely accused the publisher Bompiani of not having paid Sartre his full royalties in Italy and has attributed to him views that he has in fact never expressed. Bompiani, who is a true *gentiluomo*, corrected her statements, concisely and politely, in *Temps Modernes* (August-September 1963) and drew from her the reply that the facts as published by her had been reported to her by this or that Italian writer: "Let them fight it out between themselves." As we know, she hates gossip.

There remains the case of Albert Camus, who was Mme. de Beauvoir's and Sartre's closest friend. One can read in Sartre's *Situations IV* (Gallimard, 1964) the polemical attack that dissolved the friendship and also the fine obituary notice in which Sartre did full justice to his friend and foe. What Mme. de Beauvoir has said includes some manifest inaccuracies which Jean Bloch-Michel, who was on the staff of *Combat* at the time, has meanwhile publicly corrected (*Preuves*, January 1964). Mme. de Beauvoir, whose judgments are normally so narrowly political, puts a personal interpretation on the fact that Camus quarreled violently with Merleau-Ponty because the latter had stated in a book that, "objectively speaking," Bukharin was a traitor and that the Moscow trials had been necessary. "Why this quarrel?" she writes. "I think that Camus was depressed because he felt that his golden years were coming to an end." After the death of Camus she mourned for the Camus of an earlier period who had been her friend, and for herself who had now lost a part of her youth—but not, she insists, for the later Camus who had taken the "wrong attitude" to the Algerian war.

In the second volume the tittle-tattle was concentrated on a few persons and it had its interest amidst the unfolding of complicated personal relationships. But here in the third volume, *les choses* whose *force* she describes are supremely trivial.

> I make a very full note of the details that are called trivial. Not only are they the reality which evokes the physical presence of a person or an age, but by their very nonsignificance they provide a touchstone of truth itself. They point to nothing beyond themselves and the only reason for emphasizing them is that they have existed—and that is sufficient.

This theory of the value of the banal must come as rather a surprise in view of the violent attacks which this volume contains on the *Nouveau Roman* and in particular on Nathalie Sarraute (another writer who has fallen from grace). The mass of detail is not as in Sartre's *Nausée* an expression of the oppressive presence of objects but rather an easy absorption in trivialities and the abandonment of any kind of discrimination. Torture in Algeria, a journey to Rome a double Scotch: all facts are equal, and the only interesting thing about them presumably is that they all happened to the author. Thus, she mentions English-language authors she has just discovered—Thomas Wolfe and Peter Cheyney. Previously she listed the films she had seen and in a footnote she gave the titles of everything that was on in the cinemas that year. Where the only criterion is what the author experienced, these memoirs do in fact become rather like the giant tape recorder for which she once yearned. In the case of important events this complete lack of judgment, this indifference to values, where only the relationship to the author's own person is important, is even more striking than in more trivial affairs. The following entry is from Venice:

> Headlines in the Italian papers: DIRTY HANDS [*Les Mains Sales*]. The reference is to the execution of Nagy and Maleter. Why? We discuss the problem endlessly without understanding it. This is disastrous for France since the Communists will now become even more isolated, the Left demoralized, and Gaullism intensified. The counter-demonstration today will be lacking in enthusiasm. And Sartre—who wanted so much to forget politics for few days!

In a word: Nagy executed. Poor Sartre.

"We discuss endlessly"—the phrase recurs. "We discussed Hiroshima for a long time." "The editorial committee often meets and has violent discussions." "We discussed Koestler a little. Amazing how we always land up in the same conversation." "Evening with Sartre and Bost. We discussed events." Were the discussions very interesting? There is always agreement with Sartre in any case: "He often finishes a sentence that I have begun." Those with whom they disagree all gradually disappear from the circle. They only see their friends and only confirm one another's opinions. They were all convinced that de Gaulle could not end the Algerian war and could not crush the OAS—they even believed he had entered into an alliance with that organization. So many things have turned out differently—but that does not mean that anything has to be thought through all over again. Meanwhile there are new issues on which left-minded persons can agree. Francis Roland, one of the group, changes his opinions. Comment: "He has come into money and become a Gaullist."

The importance of the trivial presupposes an interest in the accuracy of details. But there is in this internationalist woman a very French and, possibly, aristocratic trait: she never takes the trouble to spell names correctly.

(Things are a bit better in the Anglo-American edition.) Doesn't her publisher, Gallimard, have any proofreaders? They have passed the flagrant errors: Robert Schumann always stands for Schuman, Tillon for Tillion, A. Koethly for Anne Kethly (does she even remember who this is?), Walbert for Waldberg, Guelderohde for Ghelderode, Lummumba for Lumumba, Einsenhower for Eisenhower, Beuber Newmann for Buber Neumann. The greater the detail the less care is expended on it.

Simone De Beauvoir looks back in sorrow. She now regards her most fulfilled years as lost, feels that nothing remains. After the self-creation of man in freedom by the "Project," the inescapable destiny of aging and dying has now forced itself upon her. Where she dwells on this there is a different tension, even a different language, and it reminds us that the argumentative Lady Mandarin was also the author of that very good novel, *L'Invitée*. Recently her account of the death of her mother has appeared in *Temps Modernes*, and as a book, and in it she says that for her every death is a violent intrusion and an intolerable injustice: as far as she is concerned, the time has gone when Sartre explained how it is only mortality that gives life its shape and meaning.

To age, to die; she takes a candid look at her face in the mirror and gives a frightening description of it. Sartre, who began his own memoirs with *Les Mots*, writes: "I do not know what I am living for" and he tells her (this is quoted in *La Force des Choses*), "La literature c'est de la merde" (a résumé of his later interview in *Le Monde*).[4] She herself speaks of the meaninglessness of everything, now it is all moving towards the close; and with every friend who dies, Camus, Richard Wright, Merleau-Ponty, the world contracts irretrievably.

Sartre expresses his despair with so much temperament and verve that he belies himself. It is like his renunciation of literature in the very year in which with *Les Mots* and *Situations IV* he has once again become the center of literary attention. For long stretches *La Force des Choses* is a gloomy book, whereas *Les Mots* is fascinating and reads as if it were written in one brilliant stroke. Sartre wrote to accuse the child that he once was and to show that, in spite of everything, he did become the famous "*homme de lettres*" his grandparents expected. He considers this success "a failure" but when he curses literature he also blesses it whereas to Simone de Beauvoir who, at the close of her memoirs breaks into a hymn of praise for the Word as the only "transcendence." as the only link between men, and man's only shelter and home, they are lifeless words.

One has only to read his description in *Situations IV* of a walk in Venice in the rain or the study on Wols, to see what Sartre is capable of in his moments of inspiration. Simone de Beauvoir vaguely hopes that somebody sometime will remember particular words that she has joined together. Even in his monologues there is tension in Sartre's writing, and he has the resources of an effective playwright at his command. Simone de Beauvoir's despondency is leaden (though no less honest and true on that account): "The story that befell me is not my own, I thought. I was the helpless spectator of the sport of foreign powers. History, Time, Death...." She continues: "I hated the world to which I belonged. I was banished from the future by the act of growing old. Robbed nerve by nerve of the past, my life is contracting to my own immediate present. What an icy coldness!"

This note has already been sounded earlier: "One day I said to myself, I am forty. When I had recovered from the surprise, I was fifty. The astonishment that took hold of me then still persists." What remains of all the splendors she has seen? "The Peking opera; the arena at Huelva; the dawn in Provençe; Tiryntha; Castro speaking to 500,000 Cubans; a sulphurous sky above a sea of clouds; copper beeches; the white nights of Leningrad; the bells of the Liberation; an orange moon over the Piraeus; a red sun in the desert; Torcello; Rome...?" "If I had only begotten a hill or a rocket [she uses the masculine word "*engendrer*": to beget]. As it is, nothing has happened. I see the coppice of nut trees with the wind passing over it, and the promises that enthralled me when I saw this gold mine at my feet, the life that was mine to live. The promises have been kept. All the same I look back with an unbelieving glance at this believing child and realize with bewilderment how greatly I have been deceived."

These are the books last words. What a cheerless epilogue for a life that has seemed such a model or such unattainable good fortune to so many! From total absorption in universal political struggles to this state of confinement to the transient self.... In *The Second Sex* everything that characterizes woman as woman—from seductive charm to motherhood—was unmasked as part of the slave mentality created by man. And it is true: many women, especially the more creative, do in their later years often experience a new sense of fulfillment and assurance and see it as a phase in their lives with a value all its own. Simone de Beauvoir sees nothing of the kind in her life. One is reminded of Knut Hamsun's last comment: "The years bring no wisdom, only old age...."

Some French critics have noted with sorrow or with malicious pleasure that Sartre and Simone de Beauvoir have been compelled to admit having come to the end of their tether philosophically and have confessed failure. Will a Voltaire be moved again to make a last confession?

Those who have a tranquil and useful philosophy of age and death are to be envied, but I wonder why it is only in these final pages of her book that there is a density of expression that is otherwise conspicuously lacking. She mourns well for herself and for her intimate friends—but otherwise people are either "the masses," like Castro's audience of five hundred thousand (to what extent has politics for Mme. de Beauvoir been merely part of the aesthetic pleasure of the traveler and the tourist?), or the representatives of mistaken ideas.

Simone de Beauvoir supports the death penalty for political crimes, and after the war she was in favor of the execution of all those French *"miliciens"* who had blood on their hands. The idea was apparently that once the world had been rid of this polluted race of men, there would be no more murderers and torturers left. Eternal illusion! Between the happiness of the abstract masses and the destruction of the abstract villains, humanity is reserved for a privileged few: one's own little circle.

Mme. de Beauvoir has been criticized for never criticizing herself; but self-criticism implies a detachment in which there is room for humor, and whatever merits she may possess as a writer, humor is certainly not one of them. Her extensive memoirs are marked by an astonishing measure of humorlessness. One might make allowances for the inaccuracies and the injustices if they were the byproduct of sheer high spirits. But they are offered with great solemnity as a message from the spirit of the age.

Those who attach transcendent importance to words must be taken at their word, and words are used here without any feeling of detachment from either the age or the self. Has there never been anything about the farcical comedy enacted by "Engaged Intellectuals" in the corners of the great political stage that might have wheedled a smile of self-irony out of her?

In *The Mandarins* there still seemed to be a hope that this might happen and the novel remains the best part of the memoirs of her maturity. Here in *La Force des Choses* there is no comedy, but "many nails clawing at inflated balloons," as she writes of her own aggressiveness. We could share her sorrow over a waning life if only we caught her once mocking herself.

October 1965

Notes

1. The first volume appeared in English in 1959 under the title of *Memoirs of a Dutiful Daughter* (Andre Deutsch and Weidenfeld & Nicolson, London; G. P. Putnam's Sons, New York); the second volume in 1963, as *The Prime of Life*. The third and final volume, *Force of Circumstance*, has just been published in London.
2. How one "third person" reconciled himself is suggested by Nelson Algren's comments (*Harper's*, May 1965): "Anybody who can experience love contingently has a mind that has recently snapped. How can love be contingent? Contingent upon what? The woman is speaking as if the capacity to sustain Man's basic relationship—the physical love of woman and man—were a mutilation; while freedom consists of 'maintaining through all deviations a certain fidelity'! What she means, of course, when stripped of its philosophical jargon, is that she and Sartre erected a facade of petit-bourgeois respectability behind which she could continue the search for her own femininity. What Sartre had in mind when he left town I'm sure I don't know...."

   Mme de Beauvoir's early determination 'to write sacrificial essays in which the author strips himself bare without excuses' she has since employed with such earnestness that practically everybody has now been sacrificed excepting herself."

3. See Germaine Tillion, "The Terrorist," *Encounter*, December 1958.
4. See "Interview with Sartre" in *Encounter*, June 1964.

Letter from Prague

The Empty Pedestal

> *"...One can perhaps safely discuss it now. In those days many people, and among them the best, had a secret maxim which ran: try with all your might to comprehend the decrees of the high command, but only up to a certain point; then avoid further meditation...."—Franz Kafka (1917)*

The films which have been coming out of Czechoslovakia recently have been surprising the world. One that lasts for barely forty minutes was shown me at the Film Club in the Narodni trida by its director Juranek (who, like the other new directors, Forman and Jireš, must be still under thirty). The title of the film, if I understand it correctly, means "A figure to be supported"; its subject is "the Search for Comrade Kilian"—and the search for a vanished office which hires out cats for the day and, when a young man wants to hand back an ailing cat, seems suddenly to have ceased to exist and indeed never to have existed at all.

The film opens with a young man walking through almost empty streets, to a sound accompaniment of marching boots and rhythmical applause. Then he walks down a dim endless corridor, the walls of which are plastered with old posters: a portrait of Stalin, a denunciation of "Colorado beetle Truman," an official proclamation NAŠ LID BUDE ("OUR PEOPLE WILL BE....")—but we do not find out what they are going to be, because this bill is obscured by the next, which has to do with the Korean War and the "disease germs" which General Ridgway was supposed to have dropped from the sky. So we are brought backwards into the Stalin era, so uncannily remote. Why should we be looking at all these bill posters of yesterday? Are they not today quite inappropriate to remember? These are the ironies in the attitude of young Czechs to their most recent past.

It has been said of this young generation—which has, I think, been showing more nerve and intellectual vigor than that of any other country in Communist-ruled Europe—that it consists, not of angry young men, but rather of "surprised young men." Their elders have little to offer them; they have no memory of "great figures" and see no evidence of great deeds or achievements. What is demanded of them is a perpetual capacity to forget what was laid down only a short while ago: always that unquestioning loyalty to authority that the good soldier Schweik (that permanent model of Czech irony) reduced to absurdity by taking it in dead earnest. "Authority" is an anonymous, colorless term, and quite catches the tone of the country's ruling caste. What it wants is a nation of Lethean water drinkers, aware only of what today's *Rudé Právo* (or the Slovak *Pravda*) has gone through the motions of publishing.

In young Vaclav Havel's satirical play *The Garden Party*—which after eighteen months was still playing to full houses in the small Theatre "Na zábradli" (and enjoyed a deserved success in West Berlin)—one of the characters remarks that there is nothing to choose between those who said what was required of them yesterday and those who say what is required of them today. The talk is everywhere of the "scrapping of dogmatism" and the "overcoming of the cult of personality." (What was it basically—the unintelligible delusion of a whole people, a spontaneous psychosis generated from below or only a deliberate method of government?) But the new slogans sound just as bogus in the ears of the younger generation as the former panegyrics of the "great Stalin" and the "great Gottwald," and not least because to a large extent it is the same officials, the same ideologists, who have passed from one "vocabulary" to the other. In Budapest Kadar is not Gerö and, in Warsaw, Gomulka is not Bierut; but in Prague Novotny is still Novotný. The plausibility of the change of heart, which is here proclaimed simultaneously as representing "continuity" and an "improvement," suffers visibly. What with the tragedy of trials and the comedy of the new dialectical acrobatics, there is no lack of raw material for political cabaretists.

Are these alert young people moving to a kind of nihilism that merely ridicules the past and everything connected with it? Actually, the very reverse seems to me to be taking place. The revolt is also an objection against the amnesia of "the great forgetting." "We are now gradually ceasing to battle with the 'German past' and are busying ourselves with our own," one director said to me. Thus a new Czech film, *Assassination*, deals with the killing of Heydrich without the "negative legend" officially disseminated about the killer being a "western agent" and therefore suspect. I was struck by the fact that Klima, the young author of the play *The Castle*, who spent some years of his boyhood in the Theresienstadt concentration camp, has written a book about Karel Čapek, the representative writer of the "bourgeois republic"; it illustrates the trend to revive what in this case is not the blackened but merely the neglected past.

I visited the house in which Čapek spent his last year, near Dŏboŝ Castle. The cuttings from Lidové Noviny, the good liberal newspaper for which he wrote, were a reminder that there was once a Czech daily press of world rank; all the household literary details, including the famous travel books, are a reminder of the distant time when the world was open, and of Karel Čapek acuteness, humor, and terrifying visions of the future: "the Robot," the successor to the Golem; was his creation. He died at Christmas, 1938, still only in middle age, deeply depressed by the events at Munich, and his brother Joseph, a distinguished artist, did not survive German imprisonment.

Out of the Past

How can the past mean quite the same to the Slovaks as it does to the Czechs? Still, common to both is the ultimate failure of the recent attempts to transform it.

"I called on you here nineteen years ago in 1947," I said to the aged writer František Langer, the most important survivor of Čapek's generation, when I met him at Doboïš Castle. "That is a long time ago," he said, for understandably enough he had forgotten our conversation, though I remembered it well. 1947 is indeed longer ago here than elsewhere. A year later the resuscitated "bourgeois republic" collapsed, and when I paid a brief visit to Prague in that fateful year—I had been in Warsaw, where Gomulka had just been arrested—I arrived just in time for the state funeral of President Eduard Beneš. Beneš was not "the great European" as he had been called in the League of Nations, nor was he an acute political thinker. But within his limits he was a democrat, and it was Beneš' fate twice to have to accept a death sentence on Czech democracy, the first time in Munich, under the pressure of Hitler and of the West (in whose solidarity Beneš and most Czechs had blind confidence) and the second time "a thousand years later" (as I was told) in Prague, under the pressure of his closest ally, the Soviet Union. Beneš had been very popular, and I remember the spontaneous ovation he was given when he unexpectedly appeared in his box at the National Theatre. He then seemed to be the guarantor of a gradual return from people's democracy to "the rule of law," and his personal intervention in cases of arbitrary arrest contributed to this reputation. But now he was dead, having survived his "republic" by only a few months. Mourning women in headscarves wanted to approach the coffin, but I watched young tough militiamen brutally drive them away. The formal state funeral could not be allowed to degenerate into a demonstration of sympathy amounting to an expression of hostility to the new regime.

At that time, in 1947, three portraits hung in all official places—Masaryk on the left, Stalin on the right, and Beneš in the middle. I noticed that at the trade union headquarters the only portrait other than those of Stalin, Tito, and Dimitrov was that of Gottwald, the prime minister. Masaryk stood for the humanist tradition in home politics, and Stalin provided the world-political guarantee. Beneš had placed his trust in the Soviet Union as unequivocally as he had placed it in France ten years before. In his message to the provisional National Assembly on October 28, 1945, he had said, "It is self-evident that as a small state we shall not fail to orient ourselves in the first place towards the state that offers us most security...." He had returned from London to Prague by way of Moscow, and to him the state that offered "most security" was the Soviet Union. Czechoslovakia had been in fact if not formally allotted to the Soviet sphere of influence. Did Beneš have any other alternative but to "make the best" of this alliance? The wartime Czech government-in-exile had had to wait for a whole year in London to be put on a par with the other governments-in-exile. At the time the ambassador in Moscow of independent, clerico-Fascist Slovakia was Monsignor Tiso's brother; and not till August 1942 did Great Britain and de Gaulle's Free France declare the signatures to the Munich treaty to be null and void. Such memories linger. It was (and remains) difficult for the Czechs to be a "Western democracy" knowing that the West did not care.

Beneš, Masaryk, and Stalin looked like a strange trinity, but I thought it might possibly last for a long time. A number of books appeared at that time on Czechoslovakia as "the bridge between East and West," the shining example of a new coexistence. Today we know how false were those hopes and how illusory those prospects. But I still sometimes think that this failure was not "inevitable." Had the Finnish President Paasikivi not resisted the pressure of Moscow and his own Communist ministers, would it not today seem "inevitable" to us that Finland had taken the path of "popular democracy"? If Paasikivi said no and Beneš yes, this was not a simple consequence of political alignments, though the pro-Russian feelings of the Czechs and the anti-Russian feelings of the Finns had their importance.

Beneš, the "restorer," stood for the time of defeat and collapse; but Masaryk, the "President-Liberator," had been identified with distinction and political success. Thus a systematic attempt has been made to erase the memory of Masaryk, as indeed of all recent history, a remarkable paradox in a state that was created by historians, from Palacky to Masaryk. It was at that time that the huge pharaonic monument to Stalin was erected, visibly proclaiming Moscow to be the capital and Prague the seat of a satrapy. Events had first to take place in Moscow before they could be reflected in this province. The news of Stalin's political death reached Prague only after a time-lag of years, and not till then did a truly satrapic "parallel operation" take place and the loyal Gottwald was ejected, in turn, from the official mausoleum. My Czech friends described to me the difficulties involved in the removal of the Stalin memorial. A commission had to be formed to plan the operation so that it would not cause excessive damage to the neighborhood. (One of the characters in Klima's *The Castle* is the head of a curious "Commission for the Correction of the Statue.") One morning the Caucasian's head was lifted off by ropes.

Some symbols are just too obvious. On October 30, 1956, I saw the Stalin statue in Budapest after the popular fury had dealt with it. It had been torn from its pedestal, and only the boots remained. In Prague there was no popular outburst, but only calculated, bureaucratic action. The pedestal was left where it was. Its foundations were apparently built in too deep to be removable without endangering the city's drains. What an appropriate monument for the present regime!—a ponderous stone block just standing there for its own sake, with nothing on it, not even the statue of a tyrant, a faceless incubus, weight without form, symbol of a new cult of non-personality.

There is also another pedestal—the slender granite monolith in the second inner court at the Hradčany. Someone told me that it had been erected in honor of Masaryk, whose name had been obliterated, but someone else insisted that the idea had been to erect one day a statue of liberty on it. These two pedestals, from one of which Stalin had been removed while "Liberty" had not yet been put on the other, struck me as the clear double image of Prague today.

Of course, the obliteration of Masaryk's name was more temporary than the obliteration of Stalin's. But the grotesque attempt to turn Masaryk into a "nonperson" has been made. In the so-called memorial exhibition of national literature at the Strahov monastery a facsimile is displayed of a page of the celebrated MSS. of Královy Hradec and Zelena Hora, which were revealed as a patriotic forgery in the 'nineties—a deed of moral fortitude on Masaryk's part which has always been resented by certain Czech nationalists and, like his intervention in a famous ritual murder trial, gave him the stature of a "true humanist." The discovery of the forgery is mentioned at the Strahov exhibition —but the discoverer's name is suppressed. Masaryk is also omitted from the latest Czech Who's Who, which claims to include all the names of note in Czech literature. But the omission has not been accepted in silence. The Brno newspaper *Host do domu* stated in January 1965: "To claim that Masaryk did not make a significant contribution to Czech literature is a great error. An addendum should be made in the next edition...." This could not have been stated more moderately, but the fact that it was stated is something new. One could also note in the bookshops a recent book on Masaryk's philosophy, written by a young Czech philosopher.

Historians to whom I spoke admitted that the period of the "bourgeois republic" had not (with the exception of a few monographs) been adequately dealt with in recent years, and that the time was coming for a new and more "positive" evaluation of Masaryk and Beneš. As both presidents were sociologists, the readmission of sociology—in Bratislava earlier than in Prague—was in itself a kind of rehabilitation. But how "unmentionable" Masaryk must have been was made plain to me in conversation with a member of the Academy of Sciences. We had been talking of a certain person who had been able to work in Paris. That was, he said, "thanks to a grant that President Masaryk—do you know the name?—obtained for him...." Is a name out of the past important? I suppose that this name will again become much better known and more familiar to the Czechs of a younger generation. One does not have to be a chauvinist to want to be proud of a prominent figure in the history of one's country, and of whom can the Czechs be prouder than of the Moravian *kutscher's* son Masaryk?

"Strange," a historian said to me, "our young people take no interest in recent history. We conducted a questionnaire and published the results in a popular journal. Young readers preferred turning to a book about the Hussites...." The favorite historical period does indeed seem to be that of Jan Hus and the Taborites, on which innumerable books have been written. Is this perhaps because it was the only time when the Czechs made their mark on world history? Or is it also because the historians themselves want to avoid recent history? A compilation published by the Academy states that "the most important source" of recent history is the speeches and writings of Klement Gottwald. But as this source is now officially regarded as under a shadow, the consequence must be that the last twenty years are left in greater obscurity than the medieval establishment of Tabor in the year 1419. If the younger generation does not read what passes for historiography on contemporary affairs, it surely does not mean that they are uninterested in the events; indeed, the periodicals, plays, and films in which this interest is expressed demonstrate the opposite. Also it was clear from my conversations that the scholars (including many who carry some weight in the party) would be pleased if they could abandon the "prescribed vocabulary" and were allowed to write "real history," and things appear to be moving in that direction.

Taboos remain. A historian exhibited with pride a colored map showing the site of every theatre and cinema in the country. But is there a map which shows the present and former composition of the country's various linguistic groups? Or would this be, as someone remarked, of "too great interest" (to the expelled Germans? to the remaining Hungarian minority?).

Czech and Slovak

It is freely admitted in relation to the Slovaks (not to the Germans) that the "bourgeois republic" suffered from excessive centralization. Masaryk's promise to turn Czechoslovakia into a "higher Switzerland" was greeted with scorn by the right-wing Czech nationalists. "Higher twaddle," Kramář called it at the time. And when the Slovaks took advantage of the opportunity of withdrawing from the control of Prague in 1938, this reflected a long-disregarded national feeling that was by no means confined to the followers of Father Tiso or the Fascist Hlinka. Slovak national feeling also existed (and still exists) among the Communists, and the regime prides itself on having taken it into account. The old attempts to insist on a "Czechoslovak" nation and a "Czechoslovak" language have been abandoned.

Just as the centralized Hapsburg Empire was turned a hundred years ago into the Austro-Hungarian "dual monarchy," by the "compromise," so has centralized Czechoslovakia been formally turned into a "dual republic" of

Czechs and Slovaks. But the persecution of innumerable Slovak Communists for "bourgeois-nationalist deviations"—in trials that do not date back to the years of the personality cult (now officially declared to have lasted from 1949 to 1953) but to a: more recent period in which the present President Novotný played a leading part—gave Slovak dissatisfaction an impetus and earned the Slovak Communists more popularity than they could otherwise have expected. In Prague, attention is drawn to the amount that has been spent on the industrialization of Slovakia, and that is disputed by no one. There is a parallel with what northern Italy has been doing for the *mezzogiorno*. (a party of Italian economists has recently visited Slovakia for comparative study purposes), but most Slovaks say that "grave errors" in capital investment were made during the period of the "planning cult," which nowadays is under just as much of a cloud as the "personality cult." Even the great steelworks, to which ore is transported from the Ukraine on a railway track of Russian width, is held to be an economic white elephant; and no doubt about it, agriculture "suffered heavily" under collectivization. One is unable to verify such statements, but I know that inquiries have been held and the results are still kept as state and park secrets. This is still a rather secretive place.

If the Czechs remember Masaryk, in Bratislava the role of the Slovak rising and the battles of 1944 play a greater part in people's minds. So does the memory of the executed foreign minister Vlado Clementis, to whom a memorial tablet has now been erected. His notes and diaries of his last days, including a touching account of his wife's visit to him on the day before his execution, have now been published. The fact that the dead Clementis (as well as the living Husák and Novomeský,) has been completely rehabilitated, while the Czech party secretary Slansky has not, gives a peculiar satisfaction to Slovak national pride. Clementis' widow seems to be coming in for the same kind of special honors as Mrs. Rajk in Budapest.

In the official party history the Slovak rising was played down for years; also it was claimed that the *apparatchik* Vilem Siroký (one of those who bore the main responsibility for the execution of Clementis) led it by "leaflets written in prison." I was told in Bratislava that a group of Czech historians met in "conclave" and demolished this legend quite against the party's wishes. Siroký's final dismissal came about as the result of a public protest by Slovak writers and journalists. Siroký is still on the central committee, but at receptions he is left in woeful obscurity (and his wife recently committed suicide). It was undoubtedly the Slovaks that shook Stalinism throughout the country and se liberalization going. Even if the most important impulses in this direction today again come from Prague, Bratislava retains the glory ant a special position. Hence the Slovaks can, on the whole, regard themselves somewhat more as the movers and makers of history and not, like the Czechs, merely as its object. The difference is noticeable.

Many outstanding personalities have been rehabilitated, but not reinstated. At last year's celebration at Banska Bystrica of the twentieth anniversary of the Slovak rising, President Novotný handed the rehabilitated Gustav Husák a "Remembrance Medal." The scene was recorded for television, but instructions were issued immediately afterwards that it was not to be shown. Husák, who was the only accuser in the show trials who never "confessed," had declined a small job and is now a mere "member of the Academy," writing books and articles. Novomeský, Kaliský, and other members of the former leading group are also allowed to write, to the great advantage of the journal *Kultúrny život* which has acquired such importance in this whole period; but they remain on the margin. Thus a group of men to whom the regime has admitted it did wrong has been neither silenced nor restored to responsibility. (I wonder whether Communists ever read Machiavelli, in whose *Prince* there are warnings against such half-measures....)

In Bratislava, I seemed to meet only persons who had been persecuted or victimized in one way or another. A student's "bourgeois origin," for instance, had been discovered shortly before he finished his course: he was expelled from the university. Eliminating in this way the offspring of the "bourgeoisie" (i.e., generally the offspring of able, industrious qualified people) was an act of self-mutilation that is now seen to have been such and has beer corrected. Editors had been sent to work in factories and economists became laborers; an important but inconvenient author for whole foreign publishers were competing was not allowed to have his books translated into Western languages because, in the view of the Writers' Association, his work was not "typical of our best writing." (I was told that this sort of thing would not happen today.) There are other cases: a sentence of eight years' imprisonment for membership in "Catholic Action," though the persons concerned engaged in no action whatsoever.

The new fashion now is that it is above all "the good comrades" who are persecuted. In one of his "belated reports" in *Kultúrny život* Ladislav Mnacko told the story of a man who fought for the liberation of the country; he was an air force officer in the West; on his return home he was exposed to such vexations that he regretted he had not been "a Slovak Fascist, who could have wriggled through all right...." This piece was deleted from the first edition of Mnacko's book.

Not every Communist, of course, is converted to tolerance because he has been persecuted himself. I am thinking in this connection of the director of the Bratislava Institute of Journalists who was sent to work in a factory as a "Titoist" and after a long period of disfavor managed to work his way back again. I pointed out to him that no foreign newspapers (except the various party organs) were obtainable even in the international hotels. (In a shop window opposite the Hotel Alkron in Prague I actually saw some material for blouses and trousers on which the title and headlines from *Humanité*, *Unità*, the *Daily Worker*, *Volksstimme*, etc. were printed as a pattern). Always I was assured that this could not be correct, because it was well known that the international hotels obtained foreign newspapers for tourists. "Perhaps they are hidden by the hall porter," the director suggested. "Because our policy is openness. Our press library subscribes to dozens of foreign newspapers." Later he showed me this library. I opened one of the research files and spotted an article on "The Uniformity of the British Press Explained by its Class Character." On the shelves were the same *Humanité*, *Unitá*, etc., that I had seen on the piece of cloth in the shop window. "And where are the others?" I asked. "They're in the basement," I was told. "After all, this library can also be visited by unauthorized persons...."

How strange that this spirit of censorship should still be taken so much as a matter of course. A striking contrast is provided by the journals in which a new openness to the world appears. I spent many hours in these editorial offices, both in Prague and in Bratislava, and these are impressively serious weekly and monthly reviews (which altogether have at least 300,000 readers and probably many more) and stand in the foreground of intellectual discussion.

The editor of *Kultúrny život* in 1963 (the stormiest and most difficult year) was a young man named Pavol Števček. Like others of his generation, he was taught no Western languages at school and has since been far too busy to make up the deficiency. I had to talk to him with the aid of older editors as intermediaries; several of these, like the present editor Juraj Spitzer, speak perfect Hungarian, good German, fair French, and thus recall that Bratislava once had a cosmopolitan, multilingual intelligentsia. More outside the offices than in them I learnt a great deal about the working of a censorship that treats its own existence as a state secret; when it occasionally insists that a contribution be deleted, it takes skilled care that no old-fashioned blank space appears to betray the fact. What progress it would be to have a clumsy censorship that still worked with scissors and obvious last minute cuts!—or even a modern censorship that confessed to its own existence. This would indeed fit in very well with the welcome transition that is now quietly taking place from a fanatical party state of prescribed unanimity to an authoritarian state that expects only obedience and is gradually learning to coexist with the beginnings of a relatively independent public opinion.

The *Kultúrny život* story will have to be written some day—for various reasons the time is not yet ripe—and factors such as Slovak national consciousness, unjust persecution of intellectuals and politicians, cosmopolitan tradition, distance from the oppressive capital and the closeness of Vienna (and of the Austrian and German television all will have to be taken into account just as much as individual personalities. The thirty-year-old Števček suffered a heart attack after editing for a year, and nobody was surprised.

The "Slovak Spirit" reminded me more of the Polish than of the Czech. Its people were formed by Catholicism and partly also by Calvinism, and a potentiality is there for narrow fanaticism. Tiso's regime was one of the grimmest, worse than Horthy's Hungary. Yet it has a very lively liberal intelligentsia, and there is independence and a touch of spontaneity in everything.

In Bratislava, I was shown a film called *The Organ*. The chief character is a priest who believes in the "sacredness of beauty," and takes on as organist a Polish soldier who gives himself out to be a monk. They try to hide and rescue Jewish families. (Few survived, as the uninhabited old Jewish quarter near the Pressburg castle now underlines). The only unsympathetic character is the Party secretary; but the police themselves turn against him and are on the side of "the good priest." This was, I thought, a transfigured picture of life under the Tiso regime. "That's just what our dogmatists said," my companion remarked with a laugh. But it can be regarded as a counterpart of the Slovak film *A Shot in the High Street* that was shown at Cannes, in which the Jewish deportations are depicted without any easy and obvious German villains This is a new and courageous aspect in films on that subject. But *The Organ* also provides confirmation of the deep roots of a specifically Slovak national feeling.

This emerged in a truly difficult conversation with the leaders of the Writers' Association in Bratislava. Neither of the writers present, both of whom were members of the presidium, knew any Western language. The theme was "the difference between Czechs and Slovaks." "Certainly," said M., "Czech words from modern industrial society are invading our language—but isn't it the same as the incursion of American words into French?" The comparison struck me as odd. Czech, of course, enjoys a certain precedence as the language of the majority and of the capital. Slovak books and film dialogue are translated into Czech, while the Slovaks generally do not translate Czech originals. Nevertheless Czechs have sometimes been glad to read Slovak; *Kultúrny život* published its critical reports and discussions long before the Prague journals, and copies were sold under the counter in Prague at black market prices.

Though Prague is now the intellectual center again (as is shown by journals such as *Literární Noviny, Plamen*, and *Tvar*[1])

Slovakia has somewhat greater reserves. How far do the discussions that take place here go "beyond Communism"? Eugen Loebl (another victim of persecution who now plays a leading part in discussion of economic reforms) has argued that individual liberties constitute "the only legitimate substance of all authority." But there are, generally, very clear and severe limits that are still set to discussion, and they appear plainly in Ladislav Mňačko latest articles.

To what extent do the Czechs and Slovaks in this time of great change believe in the possibility of independently shaping their own society? This is a question that cannot be asked openly, but it occupies them all the more for that reason. Two foreign ministers of Czechoslovakia, Jan Masaryk and Vlado Clementis, died in circumstances connected—in popular feeling—with the desire for "independence." The realistic feeling for "limited sovereignty" is perceptible. The centuries spent under Austrian rule, the years of suppression under the German occupation (not that the two periods are in any way comparable), and the allotment to the Soviet sphere of influence provide no foundation for great confidence in the possibility of ever really going their own way. But memories of the "bourgeois republic" are a pointer in the direction of a more independent diplomacy.

Czechs like to think of all the occasions in the past when something of worldwide importance came from Prague. The "rediscovery" of Kafka should be seen in that light (though it would have been inconceivable without Professor Eduard Goldstücker, whose only concern was Kafka's work itself). But in the case of so many zigzag East European advances, the Party invariably assents only hesitantly; it merely gives "concessions"; it takes no bold initiative of its own. Tourists are sold picture postcards printed in many languages, showing among other things, Kafka's birthplace; but a tablet has not yet been put on the house. That, apparently, would be too much. This honor has, deservedly, been granted to that remarkable journalist Egon Erwin Kisch (who was, after all, a Communist). Kafka's turn will certainly come. But putting off as long as possible what is already taken for granted is typical o f the doctrinaire regime which suspiciously regards advances as retreats.

The Two Sectors

Today "two sectors" are to be found in every field. There is collectivized and non-collectivized agriculture, a dead party press on the one hand and living journalism on the other, a partially sluggish and hidebound bureaucracy contrasting with a developing industrial society. The dividing line is not between Communists and non-Communists, but between the efficient and forward-looking and the political worthies who cling to their positions and to the past. Cestmír Císar previously Minister of Education, belonged to the former; he knows how deep the cleavage is between the generations, and his cautious behavior at the May student celebrations (with all their breakthrough to satire) showed understanding and avoided the riots of the previous year. For this and other reasons he was recently "exiled" to become ambassador in Bucharest. Jozef Lenart, the prime minister, is also included in this group. A Foreign Trade Ministry official who knows no Western languages and went out and bought expensive but unusable machinery in the West is one of the political worthies. The replacement now taking place of thousands of unqualified factory managers shows the effort that is being made, at long last, to give more scope to properly trained and competent men.

This "coexistence" is to be found throughout the country. In the Philosophical Institute, for instance, doctrinaires and critics uncomfortably rub shoulders.[2] On the whole the changes the t have taken place in a very few years have been far-reaching, and I assume that the next years will necessarily be involved with further changes; for, with all its glaring contradictions, Czechoslovakia belongs today to the advance guard of what used to be called the "Eastern Bloc."

The strongest impulse to new thinking was provided by the manifest crisis in economic management. Three years ago Ota Šik, who now condemns command planning, was himself one of the "dogmatists." It must be appreciated that the third five-year plan, which came into force in January 1961, was abandoned as early as August 1962, and was followed by a similarly short-lived "seven-year" plan and an interim plan for 1963. The causes of the crisis were manifold: qualitative deterioration of an "extensively" growing industry; decreased productivity; lack of rationalization and industrial research; production in individual enterprises over a wide variety of products (instead of being concentrated on a few); accumulation of stocks of unsaleable goods; strain caused by economic aid to "undeveloped" countries (and to Cuba); shortage of capable and enterprising industrial leaders (resulting from the system of making appointments for political services); the catastrophic failure of collectivized agriculture; the lack of proper economic planning (because everyone fought to defend his own territory and all conflicts were bucked up to "higher level," at which capacity for sensible decision was again lacking); labor shortage and bad work discipline. Thus centralization and decentralization succeeded each other as if different teams of bureaucracy were playing a game.

It is hardly surprising that in a country with a highly developed industry and agriculture this general deterioration in quality, this self-exclusion from the world market, and widespread shortages should be felt as peculiarly shocking. In a recent Austrian-Czech television discussion the Austrian side asked: why should two neighboring countries which started at roughly the same level after the war now be displaying such a wide difference in output and standard of living? The Czechs were unable to answer. The steps which have been taken towards reintroducing "elements of a free market economy" (allowing prices to find their own level in restricted fields), the solemnly celebrated discovery of "the consumer," the still timid efforts to loosen up foreign trade and to let enterprises enjoy the incentive benefits of hard currency—are all claimed by Professor Šik to represent "a further advance in socialist economic thinking," having nothing whatever in common with a "return to capitalism." But the terminology doesn't matter so long as the stubborn adoption of the Russian economic model is recognized as the cause of retrogression.

The change of heart implies, not the setting free of hitherto repressed factors of "material self-interest," but working harder and thinking harder. I have already mentioned Eugen Loebl who, as a survivor of the Slansky trial, is allowed greater freedom of speech than many others; and it was he who remarked that "the State can decree Non-thinking—but not ideas and initiative...."[3]

Discussion tends to center on such "inner assumptions" of the new economy; but at the same time contact is sought with the West, even though (or, perhaps? especially because) this involves inspection of Czech factories by Western customers, the possibility of the exchange of experiences, and foreign travel. Eugen Kindler, a computer specialist, has described in *Kulturni tvorba* how foreign exchange shortages caused the Ministry to prevent him from attending a conference in Rome, and then again in Budapest, for which he had prepared papers on his work; when he was invited to attend yet another congress in Jerusalem he was asked to produce "an exact estimate of how much money the trip would ultimately save the State." He concluded: "I have now been doing research for six years. Five of these I consider to have been wasted—because I had to discover for myself what I could easily have learnt elsewhere in one year if I had been given the chance...." Some chemists have been sent for training purposes to a Basle chemical works, but going abroad for such purposes is still exceptional. A freer economy implies open frontiers. The destruction of the artisan class (which is now deplored) and the flight from the land of the whole younger generation (and this has not been compensated for by mechanization) are developments that cannot so easily be cancelled out by reforms. Many of the old world-famous exports, viz., Bata shoes or Gablonz jewelry—have been transferred abroad, after eviction or nationalization.

The special features of the Czech economic crisis—and the problems of the human, social, and political climate necessary for far-reaching reform—exceed the limits of this report on the changing attitudes of a new generation to the future and the past. But the striking failure of "materialist" doctrine in material affairs was so acutely felt by a nation accustomed to a Central European standard of living—and had ultimately to be so openly admitted by those responsible—that these economic factors played a decisive part in the breakthrough of a radically new spirit.

In February 1947, I expected a long period of coexistence" between the Communists and other parties, and that was an illusion. Today the question is whether a long period of coexistence is to be expected between the forces of inertia and those of change, and, having burnt my fingers once, I am not going to risk a prognosis a second time.

Still it would seem that a liberalizing tendency remains a deep historic factor in this society. In the past such liberal forces had a share in state power, and this position has of course been completely lost under the new regime.

Yet its weakness may be delusive. In 1947 there was no "liberal" or "Western" youth; too much had happened to rob them of that faith, and many of the best were convinced Communists. Today the whole system of a totalitarian Communist ideology is a dead letter for the new generation (and not only for them). It commands obedience but no enthusiasm. The thoughts and passions of the young people are elsewhere. However one wants to define the "new Humanism," this is the true specter that is haunting Central Europe.

It is hard to believe that the new things so closely associated with the appearance of a new generation can simply be reworked back into the old pattern of power. However ugly the chick may look, it just can't be forced back into the egg. To be sure, belonging to the Soviet sphere sets limits to possible developments—not so narrow as they seem to many today, but still limits. As its industrial production is constituted today, the country must be glad of COMECON for in only a few instances is it capable of competing on the world market, though it used to be. Economic reforms might improve things relatively quickly, and the impediment of Soviet quantitative industrial thinking would then be felt to be oppressive (as a minister said to me quite openly). Politically a part of the Eastern bloc, socially and culturally a part of Central Europe and modern industrial society, Czechoslovakia is by its very situation hard-pressed to make greater progress. Is it because of this that the visitor to Prague finds a great deal of humor but little cheerfulness?

Even apart from foreign policy, it is hard indeed to find a way from rigid Stalinism to a looser form of communism. Leadership is handicapped by chronic moral and economic difficulties. The existing political class has such a small credit balance in its favor, and old-style democracy, still unforgotten, beckons vaguely as a possible alternative. This difficulty of finding a middle position somewhere this side of a "relapse" into democracy, which is unthinkable to the regime, contributes to keeping alive so many outdated Stalinist features in the state apparatus. Elsewhere dictatorship has been explained by the backwardness of society; here it is manifestly connected with the fear of progress. The more unnecessary the dictatorship becomes, the more inert its representatives are bound to show themselves. It is a halfway position, and is everywhere felt to be untenable. Representing the new forces are a theatre and a cinema whose creations today reach world standards. That great empty pedestal that blocks the Prague horizon on the Summer Hill remains the symbol of the forces of inertia.

July 1966

Notes

1. *Tvar* had to cease publication in January 1966 on direct party orders.
2. The Viennese monthly review, *Forum*, published (October, 1965) a letter by Dr. Ivan Svitak, in which the circumstances of his case were dramatically detailed.

Svitak was until a year ago a member of the Philosophical Institute of the Czechoslovak Academy of Sciences; the Party's Ideological Commission dismissed him. "Stringent administrative methods in philosophical discussion," he wrote, "are quite unusual even in Czechoslovakia. Publishers confiscated all my manuscripts, editorial offices of cultural publications confiscated ten of my articles, all my university lectures were banned, my passport was withdrawn...." He was arrested and then released—in order, he remarks, "to serve as a case of 'exemplary' punishment of 'revisionist orientation'...." But he remains unemployed and hence under threats of prosecution for "parasitism."

3. "Superficially we may appear not to have enough qualified personnel to fill the leading economic posts in industry. In reality the nature of our economic difficulties is different. Do we really want leaders of a New Type? ...Have we freed ourselves of the illusion that thinking must be concentrated at the Planning Center and that the function of all others is purely executive and nothing else? Do we think of men as persons or as transformers of directives?..." Eugen Loebl in *Kultúrny život*, January 1965.

Letter from Paris

The Forty Immortal Chairs

Victor Hugo's wife concluded her story of his life with the following passage:

> To become a *pair de France* you had to belong to one of the categories from which the King took his choice. The only one of these open to Victor Hugo was membership of the Académie. He applied in 1836; the Académie preferred M. Dupaty. In 1839 he tried again, and the Académie chose M. Molé. On the third occasion, in 1840, the Académie passed him over for M. Flours. Hugo knocked on the door again in 1841, and this time it was at last opened to him. So he set foot on the first step of the ladder and began a new life.

There are three things to be noted about this. The first is that a great poet who became famous at an early age—a poem he submitted to the Académie at the age of sixteen caused him to be received by the *secrétaire perpetual*—tried so hard and so often to become a member of an institution that again and again passed him over for colorless but less controversial candidates. The second is that membership of the Académie Française could count as a stage in a political career; and the third is that that august body did not feel itself honored by the candidacy of a Victor Hugo but kept him waiting on the doorstep for five years.

All the same, Victor Hugo was elected while still young. Honoré de Balzac applied again and again (whenever a seat fell vacant by death) but invariably failed—the last time only a year before his own death. Fifty years later Paul Bourget, an epigone of Balzac's and himself a member of the Académie, wrote: "Had Balzac lived longer, his genius would undoubtedly have assured him entry into the academy...." But that is feeble consolation and a questionable retrospective prophecy, for Stendhal, Flaubert, and Zola, the other three great French novelists of the nineteenth century, were never entitled to include themselves among the "immortals," any more than were Baudelaire and Mallarmé, neither of whom would have had any objection to being elected—Baudelaire was actually a candidate once. Rimbaud and Verlaine were *a priori* excluded from consideration because of their "way of life." Even the great twentieth-century dramatist and poet Paul Claudel did not find it easy to secure admission. Though at the height of his fame and an ambassador as well (this means a good deal to the Académie Française), he was passed over on his first attempt in favor of the then widely read but literally rather insignificant novelist Claude Farrère[1] Only on the second attempt did he with difficulty surmount the hurdle.

Historians of this tradition-cowered body such as Pierre Gaxotte and Wladimir d'Ormesson (both of whom are members) claim that with few exceptions the Académie has "always" accepted important literary figures, though often after "ripe reflection" and hence "some delay." But, as we have just seen, this is totally untrue for nineteenth century French literature. One of the few important poets, apart from Victor Hugo, who were members was Alfred de Musset, of whom it is related that he once turned up for one of the Thursday meetings and said to the *commissionnaire* at the door: "Are many members here?" "Oh, yes, quite a lot." "Is Victor Hugo here?" "No, there's no sign of him yet." "Then nobody's here," said de Musset, and left

If Cardinal Richelieu, the founder and first patron of the Académie, had had his way, Corneille would not have been admitted. All the same, Corneille and Racine, and later Voltaire, d'Alembert, and Chateaubriand, were members which makes it possible to claim that for more than a century-and-a-half, from the age of Richelieu to that of Napoleon, literature, if not completely, was at any rate worthily represented in the Académie, which from the outset was never reserved for men of letters alone. Figures of ecclesiastical distinction have always been sought after, and they were especially numerous in the 18th century (in 1714 they actually formed a majority). Traditionally, Marshals of the army have always had a place. But after the recent death of Marshal Juin there may not be a French marshal for a long time to come. It was also the custom under the *ancien régime* to elect to membership the private tutors of the royal family, on the courtly consideration that kings of France would obviously seek out only the most distinguished minds for the education of their children. (At least in one instance, that of Bishop Fénelon, this was actually true.)

Dukes have always been numerous in the history of the Académie, and sometimes there was actually talk of a "ducal party" inside it. Title and social rank have facilitated entry into the society of the Forty, for it was established to be a pillar of society, a buttress of order and the state. In the pith century malicious tongues were already saying that men of letters were an "unavoidable evil" but, after all, you had to have some members capable of taking on the task of preparing the great dictionary and grammar.

The Académie has made very heavy going of the making of the dictionary. It still devotes itself to it once a week, and decades have often passed between the publication of one volume and the next. One of the members of the founding generation was the great grammarian Vaugelas, who did the letter A. After his death there vas no one to carry on to B. The years passed, and an academician named Furetiere had his own dictionary printed in Holland; the Académie made a corporate protest at this as an infringement of its privilege. At the time of its foundation it had itself to contend with another body of similar mentality, i.e., the *Parlement de Paris,* which for two years refused to ratify the cardinal's edict founding the Academy out of fear of losing its own monopolistic control of book printing and selling. Some members of the parliament had actually to be *embastilles* before the seal inscribed *á l'immortalité* could be applied to the document.

The grammar made even slower progress than the dictionary. After nearly 300 years the first and so far only volume to be published appeared in 1932, and one scholar (Professor Brunot) promptly showed that it contained over 300 serious errors. And nothing has ever come of Fénelon's hope that the Academy would produce a Rhetoric and a Poetics.

The Italian and French precursors of L'Académie Française *all* had a wider scope and a more international outlook. Mersenne, whose project dates from 1623, wanted to see regular meetings and exchanges between the Academies of the various countries. Tommaso Campanella hoped Richelieu would organize not just an Academy but the City of the Sun. Frances Yates records[2] that the Academies were meant to be as interested in things as in words, but adds: "The contrast between 'words' and 'things' is a theme with a long history." (Now Michel Foucault with *Les mots et les choses* has attempted to write this "long history.")

Who are the men of the present day—women are excluded, not by statute but by tradition—who are entitled to put the word "de l'Académie Française" after their name? Among them are scientists, such as Louis de Broglie, Le Prince-Ringuet and the biologist Jean Rostand whose father, the dramatist Edmond Rostand, was also a member). The fine arts are represented solely by the film director René Clair, while nothing has ever come of the proposal that famous painters, sculptors, and architects should be admitted. The clergy is admirable represented by Cardinal Tisserant, who is not only high in the Roman hierarchy as bishop of Ostia but is also a distinguished scholar in his own right. Among men of letters the most famous is the octogenarian novelist François Mauriac (who in his *Carnets* and "Bloc-Notes" permits himself many malicious remarks about his colleagues). When it was proposed that Henry de Montherlant should become a member he refused to pay the formal calls on academicians that are required of candidates (by tradition though not by rule), and he was co-opted without doing any canvassing. The theatre is represented by the comedy writers Marcel Pagnol and Marcel Achard; the distinguished and eloquent Jacques Audiberti was never considered, and Jean Anouilh and Marcel Aymé are not members of the club either. But then, from Proust to Roger Martin du Gard and Georges Bernanos, what great novelists have been encouraged to ask for admittance?

Since World War II, the Académie's boldest deeds have been its acceptance of the poet Jean Cocteau, who in his inaugural speech described his colleagues in their uniforms embroidered with green olive branches as "fish in a strange aquarium," and of Jean Paulhan, the *éminence grise* of the *Nouvelle Revue Française,* who did not even apply for membership until he was over eighty. Before Paulhan's election an ill wisher circulated to all academicians the pornographic *Histoire d'O.* (authorship of which has often been ascribed to Paulhan who denies it). But the successor elected to fill Cocteau's place was once more a typical representative of the Establishment, the economist Jacques Rueff. It does not seem to disturb the Académie that at the present time there is just one lonely poet among its members, and not the Nobel prizewinner St.-John Perse or Pierre-Jean Jouve, whose influence on younger poets is so immense. But the Académie has never been on congenial terms with poetry. In its eyes true literature is rather a kind of written extension of the art of elegant conversation.

When Jean Paulhan was elected in February 1964, he had to eulogize his predecessor, Pierre Benoit, who wrote pleasantly readable bestselling novels which from Paulhan's point of view had nothing to do with literature. Paulhan began his speech by addressing his colleagues as follows:

> You are surrounded by the mystery or a secret society, and not the least of your mysteries is this: You decided once and for all to devote yourselves to the study of language, but for more than 100 years you have relentlessly excluded all scholars who have devoted themselves to that very study. It might be supposed that you regard the subject of language as a well-protected prey serve of your very own, or that you have the gift of interpreting it in a manner quite peculiar to yourselves....

The speech of welcome to Paulhan was entrusted to the lawyer Maurice Garçon—having great lawyers among its members is another academy tradition—and Maître Garçon mingled only a little faint praise in his general damnation. He also thought Paulhan, whose wit is famous, too humorless. This meeting of the Academy was broadcast, and listeners, of course, failed to see the play of astonishment and amusement on Paulhan's face as he listened to the lawyer's oration.

The tradition of sour-sweet reception of new members is, however, time-honored. One Clérmont-Tonnerre, an inflated aristocrat with nothing else to recommend him, was received with modest remarks which included: "If it depended on merit alone, you would not be here today...." But this was wrapped up in so many courtesies that the candidate, who had read the speech in advance, thought it "excellent." Afterwards a friend explained things to him: and the speaker was exiled from Paris for some years by the *Roi Soleil.*

The great exception in the Academy's exclusivity towards poets was Paul Valéry, the previous holder of whose seat was Anatole France, who had no ear for poetry and had actually attacked Paul Valery's master Mallarmé. Valéry managed to make a whole speech about his predecessor without mentioning his name. Only once did he remark that his predecessor had "assumed the name of his country." In the same speech (in June 1927) Paul Valéry said that he disliked an honor "for which men of the first rank often had to wait for so long, sometimes in vain, and some were among the greatest and most meritorious..."

The Académie is an institution of polite and high society into which not all writers fit, particularly since they have not infrequently been Bohemians, rebels, beatniks, or simple enemies of bourgeois society. André Breton broke off relations with Paul Valéry after he was elected. Jean-Paul Sartre, who even declined the Nobel Prize as "too bourgeois," never came into consideration, and because of his "way of life." Jean Genet is considered just as unworthy as was Arthur Rimbaud—and not because of homosexuality, but because of his lack of "respectability."

How has the Académie Française survived over 300 years and innumerable changes of regime? It is an expression of continuity in French society; and to that extent is not merely a curious fossil, as one of its members (the biologist Jean Rostand) once called it, hastening to add that there were such things as living fossils, e.g., the coelacanth. Was it, then, born a fossil? Consider its origins.

A friend of writers named Conrart (incidentally, a Huguenot) had formed a circle in his house in which literature and new books were discussed. This was the time of the great *salons* of the *précieuses,* when new ways and linguistic usages were conquering the *élite.* Cardinal Richelieu, well informed as always, decided to take them under his patronage and give them an official character. Whether he was also motivated by his own literary ambitions he wrote plays and employed dramatists to work for him or regarded with suspicion all gatherings that were not under his own control, his attitude to literature was as political as it was to everything else. He regarded the task of purifying the French language as part of the establishment of a greater France. Conrart and his friends were by no means enthusiastic, and their reply was salted with irony, humbly pointing out that "such lofty ambitions had never entered their heads and his Eminence's intentions surprised them greatly."

But what could one do in a time when there was no such thing as an independent author who could live by his writings? Corneille alone had the prestige of public success behind him as a consequence of the reception given to *Le Cid;* and Richelieu's first request submitted to the academicians—whose number he increased to forty because of the role that number plays in the Bible—was to pass critical literary judgment on *Le Cid.* Why? Was it an amateur dramatist's jealousy at the success of a professional colleague? There were deeper reasons. Richelieu had forbidden dueling, and a duel plays an important part in *Le Cid;* he was at war with Spain, and the play glorified the Spaniards. Thus it was primarily a politician's pique The Academicians at first declined, on the ground that it was not usual to pass judgment on a work in the absence of a specific request for this by the author. Corneille was therefore induced to express precisely such a request. Richelieu had the Academy's respectful criticism of *Le Cid* brought to him, and in spite of the pressure of other business spent several days polishing it.

As a man of letters, could not the Cardinal have been a member of the Académie himself? As its patron he never attended its meetings. But his intention to turn it into an instrument of the state was plain, and the tradition survived from Louis XIV to Napoleon and after (though obsequious flattery was never practiced to the extent that it was in the time of the *Roi Soleil*, when the pronouncements of the academicians remind one of the speech patterns of the Stalin era). On the Cardinal's death the Académie found a new patron in the Chancellor Seguier. This was its salvation, because the first Academies in the Pith century, when the institution was copied from the Italian models, had never outlasted their patrons' lifetime. The custom by which the patron of the Académie Française was the head of the state who exercised the power of veto over its elections passed into desuetude under the Third Republic—but General de Gaulle revived it when he blocked the election of the writer Paul Morand, who had served as ambassador of the Vichy government in Berne. (It would never have occurred to President Lebrun to oppose the election of the monarchist Charles Maurras, who in his newspaper poured daily scorn on the Republic but, on his election, was provided with the same official guard of honor as other academicians.)

Under the third republic it was normal for the Academy to be on the Right, and the 1944-5 *libération* caused several convulsions in its ranks. Members convicted of treason or felony or "collaboration"—such as Marshal Pétain, Charles Maurras, and the Vichy minister Abel Bonnard—were expelled. But this was nothing in comparison with the purge of republicans and Bonapartists that had followed the return of Louis XVIII. De Gaulle takes the Académie very seriously, as he does all institutions that contribute to continuity, tradition, and the propagation of French influence. François Mauriac, in his panegyrical book on the General, describes how tensely he awaited his first meeting with the *Liberator*, hoping to hear great thoughts about *la France* or *la grande politique*.

> What utterly surprised me was that the great drama through which we had just lived (the date was September 1, 1944) was not even mentioned at lunch. Who would have expected that? Instead, de Gaulle questioned me about André Gide. He took a great interest in the *Académie*, and who the new occupants of the empty chairs were to be...

(To ask François Mauriac about André Gide was more maliciously witty than Mauriac cares to notice.)

On the jacket of the third volume of the General's *Memoirs*, comments by men of letters on the earlier volumes are quoted, and all the quotations are from members of the Académie. One may assume that the choice was made by the author himself. Napoleon had made the Académie a constituent of the *Institut,* which it has formally remained; like the Institut, it is housed in the Palais Mazarin. The Institut meant so much to Napoleon that during his Egyptian campaign he used to sign himself "member de l'Institut et général officier comandant."

Thus the academy was founded as a state institution for the purpose of "purifying" the French language and so to prepare it to function as a world language and increase the fame of France. The extent to which this ambition was achieved is demonstrated by the way the Académie was imitated. The Berlin academy conducted all its business in French, and bestowed a laurel wreath on Rivarol for his answer to the prize question about the reasons for the superiority of the French language.

Academicians used to be paid, and nowadays they still receive a fee (the *jeton de presence*) for every meeting they attend. The penniless La Fontaine never missed a meeting if he could help it, with the result that his colleagues called him "*très jetonnier.*" The Académie would be far richer than it is today if it had not invested its revenues in state loans, but it is still a large property owner; its possessions include the demesne of Chantilly and the building round the Passage Vivienne near the Paris Bourse. It administers numerous foundations on whose behalf it distributes prizes (more for "merit" than for literature). For literature it has had to yield to its competitor the Goncourt Academy, which has only ten members and makes only one award, the prestigious Prix Goncourt.

The kind of high society and social outlook that the Academy embodies can be seen from the nature of the foundations it administers. The most celebrated of its prizes is that for Virtue founded by a M. Montyon; an Academician has to deliver an oration on the subject on the occasion of its annual award. Then there is the prize awarded annually by the Farcy van Ael Foundation

> to a French Catholic family [Catholicism is insisted on in many of these foundations] that has at least four children—who are either living or have died for France—and is poor and works in a field connected with the manufacture of corsets.

Then there are awards that nowadays seem more symbolic than anything else, such as that to "the daughter of a senior officer who is without means and has not secured a tobacconist's concession from the Government." There is the Darracq Foundation, which gives a prize to "a young girl who belongs by birth to the best society but has been forced by blows of fate to work and has preferred a life of honorable and honest toil to that other kind of life that can bring a woman immoral wealth." There are a number of prizes for those with large families, and among these as many as twenty-seven children of the same marriage are envisaged. There is also a prize for "a poor Christian family of unimpeachable morals that has adopted one or more orphans and brought them up devoted to duty and their country."

A whole social history of old France can be read from the 140 prize endowments administered by the Académie; all, with honest realism, assume an invariable connection between work and poverty. There is a prize for a workman employed for thirty years in the same shop, and another for servants who have served the same masters for forty years "without having drawn all their wages." And this reflects the same patriarchal world that French children meet in the Comtesse de Ségur's still popular books in the Bibliothèque Rose.

One wonders how the Académie manages nowadays to seek out honest French and Christian poor to whom to award these prizes, because the genuinely poor in France tend today to be Portuguese or North African Muslims. Nevertheless, it accepted Jean Cocteau and Jean Paulhan as member and it seeks out and rewards aged loyal domestics: no inflexibility here. But on is reminded of how often this astonishing range has been satirized. Barbey d'Aurevilly wrote a sharp attack against it, which has recently been reprinted, and there was Alphonse Daudet's biting novel *l'Immortel*. Between the wars the vaudeville *l'Habit Vert* was infrequently played and became a movie. Gaston Leroux, one of the best-known writers of detective stories, made the Académie the scene of his recently republished novel *The Bewitched Chair*....

All this, of course, is part of the Académie fame and legend. Many writers who have in their time scorned it have later joined it. "When we are forty, it has been said, we are ridiculed. But when we are thirty-nine, everyone genuflects...." It must not be forgotten that in the lath century the Académie was in the centre of all the Enlightenment controversies. Voltaire made the most strenuous efforts to ensure his admission and actually had himself sent a medallion blessed by Pope Benedict in order to be able to tell his opponents not to be "more papist than the Pope." With d'Alembert as secretary of the Académie the party of the Encyclopaedists triumphed (though it was one of its respected members, the writer Chamfort, who later argued before the National Convention that it should be dissolved).

There is a notable description by Heinrich Heine of a meeting of the Académie under Louis Philippe:

> Every year I regularly attend the ceremonial meeting in the rotunda of the Palais Mazarin. One has to wait for hours to secure a seat among the *élite* of the intellectual aristocracy, to which, fortunately, the most beautiful women belong. After a long wait the Academicians at last appear through a side door. Most of them are either very old or at any rate no longer very healthy; no use looking for beauty among them. They take their seats on long, hard, wooden benches. (One talks of "academy chairs," but these do not exist in reality; they are a mere fiction.)
>
> The session begins with a long, tedious speech on the year's work and the entries for the literary prizes by the temporary president. Then the secretary rises, the *secretaire perpetual,* who holds office in perpetuity like the King. The secretary of the Academy and Louis-Philippe are persons who cannot be deposed by ministerial

or parliamentary whims. Unfortunately Louis-Philippe is now advanced in years, and who knows whether his successor will maintain the blessings of peace with as much skill as he. But Mignet is still young, spared by the hand of time that whitens hair and wrinkles brows. The handsome Mignet still has the same golden locks as twelve years ago, and his face has an Olympian radiance. The present perpetual secretary of the *Académie is* one of the greatest barbers of our time. Even if one hasn't a single sound hair on one's head, he is able to conjure up a curl of praise for one and conceal that bald pate under a wig of eloquence. How fortunate are these French Academicians! There they sit blissfully on their secure benches, and they die happy because they know that, however doubtful their careers may have been, the excellent Mignet will eulogise and praise them after death. Under the spreading palms of his oratory, as perpetually preen as his uniform, lulled by the breeze of his rhetorical antitheses, they rest here in the *Académie* as in a cool oasis. Meanwhile the caravans of humanity pass by unnoticed save for the tinkling of the camels....

The Académie, having made the codification of the language its special task, exposed itself to ridicule during the last century by first refusing to accept the candidacy of the great lexicographer Littré, whose dictionary is still a standard work, because a Cardinal who was a member objected to his "irreligiousness." Since then the Académie has not been particularly intolerant. But its authority in matters of French usage is not highly rated by the grammarians who regularly discuss such matters. French, which in the eighteenth century conquered the world, is now on the defensive, trying to beat back a massive invasion of English words. But the Académie plays no special role in the operation.

The absurdity of many of the links between literature and the Establishment, between so-called culture and the state is too easy to criticize. Before the war there was a member who was an industrialist, and his total literary *oeuvre* was said to have consisted of a prospectus for a headache cure.

But this link can also be seen in another light. As Friedrich Sieburg wrote in his once-famous book *Is God a Frenchman?*

> In France it is the writer, not the *savant,* who occupies the first place among the intellectuals. His function is to counterbalance the specialist and prevent the disintegration of culture into separate disciplines. The Specialist appears as the auxiliary worker who has voluntarily left the centre of things and is only justified when he makes his way back to it. Whereas the Man of Letters is conscious of the comprehensive nature of his work and conceives his function as the common denominator of such professional activities as he may incidentally he engaged in. Every Frenchman in a leading position, whether he is a general, a businessman or a politician, feels it incumbent upon him to sacrifice to the goddess Literature and take part in her rites. He thereupon garnishes his reports with literary allusions. The important thing about it is that such quotations serve not so much to adorn his speeches, reports, opinions or orders-of-the-day, as to make them more easily intelligible. A businessman who quotes Barrès at a company meeting provokes not mirth but a feeling of solidarity. For every one of his hearers is proud to belong to a civilization which urgently calls for the writer's services instead of excluding them...The slogans and the "dressing" are essential, and they always come from literature as a source of legitimacy.

So it is that a really good knowledge of the subtleties of one's own language and literature comes to count among the foremost social virtues. It is not the (east of its anomalies. It was long ago said of the Académie that it is the "last trace of the monarchy in France." Under the Fifth Republic, in which monarchical features that had never completely vanished have become more discernible again, the French Académie seems less and less of an anachronism. The future has caught up with the past, and loves the pomp and power of it all.

Edmond Rostand's Cyrano de Bergerac (a contemporary of the founding fathers) has these lines:

"Bardin, Boissat et Cureau de la Chambre, Porchères, Colomby, Bourzeys, Bourdon, Arbaud, tous ces noms qui ne mourrort jamais, que c'est beau."

But it is only the chairs, which are never allowed *to* remain empty for long, that are "immortal." The big Larousse now includes the colloquial term used of academicians: *cul á fauteuil,* "chair bottom." Naturally enough, it is not included in the Académie's dictionary. For a "fossil," the active part it plays in the public mind is astonishing. That skeptical organ of the Liberal Left, *Le Monde,* prints verbatim in a four-page supplement the two main speeches made at the reception of every new member. All the other newspapers report the event and at least print excerpts from the speeches. However superannuated the collective mentality may seem to be, one continually notes how many serious figures of French public life, modern and sophisticated, still aspire to a chair. Ah, to be received into this most exclusive of all clubs —it would be the climax of one's life. How well the Cardinal understood his *France immortelle!*

June 1968

Notes

1. 1A tradition which is kept alive. In December 1966 the bestselling novelist Maurice Druon, much inferior even to Claude Farrère, was preferred to the poet Pierre Emmanuel (who has, however, now been elected and is the only poet in this assembly).
2. Frances Yates, *The French Academies of the 16th Century* (Warburg Institute, 1947).

Letter from Paris

Decline of the French Left

At the end of the war, during which the greater part of the French Right compromised itself with Vichy, the Left in France was practically everything. Today, twenty-five years later, it is practically nothing. How has that come about? During this quarter-of-a-century France has undergone a tremendous transformation: its industry is more modern, its commerce more rationalized, its agricultural economy less overpopulated and more profitable —a metamorphosis the details of which have been well described in *The New French Revolution* by John Ardagh. Leftwing publicists and theorists such as Serge Mallet have written books with titles such as *The New Peasants* and *The New Workers*, thus indicating the change to a more productive and more efficient society. While the middle class was formerly predominantly represented by small traders and business men, artisans, and small and medium manufacturers who banded together to resist the demands of productivity and price reductions—big industry often reacted in exactly the same way—today there is a broad middle sector of experts and technocrats who think about profitability, rationalization, and planning. Under both the Fourth and the Fifth Republics there has been a mixture of private and state economy, of free market and planning. The Renault works are an example of efficient state industry; Jean Monnet created a type of elastic, "concerted" planning which experts from other countries came to study.

The first puzzling fact that confronts us is that a country that has felt the spur of progress, that has become aware of the deficiencies and backwardness of a traditional, autocratic capitalism and, broadly speaking, has made considerable advances along the road to a modern industrial and welfare society has, unlike all the other democratic nations in Europe, failed to develop a strong Social Democratic party capable of acting either as an effective opposition or as partner or principal in a nation government. What we see instead' is a weakened and, so far as the non-Communist part of it is concerned, numerically greatly reduced and divided Left that has been more unprepared and more helpless in the face of each and every crisis of the regime that it opposes—until the disaster in the parliamentary elections of 1968. In the second round of the recent presidential election, it was unable even to present itself as an opponent.

Whatever crisis of ideology or policy there may be in the reformist movements in other societies, France is a special case. Her economic and social development is far from being so different from that of other European nations as is her political development; as expressed in the two phenomena of Gaullism and the powerless Left.

There is also another factor that makes this weightlessness of the Left seem a kind of negative political miracle to the foreign observer, namely the fact that both to Karl Marx and to contemporaries of the revolution of May 1968 France was the country *par excellence* of the Great Revolution of the Left. That was what it was from 1789 right through 1830 and 1848, and from the Paris Commune to the Popular Front of 1936, the nationalizations and social reforms of the post-1944 governments, and finally the May riots, associated with the great and well-disciplined general strike.

Left-wing revolutionism is a living tradition in France; even archconservative parties include the word *gauche* in their names. Gaullists do not want to sit on the right in the National Assembly; some Gaullist groups call themselves Left-wing Gaullists, but no one has yet described himself as a Right-wing Gaullist.

And now we have seen a presidential election in which the four Left-wing candidates together failed to attract one-third of the votes (and that in the absence of de Gaulle, who always managed personally to attract many Left-wing voters). Is this a chance, an accident, a passing eclipse, after which the light of Left-wing ideas and hopes will soon illuminate France again? Anyone who has been just as surprised by the dramatic changes in France during the past few years as any "non-specialist" will carefully refrain from making prophecies. Let me therefore not try to read the future, but restrict myself to what has happened before our eyes.

There is, in the first place, the Socialist Party, which until recently archaically described itself as the SFIO, an abbreviation for "French Section of the Workers' International," and in the immediate post-war period seemed to have legitimate hopes of successfully competing with the Communists. It has undergone a gradual and—with a few exceptions, as in 1956—steady decline from 23 percent to 5 percent of the vote, and even if this last figure—representing the votes cast for Gaston Defferre against Pompidou—is not to be regarded as valid because many Socialists voted for the centre candidate (Alain Poher) while others voted for other Left candidates, it has lost nearly three-quarters of its vote. What was the cause of this?

If we regard political developments as being attributable, not only to the working of anonymous social forces, but also to decisions made by individuals in positions of political power, it is tempting to put the chief blame on Guy Mollet, the secretary-general of the SFIO since August 1945. Mollet, an English language teacher from Arras (the mayor of which he has been for many years), originally prevailed against the candidate supported by the great and prestigious Socialist leader Léon Blum. The radical policy for which he then stood was a rapprochement with the Communists, repudiation of opportunism and reformism and resistance to the menace of *embourgeoisement*. Since then, however, he has himself contracted electoral alliances at Arras with the Radical Socialists (1956), the Gaullists (1958), the Communists (1962), the Popular Republican Party, the MRP (1965), and again with the Communists (1967). He is sharp and caustic in his comments on other parties. Of the Communists he has said: "They are not Left of us but East of us," and of the MRP: "This party should simply not exist." His, too, is the often-quoted phrase: "Our Right is the stupidest in the world." Of any Socialist who opposed him he would say that the man was nothing but owed everything to the party, and of other politicians that, in so far as they did not belong to the SFIO, they were at most "second best." Of Pierre Mendès-France he delivered himself of the pronouncement that "he is not one of us, but he is the best of the rest...." ("Il n'est pas des nôtres, mais le meilleur des autres.")

Under the Fourth Republic, Mollet was five times entrusted with the task of trying to form a government, but only once, in February 1956, did he become prime minister and during his period of office the capitulation to the French settlers in Algeria and the Suez expedition took place. In 1958 he played the decisive part in overthrowing the last prime minister of the Fourth Republic—Pflimlin—and bringing about the advent of General de Gaulle. Before the presidential election of 1965 he engineered the failure of the campaign to put forward Gaston Defferre, the Socialist mayor of Marseilles, as candidate and tried to secure support for the liberal Pinay before declaring himself satisfied with Mitterrand as a "unity" candidate. In the latest campaign he again first tried to block Defferre's candidature and then did all in his power to weaken him. For him there are three kinds of possible political allies. In presidential elections they can be sought on the Right; in parliamentary elections the favorites are the Communists; and when it comes to forming a government they are unspecified. This is not so much guile as the reflection of a definite French electoral logic, in which he is taken to be an undisputed expert.

Five days after he became prime minister he recalled General Catroux, the liberal Resident in Algeria, whom he had just appointed, and replaced him by the narrowly nationalistic Socialist Robert Lacoste, who looked only to the French settlers. But he was not the first Socialist whose only view of *décolonisation* was stubborn resistance to it. There was never a group of French Socialists similar to the Fabians in the British Labor Party who thought out the problems of Empire. Conversations with the Vietnamese were broken off under the Socialist Minister Marius Moutet; and under the Socialist Resident in Algiers Naegelen the elections were so blatantly manipulated by the administration that many Algerians who had hitherto been *assimilationistes* were turned into rebels.

It took a Nationalist general coming from the Right to carry out the decolonization in face of which the SFIO failed completely, not least because it had many members in Algeria among French officials, particularly the police, but had no idea how to respond to the slogans of the *fellagha*. The first attempt at a policy of understanding in relation to the Algerians was made by Pierre Mendès-France, who ended the Vietnam war and instituted a policy of reconciliation with Tunisia. He was supported by Gaullists such as the Minister Fouchet, and by Marshal Juin, while Guy Mollet forbade Socialists who were willing to do so to enter the only reform-minded government of the Fourth Republic.

Mallet is characterized, not only by this lack of any great reform policy, but also by a combination of practical opportunism with unchanged revolutionary doctrine. The SFIO is the only great Social Democratic party that has not had a "Godesberg" (to use the German formula), he has not revised its program or changed its outlook; only a few years ago a circular on party doctrine by the—now retiring—secretary general, stated: "He who wishes to think anew has no place in our party."

It is this association of extreme flexibility in practical politics—in the name of "Saving the Republic"—with extreme rigidity in doctrine—in the name of "loyalty to socialism"—that distinguishes Guy Mollet from: great Socialist leaders of the past, such as Jean Jaurès or Léon Blum. He is, however, no dictator, but a man of the party machine; and he is supported above all by the northern federation of the party. He has had continually to cope with sectional struggles and rivalries of all sorts, and in the process has driven many of its best minds, such as André Philip, into the Left-wing Socialist PSU; these men are thug in practice, lost to politics, because the only part so far played in them by these splinter groups has been to diminish the total representation of the Left by putting forward their own minority candidates.

So the crisis of the Socialists can certainly not be explained away by the limitations of a single individual who—unlike a de Gaulle or a Mendès-France—has no "untypical" characteristics. Before the first vote in the presidential election, Mauroy (Mollet's designated successor), hastened to announce that, though the Socialists would vote for Alain Poher, they would in no circumstances help him to form a government. Thus the French electorate was informed that, while the party desired to destroy a political order, it had no intention of substituting another one for it. So the spirit of Guy Mollet, if it can be called that, survives his power in the political machine.

In July, Pierre Mauroy was not elected as successor of Guy Mollet as everybody had expected. Instead Alain Savary was chosen, a man of great integrity who in his twenties had been the Gaullist governor of St. Pierre et Miquelon (at the time when these islands were at the centre of a tension between de Gaulle and the USA). He had resigned over North African policies from Guy Mollet's government and later from his party. Savary was elected by 31 against

29 votes, a precarious victory due—it was said—to the support of Mollet himself. The time is apparently not yet ripe for the Socialist Party to start regaining lost prestige.

The other and quite different problem of the Left is the only slightly diminished strength of the Communist Party which—unlike the Italian comrades—recently demonstrated its unswerving loyalty to the Soviet Union and put forward a very successful candidate for the Presidency of the Republic in the person of the experienced parliamentarian and veteran Stalinist Jacques Duclos, who secured twice as many votes as the public opinion polls expected and more than twice as many as the three other candidates combined (Rocard of the PSU; Krivine, the May revolutionary; and the Socialist Dellerre, who promised a Mendès-France government if he were elected). The French Communist Party has recovered amazingly quickly from the two great blows of the May revolution, during which it was isolated and attacked from the Left, and the intervention of the Warsaw powers in Czechoslovakia, which again robbed Communism of its "human face." Now it appears to be making headway against the ultra-Leftists among university staff and students.

But the stronger it is, the lonelier it becomes. The hope of the "Left Federation" that François Mitterrand wanted to forge was to become at least as strong as the Communists, and thus to be able to accept them as allies without frightening off electors who fear the Communists and without having to be afraid of them itself.

An alliance of equals still seemed possible in 1967, when combined lists were a feature of the elections and Pompidou's majority shrank to a few votes. Since the events of May, and Prague, and the collapse of the non-Communist Left, there have been no bridges between the Communist "ghetto" and the rest of political France. The more securely the Communists entrench themselves in their trade unions and their red districts, the more their embattled "protest" deprives them of political efficacy.

In spite of that the Communists are, in practice, a reformist party—though this development is still disguised by their rigid internal structure and their link with Moscow. Communist leaders such as Maurice Thorez and François Billoux felt thoroughly at ease in 1945 in the three-party governments under de Gaulle and after de Gaulle. They called for the breaking-off of strikes, sharply condemned Algerian nationalism, and when—in a changed international situation and under the pressure of the war in Indochina—they were eliminated from the government by the Socialist Paul Ramadier, they went on declaring for months that they remained in principle "a government party." Only under the pressure of the Stalin-Zhdanov line, the transformation of Communist parties into civil war parties, and the struggle against such objectives as the ports through which Germany was to be provided with food supplies did the party withdraw from all spirit of cooperation. This 1944 willingness to share in the government had been something new. In 1936 the Communists refused, to the general surprise, to take office in the Popular Front government, but critically "supported it from outside."

During the past eleven years the social struggle against the bourgeois state, combined as it was with their agreement with de Gaulle's foreign policy, has resulted in the development of a kind of schizophrenia among the Communists, for they could neither support the Gaullist regime nor want to overthrow it. To them, as part of an international movement, any alternative government, including a Leftwing one, would from the viewpoint of world politics have been worse.

It was events outside France that caused the Socialists to move further and further away from the alliance that had proved its usefulness in the 1967 elections. The Israel war and events in Czechoslovakia created a gulf between the two parties. True, the Socialists avoided deepening it, but François Mitterand did not propose to have any Communist "shadow ministers" in his so-called counter-government. Thus it was clear that the electoral alliance could lead to no government alliance.

The question remains why a nation with such a great tradition of critical thought has such a narrow-minded and rigidly doctrinaire Communist party of mass influence. Among the vast literature on the subject, the books of Annie Kriegel are particularly recommended to those who read French.[1] Whatever the causes may be, the special strength of the Communists is a component of the general weakness of the Left. The party of revolution has in practice merely consolidated the notorious *immobilisme* of French politics.

So far as political geography is concerned, the Left is much stronger in the less industrialized, "underdeveloped" parts of France—that is, in the south—than in the industrial areas of the north In 1967 it was again in the south that Mitterrand's "Federation" was relatively more successful with the peasants and in small country towns than in the more modern, expanding big towns. While the Gaullist party—which has so often changed its name—gradually spread through the whole country and continually grew in strength, the Left has been splitting up and becoming regionalized.

It is of course very natural that protest should be strongest where a sense of backwardness and neglect prevails—but that has only made the Left the defender of the small man rather than an instrument of progress. For innumerable Frenchmen *le progrès* often has brutal and inhuman aspects, while a defense of *les petits* has social and human value. But it is inadequate as a political ideal. Guy Mollet once protested against a law for the rationalization of retail trade: "We cannot ask this of our traders," he said. Defense of the immediate interests of the small man has not sufficed. It was no accident that the great success of 1956 was accompanied by a wave that brought into parliament many Right-wing Poujadists hostile to the State. The manner in which the Communists identify themselves with all the demands (including demagogic ones) of the various interest groups has often been described as a "*Poujadisme du Gauche.*"

The ideas that have been of moment in postwar France are associated with the names of Jean Monnet for planning, Robert Schuman for the overcoming of nationalism, de Gaulle for decolonization, and not with any of the names of the men of the Left to whom the field lay open in 1945 but were lacking in dreams, visions, and reforming spirit. The way from that zenith of power to the time when Jean Daniel (the chief editor of the Left-wing weekly *Nouvel Observateur*) confessed that "today it is an act of heroism to belong to the Left" has on the whole been one of gradual decline, interrupted by isolated episodes of recovery and hope. Every event from the colonial wars to the May revolution has been felt by the Left to be, not an opportunity, but a disturbance of a revival in progress.

Not long ago I had a talk with a well-known intellectual of the extreme Left, Claude Bourdet, who complained that "de Gaulle's retirement came too soon—the Left was not yet ready...." The truth of the matter was that part of the bourgeoisie dared vote against de Gaulle because the revolutionary danger from the Left had grown so remote. If history had always waited until *la gauche est prête*, immobilism would have been total. All impulses to movement, to the solution of crises, came from outside—with one great exception, that of Pierre Mendès-France. Between June 1954 and February 1955 he cut a number of Gordian knots—Vietnam and Tunisia—and was overthrown by men of his own Radical Socialist party just when he was about to tackle economic and social problems. For all his defects, he was undoubtedly the only reformer who roused political interest and inspired trust among the young. He quickly resigned from Guy Mollet's 1956 government, and one can understand why. But a good deal of his reforming spirit lives on; his leading economic adviser Simon Nora has been given a similar post in Chaban Delmas' government (Chaban Delmas was himself a member of the Mendès-France cabinet), and Nora's report on the state of the public services and state industries, which was long kept secret, may yet be a point of departure for important necessary reforms.

The two significant trends in France have been called *Mendèsisme* and *Gaullisme*, i.e., have been named after individuals, a phenomenon for which there is no parallel in other Western democracies. That is an indication of the special difficulties put in the way of new ideas and actions by the embattled self-sufficiency of the party machines. They have to come from outside, as a result of the initiative of individuals. The responsibility for every attempt to break through the two strangely mingled traditions of war between political creeds and combinations of interests has been taken, not by political artier, but by "lonely individuals," It is possible that now, after the twilight of the gods, in the more normal era of "Pompidolism," a new phase may be beginning in which France will grow more similar to the other democracies.

And the parties of the Left? The Communists are reformist-minded, but do not dare to be reformist in practice, The Socialists practice reformist policies, but do not dare to adopt reformism as part of their doctrine. Thus the spirit of practical reform in French society seeks other and sometimes unusual and unexpected outlets. At all events, if reaching a zero point is ever a blessing, the French Left is now enjoying a state of grace indeed.

December 1969

Note

1. Annie Kriegel has written a two volume' work: *Aux engines du communisme français* (Mouton & Co., the Hague) and, among several other books, a study of the French Communist Party for Editions du Seuil.

The 1970s

Letter from Paris

The Idiot, or Sartre's Flaubert

Jean-Paul Sartre has at last finished the first two thousand pages of the book on Gustave Flaubert, which he began more than fifteen years ago, and they have recently been published by Gallimard in two volumes under the provocative title *L'Idiot de la Famille*.[1] He completed them with a combination of guilt and relief. This emerged in a conversation with the two authors of his monumental biography which appeared last year,[2] the length of the conversation was almost proportionate to the length of the work, for it filled more than two full pages in *Le Monde*.

Why had he resumed work on his Flaubert, which he had dropped in 1955 after writing the first 1,000 pages? Because, he said, he had wanted at last really to finish something. The Ethics he had announced in his *L'Être et le Néant* had never been written; his novel cycle had been shelved; there would be no sequel to the first volume of his *Critique of Dialectical Reason*; and his work on Tintoretto would remain a fragment. But *Flaubert* was the one thing he was going to complete. He expected to publish two further volumes, on one of which he had made excellent progress; it would even include a history of the development of the arts round-about 1850. The last and most important volume, a structural analysis of *Madame Bovary*, was still at the project stage. He thought he would need "another three years" to finish with Flaubert's neurosis, and "two more" for *Madame Bovary*. True, the study of *Madame Bovary* could be deduced from the analyses in the first two volumes, but the interest of this novel lay in the factors that could not be so deduced. Thus at the age of sixty-six Sartre was expecting to spend five years on completing this enormous (or, as Flaubert used to say, *hénaurme*) book. Other projects, such as a play or the "political testament" he has announced, may intervene. So we cannot exclude the possibility that this work that he is really determined to complete (though not beyond *Madame Bovary*, for he is no longer interested in the later Flaubert) will remain a torso, though one larger than any usual biography or analysis of a writer's work—larger even than Sartre's over-dimensional work on Jean Genet, which began as a short introduction but grew and grew.... His pleasure that the first two volumes have been published—because of their weight and his reputation their publication was the great literary event of the spring—was expressed in this marathon interview in the sentence: "I am now faced with an agreeable obligation: that of finishing my Flaubert." The title refers to the fact that Gustave has learned to read and write rather late. Although an admirable letter written at the age of nine is known, Sartre regards this lateness as a most important symptom to be linked at once to a frustrated childhood and to Flaubert's future relation to words.

In an interview in September 1970 with the ultra-left *Idiot Internationale*, the masthead of which states that its editorial committee consists of "all the political prisoners of this regime," Sartre spoke of his Flaubert in different, almost apologetic terms. He tried to explain the extent to which the events of May 1968 had changed him, made him a "different man," caused him to break with the "classical intellectual" he had hitherto been.

> My problem [Sartre said] is that of a 65-year-old intellectual who for twenty-five or twenty-seven years has had in mind writing a book about Flaubert, i.e., using familiar scientific methods to analyze a human being. Then came May 1968. I had been working on the book for fifteen years, and I am deeply involved in it. What am I to do? Give it up? There would be no sense in that, and yet someone has said that the forty volumes of Lenin's works constitute an oppression of the masses. What am I to do? I have decided to finish the book, but that leaves me at the level of the traditional intellectual. ...I do not see a way out of the dilemma. Is there an intellectual method that is not directly accessible to the masses that can yet find intermediaries through whom it may reach them? Is my Flaubert a work that will necessarily fade and vanish, or one that may be useful in the long term? It is impossible to tell. I dislike, for instance, what some authors write, but I cannot maintain that their writings may not at some time or other be accepted by the masses, and for reasons it is impossible to foresee today...

Thus Sartre is still the Sartre who in *The Words*, the memoir of his childhood, mocked at and rejected his literary bent, but made a book (i.e., literature again) out of that mockery and rejection; the Sartre who repudiates but nevertheless embodies the "intellectual type." He came to grips vigorously with the little *Poulou* that he once was and used him to illustrate his theme. In connection with his Flaubert he says that the life of another person can be completely understood—he calls it *"totalisé"*—only when it has been completed; an interesting view, as his object is to understand, not just externally but from within, in all its intimacy, a life that (in his opinion) can be made communicable and transparent to the last degree. On this complex question he has apparently no doubts; after years of familiarity with all the aspects of Flaubert's life he "knows in advance" what Flaubert will do and, as there were no psychoanalysts in Flaubert's lifetime, he claims to know him better than Flaubert could know himself. Sartre believes the method he developed or hammered out in the course of this work to be a way, not just to assumptions about or a closer approach to a man and a writer, but to a form of total understanding. ("Nous essaierons d'effectuer la restitution compréhensive de cette existence considérée comme totalisation en cours.")

At the same time Sartre does not deny that he has written a fable about Flaubert, a nonfiction novel describing the formation and development of an individual belonging to a definite period, bearing its imprint and that of his family history. The first part deals with Flaubert as a product of that family at that particular time, i.e., as the second son (if the children who died young are not counted) of a respected Rouen surgeon who felt him to be superfluous (as the eldest son was to succeed him professionally). Also, his mother wanted a girl, who indeed arrived after Gustave and is said to have monopolized her mother's tenderness. Maurice Nadeau comments:

> It would be a senseless quarrel to ask the author how he got to know in which way Gustave's mother did her breast-feeding. He readily admits that he does not know, that nothing proves that it was really that way, that he invented a "fable." But even if I am proved wrong, he says in essence, I am nevertheless right. Supposing that things happened differently, my approach (*démarche*) is the only one that is appropriate. O method, how powerful thou art! (*La Quinzaine Litteraire*, June 1971).

The unhappy influence on Gustave Flaubert of his relationship with his parents and siblings recalls Sartre's Jean Genet, known as "the bastard" because of his illegitimate birth and therefore similarly rejected as socially superfluous. In the second part, Sartre sets out to show what a man makes of what the circumstances have made of him. It must, of course, be borne in mind that we have here only the first 2,100 pages (about a million words); but so far the emphasis is on Flaubert's compulsions and complexes, including his neurosis (and in this connection Sartre insists that Flaubert was not an epileptic, as many previous biographers have maintained, but—an hysteric).

This book, in which many chapters and above all digressions (on Hamlet, actors, laughter, which is oddly considered as conservative and even reactionary behavior!...etc.) are fascinating, contains a remarkable contradiction. Sartre, as he tells us in *The Words*, has been preoccupied with Flaubert since his adolescence. He wanted to read *Madame Bovary* when he was twelve. "Darling," his mother said to him, "if you read such books now, what will be left for you later?" To which Poulou replied proudly: "I shall live them." Sartre has written extensively about Flaubert in *Being and Nothingness* and in the *Critique of Dialectical Reason*, as well as in *What is Literature?* He disliked Flaubert as a bourgeois writer, as a believer in art for art's sake. This antipathy never excluded admiration of the novelist's greatness, but only in this work did he overcome it and replace it by "empathy." (Flaubert may have said, "Madame Bovary, c'est moi!," but Sartre expresses a profound disgust with poor Emma whom he considers irredeemably stupid and base—no "empathy" with her!)

In Sartre's view, Flaubert has been conditioned by his childhood to pessimism and to passivity, to the desire to be a woman, to be old. Sartre dwells at great length on Flaubert's erotic life and promises to write at even greater length about it in the following volumes. He finds him conditioned entirely by femininity, as if Flaubert had really been—to quote Jean-François Revel's review—"*une lesbienne.*" But what of the untiring literary work of this "passive" person? Literature—says Sartre with contempt—is "*une mini-praxis,*" a bare minimum of activity, a flight from true deeds in the real world. So a contemporary whose major activity has been writing books and who has been fascinated during the greatest part of his life by the writer Flaubert to whom nothing other than literature has ever been real, wants us to believe that to him Flaubert is just an interesting case study, and not relevant to himself. Sartre dares not say: "*Flaubert, c'est moi*"; he stops short of analyzing a fascination that has almost fumed into an obsession.

There is very little, at any rate in the first two volumes, about Flaubert's most important works; we are shown Flaubert, not as a writer, but as the second son of a French doctor in the last years of the reign of the Bourgeois King, a well-documented case both for Marxian social analysis and Freudian psychoanalysis, which here flow together into a single stream. Also Flaubert is a writer who based his work on *le Néant* and was therefore bound to fascinate the philosopher of *L'Être et le Néant.* Flaubert wanted to start out from nothingness and to reach the whole, and even proposed to write "a book without a subject."

Those who have not sufficient love and admiration for Flaubert to want to read every line that is written about him will find here no real explanation why such a monumental work is so full of the most minute and sometimes tiresomely repetitive analyses, reflections, and asides. For, though anyone interested in Flaubert will learn many new things, including material from previously unknown sources, it is surely legitimate to suggest that it is interest in Jean-Paul Sartre rather than in Gustave Flaubert that will cause many to buy the book and some to read it patiently.

For *The Idiot of the Family* is in all respects authentic Sartre, actually a *summa* of his philosophy, though so far it presents us with only a portion of Flaubert's life. The great exception is the chapter on the adulterous couple's celebrated cab-drive that involved Flaubert in a charge of pornography, though he did not devote a single word to what took place in the cab, but merely described its route. Sartre does not examine the literary significance of this famous passage, but triumphantly connects it with a story told by the Goncourt brothers of how Flaubert crudely described to them how he first had relations with his mistress Louise Colet in a moving cab and from time to time put his head out of the window in order to laugh. So the little that is here incidentally mentioned about Flaubert's masterpiece serves only to illustrate his life, even though observations about "the imagination" and about "a life whose failure led to a triumph" can conceivably lead us in the direction of literature.

I have already referred to the curious title, *The Idiot of the Family.* According to his niece, Flaubert learned to read later than other children. Sartre regards this as a determining factor in Flaubert's development, and in turn the result of the severity of his mother, who never hugged and caressed him but brought him up on strict disciplinary lines. Sartre's hypothetical conjectures about Flaubert's early upbringing are later presented as established fact, from which many other things are then in turn deduced as established fact. In Sartre's eyes we know nothing about a man or a writer if we do not know about his infancy. So he just has to be certain about child Gustave....

The book moves constantly between what its author calls prospective and regressive analysis. It is therefore surprising that Sartre has so far not "prospectively" reflected on Flaubert's literary posterity, which was so much larger than that of Balzac or Stendhal. From Henry James and Turgenev, to Proust, Pound, and Eliot, there is a constant mediation of great writers on Flaubert, a Flaubert fan school—as indicated for instance in Roger Shattuck's book *The Stoic Comedians: Flaubert, Joyce, Beckett* or in Nathalie Sarraute's essay of "Flaubert, le précurseur." Seen in the light of his influence, Flaubert must indeed appear as "our contemporary" while Sartre so far confines him rather strictly to his epoch and its limitations. Why, then, have Henry James, Marcel Proust, and now Jean-Paul Sartre himself been so fascinated by this writer, and given his work and his attitude to literature so much thought?

Sartre gives at different times different answers. For instance he claims that we can only know a writer if we have much material on his family and childhood and that Flaubert through his own correspondence and other testimonials is a unique case of a richly documented writer's life:

> And of all we know among those long since dead there is no one whom we like...Nursing, the digestive system and excretion, the first cares about cleanliness, the mother relationship: of all these fundamental things, nothing. ...Without the earliest childhood, it suffices to say that a biography is only building on sand....

It is surprising that Sartre should have erected such a huge edifice on such slender foundations, for he says depreciatingly of interpretations by others that they are like "cloud castles built on thick mist." The reader is hurtled from one period of Flaubert's life to another, and references to innumerable personal circumstances of which Sartre takes knowledge for granted. (For a chronological life of Flaubert the reader will do better to rely on Enid Starkie's biography, and for an introduction to his work on Maurice Nadeau's study of *Flaubert's Greatness.*)

One of the most successful chapters is devoted to Flaubert's fascination with "stupidity," his pinpointing of turns of phrase, which later assumes encyclopedic proportions. Sartre shows that the stupid bourgeois commonplaces that Flaubert ridiculed were reflected in his own way of thinking, particularly in his letters, and that his attitude to bourgeois stupidity, as to the bourgeois world in general was ambivalent. In examining Flaubert's lifelong fascination with stupidity, Sartre notes that there were really two kinds:

Flaubert unites under the same name two contradictory absurdities, of which one is the essential quality and the other the acid which corrodes it.

Many of the "clichés" which Flaubert jotted down for his *Dictionnaire des idées reçues* can be found in his own letters as sincerely held opinions, or as turns of phrases used without irony. Flaubert, who thought that in novel writing there was room for scientific progress and who at the same time ridiculed every belief in progress, did not escape an ambivalence which Sartre elucidates.

It is remarkable that among the factors that led to his becoming a Flaubertologist so unique in every respect there is one that Sartre does not mention. Flaubert hated the bourgeois class without ever being able to escape from it, and Sartre has often represented himself as a bourgeois intellectual who "will hate the bourgeoisie to his dying day but is unable to escape from the bourgeois world; and his denunciation of literature has actually become the very quintessence of the literary. He claims there is no connection between the paradox of Flaubert and his own, that he chose Flaubert precisely because he was a complete stranger to him. This claim might be worth subjecting to the same kind of psychoanalysis as Sartre devotes to Flaubert (or, rather, subjects him to).

But these are hasty responses to a book on which an important philosopher and writer has worked for many years scrapping many earlier versions. In these remarks I haven't attempted to offer more than a first impression of such a massive work. For the time being a "fragment" of these huge dimensions defies assessment; it confronts us almost like some natural phenomenon. Jean-Paul Sartre's Flaubert will remain an important work even though, as is inevitable, the critics question a great deal of what the author puts forward as absolute certainty. Sartre says himself that he "no longer has any views about this book." Consequently, the views of others will surely affect him little.

December, 1971

Notes

1. Gallimard, 2 vols., 110 fr. There is something striking about the usage of "Idiot" One of Sartre's favorite left-wing papers is called *L'idiot Internationale*. For Sartre, who once considered writing about Dostoevsky, there might also be an association of thoughts with the famous Russian novel. For the journalists, there could be a provocative contradiction to the French self-estimation of being so very intelligent. "*L'idiot*" might also be compared to Voltaire's "*huron*," the man who does not play the game of being clever and by his "simplicity" sees through all the conventions and tacit conspiracies which the "intelligent ones" take for granted. These are quick associations. In any case it would appear to be the case that the French Zeitgeist has got itself fixed on a new word.
2. Michel Contat and Michel Rybalka, *Les écrits de Sartre* (1970).

D'Annunzio and Mussolini: New Letters

"Every leader is an individual response to a collective demand." Thus Leon Trotsky on the subject of Adolf Hitler. But when there was a collective demand for a leader in the Italy of 1919 the response was twofold—Gabriele D'Annunzio and Benito Mussolini.

Both had seen active service in the World War, and both, opposing Giolitti's neutralism, had advocated Italy's entry on the side of France. D'Annunzio, the older by twenty years, and world-famous since the 1890s, had declared himself earlier than Mussolini, who at first had been very strongly opposed to Italy's entry. And whereas the Forli socialist, wounded on the Isonzo after a brief spell at the front, was able to return to his business as a publicist, the fifty-year-old poet from Pescara remained to the end the most intrepid of pilots, having previously served in the cavalry, the infantry, and at sea. He had made himself a legend with his flights over Vienna and Trieste, had lost one eye and was the idol of the Arditi, a mixture of elite troops and swash-bucklers with rough manners and rather criminal leanings. Later, as the self-appointed "Regent" of Fiume, which he called Quarnero, he had signed his decrees *Il mutilato di guerra*—"the war-wounded."

D'Annunzio's fifteen-month escapade in Fiume, beginning in September 1919, represented the first crack in the postwar West European order of Versailles and Trianon, the ominous foreshadowing of the era of freebooters in a world which President Wilson had sought to make "safe for democracy." Self-styled Nietzschean supermen would all be turning nationalist.

D'Annunzio—like his French contemporary, Maurice Barrès—had moved from the erotic fervor and self-indulgent egotism of the *Übermensch* to extreme nationalist passion. For the cosmopolitan whose greatest success had been gained in Paris (he had fled there to escape his creditors) and who had been influenced by Nietzsche, Strindberg, Wagner, and Dostoevsky, this was a logical step. But to the man from the Abruzzi the "Italianness" of Dalmatia was a rather less genuine conviction than the Frenchness of the sundered provinces was to Barrès, the man from Lorraine. By the boldness of his act in proclaiming the free city of Fiume to be a part of Italy (it won him the sympathy and support of the frustrated Italian army and navy), D'Annunzio furnished Fascism with a dramatic example. But more than this, he gave it much of his own style. The famous war-cry *Eja, Eja, allala* was his, as was the slogan *a noi!* (to us); and he was also responsible for the militia uniform with the tasseled cap. In a regime in which gesture, rhetoric, and ceremonial pomp played so large a part, such externals were by no means unimportant. Above all, D'Annunzio's March on Fiume set the pattern for Mussolini's March on Rome—the perfect example of how a fait accompli could be brought about.

D'Annunzio, on 12 September 1919, did not merely annex Fiume, which was recognized as a free city by the Italian government; he reached out beyond it to purely Croatian villages and islands. In fact he grabbed everything he could lay hands on, going as far south as Zara (now Yugoslavian Zadar), and in so doing won not only the plaudits of the right but the respect of even the extreme left. He was turned out at Christmas 1920, by a few warning shots from an Italian warship. This encounter, which he thenceforth described as "the bloody Christmas (*Natale di sangue*)," cost four lives. During his "regency" of Fiume he had held himself to be the uncrowned ruler of Italy, believing that he would be as warmly welcomed in Rome as he had been in the free city, and did not doubt for a moment that the Italian people would grant him "unlimited power."

To Mussolini D'Annunzio was an ally and a model, but also a rival: was there room for two freebooters? But D'Annunzio was no politician. He lacked the patience for long-term manoeuvre and indeed for any kind of activity that did not occur in the full glare of the arc-lights accompanied by resounding proclamations and a roll of drums. Mussolini was altogether more astute, more cool-headed and realistic: he was, moreover, entirely concentrated upon the achievement of real power, whereas D'Annunzio reveled in heroic attitudes and liked to think of himself as the great artist who may now and then descend to the level of politics but never loses sight of the fact that "Art comes before country." While Mussolini built his State, D'Annunzio was concerned with his statue.

D'Annunzio's writings are now going through a new period of reassessment. His influence on Stefan George, Hofmannsthal, and Heinrich Mann; on Montherlant (who acknowledges it) and possibly on Aragon and Malraux (who don't), on the film director Luchino Visconti, and many others—this is due not solely to the revival of a fashion and attitude of mind but also to the element of modernity in D'Annunzio's books which makes him appear the literary, if not the chronological, contemporary of James Joyce and Thomas Mann. His importance in Germany at his peak period (despite the bad German translations) may be gathered from Peter de Mendelsohn's recent history of the famous S. Fischer Verlag. Indeed, Thomas Mann frequently warned his brother Heinrich against D'Annunzio's "overblown versifying." The comprehensive, if not very accurate, biography of D'Annunzio by Philippe Jullian which has recently been published in France—and the numerous critical surveys of the *fin-de-siècle* "decadents," the Stile Liberty and Art Nouveau, which cannot disregard him—show him to have been part of a movement which has had an artistic posterity. It may be said, indeed, that compared with *il Duce* D'Annunzio has had the better of it. The forerunner of fascism did not become a fascist fellow-traveler but he continued to think of himself as the Duce's mentor and soothsayer. He was the great Independent living in the honorable and illustrious "inner exile" of Vittoriale on Lake Garda. But he did not feel his independence threatened by the Duce's munificence, including the very costly publication of his Complete Works. Mussolini may have been more realistic when he exclaimed:

If you can't pull out a rotten tooth, you have to fill it with gold....

The *Carteggio*, the uncensored collection of letters exchanged between Mussolini and D'Annunzio which has just been published (in Milan by Mondadori), will contribute nothing to the objective assessment of the poet. On the contrary, this correspondence of nineteen years has more to tell us about the prosaic, purposeful politician than about the faun-like, self-worshipping peacock-figure, the man who in a letter about a medallion he designed (which was disapproved of on account of its "anatomical realism"), confides to the Duce that he still exercises his "muscle" daily, and that the woman he "rode" last night is completely worn out, poor thing.

Up to 1934 it is a political correspondence in which D'Annunzio vehemently and sometimes hectoringly calls for the long-promised law protecting the rights of seamen; this was made difficult for Mussolini by the fact that he had also to take account of the interests of the big ship-owners (such as Cosulich). Later there follows a string of requests. D'Annunzio's son must be made a deputy; the Dutch lady who appears to have a valid claim to his Lake Garda property must be dealt with; the most famous of his mistresses, Eleonora Duse (who had just died in America), must be brought home and given a state funeral. But with all his repeated demands D'Annunzio never loses his sense of his own dignity and importance. He is never servile. And now and then he utters words of noteworthy political advice.

On 11 September 1915, immediately before the March on Fiume, D'Annunzio writes to Mussolini:

My dear Comrade, the die is cast. I'm going ahead. Tomorrow I shall take Fiume by force of arms. May the God of Italy be on our side. I shall rise from a bed of fever, but delay is impossible. Anyway the spirit will overcome the weakness of the flesh. Summarize the article which the *Gazetta del Popolo* is to publish, but print the ending unchanged. Give us full support while the fight is going on. I embrace you...."
[Renzo de Felice, the editor of the correspondence and a notable biographer of Mussolini, notes that D'Annunzio did not give Mussolini's *Il Popolo d'Italia* the first offer of his journalism, but merely the right to reprint articles contributed to other papers which he considered more important.]

Mussolini, on his side, utters dire warnings against communism, which D'Annunzio does not take seriously. "We must also be on our guard against Bolshevism," Mussolini writes from Milan on 18 September 1919. "There are 450,000 workers on strike. However, the majority of the workers approve of the Fiume affair."

On 25 September Mussolini advises D'Annunzio to march on Trieste, to declare the monarchy deposed and put himself at the head of a junta—in other words, to stage a republican revolution. As we know, this is not what Mussolini himself did. He seized power when the king refused to countersign the discredited government's emergency decrees—that is to say, under the monarch's personal protection.

But that was yet to be. D'Annunzio, meanwhile, was sending messages of triumph and defiance from Fiurne, to be disseminated by Mussolini's press.

> Let Italy know that my enterprise is irresistibly gaining ground....She must also know that no government, ally or friendly power can withstand my iron resolution. Wilson is going mad—what a nemesis! He is gnashing his brains with 32 teeth! Press boldly on! (6 October 1920)

When the "great adventure" was ended, Mussolini—addressing D'Annunzio as "*mio commendatore*," kept the memory glowingly alive:

> Peerless warrior, great poet, animator of the new Italian generation.... (17 August 1922)

D'Annunzio had no confidence in the success of the Fascist march on Rome and little wish for it to succeed. He had many contacts at that time with left-wing circles, and he saw Mussolini as the tool of the "agrarian enslavers." He wrote to friends, "I cannot abandon the common man." To Mussolini he wrote, "The Italy of today does not love me or believe in me." He even wrote sardonically after Mussolini was in power, "Nowadays the young grow old fast, while still singing *Giovinezza* [Youth]."

He gives vent to his frustration and bitterness in a letter dated 16 December 1922, addressed to "dear comrade Mussolini."

> The best of myself, which I offered to my country, has been falsified, defamed and trampled underfoot. Protestations of love and trust do not deceive me. Exile is the penalty of my long and wholehearted devotion. I know it well. I accept my fate and am equal to it.

During 1922 D'Annunzio was writing the Duce letters of "healthy reproach" in line with "my customary bold frankness." And when the latter protested, saying that D'Annunzio was now regarded in France as an opponent of the Fascist regime, he replied as follows:

Your telegram has a strange tone which may be fundamentally 'Fascist' but is quite foreign to my own inner nature. You also fail to perceive the extent to which my insights have become more penetrating, and the heights which my spiritual freedom has attained.... Did not all that is best in the so-called 'Fascist' movement spring from my spirit? Was not the present national revival already—and now alas—predicted by me forty years ago?

The difficulties surrounding the "seamen's pact," signed both by the Duce and the Commendatore, were still unresolved. D'Annunzio expostulates, "You know that I wear two invisible crowns, one of laurels and the other of thorns," and when Mussolini replies that he hopes to be able to settle the matter, he retorts, "Do not send me any more telegrams saying, 'I hope to overcome the last obstacles.' In my next book you will find an eloquent passage headed, 'Against Hope'...."

A particularly short message from D'Annunzio, dated 20 August 1923, reads, "Oh, good Laocoön, throttle the snakes," and is signed "The winged adventurer of 21 August 1918."

In 1924 the king created D'Annunzio duke of Monte Nevoso. Mussolini had written to him, "The matter is settled, if you wish it," to which D'Annunzio replied in deep displeasure:

My name is a lofty title in itself for our contemporaries and their successors. I cannot and should not wish for anything. It is the overwhelming duty of the government and the nation finally to acknowledge me, irrespective of my wishes and my disdain. Let it do so. Let it acknowledge the great and many-sided part I played in the 'Holy War', and how by my lonely and uniquely heroic efforts I preserved the ancient frontiers of wounded Italy. Let it acknowledge my Adriatic campaign and creation. That is the nation's duty. It matters nothing to me whether it is performed.

In March 1924, D'Annunzio was up in arms over the persecution of the writer Miguel de Unamuno by the Spanish dictator, Primo de Rivera. He expected Mussolini to share his indignation and do something about it. When the telegram of protest which he had addressed to Paris was stopped by the Italian postal authorities he wrote:

I know the Spanish political world, I know the King, I know Rivera. I know a great many things. The Bourbon nose is now grotesquely twitching like a rabbit's nose 'full of butter' as Giovanni Villani said of the Flemings. If the Directorate continues to persecute Miguel Unamuno, and goes so far as to bring him to trial and sentence him, I shall sharpen Don Quixote's lance. You should be at one with me in outrage and protest. A few years ago you would have stood at my side, as your bold paper *L'intrepido* put it.

In April 1924, D'Annunzio, abandoning all hope of a settlement of the seaman problem, wrote furiously:

We must now part company for good. I have been led on from disappointment to disappointment, from betrayal to betrayal, from hypocrisy to hypocrisy. The signing of the sea-pact was simply a sham, it was never implemented. And this ends it. You must stay on your side and I will stay on mine. As you know—the whole world knows it—in my heart and brain I have every kind of courage. You promised me a truce. You promised it to my art, which is beautiful and eternal as a river, a lake, an Italian landscape. And now you force me to make war. May the responsibility be on your head, and the bloodshed. We embraced by an open grave. We take leave of one another amid the ghoulish laughter of skulls.

But this was merely a flourish, not a separation. Before long, confidence between them was so far restored that Mussolini, suffering from the repercussions of the murder of the socialist Matteoti (and he had authorized it), could write:

Two months ago they flung a corpse between my legs, so heavy that it nearly knocked me off my balance. How I envy your solitude, peopled with splendid memories and enclosed in the diligent rhythm of your great work.... If you can spare two minutes, write to me, but not about politics. [Mussolini underlined the last words.]

D'Annunzio's works were on the Index, and the Church made difficulties when it learned that a new play of his was about to be produced. A Brescia newspaper which was to have printed his letter of protest was seized, and he wrote to the Duce:

I expressed my opinion of their shameful persecution in a few lines penned with the lofty elegance that no one in the world except myself can command. The paper was brutally confiscated, and this is said to have been done at your instigation. I demand a full explanation so that I may know whether we are comrades or enemies.

"Comrades," Mussolini soothingly replied. It was all a misunderstanding, a case of excess of zeal on the part of an underling "under pressure from the bishops."

A particularly interesting letter is the one dated 9 October 1933, in which D'Annunzio warns Mussolini against Adolf Hitler, the "marrano"[1] with his sick blotchy face, paintbrush flourished like the bladder of a sinister Pagliaccio, and the lock of hair straggling down to the top of his Nazi-nose. "That's enough. You know what I mean. In blunt, Caesarian terms, France must not disarm and Italy must not disarm...." Mussolini replies non-committally: "I have thought about the subject of your letter, and it would be worthwhile to discuss it thoroughly in the peaceful solitude of your Vittoriale."

D'Annunzio, writing in French, composed an appeal to the French people in the name of their common hatred of "the abominable England of Jonathan Swift." (Why Swift particularly?) "This appeal," he reported, "is 212 pages long, and you who know the language will find in it some of the finest pages of French prose ever penned."

Nothing more of significance happened during the two-and-a-half years remaining to him. The fact is that since 1924 he had withdrawn from active politics. If he could not be the Leader of Destiny, he could at least be revered as the great trailblazer and artist. His letters are all written in a grandiose-ornate style as "classical" as the Vittorio Emanuele monument in Rome. The only human note that emerges is contained in the passing references to his physical state of advancing age and infirmity.

The publication of this correspondence will do nothing to enhance D'Annunzio's reputation. On the contrary, it makes it more difficult to render him such honor as he deserves for his real and considerable contribution to literature. He was not the stuff of which dictators are made, because as the Hero and as the Bard he remained a dilettante to whom politics was never anything more than an attitude, a role to be played among others. It was never, as it was to Mussolini, the only conceivable way of life. D'Annunzio would probably have been incapable of having his political opponents murdered. However much he might hold forth about Power, Fame, and Imperial Grandeur, literary creation was to him always the nobler task. Even before the turn of the century, when D'Annunzio crossed the floor of the Italian Chamber from the Right to the Left, a Frenchman had called him *le deputé de la beauté*. His kind of aesthetics had many points of contact with Fascism. And yet—from the *fin de siècle*, of which D'Annunzio was an important part, certain notable impulses are still active in European culture; from fascism, none.

April 1972

Note

1. A "Marrano" in Spain was a baptized Jew; but it may also—in Italian—simply mean a scoundrel.

Letter from France

New Society, Old Politics

There were numerous political surprises in store for anyone who witnessed the recent events in France, especially that most intensive and extensive of French election campaigns. Never was so much innovation coupled with so much tradition. On the one hand, we have more technology and modernity, noticeable mainly in the lifestyle of the middle classes (which seem to be wealthier and in many respects more privileged than their counterparts anywhere else in Europe), and also some enduring progress at points of contact between state and citizen, (e.g., social security offices). On the other, one is faced with the presence of a growing foreign sub-proletariat, the persistent housing and transportation crisis that besets the millions who commute between suburbs and urban centers, and also disconcerting pockets of backward services (e.g., the dilapidated telephone system).

French politics display a juxtaposition of technocrats and old-fashioned notabilities, one of whom informed his constituents that he had made personal representations to government departments no less than 20,000 times during the previous legislative period. Mammoth public opinion institutes, staffed by bright *"Sciences po"* (political science) graduates, may soon save voters the trouble of voting because their extrapolations are becoming an ever more accurate measuring-rod of the political terrain. As for the major debates, they are now mounted between star performers on the broadcasting networks. Still, old French ways persist. Candidates parade their past services to a limited audience in nasally dramatic tones; and maladroit pamphlets and placards, quite innocent of the designer's art, commend the electoral merits of honest men and women blessed with a clear and level gaze. Even politicians who call for a new *"qualité de la vie"*—the slogan is at once justified and in vogue—fail to exhibit any feeling for such a quality in their contributions to political window dressing. Big-city *"enarches"*—graduates of the *École nationale d'administration*—contend with "notables" who are supposed to possess that much-vaunted "human touch" and "sense of personal contact" which computers and the mass media cannot replace.

There exists a whole new literature on *"la France pauvre."* Attention is focused on workers whose living standard, though higher than it was, has risen less than in West Germany and Italy; who are compelled to forgo many amenities because of the housing shortage, time lost in traveling and lengthy working hours, and whose experience of everyday life does not quite accord with the glad tidings of the sociological statistician. One of the most successful recent films, *Elle court, elle court la banlieue,* took its inspiration from the book by Brigitte Gros, a politician. It pictures the harried existence of the *"banlieusards,"* sometimes comically, sometimes critically, and ends in a street scene which portends something akin to a mass revolt by the enervated commuter.

"La vie quotidienne," everyday life—for the first time in a Fifth Republic election, this slogan ousted *"la grandeur"* from its traditional preeminence. Finance Minister Valéry Giscard d'Estaing proclaimed that the economic miracle had now to acquire a new "social dimension"; Premier Pierre Messmer conceded that the position of low-paid workers was a blot on the face of modern France. Everyone now recognizes that France's so-called "Japanese" economic growth has been accompanied by the emergence of new and glaring inequalities.

Many hundreds of thousands of peasant farmers and agricultural laborers have flocked to the towns and factories in recent years. There they encounter an often-diabolical working rhythm and scant safety precautions—a form of *"capitalisme sauvage"* which the welfare state, for all its achievements, is failing to tame. The number of French women who have to work in order to procure the now-familiar range of household appliances is larger than in other Western countries. This is compulsion rather than a symptom of emancipation; and its results can be seen in the distressing growth of hooliganism among adolescents who have no family to look after them.

Research into the living standards of the new French middle class is lacking, but some pointers can be found in perhaps the best political book to be published recently: *Le système Pompidou* by the socialist Gilles Martinet (Editions Du Seuil). This notes that the monthly income appropriate to a modern up-and-comer starts at *"une brique,"* or one million old francs (10,000 new francs, but why do sums in new francs when the French decline to?). France is commonly accepted as the country with the most "second homes." The possession of a house in the country as well as a flat in town is a minimum requirement of the middle-class living standard. Many metropolitan boutiques display shirts at 200 francs, jumpers and shoes at 400 or 500 francs; and luxury articles such as these seem to find plenty of takers—notably young customers. It was my impression that France's consumer society is comparable only with a section of nouveau-riche Northern Italy

Is it any mystery that "admires" should have been proliferating among the Gaullists? In contrast to the *"Républicains indépendants,"* the bunk of whom are materially well-to-do, many Gaullists are people of very modest background. The Parisian atmosphere tempted them to emulate an extremely expensive style of living that could only be maintained by those with links between Paris political influence and important business interests. The high living standard enjoyed by the new (i.e., "technocratic") middle class is already taken for granted. In the France of yesterday whose prosperity was less conspicuous, the difference between frontrunners and stragglers did not leap to the eye as it does now.

Another two million voters; a changed and, above all, urbanized society; old French industries gripped by crisis, and new industrial centers burgeoning in other regions (Toulouse instead of Lorraine)—these factors help to explain why France's economic miracle is associated with so much latent unrest. Equally, they make it hard to evaluate the prevailing degree of political stability. This has nothing to do with the inequitable distribution of votes between large and small constituencies because the final voting figures of last March tell the same story. As leader of the Left four years ago, François Mitterrand rallied about 45 percent of voters against De Gaulle. The same Left-wing coalition has just turned in a similar performance. The "*Réformateurs*" received as many votes in 1973 as the "*Centre*" did during the 1960s. Regroupings do occur, of course, and even small shifts can be fraught with consequences. The fact nevertheless remains that for the past hundred years French votes have been divided between the Left-wing and Conservative camps in roughly equal proportions. Grand ideological controversies count for less than "*pesanteurs sociologiques*," or the social forces of gravity; and these, in turn, have more to do with traditional modes of behavior and change more slowly than society itself.

What currently appears to be a major novelty is that the *Réformateurs*, who are all out for social change, might constitute the weight that could tip the scales. However, they are hardly a homogeneous political force. Watch Jean Lecanuet and J. J. Servan-Schreiber appear together in public (solid middle-class provincialism versus brilliant nervy sensationalism)—and become acquainted with individual "*Réformateur*" candidates (some of whom are the most conservative and old-fashioned politicos imaginable), and one cannot fail to perceive that the "*Centre des Réformateurs*" is a house of the four winds. Although this group may well contribute to a political transformation, it, too, should be viewed principally in its relationship with the old and new French middle classes whose privileges do not, despite the "*égalité*" that is so often demanded but never practiced, appear to be at risk. On the contrary, perhaps it is they who will chiefly benefit from political regrouping just as they have so far done from the economic miracle.

May 1973

Letter from Rome

Italy's "Cultural Crisis"

One always senses here the fundamental split between state and culture, and Italian culture today is both accuser and accused. Over eighty college professors are active in the political life of Italy, in both Parliament and the Senate. The president of the Republic and several ministers have occupied, or still occupy, professorial chairs. Why, then, do all Italian official publications go on and on about the "shipwreck of culture"? Why do they keep on expressing "grave disquiet" over the chasm between public life and cultural activity? Both the *Corrière della Sera* and *L'Europeo* have carried out enquiries among writers, film producers, architects, lecturers, and "cultural managers." There and elsewhere, too, the same complaint and the same indictment is to be heard; in innuendos, in polemics, and in discussions, the same spirit of resignation or revolt is to be found, and this applies even to the older generation, generally regarded as responsible. In the list of national shortcomings three points stand out: (1) the divorce between the state and the political parties on the one hand and culture on the other; (2) lack of a "sense of responsibility" among cultural leaders; (3) the increasing grip exerted by industry on the press and publishing world.

The state's lack of interest in culture is ascribed first to the effect of historical tradition ever since the Counterreformation—but also to the effect of present-day politicians who do not feel themselves obliged to be at all concerned about culture. Those ministers who still occupy professorial chairs keep them although they cannot fulfill their academic duties. Many of them occupy chairs in several different cities and employ substitutes. No great reforms are to be expected from them.

University degrees have become increasingly devalued and ready teachers of repute argue that the old "*laurea*" should be abolished. Nepotism and good connections rather than ability govern appointments to professorships, like much else in Italy. Moreover, the more gifted students no longer aim for a university career since they find that other callings can provide them with greater advantages and prestige. Research receives less support from the state or the great industrial concerns than in any other modern country. Italy can now barely produce a research worker of international repute. The poet Eugenio Montale said: "In a few years' time Italy will be full of unemployed intellectuals with worthless degrees...."

In an interview, Carlo Bo, a well-known professor and author, was deeply pessimistic: "I think there is a state of neglect, of inaction and of despair which could not more dramatic. There is no continuity. The intellectual does not get a hearing and has lost all standing. Our universities are now mere factories for superfluous degrees...."

Among those whom I asked none had a good word to say for the whole system from the primary school to graduate research (apart from some efforts being made in places like Pisa and some signs of renewed interest in the universities). Dr. Faeda, the mathematician and president of the Rectors Conference, lamented: "We have over 8,000 undergraduates. Italian universities have become mass institutions—without being organized as such...."

The older generation wistfully recalls the great hopes of the anti-Fascists and the excitement of 1945. Ignazio Gardella, the architect, said; "After the liberation we, the architects of Milan, initiated a lively dialogue between culture and politics. Now that is all gone. As far as town planning is concerned hundreds of schemes have remained paper plans only. Our best architects are people who paint the walls while the house is burning. We are bogged down in an outdated economic system and have no pattern of a new society to inspire us. We have less of a dialogue with the young than our parents had with us. Our great mistake was not that we worked within the system but that we did not exploit our successes to change the system from within...."

Giorgio Strehler, director of the Piccolo Theatre in Milan, said: "We were a generation without teachers. We hunted through the libraries and had to discover the world for ourselves. We had no orientation from the past and perhaps we invented it all. The present generation will have nothing to do with what we call orientation or the past...."

In Strehler's view, like many of the others who were interviewed, the dramatic turning-point was the decision of Togliatti, the late Communist leader, to allow *Politecnico*, the popular cultural periodical run by ElioVittorini, to cease publication; the Communists were the only major party whose cultural policy seemed to hold out some hope. Those I questioned, however, invariably emphasized that the Christian Democratic Party had been in power all the time and it could not really be called a "disappointment" since it had never had any cultural policy at all. Strehler also indulged in some self-criticism: "Very few of us took it upon ourselves to work in political organizations. We would demonstrate or sign some petition, but we would not do day-to-day low-level work. Everyone in Venice protested about the Statute of the *Biennale*, but what came of it all? Nothing. Everyone went home and busied himself with his own affairs. We have become incapable of bringing our problems to the political authorities...."

The persistent theme at present is that all this is "the writers' fault"—but this argument disregards the vital point that Italian society contains very few readers of books. Here the foreigner who rightly admires present-day Italian literature is in for a shock. With writers such as Palezzeschi, Montale, Silone, Landolfi, Piovene, and Moravia in the older generation—Sciascia, Natalia Ginzburg, and Calvino in the middle generation, and Malerba; Sanguinetti, Manganelli and Anna Banti among the younger—with critics such as Pampaloni, Paolo Milano, and Arbasino (at least twenty more new literary names could be mentioned such as Arpino, Tobino, Cassola, and Gianna Manzini)—the European reader is unlikely to have an impression of sterility or provincialism, about which there is so much tale nowadays. Moreover, many daily newspapers in Italy pay considerable attention to cultural matters and the ties between literature and journalism are closer in Italy than elsewhere. Ennio Flaiano and Dino Buzzati, for instance, were well known as both men of letters and newspapermen. The connection between literature and the films is also very close. Pasolini is an author and film-producer, Bertolucci began as a poet, Moravia is a film critic, and Malerba a scriptwriter.

Compared with most other European countries, therefore, Italy is cutting rather a good figure, their own favored *"buona figura."* The fact must not be overlooked, however, that the percentage of Italians who read at least "one book a year" is the smallest in Europe—smaller even than in Spain and Portugal. The *Corrière delta Sera* recently reported that out of every hundred adults the following had read "at least one book in 1971":

66 Dutchmen
63 Englishmen
56 Frenchmen
52 West Germans
40 Spaniards
28 Portuguese
24 Italians

This is a statistical fact which no one would suspect when visiting the attractive bookshops in the major cities or admiring the plethora of new editions (in particular the translations); certainly no one would suspect it as he meets the many brilliantly informed and highly cultivated Intellectuals in every urban centre. As Renato Guttuso says: "The average Italian, even in a senior position, is less cultivated than the average Frenchman, Englishman, or German. There are many reasons for this—our schools are worse, for instance, but another reason lies in the mechanics of education and cultural life outside the schools...."

Clearly there are two Italys; and the second Italy, that of the illiterates or semi-illiterates, the "strip-cartoon (*fumetti*) readers," is larger than the uncultivated mass in the rest of Europe. Can the writers be put in the dock because they do not make an impact on a non-reading public? The accusation reminds me of the exhortation that used to appear regularly in Spanish newspapers: "ILLITERATES, LEARN TO READ!"

It is clearly a question of schooling, of the entire educational system and structure of government and not—as Goffredo Parise, for instance, likes to argue—the fault of the writers because they use too many complicated words and are too divorced from "the facts of life." Latin American writing, for instance—today perhaps the most interesting literature in the world—is not "popular" in this simple sense; yet its good authors make their impact on hundreds of thousands of readers. To say, as the *Corrière della Sera* has done, that "culture has been ship-wrecked," as if literature had ever been at the helm, is to forget that the ship was not seaworthy to begin with.

The striking feature for me is the transition from pristine illiteracy to a neo-illiteracy consisting of *fumetti* readers and "goggle-box" addicts. Marshall McLuhan's thesis about the devaluation of literary culture does apply to Italy, but his optimistic forecast that the new media would produced fresh community of interests does not; that hasn't happened.

The problem, therefore, is that the state is not interested in culture; that culture makes no impact on the people, and that, educated society being middle class, culture comes under the influence of big-business interests. As a result newspapers such as *Il resto del Carlino* which have traditionally had a cultural background, suddenly. Turn over to strict conservatism on change, of ownership. And newspapers have always been a major factor in Italian culture.

Could the intellectuals have done more? The question is otiose, for the problem is one of the future, not of the past. It is striking nevertheless that some of the scientists and artists whom I have been questioning were not completely pessimistic and could still see certain prospects. It is discouraging, however, that basic school and university reforms are still awaited, that research policy is in decline, and that each government seems to accept its failure with equanimity. Moreover, the phenomenon of "anti-culture" does not spring merely from the necessities of a so-called backward country. Whole classes of society who have recently achieved an improved standard of living take remarkably little interest in cultural activities. The Italian "economic miracle" was admittedly incomplete, but the extent to which culture—the most glaring instance being town planning—lagged behind has been something of a "miracle in reverse." So the talk of a cultural *malaise*, of the failure of the political forces to cope with educational problems, is not without justification. It is to be seen everywhere in the "way of life" and will sooner or later exert an adverse influence even on material developments. The bitter self-criticism, the vocal discontent, has its good reasons. Strehler talks of a "slimy morass." Alfonso Gatto tries to explain: "In Italy the authorities have no interest in culture. Our rulers are basically devoid of culture. At the same time all politicians are prepared to swear that Culture is Essential. It is all the outcome of great narrow-mindedness, of the banality of conformism...."

There is, however, no point in trying to turn the intellectuals of "the 1945 generation" into scapegoats, particularly in so far as the writers are concerned. Such an indictment surely derives from a completely false concept of the duties and possibilities of literature. Writers who allow themselves to be influenced by such accusations and demands would only write worse books. Still, the challenge is clear. Can they—and how—make a contribution to the growing (and daunting) necessity to overcome Italy's cultural underdevelopment?

January 1974

Frantz Fanon: "Black Orpheus" of the Homeless Left

Franz Fanon died in 1961 at the age of thirty-six, at which time Algeria (his adopted country) honored him with a state funeral and with a boulevard and a university in his name. Fanon was a doctor and psychiatrist from Martinique; his wife Josie was a white Frenchwoman, and she still lives in Algeria with her two children. Most of his brothers and sisters live in Martinique, but one brother has a high position in the Ministry of Finance in Paris, and although a native of Martinique, which is a French Department, he is not allowed to go there because of his so-called unacceptable opinions on self-government. In Fort de France, Fanon was taught by the poet and political writer Aimé Césaire, the prophet of *"negritude"* and in France one of his teachers was Francis Jeanson, a disciple of Jean-Paul Sartre's, who became as actively involved in support of the Algerian struggle in the 1950s as Frantz Fanon himself.

Frantz Fanon came of a middle-class family of mixed black, white, and Indian blood, and his Christian name recalls the Alsatian origin of one branch of the family. Frantz was blacker than his brothers and sisters. Through his education he felt himself a Frenchman whose race and origin were incidental. He joined the Free French Army, took part in the liberation of the French "Motherland," was wounded and awarded a medal. The discovery that a black man was not treated as the equal of a Frenchman in the army, even though as a *"Martiniquais"* he was treated differently again from the Africans, led to his first book which he wrote at the age of twenty-seven: *Black Skins, White Masks*. Although thickly larded with references and quotations, chiefly from Nietzsche and Jaspers, and with a rather superficial newly acquired psychological jargon, it is an extraordinary account of his mental growth. It remains Fanon's one contribution, but an important one, to the understanding of the society in the Antilles island, and his alienated feelings, as an intellectual *"Martiniquais,"* of being both an outsider and at home in the French community.

> Some ten years ago I was astonished to learn that the North Africans despised men of color. It was absolutely impossible for me to make any contact with the local population. I left Africa and went back to France without having fathomed the reason for this hostility. Meanwhile, certain facts had made me think. The Frenchman does not like the Jew, who does not like the Arab, who does not like the Negro....

Francis Jeanson wrote an introduction to this book; and Jean-Paul Sartre, Fanon's philosophical mentor but his political pupil, wrote a foreword to *The Wretched of the Earth*. This and his preface to Leopold Senghor's poetry anthology, *Black Orpheus*, contain Sartre's most important ideas about revolutions outside Europe. (His study of Lumumba, an uncritical and basically paternalist projection of French historical and sociological categories onto the Congo, is of lesser interest.)

Is there anything we can learn today from Fanon's message, his example, or his ideas?[1]

Fanon's style and reasoning powers, apart from certain apodictic obscurities, are essentially those of a Parisian *homme de lettres*, even though he was doubly alienated from France as a "*Martiniquais*" and as an adoptive Algerian. The letter he wrote in 1956 to Robert Lacoste, the French governor of Algeria, announcing his resignation from his post as doctor in the Blida psychiatric clinic, is the manifesto of a Frenchman who deplores what is happening in Algeria and wants no part of it. A committed French intellectual therewith made a political and moral decision. From that point on Fanon spoke of the Algerians as "we"—as a leader writer on the FLN paper *El Moudjahid* in Tunis, and then as ambassador of the Algerian provisional government in Accra. Albert Memmi reports that when Fanon wrote of "*nos pères*" he somehow meant Algerian ancestors; and Memmi remarks how unusual it is for anyone with a French upbringing to make such a tribal transition, like those Senegalese and Antillese schoolchildren who spoke of "our ancestors the Gauls"! As a black man with a French education, who barely knew Arabic and was not a Muslim, Fanon had taken an extraordinary leap forward, or backward, to think (and perhaps to feel) of the Algerians in a personal ancestral line.

In Fanon's short-lived career his character proved to be astonishingly strong and independent. His writings, including a number of psychiatric publications, show a certain open mindedness and critical acumen, only occasionally subordinate to the requirements of propaganda. Of course Fanon, like Che Guevara and Régis Debray, was a theorist and militant in the cause of "tricontinental revolution," but his intellectual experience was richer than theirs, and he was also closer to reality and more down to earth. After the war, he was well on the way to a successful career as a psychiatrist. He worked with Tosquelles, a leading modern psychiatrist and director of a clinic in Normandy, and his overseas transfer to Blida was by chance. (When Algeria became independent, this clinic was named after Fanon.)

Fanon sought to express his sympathy with the Algerian struggle for independence in deeds more than in words. As a psychiatrist he encountered the effects of this awful seven-year war, with all its brutality and torture. He protected *feddayin*, helped to hide them, and became an Algerian political activist. His first book had been about his rootlessness in his own native land.

Taking root in Algeria was not only an overt political decision for him but also a deep psychological need.

The idea of *"negritude,"* extolled by Aimé Césaire in his poems, only caught Fanon's enthusiasm for a brief time. Perhaps it was not so much a color or a country that he was adopting as a revolution. In Colonel Boumedienne's post-revolutionary Algeria, it was inconceivable that he would have sat on a political council or served as an ambassador or even as a propagandist.

Already under Ben Bella (who shared Fanon's romantic belief in the peasants as the only true revolutionaries), and all the more after Ben Bella's fall, the various factions of international revolutionaries—Greeks, Egyptians, French—who took part in the Algerian struggle were expelled, one after the other. Fanon saw himself in Accra as the prophet of a future united Africa, and he would have preferred his true roots to be set in this Pan-African revolution. This, too, has not come to pass—just as Fanon's expectation that Algerian women would be emancipated after independence has not been fulfilled. But his defenders would argue that no true or deep general revolution can happen "at a stroke."

Fanon never became particularly popular with the black Africans. Even black American writers like Richard Wright and James Baldwin felt "foreign" among Africans, and probably Fanon did too. It is part of his strange story that his greatest effect as a prophet of violence was in the far-away USA. There he became the posthumous hero of the Black Panthers and indeed on the scene of the whole New Left as it emerged in the 1960s. In fact, one armed Black Panther intellectual wrote: "Our brothers who shoot from the rooftops have all read Fanon."[2]

This long-distance effect of the clever and sensitive psychiatrist from Martinique was all the more curious and remarkable when one recalls that Fanon fought as a Frenchman for France, as an Algerian for Algeria, and did not preach out-and-out racial struggle between black and white, but rather cooperation and reconciliation between races (after the "overthrow of capitalism," of course).

Fanon's advocacy of violence has often been compared with Georges Sorel's essay on violence. Yet in his preface to Fanon's last book, *The Wretched of the Earth*, Sartre angrily dismissed Sorel's book as "fascist rubbish." Fanon probably never read Sorel, and made his way to the notion of violent purification from his own experience of the long-standing contempt of the *colons* towards the Algerians who finally broke out in violent rage against their humiliation. Then he developed it into a faith and a theory. Fanon's standpoint is rather more political than Sartre's in his preface.

The Paris philosopher actually called for the physical annihilation of Europeans and spoke of Europe as a continent which had endlessly betrayed and cheated the rest of the world. Sartre sharply criticized the Algerian leaders for finally coming to terms with General de Gaulle on their country's independence—instead of carrying the revolution over to France. He expected them to set loose a permanent revolutionary internationalism, for in his own ideology the colonial nations were to replace the feeble European proletariat as the revolutionary class.

Fanon appeared to be more "pragmatic." From Europe Fanon wanted only reparation, and reparations required an intact European economy rather than a European chaos.

Yet the economic aspect was not central, and Fanon was not concerned with rapid material progress in the former colonies. He was more interested in a "new way of life." He wanted an end to "bureaucracy," to "native bourgeoisies," to the "aping of the economic modes of former masters." The old order was much better at such things. What he longed for was the restoration of a damaged collective dignity—the same idea was also central for Georges Sorel—on the basis of an austere equality. An ascetic way of life would befit men to be leaders. Nobody was to live any better than the humble peasants in the villages. There was to be no whoring after the false gods of "modernization" and "industrialization." No wonder the communists were astounded at his theories and alarmed at his influence! To be sure, the idea that virtue lay in refusing progress went back to Rousseau; but Rousseau taught—for example, in his famous bit of advice to the Poles—that an independent country's sovereign character must lean heavily on its tradition, which should even be over-emphasized and stylized. Yet Fanon refused to hark back to the past. As he wrote in *Black Skin, White Masks*:

> In no way should I dedicate myself to the revival of an unjustly unrecognized Negro civilization. I will not make myself the man of any past. I do not want to exalt the past at the expense of my present and my future.
>
> The body of history does not determine a single one of my actions. I am my own foundation.

Fanon wanted his place, and all Africa's place, to be set in a long and permanent revolution, in the future and nowhere else. If he spoke against one-party states as a new despotism it was not as if he were supporting a democratic "pluralism" but rather better one-party states, which were to be closer to the people and to be based on a separation of power between state and party. He warned against overgrown capital cities. All these were useful warnings for former African colonies—but they were completely ignored.

Fanon longed to be on the locomotive of history, but he got the railway timetable all wrong. Most of the decolonization of black Africa took place without bloodshed, and this too was against Fanon's teaching of the benign psychological advantage (and indeed necessity) of violence in the "final contest." African independence did not lead to African unity but rather to further Balkanization, except in the powerful military states of Nigeria and Zaire. A victorious political elite assumed the enormous privileges of a New

Class. As the agronomist René Dumont, who like Fanon always stressed the problem of Africa's rural economy, has written:

> In former French Africa we now see fifteen governments with more than 150 ministers, hundreds of cabinet members, thousands of members of parliament. Gabon, which has 450,000 inhabitants, has 65 members of parliament, one for each 6,000 people as compared with one for 100,000 in France—and their privileges are comparable to those of French deputies." (*L'Afrique Noire est mal partie*, Paris, 1962)

Did anything turn out as Fanon wanted it to in Africa? Very little, and very much went quite the opposite way. There is no sign of a "Pan-African solidarity of hardship and hunger" in the arid regions of West Africa—there is not even much interest in the need for it. No social group in Black Africa has shown itself to be attracted by Fanon's appeal. Where are the African intellectuals who go out to the villages to teach and help and lead the people, like the *Narodniki* in Russia or the Gandhians in India? This is simply not happening in Black Africa.

Fanon was a prophet without honor in his own country but also without honor throughout the African continent. Even the "Fanonism" in the American Black Power movement has disappeared together with its charismatic manifestations. Where is Stokely Carmichael? Who knows of Eldridge Cleaver? Some of these old militants still live in Algeria, Fanon's adopted country. But in the USA Black Panthers now preach "Ballots, not Bullets," and seek power in city council elections and jobs in the community social services. It has been a striking change of direction—and would probably have been, in Fanon's view, a bleak regression of the Black Revolution: it has been a phenomenon almost ignored outside the USA. Certain minds thrive only on the spectacle of enthusiasm and hope, and turn away from the realities of disenchantment and reconsideration. Nobody less than the Algerian vice president, Belkacem Krim pronounced these words in a funeral oration: "Frantz Fanon! Your example will always remain alive. Rest in peace! Algeria will never forget you...." A few years later Krim was sentenced to death on charges of treason and conspiracy, and was subsequently found murdered.[3]

Much of the vaunted "new politics" and the cult of "revolutionary violence" has disappeared. Of the Third World charismatic leaders only Fidel Castro and Sekou Touré remain. But this used to be the grandiloquent world of Nehru, Nasser, Nkrumah, Sukarno; all were regarded, only yesterday, as secular prophets and history makers of the first importance.

Is Fanon still worth reading? I should think there is good reason for interest in him still being so strong. For his experiences and decisions still touch us—but then we could say that after the death of any youthful revolutionary ideologist. Surely this is not enough. Fanon's dream of a united Third World is over. But today Europe is indeed "besieged," as Fanon hoped and foresaw it would be. It is not besieged however by men of revolution but by men of power. The most conservative states in the Third World have become global movers and shakers—it is the time not of Fanon but Feisal. Oil is the catchword, not Utopia. Saudi Arabia has seized the leadership, not the HQ of Afro-Asia revolutionaries. As for Libya, it really represents politically a kind of Islamic puritan restoration. It is not essentially revolutionary and does not believe in "the future" (in Fanon's sense, or in the sense of the progressivism of European radical intellectuals); and Ghadafi is proving to be simply an embarrassment. (After all, he wants to turn the clock back on women's emancipation which for Fanon was a central issue.)

Frantz Fanon, the Algerian revolutionary and the Pan-African, was in truth a typical French intellectual and remains part of the European romance of ideas. It was not a world he made, but he was made by it: made, at least partly, by European experience—European crises and contradictions, faults and misdemeanors—and also by Europe's moral imperatives and worldwide perspectives. Fanon was the "Black Orpheus" of the Parisian revolutionary intelligentsia. He was more a creature of the European system than he would ever know or admit, although he wanted to free a whole continent from it. Outside this system, and apart from the societies and cultures where it obtains, he is quite incomprehensible.

We are often reminded what happened to the foreigners who took part in the great French Revolution and the great Russian Revolution—exiled, executed, ignored, sometimes (happily) pensioned off. Every revolution begins by celebrating the freedom of all mankind, but it later comes to take a more narrow view of its tasks, and the first victims are the universalists, the comrades with all-too-cosmopolitan ideas. But this cosmopolitanism (described so memorably by André Malraux in his novel *The Conquerors*), this active sharing in the fate of other nations and people, is part of the European tradition. Militants who follow the cause are successors to the missionaries who followed the cross and sometimes preceded the flag, and they all bring a gospel of salvation. They may think of their activity as selfless service on behalf of another people; but "service," however selfless, comes to mean influence and ultimately power.

Frantz Fanon, who would have been unable to work in Boumedienne's Algeria, might well have become an adoptive "Palestinian" next, for he could only find a place for himself in a movement and a struggle and not in an established order. As a psychiatrist who was against "long-term institutionalization, and in favor of "community care," Fanon would probably have made louder protests against Russian political psychiatry than many influential doctors in the West. Did Fanon, the world revolutionary, belong to the "Homeless Left," as Herbert Luethy once described it? Perhaps it should nowadays be referred to as the home-seeking Left. For Fanon rootlessness was not the normal state of a revolutionary seeking to liberate mankind; it was only a personal misfortune. How could France ever be a true home to him? This was impossible, as he showed so movingly in *Black Skin, White Masks*. But France was more important to his spiritual and political development than he cared to admit.

It could well be that Frantz Fanon is no longer important—if he ever was—for the understanding of what Africa is and is becoming. But for the understanding of what Europe was and could be, this intellectual from Martinique who "explored the frontiers" and lived in "extreme situations"—this pupil of Marx, Nietzsche, Jaspers, and Sartre—is eminently important. He should not be forgotten, although a mere dozen years after his early death his prophecies about a new world to come—not for the first, or the last, time in the history of the romantic intelligentsia—are, or at least now seem to be, illusions.

August 1974

Notes

1. Most of Fanon's works have been widely translated and put into paperback circulation. In the original French they have run to many editions and printings, and there are also now a number of interesting and important studies, including Albert Memmi's essay in *Esprit* (September 1971), and two American biographies: Peter Geismar's *Fanon* (1971) and—the one indispensable book—Irene L. Gendzier, Frantz Fanon: A Critical Study (1973). Simone de Beauvoir's recorded memories of Fanon—in the second volume of her memoirs, *The Prime of Life* (1962)—are perceptive and revealing and they give the impression that Fanon had a frantic craving for argument and action, at a time when he was already doomed to die of leukemia.

    For my own part, I have attempted to situate Fanon in the line of Jean-Jacques Rousseau rather than of Karl Marx or Lenin, in my book *Der Rest ist Schreiben* (Vienna, 1972). I should also mention David Caute's rather simplistic study *Fanon* (Fontana Modern Masters, 1970), and a ponderous book on Fanon published in Germany: Renate Zahar's *Kolonialismus und Entfremdung, zur politischen Theorie Frantz Fanons* (Frankfurt, 1969). It has been translated into French, and it is, inevitably, overloaded with not always relevant quotations from Adorno, Horkheimer, and Marcuse.
2. About this "Americanization" of Fanon, the political scientist Aristide Zolberg has written incisively in *Encounter* (November 1966).
3. He was strangled to death in a Frankfurt hotel room in October 1970.

Letter from Paris

As Sartre Grows Old

Jean-Paul Sartre's name has now disappeared from the daily paper *Libération* and from all other remaining publications to which he used to lend his name as *directeur* in order to shield them from government reprisals. As General de Gaulle once remarked: "One simply does no lock up a man like Sartre...." Yet General de Gaulle did manage to get a sly blow in, however, addressing him as "*cher Maitre*"—as if the revolutionary (who had scornfully refused the Nobel Prize) was a member of the French Academy.

Admittedly Sartre had bemoaned his "impunity" but he nevertheless exploited it to protect revolutionary publications. Still he evidently had no deep wish for his name to be constantly linked with *causes célèbres*. Now, his output much reduced by weariness, age, and an affliction of the optic nerve, Sartre is withdrawing into himself; he no longer wants to be identified with publications which he scarcely reads any more.

Sartre has recently talked to two revolutionaries—Philippe Gavi, the thirty-three-year-old editor of *Libération* and Pierre Vicot, the twenty-eightyearold leader of the "Maoists"—for their book *On a raison de se revolter* just published by Gallimard. One conversation here recorded may well be regarded as Sartre's testament. He looks back to the time when he was a Communist fellow traveler, when he dreamt of a libertarian revolution (yet with no hope of seeing more than the first beginnings of it); and he spoke with a disarming candor (and admitted inconsistency) which has not always characterized his political pronouncements.

Talking recently to his biographer, Francis Jeanson, Sartre had outlined his attitude to force: "There is also a type of force which genuine present-day revolutionaries will have to use against those false revolutionaries, the Communists...."; On the one hand, as he said: "Force only comes into the picture when all arguments have been exhausted and I have invariably maintained that there are arguments." But then, on the other: "Theoretically I still maintain that force offers the only opening for a society fundamentally different from our own...."

What would this fundamentally different social order look like? To be sure Sartre never explicitly repeated, in the old phrase, that the Movement is everything and the Aim nothing. But he is not so far from that attitude of mind when he says: "I do not know what should be the nature of the new order which will come. Will it be a dictatorship of the proletariat? I do not think so, for dictatorship would be exercised by the representatives of the proletariat, and that is something altogether different." In the talks which he has been holding with the two revolutionaries (every Monday, since November 1972) and in which he plays by no means the principal part, Sartre continually refused to be "specific." He had no theory, he said. He refused to paint a picture of some alternative system. He has a compelling belief in "freedom for all," in the power of the individual, but it must never develop into coercion of other people. He does not explain, however, how this power without coercion can be exercised. His own thoughts he regards as provisional and transitional— "One must give vent forthwith to relevant thoughts, for if you produce ideas in twenty years' time, they will be of no practical value...." One thing he is sure of: "To be free means acting in the service of something which does not yet exist" ("agir en fonction de ce qui n'existe pas encore, c'est precisément être libre").

Today the revolutionary is a man conscious of his alienation, who looks at human life from a distance and anticipates that man will live in a non-alienated society. On one subject, on which he previously vacillated, Sartre is now uncompromising: elections are invariably bad things, invariably counterrevolutionary. To allow oneself to be represented by someone else instead of oneself taking action within one's own environment—that is the essence of *aliénation*. Even if it is a vote cast for left-wing parties, then the associated self-deception would be all the greater and the ultimate disillusionment more bitter. What is essential is to "invent" some other form of political behavior.

Nevertheless, now for the first time Sartre reverted to the moral problem, having refused to write the work on Ethics forecast in his *L'Être et le Néant* (1943). He has stated that development of a viable moral doctrine in a classridden society was an impossibility. Morality, so he now says, must show itself at the workbench level, in production; it will be materialistic. But it is a primary fact of social life, and the Communists underestimate it. "When I was eighteen I was a prisoner of an idealistic irrealism. By the time I was forty-five I was an amoral realist...." Now, however, morality appears to be the very basis of realism in his eyes.

To the two young men of the far left to whom he was talking Sartre drew attention to the fact that after victory the revolutionary could indeed turn into an oppressor. But they only asked how resistance to such a new force could be possibly guaranteed now. Compared to them Sartre is a libertarian spirit as in the old innocent days of anarchism or early syndicalism:

What are the personal plans of the ageing revolutionary? He proposes to go on with the fourth volume of his Flaubert[1] as long as his strength allows. At this his two young comrades said: "You ought to write a popular novel instead." Sartre objected: "I have already written three volumes and the fourth needs to be done. A popular novel? I should first have to find out what that is. Can such a thing be of any use at this time? When have popular novels ever aroused revolutionary fervor in their readers?" Then it was his age that showed: "You are asking a lot of me, and I work that much less. I shall think myself lucky if I finish my Flaubert...." The writing of a novel means being in sympathy with its hero's future, he went on; it means expressing one's own feelings about the shape of things to come through his experiences. "But for me the future is a sealed book—and then you expect me to start a new literary career...."

Sartre now maintains that he never pretended to have had all the valid answers; he frankly questions his own views. But is his refusal to clarify in any way the relationship between revolution and the brave new world authentic candor? His very refusal has almost become an obsession. Sartre seems to be expecting some new force "which is in no way a political force such as we know it." Does not this at least presuppose the elimination of that *rareté* which was one of Sartre's basic notions in his *Critique de la raison dialectique*?[2]

Admittedly, Part Two of this *Critique* will not now be written, any more than the treatise on Ethics which he once promised. So it is perhaps all the more understandable that Sartre does not want to leave his Flaubert as a limbless torso. Sartre now appears to be convinced that his political ideas will not remain valid for very long, but that his book on Gustave Flaubert will be read for a long time to come. Who would care to contradict him?

November 1974

Notes

1. See my account, "Sartre's Flaubert," in *Encounter* (December 1971).
2. See Raymond Aron's critique of this work, "Sartre's Marxism," *Encounter* (June 1965); and Maurice Cranston, "Sartre & Violence, *Encounter* (July 1967).

Letter from Zurich

"What Thinketh Solzhenitsyn?"

Wherever I go these days the moment the deep dark secret that I come from Zurich is divulged there come the inevitable questions: "Do you know Solzhenitsyn? What is he writing? What is he thinking?" This is the way we Swiss are cross-examined these days, and I was hard pressed in London, recently, and again in Washington, to come up with some proper answers. What do they really believe: that the illustrious Russian exile conducts some kind of literary salon along the Limmat (which James Joyce once besang)? Or perhaps it is a matter of "status" or prestige, for after all anybody who is anybody in Zurich town must be running across Solzhenitsyn at parties or in cafés (the "in" ones, of course). How embarrassing it all is when one has to confess, again and again, that unfortunately one hadn't yet, or quote, or up till now, had the happy opportunity of... etc. After that, interest in a Swiss visitor sinks to zero.

I was forced to think back to another, not unrelated incident I was then living in Paris, and was doing a broadcast on French cultural affairs in a West German television studio. Couldn't I tell them all about Sartre and Aragon and Beckett—what they were writing and what they were currently thinking—as if I had just left them in some Left Bank salon or café? How could I confess that I had run into Sartre (at least as far as a serious conversation was concerned) only once—and that happened to be in Zurich. I once called on Louis Aragon and all I learned from him for a full hour was the importance of being editor-in-chief of a Paris evening paper. And as for Beckett, what I knew about him (what he was "really" thinking) came from one of his translators, Tophoven, and from the philosopher Cioran, and the painter Bram van Veld. I couldn't help feeling like that nice American lady in Washington who, in a Georgetown cocktail party discussion of some recent best-seller, was asked whether she had already read the book in question, and replied: "Yes, but not personally."

In the case of Solzhenitsyn one couldn't even resort to that familiar (and nasty) intellectual nose: icy supercilious indignation. One has encountered enough of that: the outrage against a Russian dissident who is applauded and cheered by "the wrong (i.e., conservative) side"; the hate/envy of an author who has earned a lot of money and still calls on our sympathies: the hypercriticism of an intellectual who may be a source of some relevant information but who is basically a mediocre (and, in any ease, "reactionary") novelist. Alan Brien, busy with porno-culture in his *Sunday Times* column, is quickly bored by Solzhenitsyn; German intellectuals, still tilting their lances at the Axel Springer press empire, find Samizdat keeping bad company on the Elbe. But surely these, and other similar efforts, count for very little when compared to what the Russians and all the East Europeans themselves feel about Solzhenitsyn's body of work. How silly the West can be!

The silly season took a new turn for me in the Garrick Club in London where I happened to meet a distinguished English scholar. Surprisingly his first question was not, "Have you seen Solzhenitsyn?" But, rather, he explained and apologized: "Sorry I didn't call you in Zurich last week. But I happened to be meeting Solzhenitsyn over the week-end, and we talked all the time...." So, at long last, I could turn the tables and promptly did: "What thinketh Solzhenitsyn?" My friend hesitated for a moment, and then went on with admirable academic thoroughness: "Before I can properly give you an account of that, I must clear up certain widespread misunderstandings about the nature of Pan-Slavism and traditional Russian Nationalism (and one or two other things as well)...." This took a fascinating hour, but we never even reached St Petersburg in 1917, let alone Zurich of the weekend before last.

In some desperation I tried making a last-minute telephone call. I simply could not return to Zurich without some proper scraps of information. My persistence was rewarded. "Oh, you want to know what Solzhenitsyn is really like? Well, in the first place, I've never met anyone, in East or West, who has his kind of concentrated intellectual vitality. It is a rare mental intensity.... When I put some theses to him—of some seriousness and complexity he listened to my long, rather rambling remarks with patience and attention. He then apologized for withdrawing for a minute or two to his own study to ponder the matters in question for himself alone. When he returned he made a breath-taking one minute resumé of my position and then stated his own views methodically, point for point, with exhaustive precision...."

This much, then, I can pass on to all curious spirits. Before I return home I will be listening in on such literary conversations as go on in New York and Palo Alto, and it could be that before I am back in Solzhenitsyn's Zurich I may well have a scrap or two more to report.

February 1975

The Quest for Serendip

The new name is Sri Lanka, but Ceylon was once called Serendip, and there was an Indian fable entitled "Three Princes from Serendip" which recounted the agreeable adventures of a trio who kept on encountering men and places they neither sought nor expected. This presumably was Horace Walpole's source when coining the word "serendipity" (1754), for the talent to run across nice and pleasant things. I am not quite certain how long in the unhappy England of today the phrase can be sustained, but for a long time now it has been—especially for foreigners—a much-admired and envied word-coinage of the English language. Perhaps (as Goethe thought) America does have it better, for in post-Nixon Washington recently I heard it twice in one day and also found it in a newspaper column.

Little point in underlining that every language has certain special words of its own to describe a shade of feeling or a stroke of fortune, and that other tongues don't quite manage to catch the inflection. They become *Leitmotifs*—to use a German word that has been taken over by the French and the English languages for lack of an exact rendering of their own.

Anybody, therefore, for serendipity? Once we have learned that there is indeed a word for happy surprises in a world full of most unhappy turns of events, then there is a strong temptation to transliterate. In German, I suppose, it would become— taking advantage of that hovering little umlaut—"*Serendipiät.*" But surely serendipity has rather a lighter touch about it, as if good luck had wings. The German rendering sounds too grave, too heavy, as if that cloud with a silver lining never could float.

But not to worry. Our very inability to take over what is necessary may save us from the kind of unnecessary borrowing which has made "Franglais" and "Amerenglish" so notorious. Why do we say in German "*unterprivilegiert*" when it is in any language Just a six-syllable way of saying "poor"? It betrays the same kind of verbal inflation in which the Americans say "senior" for "old," in order to suggest that there just aren't any old people but only "senior citizens" who then take on almost pseudo-senatorial rank. A slight stroke of the pen and a minus can become a plus.

To be sure, coinages like "underprivileged" sane the purposes not merely of semantic euphemism but of social protest. It suggests that it is the right of every citizen to possess fully all the privileges going, and that a part of the citizenry is regrettably deprived of some of same. A privilege is no longer something special but belongs by revised definition to the rights of all. What will happen to that small remnant of the old European aristocracy, still trying to clam to the distinction of their traditional names, when we suddenly come to realize that we, who have no "de" or "van," are really under-nobled and hence grievously hobbled in our essential human dignity? This may well become the game of name, and a bitter class contest it could turn out to be.

But there is nothing untoward about serendipity. It was always precious, and may nowadays become increasingly rare; but it does run trippingly off the tongue. And surely every child knows that it is rather easier for fabled princes to find happy ends than for Western man caught between the dangers of the Gulag Archipelago and the Post-Industrial Society. Perhaps if our lives are to enjoy a touch of the serendipitous then serendipity may well have to return as a privilege, as that special and not widespread quality which Napoleon used to call "*la Fortune*."

But there's the rub. Can our mass-democratic society afford even a bit of good luck for the few? Shouldn't serendipity—and all its felicitous means of production and distribution—be socialized and thus put to the benefit of all the people? Arise, ye prisoners of misfortune, you have a serendipitous world to win....

You see, I knew that playing with words would come up with an agreeable surprise.

April 1975

"Where Have All the Flowers Gone?"
—The New Left Today

What other thoughts should preoccupy one on the trip back from Berkeley, California? It is quite ten year since the stormy beginnings there of worldwide student revolt. Berkeley was the soil of the flower people who then transplanted themselves to San Francisco's Haight-Ashbury and withered on the vine. It spawned the cult of the four-letter word under the banner of the "Free Speech Movement," and it won its first victory over the hated academic enemy in the purge of University Chancellor Clark Kerr. Thousands danced, chanted, struck, dreamed of a brave new world. And where are they today? On the plane back East I read an inquiry by the editors of *Business Week*, who should know, and the conclusion was that most, if not all, are today gainfully employed. They have jobs in industry, and if they haven't been laid off in the current recession they are quite dutifully putting in their nine-to-five. But still, they do have special characteristics: they appear to be "more intelligent": and have "more style." A great many others have remained on the old battlegrounds of the campus, and constitute the new generation of university instructors searching for nice students to teach in a time of academic retrenchment.

But perhaps too much attention has always been paid to the campus rebels who were so effectively noisy and visible. What of the "Negro Revolt," the radical forces of the so-called Black Panthers? Here, too, there is a deafening silence. Novelist-pamphleteer James Baldwin appears to have converted himself from revolution to reform, and the old stormy petrels seem so anachronistic as they operate over still waters. I spoke to one black journalist who said, "Why did everybody constantly write about our Cult-Heroes of Violence, instead of paying attention to our engineers and executives and politicians who were beginning to make good?..." No, the era of Radical Chic is gone, and one suspects that the savage piece which Tom Wolfe wrote at the time about Leonard Bernstein's cocktail party for the Black Revolution may well go down as one of the polemical turning-points of current affairs. Fashionable moods are so transient.

Seven years have elapsed since the assassination of Martin Luther King (the killer is behind bars, but his paymasters have never been unearthed), and it could be that his political star was then waning. Malcolm X's message of blood and thunder was carried forward by Eldridge Cleaver and Stokely Carmichael, and the later (if with more muted Marxian orthodoxy) by Angela Davis. Those were the days when the *New York Review of Books* was the central organ of the New Left, and it dutifully put formulae for Molotov cocktails on its front page and reprinted the rousing manifestos for the Brothers and Sisters of the Movement. Times change. The *NYRB*'s review of Angela Davis' recent autobiography was something less than enthusiastic, and no tears are being shed for those martyrs of prison revolt, the "Soledad Brothers."

It could be that only a mix of black and white could have sustained a radical New Left ideology. But the radical blacks made a special target of the white liberals, and it would have taken not merely idealism but a sick portion of masochism to accept every insulting attack with another confession of white middle-class guilt and yet another generous check. It was an uneasy, unhappy alliance for a few years, but it's an over now. The reaction I have heard from coast-to-coast was: "Well, if they didn't want us, then we were no longer obliged...." The white liberal support—now along normal, conventional electoral lines—goes to black urban personalities who are qualified to do a job of effective work as a mayor or an educationist or a judge. It is they who get the votes, and the kudos when they prove successful. But who knows or cares who is still holding court in Algiers (or are they in jail, or have they been deported)?

Pioneers often get out-distanced. The blacks can be said to have started the "Ethnic Revolution," but then it caught on elsewhere like wildfire. Black may have been beautiful, but now the slogan is also (and I have seen the graffiti evidence) "SLOVAK IS BEAUTIFUL!" Every minority group—and "ethnics" has become a catchphrase to displace "beatniks"— is set on the glory road to fulfill its culture and heritage. The most powerful among them are perhaps the "Chicanos," or Spanish-speaking Americans, and they are now even succeeding in having Spanish accepted as the basic language of instruction in their neighborhood schools. If "Black English" is to be taken seriously, what of the language of Cervantes? So has the ethnic consciousness expanded and crowded out what was once a black monopoly of demands.

Can it then be that a kind of "cultural revolution" has displaced the longed-for revolutionary class struggle? The figures of American unemployment have been mounting from 7 percent to 10 percent, and so far as l can see there is no new outburst of proletarian militancy, no developing consciousness along New Left lines which would open a perspective of Changing the System. They may all be Keynesians now, but not socialists. The miners of West Virginia went out on strike for more money, for a "bigger piece of the national cake," and at the same time militantly campaigned against certain tendencies in the new school textbooks that were "corrupting" their children. Boston has been torn apart by the conflict between the Irish and the blacks over bussing and integration, but where were the voices that could be expected to preach to them that they really had "common class interests"? Passionate things are in the saddle.

I also read through a few recent numbers of *Ramparts*, once the muckraking journal of those who had all the simple solutions; and there, lo and behold, was a moderate tone, cautious analysis, differentiated argumentation. Will wonders never cease? Men of violent action are becoming men of prudent thought. It is an altogether remarkable phenomenon, for how is it that the demonstration of the moral bankruptcy of the Nixon regime—and with it the discrediting of so many in the liberal-conservative Establishment—proved to be of so little profit to the Left? What a moment for Protest! Here is the proverbial "Crisis of Capitalism," with the excess profits of oil millionaires and the corruption of the ruling class—and yet one can only conclude that the crisis of the System is rather less severe than the crisis of the Left.

Its main deficiency may well be an intellectual one: its failure to learn. The Bourbons of ideology go the royalists one better, for they forget everything and learn nothing. Consider the recent failure in New York. Senator Javits was destined for electoral retirement in a time when the swing is vast from Republican to Democrat. Anybody could have beaten him—except the McGoverntype ideological radical put up as the candidate, Ramsay Clark, who ran a million votes behind the ticket. There is also a painful emotional vacuum as no new loyalty or allegiance emerges to fill the empty ideological space. The "Third World" is a tired, exhausted cause. The kids can put up posters of Che Guevara—but of King Feisal? And on Central Park West?...The youthful Jewish rebels, once so prominent in the radicalization of the American youth, were quite prepared to be critical of a triumphant and apparently arrogant Israel, but they are not ready to preside over the threatened "liquidation of Zionism." Wherewith will the salt be salted, and the secular religion be given its note of prophetic determination, if the Mosaic remnant should withdraw? This is an important element in the split between left and left and the disintegration of militant confidence.

So it is that the flora and fauna of yesterday are hard to find on the American scene today. The flower people have had their day, and it turns out to have been a moment of horticultural, rather than political, history. "We are all weeds now," one sad Berkeley veteran told me, and he had once planted roses in the barrels of National Guardsmen's rifles in the famous People's Park confrontation. I could not help recalling what one sad surrealist told me once in Paris as he looked out at the French shop-windows and billboards, "They are all surrealists now...." I was told of a prospering little agency in California that makes its money packaging advice on how ambitious little Groups can organize flourishing Communes.

In the last analysis, it could be that the revolution which failed for the New Left was the vaunted "revolution of rising expectations." Everybody in America is brought up to count on "more" and more has tended to mean less: less idealism, less materialism. Expectations are sinking. The real struggle is to keep what you've got: your job, your present living standard. Who thinks of the Revolution of only a decade ago, "The Fire Next Time"? On my return to Washington I watched an orderly procession along Pennsylvania Avenue in front of the White House. It was supposed to be a protest march. A few policemen held it up quietly for a few minutes. The president in his black limousine was driving out to the Capitol.

May 1975

Ignazio Silone at 75

He was born as Secondo Tranquilli, the son of a poor family of peasants and weavers in the Abruzzi town of Pescina, on May 1, 1900...a date that even the most absent-minded would remember. His alias as a revolutionary and his nom-de-plume as a writer was perhaps derived from an Abruzzi mountain rebel named Quintus Pompaelius Silo who led a successful insurrection against Rome in 90 B.C. on behalf of the rights of the Marsers. In any case, we know how deep are his historic roots in his native region from one of his later works, a success both as a book and a play, *The History of a Poor Christian*, which deals with the tragedy of the Abruzzian pope, Coelestin.

His mother and five other children, perished in the earthquake of 1905. A brother died in a fascist prison. But no less strong in his memory remains the picture of those "*cafoni*," the poor workers in the fields, who lived in the villages around Pescina, came to town to market and passed by his childhood house.

Silone's career as an Italian communist and his break with the Stalinist Comintern has often been described, and nowhere better than in his own still valuable account in Crossman's volume called *The God that Failed*. The occasion—and it is a detail that one forgets—was his refusal to sign a document that he had not been given to read. He fought for the honor of his signature, even for the dignity of a name which was not originally his own. In the Mussolini years he lived in exile in Switzerland (1930-44), mostly in Zurich. In a sense he was "doubly alienated," having broken with both comrades and country, and it left literature as his only home. It was his very loneliness and isolation, deepened by illness, which gave a special character to his novel *Fontamara* and possibly gave it a note, which in those days facilitated its immense popularity. It was translated into several dozen languages, enjoyed both literary and political favor (and Leon Trotsky, himself a refugee, hoped it would be circulated in millions of copies).

Still, his essential temperament—for all his political commitments and ideological polemics—was far from abstract word spinning. It was that of a teller of tales, as any one who has enjoyed hearing an anecdote from his lips knows; and he continued as a fabulist, a writer of stories, plays and novels. Even in his non-fiction his mind turns always to the specific example, the human fact, in setting out an analysis, as in his very early and still Marxian book on "Fascism, Its Origin and Development" (Zurich, 1934). In his subsequent work entitled *The School for Dictators* (reissued some years ago by Gollancz) this trait was reinforced by his distaste for his countrymen's habit of grandiloquent rhetoric. His anti-fascist bitterness was tempered by his ironic wit.

> In our Italian literature there is the figure of Don Ferrante, a Milanese ideologue of the 18th century, who reflected long and deep over the cholera epidemic which had been sweeping through the Northern provinces. According to Aristotle, as he well knew, there could only be two categories: accidental things and substantial things. But inasmuch as the cholera symptoms and consequences appeared to fit into neither of these fundamental categories, it could therefore not exist. This conclusion, however, did not prevent him from being infected and passing away....

I felt for a long time that *Fontamara* (1933), *Bread and Wine* (1936), and the other novels centered around the revolutionary Pietro Spina constituted the real heart of Silone's body of work. Reconsidering his career, I wonder whether that place should not rather be given to his autobiographical contributions, his personal memoirs as well as his general reflections (*Encounter* once published his long memorable essay on "Re-thinking Progress" [March/April 1968]); for they do, taken together, constitute something of an "Uscita di sicurezza," an emergency exit for twentieth-century man.

Silone always preferred to be an old-fashioned, rather than a fashionable, writer. Yet he always appeared to be spanning a vast arc from the ancient past to the imminent future, from a bygone world of feudal and Christian values to the "Post Industrial Society." When I first met him he was only forty, and I remember being so struck by his capacity to maintain long silences, punctuated every now and then by sudden bursts of reminiscence. His withdrawal was not indifference or timidity but modesty; and his communication was, when it came, deeply personally felt. It was, as I came to know, the very rhythm of a master, and the special quality that bound him to all his readers as a "*compagno*." His companions greet him on his seventy-fifth birthday in Rome.

August 1975

European Notebook

What's Left

On the one hand, we can tell which is right and which is left; on the other hand, the troubles begin. Nowadays in Portugal, France, and Italy, the sense of political direction is beginning to become strangely blurred. In Portugal, where none of the new parliamentarians want to sit anywhere but on the left of the elected chamber, the Socialist Soares is locked in a struggle with Communist-supported Army officers. But in France the two great parties of the left are associated in a "common front" and their candidate François Mitterrand was almost elected president. Yet even by they general chances have improved—according to the pollsters—a Left government seems increasingly unlikely, for if a majority of Frenchmen might have confidence in Messrs Mitterrand and Marchais, they do not appear to have any confidence in each other.

Mitterrand is accused by Georges Marchais of seeking new allies "on the right" but in Italy it is the Communist Party who is offering the Christian Democrats a "Great Coalition." So, for those who can tell their left hand from their right, we have barricades in the middle in Portugal, an inflexible line between government and a split opposition in France, and in Italy an "aperture" wide open to the centre. Have these differences something to do with the individual Latin complexities of each of these volatile Mediterranean political cultures? Soares was forced to break with "revolutionary" comrades under heavy pressure; Mitterrand still strains to maintain a fiction of unity and agreement; and the Italian socialist Martino faces increasing losses in political support as the Italian Communists effectively present themselves as the very best of social democrats.

Unlike Cunhal who is an old Portuguese Stalinist with nothing but contempt for bourgeois democracy and its ways, Marchers recognizes (or at least says he does) the importance of a pluralistic democracy— and then goes on to praise his comrade in Lisbon. Not so Enrico Berlinguer who has openly criticized the intolerance of the Cunhal line, which is proud of being "armed to the teeth" and whose toughness is throwing a shadow over a Communism *all'italiana* with all its hard-working mayors and local councilmen. To be sure, there are Italian militants (in the metal unions, for example) who would much prefer a Cunhal to a Berlinguer. One would suspect that the "liberalism" of the Italian Left is more popular at the top than at the bottom of the movement.

Why is it that the French Communists appear so stiff and inflexible and the Italian comrades so tactically agile? One theory has it that in the moment that the French Communists abandon their "hardness" then the whole movement in a modernizing France dissolves into reformist and meliorist groups. In more backward Italy, however, there is a political space for reform-minded revolutionaries. Be that as it may, one still has to puzzle out why, then, does the leader of the Communists in Spain, Carrillo, seem so "democratic" and Portugal's Cunhal so totalitarian? At the risk of making a cult of personality in the West, perhaps the character of the various individuals concerned plays something of a role.

According to Berlinguer, "Italy is not Portugal." And Marchais also insists that "France is not Portugal." There are even voices in Lisbon that ore heard to be claiming that "Portugal is not Angola." In Luanda the warring factions on the left are accusing each other of thinking that Angola is Russia or, alternatively, China.

We need to make new maps for this new political geography. Our old ideological Mercator projections whereon we could make out East and West arid Left and Right is now simply too flat.

Dante might have suggested abandoning all hope if one tried, as an outsider, to enter into the internal political problems of Italy nowadays. I hare immersed myself in the Italian press the *Corrière della Sera* of Milan, the *Stampa* of Turin, the *Messaggero* of Rome—and was puzzled to distraction. Why, then, did Signor Fanfani resign as leader of the great center party, and what did it all mean? The more one read, the less one understood. I had to make for myself a little dictionary that could translate some of the confusion into meaning. Here are a few excerpts from the lexicon, just to discourage the others.

1. *Trasformismo*. I take it that this derives from the old politics of the pre-Fascist Italian statesman Giolitti, and it referred to his eagerness to absorb all the new forces on the scene, whatever their program—or ideology, and make new arrangements. Today it suggests the hope of Stability through Change "*trasformazione*." Particularly useful in trying to make out the old and new opinions of rearranged Italian newspapers.

2. *Ridimensionnamento*. Another of the polysyllabic concepts without which Italian politics cannot survive. It underlines the shrinking of a group's political power and, the frank recognition thereof. The process of "re-dimensioning" never refers to the expansion of power and influence, only to its diminution.

3. *Strumentalizzazione*. Always employed when an event of the day is used against an opposing political party, that is, a pro-fascist bombing as an argument for the Left, the terrorism of the ultra-Leftists as an argument for

the Right. Always refers to what the others are up to, never what you are doing, and thus polemically indispensable in the current debate.

4. *Egemonizzazione.* The way in which the major parties deal with the smaller allies in order to maintain their hegemony.

5. *Caotizzanione.* Making a chaos of the remaining orderly areas of Italian public administration—accidentally, or on purpose.

6. *Equilibri avanzati.* A tricky operation to readjust the political equilibrium to the Left, going beyond the old "aperture" approach which Fanfani once advocated and now has rejected (see *"trasformismo"*).

7. *Parallelismi convergenti.* Here Euclid may well be turning in his grave, but the converging parallel lines indicate that groups can work together towards a common end without becoming allies. Probably a curious Romanesque conception of Einstein's relativity.

8. *Sottogoverno.* A suggestive word to underline the building up of power positions outside the musical rules of the game, but with the connivance of the powers that be. Its effect appears to be the dissolution of the Republic into a congeries of political and economic principalities. Burckhardt might have sensed here a return to Machiavelli's Renaissance.

9. *Populismo.* Good catchall for unpopular but very active minorities—who speak in the name of the whole people to justify their power-struggle (via intimidation, and worse) for key positions in the trade unions, the city councils, etc. Some hold that Fascism itself was a *"populismo"* and led to the Duce's- (and caudillo-) type dictatorship. Others claim that today *"populismo"* is deeply anti-fascist. Nobody lets on exactly where it will lead this time.

But then Berlinguer is not Mussolini. Italy is not Spain. Nor is the European political vocabulary what it used to be.

November 1975

European Notebook

Arguing about Fascism

Is fascism still fascinating? The historical phenomenon of twentieth-century Europe appears, if one overlooks its rhetorical uses in propaganda battles, to have faded—except in the place of its origin, Italy. In Germany they would seem to have "mastered the past," and even the recent so-called *"Hitler-Velle"* of biographies and memoirs is approaching an end. In France the era of the Nazi Occupation and the Vichy regime is taken to be "so long ago" that even the national celebration of Victory days is being abandoned. But in Italy there was neither a popular resistance movement nor a Nuremberg Trial of war criminals nor an Anglo-American "Re-education" program. What happened in the two decades of Italian history under Benito Mussolini still needs to be confronted, considered, criticized.

The first controversial step in this direction has now been taken by an historian of the younger generation which, neither pro- nor antifascist, is simply post-fascist. Renzo de Felice is forty-six, but he is not without personal commitment as his first book, *A History of the Italian Jews under Fascism*, testified. He went on to produce a four-volume biography of Mussolini, and it has already gone into several editions, with much attention in the specialist historical journals. Renzo de Felice has now been interviewed at length by an American historian, and the slim book just published by Benedetto Croce's old house, Laterza in Bari,[1] has provoked a nationwide storm of controversy and debate.

Here is no conventional repetition of the old well-worn theses about fascism, totalitarianism, late capitalism, charismatic leadership, and the like. This act of revisionism has proved to be little too much for Italy's ideologized intellectuals. A massive counterattack has developed, and De Felice's friends have even been talking of a "witch-hunt." Nearly everybody I spoke to about it is either passionately For or Against. Perhaps his most daring piece of research was to actually try and locate the survivors of the Mussolini regime and gather their testimony; and only Federzoni, the ideologue of strict nationalism, refused to be interviewed. Not that he has published any of this material, but obviously the "personal" insight into motives and characters has been helpful to "understand" history rather than simply to sit in judgment on it.

De Felice's historical approach is to make certain important distinctions—for example, between the Movement, the Party, and the Regime, with Mussolini's person supplying the only connection. Here he sees the Duce as a "revolutionary" figure. This is, of course, explosive stuff in contemporary Italian politics where Revolution means Left and the Right stands only for Reaction. But De Felice argues that it was indeed a revolutionary factor in Italian society to recruit new popular elements and classes—the "masses," if you will—into participation in the political process. One notes that Aldo Garosci, the respected anti-Fascist and historian, recently ascribed the high participation of the voters in national elections (90 percent) to the lasting influence of the earlier "activization."

More than that, De Felice argues that the Fascist Revolution did manage to win a popular consensus: Mussolini, until the last disastrous period of World War II, enjoyed the support of a majority, sometimes silent, often acclamatory, but not simply a popularity based on force and manipulation. One of the volumes of the work on Mussolini is called "The Years of Consensus." De Felice, accordingly, places emphasis on the peaceful pro-Western foreign policies of the regime until at least 1934; and he doesn't believe the later involvement 'in aggressive war to have been "inevitable," or "in the logic of events." It was Mussolini, at a time when the Western powers showed no interest in what was happening, who mobilized troops on the Austrian border to warn Hitler. Here, as in many other places, De Felice sharpens his pencil point until it almost breaks. The war of conquest in Abyssinia, the demands for Corsica and Nice these surely were not pieces of rhetoric, but like the invocations of the heritage of ancient Rome were part and parcel of an expansionism which expressed itself in the Fascist cult of war, an "ideological twist" which had historic consequences.

The "ideological twist" which De Felice does emphasize, even to heretical proportions, is the cult of youth. The addiction to youthfulness, he holds, was real and deep; and in point of fact Mussolini allowed a little more freedom to the youth movements (and their periodical publications) than was his wont. This is arguable. But the thesis which has caused the most controversy—involving all the major newspapers of Italy, as well as radio and television broadcasts—was his insistence on the singularity, the uniqueness of Fascism, and the worthlessness of the comparisons so often made to other "right-wing" movements, from the Rumanian Iron Cross to the Juntas in Greece. Here the polemic is with the classic presentation of Ernst Nolte in his book *Three Paces of Fascism* (1965). Others have gone on to use "Fascism" as a catch-all, And De Felice seems to be curiously keen not to give up Italian specificity.

Historians, especially German ones, will be surprised by this claim of national exceptionalism, and it is more forcefully than persuasively argued. Italian Fascism was Left, German National Socialism was Right. Mussolini never forgot his experiences as a socialist, continued to believe in a "progressive future," while Hitler remained untouched by such sentiments and was bound by past traditions. De Felice even contends that only Mussolini had the true charismatic style as leader, and suggests that Hitler thought of himself as dispensable. If there was an identity between the two dictators it was in what they rejected, not what they shared. The Fascist and the Nazi were two quite different species of political animal.

Needless to say, the usual view of historians has been the very opposite. Where but in Italy were the traditional institutions, like the Papacy and the Monarchy, powerful and influential, and ready to play a role when the Fascist regime began to disintegrate? Who was really more "independent of the past," the relatively conservative Mussolini or the radical Hitler? Like all strong-minded historians offering a simplistic interpretation, De Felice picks and chooses among the available facts, often ignoring the obvious ones and not even attempting to explain them away. For him Fascism is revolutionary because it transformed the old political structure by bringing al new class into the social struggle for power. This was, he claims, a specifically Italian phenomenon.

There have, of course, been critics galore. Not a few have spoken in terms of a "stab-in-the back" to anti-Fascism. Rather more calm was the evaluation in the *Corrière della Sera* by Leo Valiani, an historian of the older generation. Valiani was in Mussolini's prisons for some ten years and in fact was, after 1943, a leader of the "military underground" in northern Italy; his work on the Habsburg monarchy is widely respected. The differences between Nazism and Fascism, according to Valiani, are not greater or different in substance than the differences between Germany and Italy. Valiani does not subscribe to the notion that Italy was "youthful" and "optimistic" and Germany merely lost in visions of a *Götterdämmering* and an *Untergang*. Who after all had a *Kraft-durch-Freude* movement, proclaiming strength through joy? Indeed the De Felice theses could be stood on their head, and have in fact already been. In Ralf Dahrendorf's well-known work on German politics,[2] it is Nazism which is seen as a truly revolutionary force, if an unwitting destroyer of old social forces and attitudes, and thus a preparatory stage for Germany's subsequent postwar democracy.

The most formidable defense of De Felice came from Rosario Romeo, an historian of high repute, writing in the *Nuovo Giornale*, and troubled by the "hysterical" and "denunciatory" character of the national debate. He disagreed with many of the contentions, but felt no serious historical interpretation should be placed beyond the pale of intellectual discussion. One leading Communist—possibly in the general mood of making historic compromises—even tried to mediate between the polemical camps. Giorgio Amendola, the son of a liberal politician who was murdered by the Fascists, insisted in an article in *Unità* that Fascism was not simply a matter for outrage and indignation, that it had to be comprehended, indeed, "integrated" into the course of

Italian history. It is not enough to trace only "the thin line of erstwhile anti-fascist resistance." He uses, however, this argument to play down non-Communist anti-Fascism. There was, according to Amendola, a "Left" element in the early rallying of the Fascist movement (here he is only following Togliatti's *Lezioni sul Fascismo*); and there were many, like the Communist Delio Cantimori, who in fact thought they saw in it a hopeful revolutionary future for Europe and, like Ingrao, today a gray eminence in the Party, who were active in Mussolini's student movements and felt themselves to be "progressive" rather than "reactionary." Surely this is tricky and dangerous ground for ideological forays, in view of the old Jürgen Habermas formula of "Left Fascism." If fascists turn out to be communists, may not communists mutate into fascists (in Portugal, Cunhal is in fact being denounced on the Left as a "fascist" in method and principle)? In an exchange (in the weekly Espresso) with Leo Valiani, Amendola amplified the sense in which antifascism was "too thin a thread." Only the Communist party—he contended—had a clear policy while all other antifascist movements were utterly confused and grievously mistaken. Suddenly the argument about fascism and antifascism took on a different aspect. The apparent liberalism of Amendola's defence of De Felice had a very different meaning and motive: the desire to diminish the political and ideological role of the noncommunist anti-fascists.

As for De Felice in this whole altercation, he notes with a melancholy tone that "among the worst evils which Italy has inherited from the Fascist epoch is the heritage of intolerance the anti-fascists have taken it over, nationalizing the habit of discrediting and destroying one's opponents...."

Why is it that only now in Italy, "thirty years after," has such a controversy broken out?

There are, to be sure, Neo-Fascists on the Italian scene; but the chances of their seizing any kind of power for themselves is just about nil, although the Left (and especially the far Left) is constantly shouting about the imminent dangers. Thus De Felice's approach, which is that of an historian who thinks of the phenomenon he is dissecting as a thing of the past that can be looked at objectively, is a kind of ideological provocation. To be sure, there are "dangers" on both Left and Right, and both have been involved in the wave of terroristic violence which has swept Italy in recent years: *"trame nere"* and *"trame rosse,"* conspiracies both red and black. But politicians and even judges in Italy have a keen nose for the way the wind is blowing, and the tendency is to deal with Left violence most circumspectly. The ideological atmosphere suggests that "only from the Right" can come threats to the democratic social order. The mantle of anti-Fascism thus offers a protective coat for all the elements on the so-called Left who are operating extra-legally. How disturbing, then, to hear it argued by Renzo de Felice that the total simple-mindedness of "anti-fascist" articles of faith has nothing to do with understanding the past or effectively dealing with the present (Here is a break with Italy's grand rhetorical traditions in politics.)

Some fifty years ago there used to be an angry cry, "Ha detto male di Garibaldi!," for even to seem to speak ill about Garibaldi was tantamount to sacrilege. Italian political life has always had its secular saints. Now the idea has been put about that Renzo de Felice has spoken well of Mussolini (which he hasn't), and this too is to be reckoned among the sinful perfidies.

Still, it remains something of a paradox *all' italiana* that an historian who thought he could put some distance between the past and the present should have been so passionately caught up in the current twists and turns of political life here. To try to revise an interpretation of bygone events is obviously to be a "revisionist," a dangerous thing in a world of embattled orthodoxies. Perhaps someone at Laterza in Bari should have reminded Renzo de Felice of Benedetto Croce's old dictum that all history is contemporary history.

December 1975

Notes

1. Renzo De Felice, *Intervista sui Fascismo* (ed. Michael A. Ledeen), published by Laterza (Bari, 1975).
2. See Ralf Dahrendorf, "The New Germanies: Restoration, Revolution, Reconstruction," *Encounter*, April 1964.

European Notebook

Giants on the French Left: Thorez and Aragon

Monumental biographies have just been published, devoted to the two best-known French Communists: 630 pages (from Fayard) to Maurice Thorez, the Party's former Secretary-General, who outlived Stalin but did his very best to remain true to his example; and 440 pages (from Le Seuil) to Aragon, the Party's "Bard," who has veered between inquisitorial dogmatism and a belated protest against post-Stalinist persecution (at the trial of Siniavsky and Daniel and the occupation of Czechoslovakia). Louis Aragon referred to the effects of the 1968 invasion in *Les Lettres Françaises* as "a spiritual Biafra," whereupon his periodical forfeited Party backing and was compelled to cease publication (mainly because it lost access to its numerous subscribers in the East). The same week, he accepted a high Soviet decoration. He is still a member of the Central Committee of the Communist Party.

Maurice Thorez, "un fils du peuple" (to quote his thrice-revised and in fact ghostwritten "autobiography") died in 1964, shortly after his sixtieth birthday. The biography devoted to him by Philippe Robrieux, once a young and ardent Communist, is thoroughly documented and is of considerable interest. It bears the subtitle: "Secret Life and Public Life." "Secret" might have been replaced by the less sensational but more apt "private," for little secrecy surrounded the fact that he was the illegitimate son of a grocer and a working-class girl (and her husband later made him an excellent foster-father). Nor was it such a secret that his marriage to Aurore (their son is now an architect of some repute) was soured by his lengthy stays in Moscow; and that his long association with Jeanette Vermeersch, who was nineteen when they first met, developed into a political factor because Jeanette was abrim with political ambition and indeed became de facto head of the French Communist Party (after her consort's stroke) without any mandate save his personal faith in her.

The features of Thorez's career which used to be "secret"—his sympathy for Leon Trotsky and his links with that early Bolshevik dissident Boris Souvarine—have often been reported in the past. As to what was unknown, for example, where Thorez hid after deserting from his French Army regiment on Party orders in 1939, the present biographer is incapable of anything but conjecture; but it can only have been a short time before he made his way to the Soviet Union via Hitler's Germany.

What is noteworthy is Thorez's long-standing association with the Czech-born apparatchik Eugen Fried, his mentor (and, perhaps, only friend), who subsequently married Thorez's divorced wife Aurore. Fried played a major role in the Party, but he received no mention whatsoever in the history of French Communism written by Jacques Fauvet, the editor of *Le Monde*. His importance was probably aired for the first time (in an article in my old review *Preuves*) by the former leading Communist André Ferrat. The circumstances under which Fried was shot by unknown persons in Brussels in 1943 suggest that this was a Soviet secret service operation, it being extremely improbable that the Nazis would have failed to interrogate Fried and his wife if they had been aware of his identity and function. *Apparatchiks* with careers like that of Fried were not infrequently murdered or executed by their own organization.

"A miner" (according to legend), Maurice Thorez was in reality a bright schoolboy who later went to work in an office; he was a self-taught man who was so quick to learn that he could acquire remarkably good German even after sustaining a stroke in middle age. Although devoid of originality and political ideas of his own (not to mention familiarity with the Marx, Engels, and Hegel texts which he so often quoted), he did accumulate a certain amount of intellectual baggage.

Thorez is said to have had in all his great Communist career only two private interviews with Stalin, who always commanded his unqualified allegiance. It is extremely interesting to observe how a Western Communist leader of those years had to dichotomize himself between the Great Man role assumed for the benefit of his militants and voters at home and the abject and unwavering vassalage which was *de rigueur* within the Kremlin's orbit. "De-Stalinization" came as a blow to Thorez, from which he never recovered. The man who had always prudently trimmed his sails to the wind became an overt foe of Nikita Khrushchev, and he did all he could to postpone disclosure of Stalin's "crimes" and to defer all attempts at "thaws" and "liberalization."

One still finds it curious that this trend towards liberalization and de-Stalinization came, not from the "civilized West" but from the "primitive East"—from the higher reaches of the Soviet regime and the Bolshevik Party. The large French Communist Party, with its many prominent writers, artists and scholars, was paleo-Stalinist. The post-1954 Soviet system, by contrast, was a cauldron of unrest, of ideological debate and even receptivity to a few new ideas.

Perhaps one must have experienced this paradoxical situation at first hand to appreciate it fully! However, Robrieux's biography not only confirms what we already know; by interviewing numerous witnesses and thoroughly researching his subject, he has unearthed many new particulars and shed much new light. That a veritable cult should have grown up round this very averagely endowed man (if an able speaker and organizer), that his fiftieth birthday should have become an occasion for nothing short of a ritual homage, and that he should altogether have failed to stage an equally moving celebration in honor of his sixtieth birthday (after Stalin's death)—all these things contain grotesque elements of human comedy.

Here is Thorez in his luxurious villa in the South of France, carefully noting what gifts and letters are sent to mark each of his birthdays and bestowing due favor or reprehension.... One cannot help being reminded of the *Roi Soleil* and his chronicler the Duc de Saint-Simon (mentioned, by the way, several times by Robrieux himself). Everyone knows that General de Gaulle had a touch of Louis XIV—and indeed the satirical magazine *Le Canard Enchaîné* for years published reports on the General's "court" couched in Saint-Simonian language. But wasn't the "opposing camp" also a very French court, complete with its own favorites and etiquette? Maurice Thorez was a fabricated figurehead, a leader behind whom others did the thinking and others made the decisions, and others even produced the ghostwritten memoirs. Still, he was not an un-person, and he makes a fit subject for biography. Maurice Thorez called the Soviet Union "my home," yet his stature as a Frenchman moved General de Gaulle to extol his "feeling for *l'État*." He has personified a remarkable chapter of contemporary political history.

Louis Aragon—as an author known simply as "Aragon"—considered himself a particularly close friend of Maurice Thorez, and he celebrated Thorez's return from a lengthy spell of recuperation in the Soviet Union with one of his most embarrassing dithyrambic encomiums. Still, he is a major French novelist and poet. His biographer, Pierre Daix, used to co-edit *Les Lettres Françaises* with him. Unlike Aragon, Daix left the Party after the ousting of Solzhenitsyn; he was his first translator and has published a notable book about him. His biography of Aragon can scarcely be called that. A better adjective would perhaps be "respectful," and that surely is not the best or even proper basis for biography; but it characterizes almost all the books devoted to Aragon, as if that literary eminence drew unto himself only those so dependent on him or spellbound by his power and influence that they write of him on their knees.

Like Thorez—but in this case more importantly—Aragon is an illegitimate child, being the natural son of a senior government official and *homme de lettres*. The fact was long concealed from him. He knew his mother as an "elder sister" and did not discover the true circumstances of his birth until much later. Aragon has been more of a virtuoso than a creative spirit in terms of intellectual and artistic achievement. His friend André Breton (the two young medical students became: acquainted during their military service in a Paris hospital during World War I) was less talented as a poet but vastly superior as a human and artistic force in the world.

Aragon was one of the best and most effective writers of the Surrealist school, which he repudiated and denounced at a congress of the Communist International in Kharkov in 1930 without ever cutting adrift from it entirely. He then became the French Communist Party's keenest polemicist and most virulent inquisitor. He who had experimented so freely became the dogmatist of socialist realism, denying to the young the very right to go their own way—wrong track or not—of which he himself had taken full advantage. A group of Communist intellectuals, who were associated with the newspaper *Action*, rebelled against his literary despotism in 1947 and then later capitulated—a significant episode completely omitted in Daix's account. A zealous champion of Lysenko, as of the Great Purges' show trials in Moscow and Eastern Europe, Aragon took on the strange proportions of an inquisitor with the soul of a heretic, a dogmatist with the soul of an artist, a connoisseur of power and language alike.

A dash with the Party occurred after Stalin's death (1953) when Aragon published a Picasso drawing in *Les Lettres Françaises*—this showed a youthful and Asiatic-looking Stalin of a type which the Party found incompatible with their image of the venerable "Father of the People." Aragon stood up for Roger Garaudy, initially a doctrinaire, then a dissident ideologue, but he did not oppose his expulsion from the Party. In 1966 *Les Lettres Françaises* identified itself with the "Prague Spring" and the new liberalization movement in general, but Aragon never attacked the Party head on. He was, and still is, tolerated as an elderly enfant terrible, a Party adornment for whom every allowance is made.

Among Aragon's many pieces of defamation there is one which occurs in the first version of his novel cycle *Les Communistes* (later revised). This was leveled at his erstwhile friend Paul Nizan, who left the Party after the Hitler-Stalin Pact and was killed in action in 1940. Aragon denounced Nizan posthumously as a "police informer," without a shred of proof. The Paris atmosphere in which he did so—subsequently described by Jean-Paul Sartre—was one that brooked no contradiction from any quarter; the Communist Party in post-Liberation France exercised a cultural dictatorship.

Aragon's union with Elsa Triolet, a Russian authoress whose sister was the mistress of Mayakovsky, created just as exemplary and power-conscious a "royal couple" as were Maurice Thorez and Jeanette Vermeersch. Elsa was very well informed about the persecutions in Stalinist Russia. It was noticeable that, when drawing on these experiences after Stalin's death in a novel entitled *The Memorial*, she felt more at ease than under the earlier restrictive Party guide lines with which she had so rigidly complied.

Pierre Daix does almost nothing to dispel the semi-obscurity surrounding much that one would like to know about Aragon's political activities and his wielding of cultural power at the head of the Communist-led writers' association *Comité National des Écrivains*. He reverentially quotes from good, bad, and indifferent poems without any attempt to discriminate. Perhaps we shall have to wait until after Aragon's death for an objective portrait and discerning interpretation of the man and writer. Like those before him but on an even grander scale, Pierre Daix has missed his chance. Even Communists with feet of clay should be seen upright and in the round.

March 1976

European Notebook

Porn-O; A New Prince?; Régis Debray's Novel

In his foreword to *l'Histoire d'O* Jean Paulhan invokes Nietzsche, but with a difference. By all means take your whip when you go to a woman, but not to tame her—to avoid disappointing the poor creature. So do women cry out for the whip, claims Paulhan. Carry this only a stage further and the man who denies his woman the whip becomes a veritable sadist.

Having had the pleasure of knowing Jean Paulhan and, so I assume, the pseudonymous "Pauline Réage" who wrote the novel, I am all the better equipped to know what is so disappointing about the film version of *l'Histoire d'O*. The book's contrast between "hot" action and a classically frigid style produced a subtle and perverted effect that is dispelled by stark "exposure." Anyway, legalized pornographic movies simply lack the appeal of exclusiveness and profanity. In America's "hard-core" productions the frontier between illusion and reality, performance and arena, is flagrantly transgressed. Real blood flows in the arena, real semen on the silver screen.

Jean Genet, a self-proclaimed enemy of pornography (like D. H. Lawrence and Henry Miller), forbade his actors even to light a cigarette on stage. No theatrical gesture was allowed to be realistic. So don't mention *Deep Throat* in the same breath.

Why are French cinemas currently inundated with pornographic films? The flood stems from a process of permissive liberalization whose counterpart—a desire to promote and create scope for "films of quality"—has been forgotten. Having stepped on the accelerator, President Giscard d'Estaing now yearns to apply the brakes. In many French towns and cities, the list of forthcoming attractions offers nothing but porn. Henri Zophiralos, the porn-film distributor, cynically comments that after all people can always seek refuge in TV. But can the French State simply sit back and watch while the new freedom metamorphoses itself into an optical tyranny and yesterday's "forbidden fruit" becomes today's compulsory fare? What is obscene here is the rugged individualism, that is the free operation, not of sexual impulses, but of market forces.

What follows—censorship? In Rome, a feminist organization has sought an injunction against Berlanga's film *Life Size*, with Michel Piccoli, in which a man devotes himself to a life-size doll. This is supposed to be a "debasement of womanhood," but surely this is utter nonsense, for since when has masturbation been an expression of male chauvinism?

Brutality appears to be in greater demand than sexuality. Audiences want to see naked violence, not naked women. But more and more pornographic films and films of violence have been going together. "Killing for pleasure others endless variety," wrote the Marquis de Sade. One American underground movie, which actually documents prostitutes being murdered, bridges the gap between stage and arena. And so it is that one must record the end of International Women's Year under the auspices of the Whip! No wonder Françoise Giroud, France's minister for women's affairs, has withdrawn her name from the editorial board of *L'Express* with which she was associated so long. It reprinted *l'Histoire d'O* complete, with what are still euphemistically called stills from the film.

* * *

Is Rome's Pro-Communist censorship already at work in Italy? This question has been raised by a programme on RAI, the Italian State Radio and television network, after an interview with Andrei Sinyavsky (the writer who now lives in Paris and teaches at the Sorbonne after spending six years in a Siberian concentration camp and forced. to leave his native land). The program was stripped of precisely those passages which were bound to show Communism in a bad light. The Italian parliament is supposed to debate this scandal, after a parliamentary question was tabled by most of the political parties including fifty Christian Democratic senators, the Liberals and the Social Democrats. As for the Socialists and Communists they have been keeping mum.

Social Democrat Belluscio's query reproduced the censored passages. They concern the position of the Russian Church, the persecution of Soviet intellectuals, artists' working conditions and limitations on freedom of speech inside the USSR. For example, the following sentences were consigned to the censor's waste-bin:

> Sinyavsky: "I refer to Mandelshtam, the great Russian poet who died in a camp. I refer to the novelist Babel, who also died in prison, and to Marina Tsvetayeva, a poet whose works were never published and who was subjected to so much privation and humiliation that she hanged herself.
>
> "We are now in front of the viewers and can discuss this subject with complete freedom.... I couldn't even conceive of a similar situation in Russia.... The State regards the slightest deviation from a compulsorily prescribed line of conduct as blasphemous.
>
> "At home, for example, there is a ban on so-called left-wing art, on Cubism, Abstractionism, and Expressionism—in short, on anything slightly to the left of Impressionism."

Intellectuals, as Sinyavsky went on, who refuse to yield to the adamantine directives of the Communist Party are scornfully characterized as "spiritual emigrants," a term essentially tantamount to "potential traitor."

> "There has for many years been an attempt to destroy the Church. This destruction is implacable. Churches have been turned into stables, or at times even blown up. Not only is the Church condemned to servitude by the State—it cannot utter a free word. No priest can visit a hospital to comfort the dying. No priest can officiate at a cemetery burial. All such acts are punishable as offenses under the penal code.... Everything began with the Revolution and is ending in a counter-revolution of such savagery that any manifestation of human thought is suppressed and extinguished by force."

Also deleted from the Italian interview were remarks made by Maria Sinyavsky, the author's wife. "I was a devout Communist from childhood onwards," she began, but never concluded.

> "I was an activist in the Union and the Communist youth movement. I cherished a profound faith in my State and government.... All went well until I enrolled at university. I suddenly discovered that my best friends, who were Jews and a hundred times more knowledgeable about everything than I was, invariably gained far worse marks in the entrance examinations. That was my first encounter with the conflict between words— between the theory as officially proclaimed—and the facts as they really are."

Signor Speranza, the Christian Democratic deputy, associates this arbitrary act of censorship with the spread of "Left-Fascism," in other words, intolerance towards any criticism of Communist ideology and practice. The Communists, he points out, have yet to enter government—but even men of moderate political views are bending the knee to "the new prince" (an allusion to Machiavelli's *Il Principe*) whose approval is so often indispensable to decisions in parliament and elsewhere. Hasn't the time come, he asks, to react?

Who was the censor? So far, nobody really knows. Some people allege that "television technicians" demanded the cuts when the program was being edited. According to another version, what underlay this incident was a manoeuvre in the shadows of the imminent "historic compromise" by various political factions inside the TV network (some of those responsible being senior members of the majority parties). The initiator of the interview, Enzo Forcella, has accepted "full personal responsibility "; he declared that he made the cuts on his "own initiative': without any "orders from above."

Forcella has been taken to task for not having even tried to agree the cuts with Sinyavsky in advance. The Russian author was unsparingly critical when he learned how matters stood. His wry conclusion:

> "To escape one censorship, only to end up under another—what a strange fate!"

* * *

"The Underground aristocracy is that of the ever-absent, and its supreme rank is death: murder or execution. This is what gives its dignitaries their real names and faces...."

Thus begins *L'Indésirable* (Le Seuil, Paris), the awaited but unexpected novel by Régis Debray, erstwhile comrade-in-arms of Che Guevara. Debray, who spent months in a Bolivian death-cell, was not only a guerrilla but one of the theoreticians of the guerrilla campaign, as recorded in *Revolution in the Revolution?* (1967), *We, the Tupamaros* (1972), and other similar pamphlets. Released through the intervention of the French government, Debray became an adviser to Allende in Chile. Today, as I hear, he is supposed to be one of the influential political theoreticians of the French Socialists. If he is, it suggests two things: first, that Mitterrand's party is not superstitious, because anyone who worked with Guevara and Allende must surely be devoid of the *fortuna* which Frederick the Great used to require from his Prussian generals, and secondly, that Debray the revolutionary has now converted himself into a reformer. This appears plausible from the new detachment which his novel maintains from the *aristocratié d'illegalité*

But is Debray's approach to his *guerrillero* experience glorificatory or ironical? The novel implies both, an ambivalence which is politically questionable but obviously has some literary advantages for the author.

The principal character in this disguised autobiography is a Genevese *petit bourgeois* named Frank, who is working on a dissertation about the history of Communism. He flees from the personal complexes that beset a snug Swiss "voyeur" of history by subjecting himself to the discipline of a Latin American organized guerrilla commando. There he is concerned less with combat than with supply: i.e., with the securing of weapons from Europe, more particularly with the measures needed to ensure that an arms smuggler keeps his part of the bargain, and with the distribution of arms between *guerrilleros* in the maquis and those in the metropolis. In the end, the perfidious arms smuggler is executed, and Frank is shot by the police.

Stories and novellas by Debray appeared while he was still imprisoned at Camiri, and they hinted that the author of manifestos also had creative talents. (We are now promised a book by Debray on Claude Simon, the French author whose *Le Palace* is the most individualistic nouveau roman to have been written about Civil War Spain.) However, no reader of *L'Indésirable* will be able to forget the author's career and distinguish between the novel and the revolutionary's exploits as strictly as "textual analysis" requires. As that witness and novelist of revolutionary events André Malraux said (according to the memoirs of his first wife, Clara Malraux): "If an author is to become famous, there must be something a little more interesting about his person than his books...." Régis Debray is no new Malraux, as the novel's attempt to mock Malraux makes only too plain; but he does possess that "little extra" as an author.

Debray now views himself with a measure of ironical detachment. His hero Frank is lower middle class; the author himself comes of an upper middle-class and politically influential family—like so many members of the "Underground aristocracy," from Edern-Hallier (who published *La Cause du peuple* and whose family owns property in the Champs Elysées) to the Italian publisher Giangiacomo Feltrinelli (to whom Debray's novel alludes). Debray himself becomes a topic of conversation at one point in the novel. But these coy and jocular real-life allusions only impart an aura of "radical chic," and the Underground's "society talk." In this spirit how can the operations described be seen as part of a revolt by oppressed peoples? They appear, through the involvement of the principal character, as an alien impulse towards commitment for its own sake.

Alternating between the first and third persons, Debray uses one of the first-person passages to cogitate as follows:

> The whole of Europe is a de luxe casino, not just Switzerland.... Where was I when sandal-shod peasants stormed Dien Bien Phu? When Frank Pais was shot by Batista's pigs and collapsed on a pavement in Santiago de Cuba? Where was I when the first Yankee bomb fell on a Vietnamese thatched roof? Busy quaffing *vin du pays* fondling the breasts of a blonde, looking for a quiet summer lakeside resort. It was revulsion rather than volition which prompted me to accept Arrnando's proposal [to take part in a guerrilla operation].

This intellectual figure lacks substance even when he kills—and even when he dies. I was inevitably reminded of the middle-class revolutionaries in Sartre's plays who find compromise "dirty" and killing "clean." I also find it curiously characteristic that a novel which attempts to translate experience into fiction should owe more to specific French literary models than to personal points of departure. Debray writes in a conventional Paris manner. There are some vivid descriptive passages but the dialogue is largely wooden, only the soliloquies are striking:

> We've had our fill of them [says one native revolutionary to another, deriding their imported European comrades] ... these empty dreamers who call themselves the New Left and rediscover the sun also rises every morning!

When Frank gets killed, the patrol commander picks up the notebooks that were in the dead man's bag and are marked "Strictly personal, not for publication." Laboriously, he deciphers what we have already read on the first page of the book: "The Underground aristocracy is that of the ever-absent...." Like Che Guevara, Frank has left a manuscript behind: it is the novel we are reading.

Worth noting among the Paris comments is that of Maurice Nadeau, a critic close to the anti-Stalinist Left and a major discoverer of new literature, who passed this disappointed verdict on Debray's novel:

> The guerrilla chiefs are nebulous lay figures. If we did not already know the purpose of their struggle it would elude us, yet they are the ones we should have liked to meet, not the loquacious scribbler who so rarely lets them get a word in....

Only on reading this rebuke did I realize why, for all its failings and ineptitudes, *L'Indésirable* strangely appeals to me. Far from being the fictionalized account of a struggle and a successor to Malraux's *La Condition humaine*, it portrays the insurmountable gulf between personal motive and political action, between the revolutionary tourists and their sanguinary guest appearances in the history of foreign far-away lands about which they inevitably know so little. It is the portrait of a young intellectual who arrives too overloaded to become a true brother to the mercurial band of native rebels and who, precisely because he cannot shake off his burden, is found wanting—not least by himself. He fights and dies because he wanted to prove something to himself. Still, to transform a heroic legend into a grotesque tragic-comedy must have called up in Régis Debray almost as much courage as did his role in that ill-starred guerrilla campaign in Bolivia. Courage of a different order, of course, but one that belongs to the essence of literature: the willingness to face unpalatable truths.

April 1976

European Notebook

On the Death of Pasolini

When Pier Paolo Pasolini was brutally murdered here by a casual homosexual pick-up in a suburb of Rome it immediately became a crime which the majority of Italian left-wing intellectuals insisted had some dark undercover political motive. At about the same time Pasolini's last film, based on de Sade's *The One Hundred and Twenty Days of Sodom*, became the subject of violent discussion and a target for the local censor. As a result the writer and film director has hardly been referred to except in connection with something horrific or scandalous. This will pass. Several of Pasolini's last books have just been published; some are new works and others new editions, but taken together they do provide an occasion to consider the best of Pasolini, poet and essayist.

Einaudi has published a small volume, *La Divina Mimesis* (echoing *The Divine Comedy*), which concentrates on the depravities and wickednesses of present-day capitalist society following the "Inferno." Garzanti has produced three volumes of poetry, the collected Italian poems making a handsome 700-page book; there is also a thin paperback containing three well-known sets of poems, "Gramsci's Ashes," "Religion in My Time," and "Poetry in Roses," together with—most important of all—"La Nuova Gioventu"; the latter is written primarily in the dialect of Friuli interspersed, in the case of the later 1974 poems, with poetry in standard Italian. Garzanti has also published a collection of essays, *Scritti Corsari* (Writings of a Pirate), sub-titled "The Most Controversial Views of a Provocative Observer."

The poems in dialect seem to me to be admirable. "Furlano" was not Pasolini's mother tongue, but his mother's dialect. He himself only learnt it, including its different local variations, after the family had been evacuated from Bologna during the War to the village of Casarsa near Udine. As with his use in his later novels of the lower-class Roman dialect, Pasolini regarded the language of Friuli (which sounds not unlike Provencal and has echoes of Venetian) as something authentic, as a method of enrichment of the standard language, now so colorless and abstract. Use of the Frinli dialect was also a tribute to his mother (whose other son had been killed by Tito's partisans) with whom Pier Paolo Pasolini lived all his life. Pasolini's use of dialect may be taken as a protest against the severance from the past, against his uprooting.

Pasolini selected and wrote the preface for the collection of essays, and fortunately he did not include the numerous articles which he has written in the previous year for the *Corrière della Sera* demanding a spectacular "People's Trial" of the Christian Democrats, arguing that they should be brought to book, not only for corruption but for promoting "a soul-destroying consumer society." The other essays are replete with provocative eccentricities, studded with reasonable insights and wild illogicalities; in contrast to those of his newspaper polemics most of them contain an element of perspicacity and are not advanced solely in a friend/foe context. Pasolini always mourned for the lost archaic Italy, which he pictured as a Franciscan idyll. It is a nostalgia that is shared by many present-day Italians—Alberto Moravia, for instance—though they all describe it differently. Pasolini abhorred "modern development" which seemed to him misdirected, although he had no dear alternative to propose. As a romantic revolutionary he was rather closer to Rousseau than to Marx, although he liked to call himself a Marxist and hoped for salvation from a fresh generation of communists; at the same time, however, he poured scorn on Communist theories and attacked the Party's ideological orthodoxy. Pasolini became increasingly unsure of the real dialectical meaning of history, and indeed of his own radical commitment, which became more and more frenetic and, in the end, he fancied it all to be a kind of game. I suspect that he sensed that the sources of his poetic inspiration were drying up; and he bemoaned the fact that in this self-alienated Italy, devastated by progress, a writer had to become a linguistic island unto himself.

Pasolini always acknowledged that he held religious views in the early Christian sense. It was no accident that one of Italy's Catholic institutions awarded a prize to his scabrous film *Teorama*. His spirit was caught in theological despair rather than in plain paganism. Many of his later poems are, unfortunately, hard to translate without losing their real essence; they are no more than prose divided into verses and were really part of his journalistic activities. In one of the poems of the series entitled "Murky Enthusiasm," Pasolini pictures himself and his friends being condemned by Orthodox Marxists (inverting a famous Brecht scene in *Die Massnahme*), and he holds them up to ridicule with the verdict which he puts into their mouths. It begins as follows:

> Severe sentence must be pronounced on those who
> believe in kindly affections and innocence.
> Equally severe sentence must be pronounced on
>   anyone who
> loves the sub-proletariat and who therefore
> has no class-consciousness.
> Particularly severe sentence must be passed on
>   anyone who

detects these dark scandalous emotions in himself
       and gives expression to them.
The words of condemnation began to be heard
midway in the Fifties and are still resounding.
Meanwhile: innocence, which in fact existed,
has begun to lose itself in corruption, denials,
            neuroses
Meanwhile: the sub-proletariat, which in fact
          existed,
has become the reservoir of the lower middle class.

There are nine further "stanzas," if that term can be applied to them. The interest, however, lies in what he was trying to say. Pasolini regarded the "sub-proletariat" as the People; in his eyes the organized working class had already become accomplices of the new consumer capitalism, in which a sense of community no longer existed. He referred to *consumismo* as a new form of "fascism" which he felt to be far worse than the old one because it leveled millions of Italians to the same standard and demoralized them, whereas the old fascism had been merely a veneer which never penetrated deep into the masses and so did not ruin them.

Many of Pasolini's earlier provocative statements had shocked Italians but they had also sparked off pertinent discussion. In 1968, for instance, when during the student revolts he wrote a long poem saying that he himself was wholeheartedly on the side of the police! They were, after all, "sons of the People" as opposed to the pampered sons of the bourgeoisie who were now playing at revolution. The last few months of Pasolini's life was marked by angry polemics with his friends, with Moravia (with whom he had edited the newspaper *Nuovi Argumenti*), with Italo Calvino and with Natalia Ginzburg.

I somehow find the comparison with Norman Mailer apt. Mailer also liked punching left and right, and curiously associated brawling with an ideology of mysticism; Mailer once wrote a violent pamphlet against his girlfriends in "Women's Lib." Pasolini could be found campaigning *against* the law, supported by the whole Italian Left, for the legalization of abortion, basing his case not only on the sanctity of life but on they fact that every man retains in his subconscious something of his pre-natal history.

The Left, including certain leading bourgeois newspapers which are now edited by left-wingers, replied to Pasolini with conventional formulations, accusing him of lack of sound insight into social problems and indeed the laws of history; and in response he would confess his immaturity, his permanent youthfulness. He even confessed to "*mammismo*," the Mother-cult now so taboo and scorned in Italy. In one of his poems he wrote that for him his mother was the only woman and his only love.

No one was more conscious of the poet's irrationality, often carried to absurd lengths, than Pasolini himself. His ideas will not be remembered; but memorable is his mistrust of the newfangled Italian rationality, now in possession of final clarifies; and this will possibly remain as a provocation and a vexation. I think that, on balance, he provoked his friends more than he did his enemies. He accused the antifascists of being fascists themselves; he pointed out that young fascists were in no way different from young antifascists in physiognomy, physique, fashion or foolishness. Those who referred to fascists as if they were quite another race of Italians, he said, were just unable to see themselves. He also ridiculed the Left for substituting for a real knowledge of class a merely rhetorical class-consciousness. Pasolini was a very embarrassing fellow. He might have played the role of revolutionary court jester had he possessed any kind of sense of humor. Still his desperation was no play-acting, no pose.

Pasolini was a figure who could at once elicit anger and admiration. He longed for a communist victory and at the same time feared an insipid, slogan-filled, conformist future. Nevertheless the smooth self-assured counter-arguments continuously hurled at him by the disciples of History and Progress, their rigid dialectics unruffled by any self-questioning, have a less human ring about them than Pasolini's poems or prose.

How hostile was Pasolini's supposed "hostility to the consumer"? Three of his films, *Decameron, Canterbury Tales,* and *The Thousandth and First Night,* made considerable concessions to his audience and were definitely commercial box office successes. In his preface to the scripts, however—one of the last things he wrote which was published posthumously—he dissociated himself from these films and hinted that he was going to try to regain his capacity as an artist by retreating to write another novel. His *Ragazzi di vita* has a permanent place in present-day Italian literature, and it is saddening that since his death most references to Pasolini should have been concerned solely with so disastrous, even on the purely technical level, a film as *Salo and the 120 Days of Sodom*. Pasolini here is neither erotic nor sensual. The ponderous obscenity of his travesty of a film version of the "divine Marquis" gives an oddly dilettante impression. So do the explicit references to literature about de Sade (from Simone de Beauvoir to Roland Barthes), and the quotations from Nietzsche in the mouths of mediocre fascist dignitaries have an unintentionally grotesque ring about them, as if the director had felt that he had to legitimize his interest in the subject by highfalutin' intellectual allusions. As for his vaunted uncompromising radicalism, Pasolini was not quite bold enough to picture the final "blood cycle," the torturing to death, except in miniature through an observer's telescope.

If pornography is a matter of lubricity and sexual stimulation and not of horror and evil, then the *120 Days* need only be banned for addicts of "coprophilia." For other viewers a government health warning that during the film they might well be overcome by nausea would be sufficient, especially if cinema managers (as John Weightman once suggested) would thoughtfully provide little air-sick bags under every seat.

All this may not quite be necessary. The controversial film has already fallen foul of the censor in several countries. Who will fight for it? It certainly cannot qualify either as a kind of Brechtian *"Lehrstück"* on the relationship between Fascism and Sadism, even less so than that other controversial Italian film, *The Night Porter*, could be taken as a serious inquiry into modern masochism (a woman who becomes the postwar sexual captive of one of her tormentors in a concentration camp).

The trouble with Pasolini was that he endowed his villains, all mediocre lower-middle-class dignitaries, with an overflow of imagination, with intricate obsessions and with an avant-garde erudition—they portray Sade because they have studied him (and Beauvoir, Barthes, etc.) in such detail!—whereas in fact the most apt comment on the subject is that of Hannah Arendt: "the banality of evil." The impression persists— and it is reinforced for me by a book of memoirs recently published by one of the Italian actors in the film—that as a film director Pasolini was transferring his own erotic fantasies and obsessions to the screen with vast self-indulgence and no artistic selfcriticism at all. The supposedly political and social context was no more than a contrived studio setting.

By my count Pasolini made at least twelve films that were incomparably better than this posthumous production. I prefer not to regard it as the "last will and testament" of the artist but only as a helpless expression of the man's personal (and ideological) crisis. Still, it remains his "last word." The tragic, vicious, violent aspect of his death in Rome had been imagined and portrayed in both his films and his novels, and was indeed inherent in the way of "living dangerously" at the mercy of a *Ragazzo di morte*.

June 1976

European Notebook

Le Monde; Italian Censorship; Solzhenitsyn and Spain

Le Monde

Paris

If France's most prestigious newspaper can be charged with something so vulgar as crude bias, then nothing Gallic is sacred. The paper in question is, of course, the Paris daily *Le Monde*, and the *j'accuse* is made in a book, *Le Monde tel qu'il est,* by Michel Legris, a "defector" who was a member of its staff for sixteen years till his resignation in 1972.

This newspaper of extraordinary quality has a large circulation—between 500,000 and 600,000—and unlike most ailing French newspapers it makes a profit. As part of the establishment and also of the opposition it is at once respectable and disrespectful. For anyone in an influential position or profession it is compulsory reading.[1] It is more than just a newspaper; it is a power in the land, an institution, and indeed the only one in France that since May 1968 has not had its own round of contestation. Now it appears to lack altogether that spirit of enlightened self-criticism in the face of an attack that it expected to be rigorously displayed by the Government, the Church, the Army, the Courts and the Universities. It appears to regard any critique of itself as motivated by plotters and intriguers, the result of dire machinations by darkly envious reactionaries. In a box on the front page of the issue of 24 March its founder M. Hubert Beuve-Méry, the present editor M. Jacques Fauvet, and the general manager dismissed the book. They did not mention its author or title, and simply announced tersely that vilification always rebounds on the vilifier. On page 17 the book was also given a short trouncing without going into any details. Later it was announced that M. Jacques Fauvet would deal with the book again—in *Le Figaro*, as a reply to Raymond Aron's critique.

Vilification? Michel Legris's book is a piece of polemical pamphleteering, but it uses many exact quotations and is never crudely argued. *Le Monde*'s almost hysterical reaction in fact provided Michel Legris with his best argument; and it turned the book into a *cause célèbre*. To what does the ex-*Monde* author take exception? He indicts his old newspaper for its mixture of prejudice and pseudo-objectivity, and he concentrates on a few examples—first of all Portugal where it consistently supported the military dictatorship of the generals and Cunhal's Communists against the democratic parties that ultimately won the elections. Jacques Fauvet wrote a reply to his critics on the Right (*Le Figaro*) and the Left (*Nouvel Observateur*) which only revealed how offended he was.

Michel Legris' book, though not nearly as good as it might have been, has been for weeks on the Paris best-seller list. And the crude reaction of the editors has provoked criticism on the intellectual Left where the paper could least expect it. Jean-Marie Domenach (editor of the monthly *Esprit* and a regular contributor to *Le Monde*) has joined the attack in unequivocal terms in his review; so has the historian Pierre Nora (editor of two famous Gallimard series, the "Bibliotheque ties sciences humaines" and "Archives"), who expressed, in *Le Nouvel Observateur*, his dismay about *Le Monde's* incapacity for taking criticism seriously.

One apt point against Legris' book was made by Jean-Jacques Servan-Schreiber in his *L'Express*. The deputy for Nancy recalled that *Le Monde* under its previous editor, Hubert Beuve-Méry, was as biased as it is today; and he suggested that the old presence of "objectivity" was more damnable than the present open "commitment." (One remembers the scandal in the 1950s of the faked "Fechteler report" in which a U.S. admiral was supposed to have revealed America's imminent abandonment of Western Europe!) In an inconclusive TV debate editor André Fontaine was confronted with Michel Legris—on the biased reports on Cambodia, Fontaine's excuse was that, after all, they were of much the same tendency that was reflected in the widely respected liberal *Manchester Guardian*! Q.E.D....

Legris was also outraged by the reporting from Phnom Penh: that capital's popular enthusiasm for the Red Khmer was followed by the expulsion of the whole of its population, including all the patients in the hospitals. "How many of these patients may have died in the streets?" the *Le Monde* reporter wrote sorrowfully, only to find prompt consolation in the thought: "How many would have died anyway in the squalor of those hospitals?"

There is a shock of recognition here, for more and more readers are finding that the newspaper that was once their Bible is no longer so "authoritative" and completely "reliable." True, it remains "indispensable"; but once it was generally read in a spirit of awe and devotion. Recently many of its readers have been adopting towards it the skeptical attitude that the French have towards their other awesome authorities. Like the President of the Republic and the professors, the generals, the judges, and all the other pillars of the establishment, *Le Monde* will have to learn to live with contestation.

Italian Censorship

Milan

"It makes no great difference whether the price is in power or is only the presumed successor of the ruling prince. In the contrary, the presumptive heir enjoys more prestige and stimulates so many people to throw in their lot with the man of the future..." Those words were written a decade ago by the brilliant Italian critic Nicola Chiaromonte.[2] He noted at the time that communism offered Italian intellectuals "a substitute for social conscience without any testing or criticism of ideas, a new conformism, a way of putting oneself in the service of 'progress,' 'history,' the 'proletariat,' without having to make the slightest change in one's way of living or thinking."

Ten years later these remarks are more applicable than ever. There are many cases—though few are publicly known—of insidious pressure on publishers and authors, of pre-censorship. I referred in these pages a few months ago to the drastic blue pencillings of an Italian state television interview with Andrey Sinyavsky; and he protested against the cuts in vain. As he put it to the Naples conference of the Italian liberals, "It is horrifying to find Communist censorship already at work in the country even before the Party has come to governmental power...." Several big publishers practice what is known in Italy as *"Feltrinellizzazione"* (after the leading publishing firm of that name), and the process is also known as *"instrumentalizzazione"* and *"egemonizzazione,"* that is, everything is being judged by its "instrumental" value in bringing about a certain cultural-political hegemony.

The most dramatic victims (not unlike Lenin's first Russian purges after October 1917) are figures on the Left, intellectuals of dissident Marxian or radical persuasion. In the current "Settembrini Case" the D'Anna publishing house conceded that it was leaning backwards in order to avoid offending the sensibilities of Communist readers and especially orthodox young Marxist students. Among the editorial changes it insisted upon, in an anthology of socialist and anarchist writings, was the omission of a reference to "human degradation in Stalin's Russia." "Our culture is already on its knees," Domenico Settembrini has said, "and I can't see why the Communists are going to 'liberalize' an already illiberal atmosphere...."

A similar experience was that of Armando Saitta, professor of history in the University of Rome, who is the author of many widely read textbooks. His latest book, published by La Nuova Italia, headed by Tristano Codignola, was censored and altered. In addition, extra matter was interpolated which was not written by him; his permission was not sought, nor was he even informed. When the weekly *Europeo*, which is itself on the Left, took up the matter it was admonished from several quarters not to break the "left-wing front" by publishing anything about it. Codignola himself bluntly declared:

"I know where Saitta now stands—the whole thing is obviously a Fascist provocation—and to avoid getting involved in his manoeuvre I refuse to say any more about it."

The censored passages included comments on the various Italian regions, the political parties, and the trade unions. Here is an example: "The danger exists that the regions are turning into preserves for party clienteles instead of into the centers of democratic life which the constitution intended." Everyone knows that that is true, but it was not allowed to be printed. Why, Saitta asks, didn't the publisher at least remove my name from the jacket? To this Codignola has merely replied: "We have our publishing and political dignity to preserve."

Dignity *all'italiana* is like the Sophia Loren divorce in the well-known film which similarly swept an difficulties under the carpet. Still, there are a great many small publishers who are struggling to preserve an exemplary independence. I spoke the other day to the art historian Vanni Scheiwiler who publishes in Milan. But Signor Scheiwiler is pessimistic; he says that under the influence of the new conformism the city, after all the cultural centre of Italy, has been undergoing a decline in intellectual vitality. "Anyone who comes up with something that does not fit in with the line is promptly put down by being called a Fascist. The word Fascist is repeated so often that one wonders whether it hasn't lost all meaning!"

This reminded me of what Ignazio Silone said in 1945 soon after he returned to Italy from his Zurich exile: "The Fascism of tomorrow will never say 'I am Fascism.' It will say: 'I am anti-Fascism.'"

Solzhenitsyn and Spain

Zurich

Alexander Solzhenitsyn told the Spaniards on Radio Madrid recently not to feel too badly about their present post-Franco political transition and to enjoy certain personal and cultural liberties which Soviet subjects hardly dare dream about.

Evidently they should not jeopardize that happy state by unconsidered political activity, for behind the illusion that still greaser freedom was attainable lurked the danger of an irreversible plunge into a real species of totalitarian dictatorship.

In his speech to American trade union leaders he regretted and deplored that the Americans had ever allowed themselves to be involved with the Soviet Union, for the threat from Hitler's Germany had never been dangerous enough to justify it.

In his interview on the BBC which attracted so much notice he said that the strength of people who had lived under a totalitarian dictatorship was that they were able "to see things in their true perspective"; and this was something which the people in the West were incapable of...in spite of—perhaps because of—their freedom.

Such utterances, based on little knowledge of the West and lamentably untouched by self-criticism, may well suit those who have always been made to feel uncomfortable by Solzhenitsyn, the witness and chronicler of the Gulag horrors, but could not say so; but they are also increasingly embarrassing to those who admire his character and spirit, among whom I number myself. The recent critiques by Raymond Aron, Heinrich Böll, and Richard Lowenthal[3] have discussed this fairly and thoughtfully, but now that more and more provocative statements are in circulation there is something that must be added.

In the first place, Solzhenitsyn has expressed definitive views on complex matters on which he lacks anything that can be called empirical knowledge. That is no reason to pay him back in the same coinage. Those who have not read *Gulag*—the third (and, in my view, greatest) volume is now available in French—and his other books should beware of passing a sweeping judgment on him. He was discomfiting enough when he confronted us with truths. Now that he at once expresses views that we must applaud and others that we do not accept (or indeed actually oppose) he forces us to differentiate. The Solzhenitsyn testimony remains; the political implications remain to be discussed, or perhaps to be ignored.

But there is, I think, a "bon usage de" Solzhenitsyn, and it presupposes a detailed knowledge of his works. For instance:

"The seal of compulsory thought has deformed us all, has not left a single brain unwounded."

And this (also from "*Voices from the Rubble*"):

"Nowhere in our spiritual isolation can we test our views against each other."

In the East, he argued the inevitable limitation of perspectives, and in this he exhibited more insight than in all his long-range statements on radio and television in the West. If after ten whole days in the country he tells the hapless Spaniards that they are rather well off in comparison with the regime that he knows, an answer presents itself:

"Each of us wallows in his own squalor, and no one's misery is mitigated by his neighbor's."

That too was written by Solzhenitsyn.

August 1976

Notes

1. See, Richard Mayne, "Demi Monde," *Encounter* (October 1969).
2. He died in Rome in 1972 (see the memoir by Paolo Milano in *Encounter*, May 1972). A collection of his articles, some of which appeared in *Encounter*, has recently been edited by Miriam Chiaromonte and published by Harcourt Brace Jovanovich (New York and London) with a preface by Mary McCarthy: The *Worm of Consciousness & Other Essays* (1976).
3. See Raymond Aron, "A Reply to; Solzhenitsyn," *Encounter*, September 1975, Richard Lowenthal, "Solschenizyn in Amerika: der wahre Prophet und die falsche Botschaft," Merkur (Munich), November 1975; Heinrich Böll, in *Die Weltwoche*.

European Notebook

Telos

Let me call my island "Telos," and happily my annual voyage there is difficult and complicated. First one has to land on another island, and only from there is there a ferry available to cross another bit of the sea. The ferry's schedule has proved over the years to be consistently unreliable; and this summer I learned, as if it were some dark Hellenic secret, that the journey would be made four, rather than three, times a week. Paradise has its little odd rules and regulations that one gladly puts up with. There is a place for an automobile (some of Telos' best beaches are several miles from the village), but how to go about reserving it remains a perennial Mediterranean mystery. Only one Athens travel agency knows anything about the intricacies of coming and going, and there appears to be a feud between mainland and island. After all, Telos has so little to offer. There is no "comfort," not to speak of "deluxe" unless one brings it along oneself on a yacht to be anchored in the port of Polaria. There is still a kind of Grand Hotel around, gently declining and falling for decades now; and its kitchen is, as Michelin used to say, "worth the journey"... to any *taverna* on the sea or a *souvlaki* stand in the village....

I meet from time to time somebody who has actually made it to Telos, heard them moan about the "miserable panorama" of a church and a cemetery on a bare hill: they know that, after all those other dozen islands on the Mediterranean Tour, nothing special is happening here. The single tiny village of the isle is perched almost inaccessibly on a hilltop, and coming from the port there is no way of knowing it is there (which must have discouraged all kinds of piratical raids over a thousand years). From the other side the view is sharp of the medieval castle and the monastery on the cliff side. When I stare at the picture of white squares and flat roofs I think of combinations of Mont St-Michel and Sidi Bou Said; but then one begins to register more and more the angular red-brick tops of the large new villas being built (after much struggle with planning permissions) by rich mainland Greeks, and each of them has at least three or four antennae protruding.

The village itself still remains something of a children's playground. Morning and evenings a dwarf-like village announcer shouts out the program in the cinema and other important local events. The women spin and weave in the open doors of their houses (glimpses of lovely painted plates hanging on walls behind theme; the old men string beads and pearls. The missing middle generation can all be found in Düsseldorf and the environs of the Ruhr, busy working and remitting. The flocks of sheep are guided by a few shepherds with marvelously crooked croziers, and the herds of wild goats seem to manage quite by themselves.

A handful of foreigners come here year after year, and a few have houses of their own through the connections of their Greek relatives. But wars and political crises inconveniently intervene to keep things as they were. All the old ferries were requisitioned for Saloniki during the Cyprus difficulties. But little is taken as tragic: except, possibly, that bewildered Telos soldier who happily returned home; but, with his raspberry-smeared face, was taken to be the first casualty of the Turkish invasion. The outside world doesn't seem quite real, and on the day the Junta fell in Athens one of the locals (who happens to be a French art dealer) suggested that the old pictures and placards of the Colonels' regime be discreetly removed: "But not to worry, I've lunched regularly with Karamanlis in Paris...."

And yet the place seems to be of some military importance, and it is no secret since the towers of the radar station can be easily seen by anyone; even a little military airstrip is being built. Curiously bearded young Dutchmen and Danes no longer find the little rooms to stay in, as soldiers and workers move in. For the moment, theft, the old cries against Tourism as the Enemy of Native Culture seem almost to be stilled. "Morally dangerous elements" used to convert all the nice young Greek adolescents to Gigolos and Junkies (the newspaper I am reading calls them "Junkers"—what would Düsseldorf think?). Now it seems the struggle is only a matter of the new souvenir shops. Should they sell such junk, and agree to accept oddly colored credit cards in strangely bartered payment?

I think back, in Telos, of some three postwar decades of Paradise-hunting. How many lost Edens have there been? Will Telos go the way of Ascona, and of Forio? We drove, having found a ferry place for our hired car, some four kilometers out of the village, and then walked into the cool sea alone, on a golden beach as far as the eye could see.

September 1976

European Notebook

Heidegger; Amalrik

The German press is, of course, crowded with appreciations and re-evaluations of the life and work of Martin Heidegger (who died on 26 May at the age of eighty-six). But I was especially struck by the obituaries in the *London Times* and the *Paris Monde*. One headline read: "A MAJOR GERMAN PHILOSOPHER" and the other had it: "LE PLUS GRAND PHILOSOPHE DE NOS TEMPS." In the *Times* it is one of several obits on page 18; in *Le Monde* there were three long articles beginning on the front page.

In France, the fascinated intellectual preoccupation with Heidegger's philosophy could be found among poets as well as thinkers and it was especially striking on the intellectual Left—where in Germany not a book of Heidegger was ever cracked (at least not since the young Herbert Marcuse was a Heideggerian). A goodly number of French studies link the names of Marx and Heidegger as if they comprised the two greatest thinkers of the modern world who conveniently complemented each other. Both the older generation (above all Jean-Paul Sartre) and the younger French intellectuals like Michel Foucault and Gilles Deleuze turned to him again and again over the years as "a key figure." It was enough for Sartre to have written in *Les temps modernes* on the death of its co founder, Maurice Merleau-Ponty, "We both had gone to see Husserl and Heidegger...." It was a curious relationship, a strange trans-Rhine brotherhood.

I saw the other night a German TV documentary glorifying Heidegger and his life work; in it a young French philosopher was interviewed and he even went so far as to praise the intellectuality of Heidegger's notorious speech in 1933 as rector of the University of Freiburg which signaled his (short-lived) acceptance of the Nazi cause. At least there is no one in Germany today who could be found to go that far. German intellectuals today know better, and they have at hand Alexander Schwan's excellent critical book on Heidegger's political "engagement"; the French have neither translated nor discussed it.

Much about the "French Heidegger" is a puzzlement. To read Heidegger in his original German, with its recondite researches into outlandish etymological roots (almost a kind of philosophical punning) is to come away with a lesson in tortured semantics which is surely untranslatable. I have never ceased to be astonished, and I spent fifteen postwar years in Paris, at how powerfully Heidegger seems to have affected even those French intellectuals who couldn't read a word of German or make out the difference between an umlaut and a colon.

It is a most strange phenomenon of French-German cultural exchange, and it suggests the mutual fascination with what is foreign. For the German literary critics of today the most decisive commentary on their great poet Hölderlin is the work of the French writer Pierre Berteaux. But for the French, as a glance at the French edition of Hölderlin reveals, it is only the interpretation of Heidegger that counts. When M. Robert Minder produced his formidable critique of Heidegger's language and literary studies, it was treated in France (especially on the Left) as "irrelevant." Nor has anyone in Germany produced anything to stand beside the three-volume work on Heidegger by Jean Beaufret. Cultural exchange has many cunning passages, not the least of which being that the one German poet whom we know to have been in "*Gedankenaustausch*" with Heidegger—Paul Celan—lived in Paris.

Could it be that this amazing cross-cultural echo, this brotherly trans-Rhine resonance, was all based on deep misunderstandings? Dare one think that the whole of French Existentialism—which puzzled Heidegger and left him cold—proceeded from erratic eccentricities?

I am certain that Europe's intellectual history could never be that melodramatic. Still, there remains the question of what it was that the author of *Sein und Zeit* (translated only decades after it was first published in 1927) offered the French spirit? I won't even attempt an answer. Let me merely say that I find the episode "Heidegger en France" one of the most exotic in contemporary cultural history. For it belongs not to the history of debate, argument and analysis, but to those private gardens of the European intelligentsia where confessions, cults, and fashions flower.

* * *

I had the opportunity to spend a day here with Andrew Amalrik and his wife, Gyusel, both freshly arrived after their cliff-hanging ordeal in Moscow and not knowing until the last minute whether they would be "voluntary released," involuntary expelled, or delayed or detained once again". We chatted lightly in German which he speaks correctly, if slowly; but in the long and serious exchanges, in which the sculptor Ernst Neizvestny also participated, there was alas a "translation screen"; and here, I have always felt, much gets lost in the effort to understand a writer from a different political and intellectual culture. One is always thrown back in such situations to tile books and articles from which one can get a clear and, one supposes, a definitive impression.

And yet, after some seven hours of talk, one could not help come away with a sense of new and surprising aspects of the man. It does make a difference if one can put supplementary questions and even go on to discuss. At one point one Russian who was present (he happens to be living in Perugia) mentioned the problem of Italy on the eve of so-called Euro-Communism. I wasn't quite prepared for the temptation which some Western ideological heresies on the traditional totalitarian Left could still offer even those most radical of oppositionists to the Soviet system. As Amalrik said, "For us Palmiro Togliatti remains the first dissident. His political testament, which demanded a pluralism as against the Soviet domination of the Communist movement, gave us new perspectives...."

How, then, does Amalrik see the change in the System (even if it should, as he now concedes, be able to survive beyond 1984)? Perhaps through a return to the original non-party Soviet councils; and out of a decentralized network of local councils a form of Parliament could develop. But, in the neo-pragmatic style of the new Russian intelligentsia (or, at least, some part of it), he quickly added the to this could only be an "ideal model," more of a benchmark than any kind of blueprint or prediction. In any event, for all his anti-Bolshevism, he would clearly reject any regime that would deal with the Communists the way they deal with other politics I parties when they have State power, namely, drive the opposition into illegality. In the event of free elections in Russia, he estimates that the Soviet Communists might well receive as much of an electoral percentage, as, say, the Portuguese C.P. did recently (12 percent). He made a point of not suggesting a "purification" of post-Communist society, but a genuinely liberal and tolerant pluralism.

Thus, among the various basic currents of anti-Soviet dissident thought—the religious-traditional; the liberal-libertarian; the back-to-Lenin revisionists—it seemed to be that Amalrik, always formulating carefully and undogmatically, belonged to the spirit of Sakharov, rather than Solzhenitsyn or Medvedev. At no point did he suggest, as I have heard it put from other Russian dissenters, that "the overwhelming majority of the Russian people" (90 percent, no less) felt precisely as he did. But after all, I chided him, he was an historian and surely that gave him perspective and a long view. "Historian?" he laughed, "with my interrupted schooling, two incomplete semesters, and no degree—you must be joking...."

Dissidence, then, was a patchwork quilt of many colors. It stitched together everything in a huge land that was crying out to be seen, heard, felt. And that included extreme Russian nationalism; growing ethnic consciousness among the non-Russian minorities (read: majorities); diverse ideologies of bourgeois liberalism and social freedom; strange mixtures of authoritarian communism and national socialism. Indeed these can be found not only among the oppositionists but even within the regime's representatives. Dissidence, accordingly, is not a single movement at all; rather, a variegated expression of deep dissatisfactions and hopes throughout a hard-pressed unhappy social order. Don't ask what vision of the future it has, because it's not One but Many, not a color but a spectrum.... As Amalrik put it to me, "Caught in a closed system one tries to get out somehow—moving forwards, or backwards, or sideways—indeed any which way.... For many Western observers, with simple notions of progress in history, this must be very difficult to understand...."

Was Communism still a belief, a faith ? No, it was almost exclusively an opportunistic adjustment to, and acceptance of, certain Established conditions; still, it had qualities of strength and resilience so long as there was no challenge from other ideas and beliefs. Not some spontaneous "wisdom of the People" emerging from the suckering masses. Rather, strong convictions held deeply and pronounced publicly by individuals who are quite ready to accept their intellectual and moral responsibilities. Some kind of break-through to "Freedom" without a proper prelude of an Enlightenment, a preparation in critical ideas, could only be dangerous.

I will not judge here Amalrik's views, and only record that he tried to face every argument and counter-argument, concentrating and relaxing by turns. And what an impression of personal liberty and intellectual freedom one comes away with! Here is not a man with yet another Message, or an author who can only add to his published books by scribbling his name on the flyleaf. One could not miss here the pathos (in one ancient sense of the word) of a man and a woman who, under the most trying and appalling of circumstances, managed to survive with honor.

October 1976

European Notebook

Doris Kearns and Lyndon Johnson; Polish Democracy; Andrey Amalrik

Bedtime Story

I happened to be in Washington at the time, but had no more to do with it than that. In spring 1967 an attractive, red-haired twenty-four-year-old Harvard student of lively intelligence was told that she had been selected to take part in the program "Young Staff in the White House." A number of young Americans would become "Special Assistants" and so watch the president and members of his cabinet at work from close quarters. President Lyndon Johnson had made the acquaintance of this new "Fellow of the White House" at an evening ball and had danced with her. Doris Kearns was then active in the anti-Vietnam protest movement. She had just written an article (and the president knew this) entitled "How We Can Get Rid of Johnson in 1968."

When I met this high-spirited young lady in Washington last year she had already (at thirty-two) become a "full professor" in Harvard on the strength of her book-length study of Lyndon Johnson. Until shortly before his death Johnson spent many hours with Doris Kearns both by day and night; sometimes he would arrive before dawn, lie down in her bed, pull the blanket up to his chin and talk while Doris sat and took notes. She was also a "resident" of the Texas ranch to which Johnson withdrew after refusing a second nomination. Since there have recently been so many revelations about "affairs" from Franklin D. Roosevelt to John F. Kennedy, it should be added that Miss Kearns was Johnson's Boswell—or perhaps to avoid the lit. crit. confusion, his "Eckermann"—and that even the gossip columnists have never whispered about "improprieties."

Lyndon Johnson talked about his youth, his mother, his dreams, his successes and his disillusionments. His listener was fascinated by the president's candor and energy (and also his honesty in his fight for civil rights for colored people). Johnson, thinking of history, wanted to leave some testimony behind him to show what he "really" was. His sharp-eyed partner, thinking of historiography, spied the outlines of a book combining intimate details with political interpretation. Publishers were alerted and offered huge advance royalties. Doris had meanwhile taken up with a philosophizing "speechwriter" for Democratic presidents and, to Harvard's consternation, revealed that her book was their combined work. Somehow her co-author (Richard Goodwin) was dropped, and what has now appeared is presumably her own account.

But her own historical account of what? Is she quite clear in her own mind that Lyndon Johnson might never "really" have let himself go? Couldn't it be that he was always calculating what to say to her and what its effect would be? Nevertheless the enormous vitality of the late president comes through, as does his sense of failure and his bitterness.

Compared to the latest biographies of Jack Kennedy, which concentrate on long-concealed histories of illness, or to the *romans à clefs* with which Agnew and Ehrlichman have taken their revenge on Nixon, Miss Kearns' bedside manner is impressive. The bedroom might well be a more suitable place for primary-source research than the doctor's office or even the Oval Room.

In his autobiography published for the presidential candidacy Jimmy Carter announced his discovery that "Presidents too are human beings." He refers to himself in the book's title, *Why Not the Best?* and a report about him in a somewhat hostile newspaper was furiously attacked by his staff (and friendly magazines such as *Time*), for the "Best" always take more trouble about their "image" than the facts. What price intimate reportage? Friendly or hostile, it succeeds at best in getting tantalizingly close to the bedside. The truth may still be under cover. Presidents and candidates, however closely observed, remain riddles, not least to themselves.

That greatest of American presidents, Abraham Lincoln, was in the estimate of Karl Marx only "eine Durschnittsnatur von gutem Willen"(an average character of good will). Which suggests that not even the vaunted dialectic manages to get under the skin, or the bedsheets, of history.

Scapegoats

Poland is a "People's Democracy." It may have certain difficulties with the workers, the farmers, and the intellectuals. But otherwise it undoubtedly represents the people.

Six years ago Poland experienced a prolonged, bloody and, within obvious historic limits, successful workers' revolt such as had never been seen before in the Eastern Bloc. I recall the following joke, which went the rounds in Warsaw at the time. Napoleon, Tsar Nicholas II, and Lenin were watching events in Gdynia from paradise (or elsewhere). Lenin enthused: "What a proletariat—militant, full of solidarity—flinching before no sacrifice as it mounts the barricades—what a prospect for socialism!" Tsar Nicholas was enthusiastic too: "These policemen, how sturdily and purposefully they go into action without any fake sentimental tentativeness. With police like that Russia today would still be a Tsarist empire!" Napoleon too was overjoyed: "This

Polish press! Had I had such a press, the French today would still not know who lost the Battle of Waterloo!"

But things as they happened were not quite so amusing. Gomulka, the rebel of 1956 who had degenerated into the most ossified Communist functionary, fell as a result of the revolt. On other occasions when: things were going badly in Poland, a call had gone out for the "*voivods* of Silesia," the most progressive of the provinces. So it was in this case. The man was Gierek; and at the end of June he was faced, like his predecessor, with similar strikes and disturbances; but he gave way to the demands, quickly and flexibly. The cause of the trouble was the sudden rises in food prices— and they were cancelled. After such a concession—which the grievous economic situation did not in fact permit— repression inevitably followed. Exemplary sentences were pronounced against "vandals" and "hooligans" in closed courts (although in 1955 foreign reporters were allowed to be present at the trial of workers in Poznan). In the factories, without a word being said, "ringleaders" were laid of work for three months without pay. It looked more like a general attempt to eliminate the opposition than a precise punishment of "anti-social elements." *Polytika* publicly laid the blame on "lack of political consciousness among the workers." I couldn't help being reminded of Bertholt Brecht's sarcastic advice to Ulbricht in 1953 that one could, after all, simply dissolve the people and elect another.

Poland's workers tend to take literally the talk about the "Workers State"— and therefore demanded free elections of trade-union officials (which Gierek promised them in 1971 but had not granted). The peasants are not collectivized, and it has been known for them to feed state-subsidized bread to their cattle since it is cheaper than the grain that they deliver to the mills. Increased purchasing power resulting from massive wage increases since 1971 has gone almost entirely on foodstuffs owing to lack of other goods for sale. Both productivity in the factories and deliveries by the farmers fell simultaneously. At the same time Poland must export meat to cope with her indebtedness.

The intellectuals are proving equally tiresome. Many of the most reputable scientists and artists, including some in senior positions, protested against a change in the constitution. In this case protest against the renewed show trials ranged from young Kuron (a sort of Eastern Cohn-Bendit) to Lipinski, the famous economist. The Catholic Church is both restive and influential. But with so many stresses and strains, Poland's Politburo needs more "agents," "spies," and associated ringleaders to explain away its failures. Now that "imperialist America" and "revanchist Germany" have ceased to be "cold war enemies," even these are no longer readily available. Pity the poor Five-Year-Plan that even has a shortage of scapegoats.

Yet Another Exile?

Ask any observer of the Soviet intellectual scene to come up with, say, twenty names which he associates with some Russian book or other. He will in all probability think at once of at least fifteen who have been subjected to arrest, labor camp, banishment, psychiatric wards, compulsory exile or, at the very least, muzzling or vilification without right of reply. Among the remaining five there would certainly be two or three names of writers whose works have admittedly been published but who have never held office or been asked for their opinion by the monolithic Writers Union, a closed shop which can at a stroke stop a writer's career cold.

I often hear the argument that, for the moment, just too much emphasis is being laid in the West on the critics of the regime, on the "dissidents." If this is so their prominence over here would be the expression not so much of genuine intellectual interest or literary merit as of a more or less manipulated process of propagandized distortion. Let us not exclude this supposition even if it makes us uncomfortable. But in any case there are certain figures—e.g., Boris Pasternak, Anna Akhmatova, or Solzhenitsyn, who are regarded as "important" by Russian intellectuals of all shades of opinion. I have talked to enough of them to know that the treatment meted out to these authors, both yesterday and today, remains distressing. This applies to the poet Joseph Brodsky, still a young man, who has been forced to emigrate against his will; one day Russian literary historians will register with astonishment that, before being handed an unwanted visa for "emigration to Israel," he was condemned as "a parasite" by a court and banished from Leningrad.

One of the youngest and best known of the exiled dissidents, representative of a broad spectrum of opinion—including "the right to pay homage to no ideology at all"—is the thirty-seven-year-old Andrey Amalrik who has now emigrated to Holland. Eleven years ago he was sentenced to hard labor and banished; he was sentenced again after writing an account entitled *Involuntary Journey to Siberia* and a small book *Will the Soviet Union Survive Until 1984?* (I learned from him recently (see *Encounter*, October) that his great-great-grandfather was an immigrant from southern France, and his great-grandfather founded a factory still in existence today.) All sorts of tricks have been played on him including arrest on the street without warrant and for several months emigration was "proposed" to him. The authorities were so anxious for Amalrik to emigrate that, when he protested, they agreed to remission of the high rate of duty applicable to personal works of art taken out of the country.

The difference between Andrey Amalrik and many other famous dissidents is that he did not substitute some cult of The People for faith in The Party. He merely doubted whether a majority of Soviet citizens were yearning for democracy or could even visualize anything other than a rigid authoritarian state. There was no mysticism or mystification here, the author himself has since criticized his own use of the provocative "1984" in his book title. He hopes that certain definite "new tendencies" will emerge in Russia but he fears certain other ones; although he has much to say to us, he regards himself (as I have already reported here) as someone who must study and reflect further.

Has he been overplayed by the West? A few years ago the influential German newsweekly *Der Spiegel* published certain slanderous and spiteful rumors about him. Amalrik then replied to the editor that he hoped to be freer, even in prison, than "your countrymen, and mine, who freely shouted Hurrah for Stalin and Hitler!" Amalrik is neither religious nor nationalistic nor Marxist. He is less inclined than many other dissidents to try and associate a new Russia with some period of the national past. In his controversial essay he published his Moscow address, and he refused to have anything to do with anything conspiratorial. Why in the world should the fact that he has now "voluntarily" changed his abode affect the interest of what he has to tell us?

November 1976

European Notebook

Miracle in Milan

There was almost something "un-Italian" about the whole affair. It is very rare indeed that a journalist suddenly invades the precincts of traditional party management, announces himself as an independent, and manages to get himself elected as a senator who would defy the old Party machines. I found the successful candidate still writing his editorials here for the *Giornale Nuovo*. But it could be that the senator's voice was proving to be more decisive than the leader writer. It was Enzo Bettiza who persuaded a group of liberals in Rome to lend support to Andreotti's attempt to form a non-Communist government. That left only the neo-Fascists, the "Missini," on the negative side (and possibly because Andreotti, in a devious Roman maneuver, expressly demanded that Almirante say no); for the Left would never have benevolently abstained if the "Missini" had not been against. Is that complicated? He who would understand Italian politics has to begin with such simplicities. I find Bettiza, no simplistic spirit, an excellent guide through the Roman ideological jungle.

And how could he fail to be, being one of those sensitive outsiders: his Slav family was "Betica," a border-Italian consequently, and like many Dalmatians quite at home in Croatian, Slovene, and Italian. In the years he spent in Russia it was an obvious advantage. He published, as the correspondent of *La Stampa* (Turin), one of the very best books about the Soviet Union, a "Moscow Diary"; and indeed Ignazio Silone thought so highly of it he published most of it in his intellectual monthly, *Tempo Presente* (and how sorely is that journal missed these days!).

Bettiza has also written a novel, *The Ghost of Trieste*, which has since been translated, with success, in both West Germany and France; and even his first novel, composed shortly after his break with the Italian Communist Party in 1950, has now been reprinted.

A few years ago Bettiza was one of the central figures in the editorial breakaway from Italy's leading daily newspaper, the *Corrière della Sera*. They wouldn't go along with yet another change of line (this time towards the New Left); and he and Indro Montanelli organized a new daily. Who would have thought it could succeed? Everybody was compromising; trimming was the order of the day. Montanelli and Bettiza produced a daily paper of style and brilliance and—how rare in Western Europe today!—political integrity. Bettiza himself, formed by his own experiences of Communists (in the Party and in Eastern Europe), must surely be one of the few active figures in Italian public opinion who do not deem it "inevitable" that the Communists come to power. Bettiza's election as a senator was associated with a number of other surprising returns that put a group of other "Independents" into Roman parliamentary life. They are the knowledgeable ones on the scene. "After all," Bettiza says, "it was old Gramsci, in a fascist prison, who worked out the resourceful strategy, namely, to move forward not by storming the commanding heights but by taking over the cultural sector. And it is precisely here that we are gaining our own strength to resist—among the intellectuals, in the universities."

His national popularity was a curious accident. I have already reported here on that disgraceful episode in which the Italian Television crudely censored Andrey Sinyavsky's broadcast (*Encounter*, April). It was Bettiza who first called my attention to the bowdlerization which he had attacked in his *Giornale*. As the campaign mounted, the Italian "RAI" was forced to allow Bettiza to debate with Enzo Forcella on whether truth-telling or expediency was to prevail, whether the Italian right to free speech was to be trimmed and curtailed "even before the Communist Party has come to power"! Bettiza became a national figure; and perhaps it was what was called his "Montenegran toughness" that proved attractive. Who else was speaking up for traditional and hard-won liberties?

I talked to Bettiza in his Milan office. Isn't being a senator, then, a full-time job? Well, evidently he is still stealing a leaf from Gramsci's old notebook and securing his political strength in the cultural sector. He was putting the next day's *Giornale* to bed, going off to do a radio broadcast, and mailing to his publisher a long introduction to the collected works of Guidon Piovene. I am not so sure I understand this kind of tough-minded political animal on the Italian scene. Militant libertarians don't exactly grow on trees around here. In Rome the calculating courtiers of the "New Power" are already maneuvering to take their places. Small wonder that Enzo Bettiza's courage and independence is being called "Montenegran."

December 1976

European Notebook

Dictatorships and the EEC; Religion in America; French Elections

Europe's Mezzogiorno

For years now three dictatorial régimes in non-Communist Europe presented European democrats with an embarrassing problem. Reference to the East European dictatorships, imposed or supported by the Soviet Union, were countered by reference to "Portugal," "Spain," "Greece," whose rulers were on the best of terms with their common protector the United States as well as with some West European democracies. They belonged in different ways (two of them directly), to the Euro-American defense community known as NATO, of which two of them formed an integral part. Thus the neat contrast between Western freedom and Eastern oppression, true in general but not in detail, was spoilt by a *Realpolitik* that bore the amoral marks of cynicism.

The years have brought a piece of luck for the European idea Two of those dictatorships have been overthrown while the third, in Spain, is giving way to democracy. In Portugal an abrupt extremist change from one kind of dictatorship to another—based on an ideological military cadre and a minority Marxist party—was prevented. In this case West European democrats strongly committed themselves.

But the European democracies can claim no credit for the collapse of the compromising dictatorial regimes, and the Americans have even less right to do so (except, possibly, in the case of Greece, because of the naively with which they supported rather than prevented a suicidal adventure by the *Junta*). But it must be emphasized that leading economic circles as well as the people of those three countries looked increasingly towards the European Community. The realization that dictatorships could not become "members of the European club" played an important part in the erosion of those regimes.

These three strokes of luck for Europe have, however, presented the Brussels Commissioners and the Community governments with a whole complex of problems that they would much prefer to be without. By its expansion northwards the relatively close-knit community of the Six assumed tremendous burdens—Continental taxpayers are now financing a quarter of British food imports—and Southern Europe holds out a prospect of competition that is alarming to Italian and French farmers. Also Turkey, with a population increase of a million a year, is knocking at the door, and claiming unrestricted entry for all its jobless seeking work in all the community countries—a prospect deeply alarming to the West Germans.

Eurocrats and politicians are wondering here how much the Community can expand without bursting. How many nations with different economic structures and a much lower standard of living can it "integrate" without disintegrating? Just how much Mezzogiorno can it absorb? The Greeks, the Portuguese, and the Spaniards now point out that they need the "European model," the "solidarity" of the European democracies, if they are to survive in freedom. Were they not continually urged to liberalize and democratize themselves? They are now doing so. Should not the bargain be honored?

I am afraid it will be more and more necessary to make a fine distinction between European "solidarity" and European "integration." The first thing that this presupposes is a measure of un-habitual political imagination and some new initiatives on the part of the "Europeans." Is that too much to ask for, too much to hope? One can only ask, skeptically, worriedly, here in Brussels.

"I Love You!"

I am reminded here of the Goethan question: "Wie haelst Du mit der Religion?" (Where do you stand in regard to religion?) That question, put to Goethe's Faust, became proverbial. But no American Gretchen would ever have had to put it to a candidate for the U.S. presidency. On this last electoral occasion all of us, voters and onlookers alike, were far better informed on this theological matter than we were on the candidate's political plans. Jerry Ford is a conservative Episcopalian.

He adopted radical evangelism, and he has a son at a theological college. As for President-elect Jimmy Carter—his irresistible advance forced us to become experts on the Baptists, the Revivalists, the Faith Healers, et al. in the Old Bible Belt of the Deep South.

True, the present strong "revivalist movement" is the third or fourth such wave in recent American history. U.S. historians have recently been studying the relevance of "politics of faith," of millenarianism and messianism, from the Founding Fathers to Woodrow Wilson. In spite of Dr. Reinhold Niebuhr (whom Carter quotes in his book *Why Not the Best?*), articulate theology plays a much smaller part in American Protestantism than it does in Europe. For many years past "revivalist" preachers (from Dwight Moody to Billy Sunday to Billy Graham) have been among the most famous and successful Americans.

Behind Jimmy Carter's certainty of direct contact with the Almighty—he calls his prayers "talking to God," and feels that no monologue but a beneficent partnership is involved—there is a tradition which goes back more than three centuries.

But why is religion in America so much more strongly linked with "hot gospellers," with "speaking with tongues" and the sense of "rebirth" than it is elsewhere in the Western world? Is it more "Christian"? A hundred and forty years ago the nation's most celebrated interpreter, Alexis de Tocqueville, gave a great deal of space to religion in his book on *Democracy in America*. He regarded it as a necessity, and indeed an advantage. He also wrote: "Here and there strange sects arise that seek to open unusual paths to eternal bliss." And why? "If circumstances of social status did not tie the American spirit so closely to the search for prosperity, that spirit would show more reserve, experience and moderation when it concerned itself with nonmaterial things." In other words: materialism calls for mysticism. The two belong together.

Revivalist religion seems to radiate a sustained and inexhaustible love. "Rosalyn and I love you" were Carter's opening words at an election meeting in a small southern town. Is there a relationship between the religion of Revivalism and Love and such problematical movements as the sect of Moon or Hare Krishna? In one respect there is. What matters is less the content of a faith than a mood, a "good feeling," a sense of power and security. It is "faith in faith," because faith—any faith—moves mountains.

What do America's enlightened, critical intellectuals say to this? They are far from mocking the "revivalists" as Paris anti-clericals, for instance, ridicule French priests. They are not faced with the difficulties of ancient institutions and traditional compulsions, for here everything comes "spontaneously" from the People itself.

But can one, in the last analysis, quite overlook that one faith is not exactly equivalent to another? America's leading politicians used to be Puritans with a troubled sense of sin; and their Christianity was considered to be a "repressive inhibition." Now, I am told here, they are complex-free men who have been "reborn" and their Christianity is a happy self-confirmation.

Well, Goethe did once believe that "*Amerika, du hast es besser*," so one shouldn't wonder about the possible bewilderment of his Gretchen to the varieties of religious experience.

Kiss of Death

Under the fifth republic, becoming a member of the government automatically involves losing one's parliamentary seat. It is taken over by the "deputy" (or substitute) who is elected with every deputy. On resignation or dismissal from the government one calls on one's substitute to withdraw and submits oneself for reelection. Thus the switch from a Chirac to a Barre government forced seven under-secretaries of state to go to the hustings and find out whether they still enjoyed support.

Six of the seven survived the test. In the case of the seventh the substitute had made himself so popular that the constituency refused to let him go. For governing majorities to suffer such setbacks in mid-term by elections is normal; it happens to Socialists as it does to Conservatives. So why were these elections, which affected fewer than one per cent of the electorate (and in which the vote was far less than it is in a general election) felt to be a slap in the face for the president and leader of the majority?

Giscard d'Estaing's majority consists of two elements (1) the Gaullist *bloc*, which the dismissed Prime Minister Jacques Chirac (in the old Gaullist tradition) wants to turn back into a *rassemblement*—its forces gathered in Paris in December. And (2) right-wing, center and left-wing non-Gaullists out of whom the President and his Minister of the Interior Poniatowski would very much like to make a "counter-force." But, like many a Central American republic, these groups have more generals than soldiers, and an abundance of claims to leadership is not accompanied by any willingness to be led. That's the main trouble with the second *rassemblement*.

In these by-elections there were three highly topical and explosive questions. Let me enumerate them:

1. How was the national majority faring in relation to the opposition of the Socialists, leftwing Radicals, and Communists? The answer is: not very well. The Socialists increased their votes everywhere and gained one seat; in spite of many predictions, discipline between Socialist and Communist voters was rather well maintained.

2. How was Giscard's majority of reformers faring in relation to the Gaullists? Answer: badly. The only candidates who got through on the first ballot were the two Gaullists (including Chirac himself). When they entered the Chamber they were received with ovations, in which the Giscardists half-heartedly joined.

3. How was Giscard's own party, the Independent Republicans, faring in the non-Gaullist group? The answer is: disastrously. A member of that party who scraped home by a few hundred votes said after the first ballot: "What harmed me was my image as a friend of the President." The other Independent Republican was defeated. Once upon a time during the triumphal era of de Gaulle, the President's name was enough to ensure victory on the first ballot to hundreds of candidates who were often unknown in their constituencies. They flew into the Palais Bourbon on his coattails. President Giscard d'Estaing has no coattails. His friendship is what in American gangster films is called "the kiss of death." Is the new year beginning with the "twilight of Giscard"? I am afraid that his majority is "unionizing" itself apart. In view of its small popular margin it means that most of the disputants involved, incapable of "hanging together," will probably be hanging separately.

February 1977

European Notebook

Budapest's "October"; The Two Cultures; Nathalie Sarraute

Budapest's "October"

On that melodramatic first Saturday in November twenty years ago we drove back hectically from Budapest in the Buick that had been, more hopefully, hired in Vienna. Other journalists remained trapped in the Hungarian capital as the Red Army attacked.

There had been no room for us in the Hotel Duna (formerly the Bristol) where most of the foreign correspondents gathered. Instead we had put up at the Astoria which had been half destroyed in the first round of fighting (in October) that had led to the temporary Soviet withdrawal. An icy wind blew through the lobby and halls, and the usually so elegant hotel manager shivered in a sheepskin coat. A small altar (with a red cloth and four candles) commemorated the reception-clerk who had been killed. In the town centre the telephone wires were down and the rusting wrecks of tanks had bitter slogans written on them in red letters: *"This is Soviet Culture."* The Russians had carried away their own casualties; but dead bodies of AVO secret policemen were still hanging and rotting. Barricades had been built of overturned tramcars. At night there was no lighting in the streets, and nothing was open—unless open means accessible through smashed windows. (Yet nothing was stolen: there was no looting.)

A week later in Vienna I listened to the broadcast of the meeting of the United Nations at which the present French Foreign Minister, M. de Guiringaud, sharply condemned Soviet aggression. The Bulgarian representative declared, with some pathos, that it was the duty of the USSR to protect Hungary from the reactionary vandals who had actually destroyed the Red Army memorial. He prudently refrained from mentioning the gigantic statue of Stalin that had been toppled.

After that hectic dash to the West on the 3rd of November, our papers were cursorily checked by a Soviet patrol between Gyor and the Austrian frontier, but cars behind us were not allowed through. Tibor Dery, still the "grand old man of Hungarian letters" in Budapest, was then about to be condemned to a two-year prison sentence; and in Vienna I gave, as promised, his greetings to his friend Ernst Fischer who broke with the Communist Party—or, more correctly, it broke with him—only much later. (But he did at the time mumble something about already regretting the play in which he allowed Marshal Tito to strut on the stage as "a Fascist.")

I had spent many hours at the Hungarian Writers' headquarters, which happened to be next door to the Soviet Embassy. Indeed it acted as a kind of brains-trust for Prime Minister Imre Nagy. (Khrushchev later said: "If we had shot a dozen of them in advance, there would have been no counterrevolution....") I remember that on 1 November there was a long, detailed, and intense discussion about the form that some future literary journal was to take. Soviet troops were already surrounding the city; but I can remember no sense of premonition, only cheerfulness and optimistic plans for the morrow. Both Georg Lukàcs, the minister of culture, and the president of the Club, the peasant writer Peter Veres, were full of new projects, all to be informed by a free and new post-Stalinist spirit.

"We don't want to politicize ourselves completely," he surprised me by saying. "An author's right to silence on political questions is new and unprecedented, and must be defended!..." A peasant from the Gyor district (with dung-stained boots and a big file under his arm) interrupted: "I spent many, many hours at night working on this manuscript! It must be printed at once!" Veres explained that in the circumstances he must be patient.... But he only went and stood in a corner, sulking and muttering indignantly.

The dramatist Julius Hay—who spent a long time in prison and shared a cell with Tibor Dery, but was later allowed to emigrate (and died last year at Brissago on Lake Maggiore)—told me why he, an old Communist, had dared to raise his voice in criticism under the terrible Rakosi regime. It was not bravery at all. On the contrary, he said. "The young were indignant—they put irresistible pressure on us of the older generation— and we just had to raise our voices...." It was ironic humor, and it impressed me more than any of the standard bits of revolutionary rhetoric.

The term "People's Democracy" is of course a pleonasm, since demos means people. But it struck me in retrospect that if it means that "the masses" proclaim their will, express themselves, and act, we who were there experienced something at that time that otherwise is merely an empty phrase—ten days of people's democracy, in Hungary, twenty years ago.

The Two Cultures

It is almost two decades now since C.P. Snow launched, in *Encounter*, the debate about the two cultures with his pitying critique of literary men (and associated humanists) for being so ignorant of and indifferent to the methods and conclusions of the natural sciences. The ping-pong game of self-defense and counterattack has gone on, but some recent articles which I have been reading seem to me to offer a number of interesting new twists and turns.

One needs, as with one of his page-long sentences, a little time to catch up with the views of Isaiah Berlin, and in an essay which I just came across in a quarterly called *Salmagundi* (published by Skidmore College, Saratoga Springs, N.Y.) Sir Isaiah deals with the "great divide" between the social and the exact sciences. Why should these two great areas of human concern be called "cultures" simply because they deal with different questions by different methods? How sound is the Western tradition from Descartes to H. G. Wells (and B. F. Skinner) which has contended that anything outside the efforts of exact calculating thought was really only "words" and "illusions"? On the other hand we have the example of that old Neapolitan Giambattista Vico for whom the fables, the myths, and the metaphors were of the profoundest significance. Heidegger, not unlike Vico, also devised the strangest kind of etymology which found truths in the most unlikely verbal associations. The sounds of human voices in history needed to be listened to, pondered and studied, if more with the insights of an "experienced understanding" than with the techniques of sociological and psychological field-workers. Has, then, the Two Cultures debate been raging for centuries?

For Jean Fourastie it is the French intelligentsia who exhibit the most unfortunate shortcomings. In his critique (in Roger Callois' review *Diogène*, No. 75, 1976) his colleagues never quite saw either "truth" or "reality" whole, confused as they became in the mix of inherited rationalism, modish existentialism, and the habits of precise formulations leading to calculable solutions. But is science, in its experimentalism, truly "rational" in this sense? Doesn't it more often than not lead only to insights into insoluble problems? "The more we are taught about Man the less we seem to recognize him." Is, then, the way forward to more doubt and less certainty, more modesty and less self-confident pragmatism? One finds it curious that where for Sir Isaiah "rationality" is the essence of the natural sciences, for M. Fourastie it represents its greatest danger.

The battleground between "Skeptics and Believers" is worked over by William Nichols in an article in the *American Scholar* (Summer 1976) which deals with the intellectual infatuation with, indeed the "religion" of, Progress. Here too the echoes of the argument are old. Carlyle's essay on the Spirit of the Times (he was writing in 1829) warned against the Model of the Machine and its awful abstract implications for our ways of thinking. One of his critics a few years later put it to him (in an American declaration of faith): "We remain firm in our faith in the steadily increasing improvement of Mankind, and no small part of this faith is the result o f mechanical inventions." From Carlyle to Snow's furious critic, F. R. Leavis, there has been a century of anger against the possibilities of spiritual stagnation and even intellectual degradation in both art and philosophy as a result of such naive Scientific Religion. But is there not a problem here in the very nature of that "humanistic" outrage? Lionel Trilling once asked whether it was not in point of fact the combination of ignorance and uncertainty of the nonscientific intellectual, faced with exact and exacting mathematical methodologies, which led his unconscious into open cries of indignation. Shouldn't we, then, be skeptical of the Skeptics?

In the latest issue of the German *Historische Zeitschrift* (Munich), Richard Konetzke throws a skeptical glance at the historical development of certain scientific ideas in biology and the theory of Evolution. Evidently once-clear notions like "selection" have been overcast with shadows, and biologists have begun to study the literature of their own past for the "insights of experience." Not unlike poets and biographers they are turning to the problems of very human turning points and even to the traps of style and language. Didn't Charles Darwin confess in his autobiography that because of his strenuous scientific efforts he was no longer capable of reading Shakespeare with the pleasure that he did in his youth? This he felt to be a spiritual deprivation.

Perhaps it will be, not the sense of Snow-like guilt about intellectual indifference to the vast riches of scientific progress, but a shared sense of mutual impoverishment, that will lead to some reconciliation in the conflict of the Two Cultures.

Sarraute and the Master

It happened to be Nathalie Sarraute's seventy-fourth birthday, but she dislikes to be reminded of the occasion. After all she is still writing with all her wonted freshness, enthusiasm, and *élan,* and has even begun a new career as a dramatic writer for the stage. There is no "serenity of old age" here, as she moves yet again to the attack on the conformities of the life around her. Gallimard has just published her latest novel, entitled *"...dissent les imbeciles"—Fools Say.*

The theme is her familiar one of authority, domination, dissent. In *The Golden Fruits* (1963) it was the problem of opinion-forming literary coteries which can decide the success or failure of a novel, and her protest against their manipulation. This did not hinder one Paris critic from easily dismissing Mme. Sarraute's new work as just so much "knitting," with little strands of faded gossip holding together a "typically female" design.

But her world is far from being "little," although she examines it with minute attention as if under a microscope. It produces authentic horrors, and the storms she records are genuine storms and the damage is not easily set right. "Microbiology" is of first importance in the laboratory, and Nathalie Sarraute has for decades now been doing "micro-literature."

Her current theme, treated with considerable wit and sarcasm, is the rise and fall of the prestigious Personality. Language itself, is, of course, one of the keys to the whole vanity fair: phrases which destroy and new words which try to heal. As I read it I could not help wonder what the hapless European translators will make of the complex and subtle play with French clichés. Even the language of the great nameless Master in the background has to be deciphered—especially that little phrase in one of his polemical writings which gives the novel its title: that's only the way idiots talk. The Master was irritated by some disagreeable viewpoint, and instead of analysis and criticism he simply vulgarizes the argument and dismisses contemptuously its protagonists. This kind of dialectic implicitly assumes: I am very wise, as is well-known, and when I say that these are chattering morons, then that's the end of the matter (for that finishes them off and intimidates at the least any one else from being tempted by such nonsense).

But here, in a very Sarraute-like challenge, just that technique is rigorously questioned, and with it the whole system of vanities in the cultural world, the terrorism of fame and prestige, the empty-minded deference to a Master who is thought to represent intelligence at its brilliant best and thus by definition quite incapable of simply saying something stupid.

Or perhaps not. Awful ingredients of doubt begin to eat away at the living statue of the Master. And here I must record that apparently no one in all the French reviews I have read—and all those Paris reviewers know the complete polemical literature in question—has called attention to the fact that the "little phrase" of the title is actually a quotation from a famous put-down by Jean-Paul Sartre. In point of fact, Sartre, when pressed in an argument, very often discovers the ineffable idiocy of those with whom he disagrees. They become not thinkers to be earnestly considered, but mere figures of fun.

Well, in a way, in this novel the knife-like weapon has been turned the other way, and almost literally, for wasn't it Sartre's preface to her first novel which helped the author to her own fame and prestige? Nobody has dared to take on this Master on anything but his own terms: by the time the whole vast *oeuvre* has been mastered, and due respect for its quantity and quality offered, the critics can only take their stand on his home grounds. Here, at long last, one dissenter from the Master has felt free to step outside the framework and look at the whole picture. Every little swish of the brushwork is examined from the outside. Mme. Sarraute makes quite a drama and a farce of it.

Still I don't really see this as a roman à clef or even as yet another Paris polemic. The pleasure to be derived from this portrait of a Master—and one is even at times also reminded of, say, Jacques Lacan's famous punning—is quite independent of local Left-bank anecdote. Here is the linguistic power of critical semantics linked to the narrative entertainments of a novelist who seems to be renewing herself with the years. As in the work of Franz Hals, the last efforts take on a sovereign youthfulness.

March 1977

European Notebook

Le Canard Enchaîné; Murder in Rome

Public and Private

One evening M. Escaro, a member of the staff of *Le Canard Enchaîne*, happened to notice some strange plumbers at work in that journal's new offices in the Rue St Honoré. It turned out that they had not been repairing the pipes, but had been installing microphones in the chimneypiece; and the men were later identified as agents of the security service (DST). The latter, and the minister of the interior of the time, protected the four men concerned, who refused to appear for a confrontation in the chambers of Judge Bernard. Because of "reasons of state," the forces of law and order were unable to compel them to do so. Had there been a similar relationship between the executive and the machinery of justice in the United States, the Watergate "plumbers" would never have had to confess.

Now, three years after the affair, which caused a great sensation, Judge Pinsseau (Judge Bernard's successor) has dismissed the journal's action at a hearing held at a date that very nearly prevented the plaintiff from appealing. In the hope of depriving them of this opportunity; all the usual practices (e.g., previous consultation between the lawyers) were omitted. Judge Pinsseau's reasons for dismissing the action deserve to be permanently recorded in the annals of justice—they remind one of the story of the broken jug which, in the first place, the borrower never received and, in the second place, was broken beforehand in any case.

First of all, the judge held that in the absence of a confrontation no one could be personally charged with the offense; then, on the other hand, he held that no offense had been committed. This for two remarkable reasons. For one thing, the penal code did not exist "to protect buildings even from violent measures"—those were his words—and M. Escaro had just happened to be passing by and was not using the premises for professional purposes. For another, it was obvious that "journalists in editorial offices conducted only political, general, or professional conversations"; hence there could be no trespassing on their "private sphere" by secret telephone tapping. After this judgment it is clear that journalists in newspaper offices never discuss private matters either among themselves or on the telephone, and that any discussion of political, general or professional matters can legitimately be tapped. This would seem finally to have disposed of the awkward problem of the "agents" who had to be protected.

There is an argument on the other side that deserves to be noted. A journal such as *Le Canard Enchaîné* is not exactly bashful about publishing details about the private lives of individuals in the public eye. Why, then, should it make such a fuss if, for once, it is itself the object of indiscreet inquiries?

But so far neither the government nor any private individual has brought a successful action against *Le Canard* for an infringement of secrecy or of the private sphere. An "abyss of treason"— to use Dr. Adenauer's phrase in connection with the famous *Spiegel* case—has never been attributed to it.

True, the private sphere is a vague term. I note in one authoritative text, "what belongs to that sphere can be stated neither in general nor once and for all." Secret tapping of conversations in French newspaper offices does not apparently count as an infringement of that sphere. Not only the press will anxiously await the outcome of the appeal.

French judges recently complained of the public announcement by the police and the Minister of the Interior of the guilt of certain persons accused of murder before they had even been charged by an examining magistrate. This was indeed extremely shocking. But how can Judge Pinsseau credibly take offense at any governmental irregularity?

Italian "Western"?

Somebody who saw the young man collapse as he was shot by the storekeeper shouted, "But that's Re Ceccone!" It was indeed the famous young football star, idol of the Roman fans of the Lazio team. One sensation followed the other. Now the jeweler who killed the Lazio *"calciatore"* (he leaves a widow with two children) has been acquitted of murder.

The cries are loud of "Class Justice"—a jeweler can fire at will and pay no penalty. But, as I follow the story, it reminds one of the classic Japanese film in which the tragedy appears differently from each differing personal perspective. The Italian district attorney saw a trigger-happy "bourgeois self-made-man" and "upstart" who, when he spotted a long-haired *"cappelloni,"* reached for his pistol. Why was he armed anyway? "He simply wanted to get rid of chaps who were different."

It appears to be true that Bruno Trabocchini, our jeweler, reached quickly for his sidearm. Once he fired some warning shots at a *"scippatore"* who was running away with a woman's handbag (he thought it was his wife who was being victimized). What was Trabocchini's defense? *"Ho famiglia!"*—the reply of every Italian in trouble. After his acquittal he sold his jewelry shop and left Rome. It was said that he feared the revenge of the Lazio sporting club, which had actually put in a legal claim for compensation for the loss of the athletic services of a soccer star. Luciano Re Ceccone was a fellow of infinite jest, and when he and a friend barged into Trabocchini's shop and shouted "Hands up, this is a stick-up!" he was knocked off in a blink of an eyelash.

Of course it was a stupid joke, especially in a city where shopkeepers, with or without jewels in glass cases, have been robbed left and right. It could be that football stars allow themselves special bits of theatricality because they think they have faces with instant recognizability. And why shoot at all? Was the jeweler not adequately insured against all possible losses? Even if it had been a real robbery it wouldn't have ruined him. Was it, perhaps, a case of self-defense? "But," thundered the district attorney, "we aren't in the Wild West (*in un paese di frontiera*)!"

This was probably a bit much, for he failed to convince the court in Rome. Can a shopkeeper, and especially one with diamonds in the window, ever feel unthreatened? A few days after the tragic incident in Rome I noted the report in a newspaper of the murder of a jeweler named Candido Bressan in San Giovannia Lupatoto near Verona who had, on command, quickly put up his hands and handed over the loot. On the day of Trabocchini's acquittal I saw another news item about a shooting in a Turin furrier's shop; the victim was a poor girl who had come to serve the morning espresso. It would seem that not only Clint Eastwood in the so-called "spaghetti Westerns" shoots at the drop of a hat. This morning I see that two young Italian policemen were shot at an Autostrada control point.

It happens to be my impression, for what it is worth, that the so-called villains of the "Class Justice" system—the judges, the policemen, the prison wardens—are less repressive than simply intimidated. Beware of out-dated slogans in trying to understand Italy today! The notion that a shopkeeper ought to understand a joke and not always think of self-defense (because, after all, "Italy is not in the Wild West")—Well, the realities are rather different.

April 1977

European Notebook

Alain Peyrefitte; Death of Prince de Broglie

Evil Thoughts

In one of his recent press conferences the French president called attention several times to a new book which had become one of the nation's best-sellers, although its pessimism in the analysis of old French difficulties is in sharp contrast to the official optimism. The author of *Le Mal Français* is a former minister and was once the general-secretary of the Gaullist Party; his previous best-seller was a book on the awakening of China, based only on a short trip and quick research. So how much expertise can one expect from Alain Peyrefitte?

When he was minister of information, an Orwellian job that most Western democracies hesitate to create, the country was not exactly deluged with fresh facts about thorny issues and grievous problems. He also had the bad luck to be the minister of education during the "May Troubles" of 1968 and was one of its first victims. Expecting only a feeling for anecdotes and an irrepressible cleverness, the reader is quite surprised by *Le Mal Français*. No doubt about it, it is an important document, compiling as it does—and with some drama and tension—incident after incident of political life at the Top, illustrating inertia, willfulness, waste, arrogance on the part of the mighty who were otherwise quite honest and intelligent public servants. The pages on the seven-year struggle to push through a long-needed statute governing work in the French clay-pits (it was finally won by a devious "blackmail" manoeuvre using the budget of the Education Ministry) is a hair-raising account of Paris maladministration and will take its place in the history of French governmental scandals.

It is all very much of an "inside" story. On 15 April 1962 Peyrefitte was led into his office by his predecessor, Christian de la Malene, and briefed on the various buttons and bells: how to ring for the butler, the *chef du cabinet*, the director of the French TV, the editor of the TV News, the head of the Radio bulletins. "At five o'clock you will be giving them all their instructions and guide-lines...." Soon Peyrefitte, as he tells it, found himself part of the system against his own will, shaping each day the French picture of the news of the world.

I was struck by the fact that Peyrefitte refers, always favorably, to Herbert Luethy's old classic analysis of French evils, *Frankreichs Uhren gehen anders* (1954), and I can recall that at the time even Raymond Aron, who was responsible for its being published in his Calmann-Levy "collection," thought the sharpness excessive and the pessimism outdated. Over two decades later a piece of French self-criticism is not dismissed as "anti-French masochism" but evidently welcomed as a patriotic act from a member of the Paris establishment. Reform tendencies among the powers-that-be are not exactly widespread, but the Peyrefitte book conforms the diagnosis of the reformers, and is consequently more than a best-selling title: it is a political act with a dash of old-time Gaullist energy about it but closer in content to the new "giscardism."

Death of a Prince

Evidently the murder of Prince Jean de Broglie did him a good deal of harm. No soldiers were dispatched to carry his coffin, only firemen turned up. Three ministers and the president of Parliament, Edgar Faure, failed to show at the last minute because of "the weather," namely a flurry of snow. There were precious few "last honors" for the Prince de Broglie at his funeral in the Norman village of Broglie. After all he had been minister several times, was a Paris deputy, a member of the European Parliament, and on the board of directors of some forty-two companies. And on the historic family tree there were three marshals, a prime minister, two famous physicists, as well as branches which featured Mme. de Staël as well as Rothschilds. The village of Broglie buried its mayor in the presence of his widow and three sons.

Once he had the glory of the successful French diplomat who had negotiated the recognition of Algeria at the Evian conference. Then came a certain coolness from both Pompidou and Giscard d'Estaing as he became a businessman with suspected deals in Middle East armaments. But the circumstances of his death put paid to the ancestral aura of distinction. It happened on a Paris street, the rue des Dardanelles, in front of No. 2, a house in which two very shady characters, Allenet de Ribemont and Pierre de Varga, continued to reside although they had more than once faced fraud-squad inquiries and police arrest. What was the nature of their "complex" business deals?

The name of a chief police inspector, Guy Simone, was found in all three address books. Who had been protecting him over a long career in the police (which, strangely enough, had no file on him) marred by serious charges of attempted murder and other suspicions? When Simone was arrested he was drinking champagne with two underworld characters; and he promptly confessed "everything," although his friends in the rue des Dardanelles quickly denied "everything." At this point Prince Poniatowski, the minister of justice, made up his mind; and blithely ignoring all the great traditions of innocent until-proven-guilty he announced the names of all the guilty ones. M. de Ribemont has meanwhile been released from custody.

What was quite clear for the minister of justice was neither clear nor proper. As the details of Jean de Broglie's financial machinations came to light in a network knotted by cheap hoodlums and hit-men, one couldn't help thinking of at least the title of that Balzac novel: *A Shadowy Affair.*

"Let us have an end to the Republic of scoundrels and accomplices!" This was once Poniatowski's warning cry to the Gaullists. More Balzacian light on this shadowy affair will have political as well as criminological implications. I suppose that those brilliant artists of family trees, France's genealogists, will also be troubled, for *"Noblesse oblige"* was not exactly the motto of the life and death of this Prince de Broglie. I have just looked again at Larousse where there are pictures of at least five of his illustrious ancestors. Who will come forward to explain how he died shabbily on a Paris side street and why he was buried in his ancestral village in disgrace?

May 1977

European Notebook

Boris Souvarine; "Gambizzazzione"; "Execution" in Turin; On the French Left

Boris Souvarine

"The Hitlers come and go..." was once Stalin's refrain about a dictator who ruled only twelve years and departed unmourned. The *Vozhd* of Moscow made his exit in triumph, and even in the *Times* of London and the *New York Times* there were, as I recall, praise for certain "undeniable achievements" and reports of saddened masses in tears. Whole sectors of European intellectual life, vaguely brought up on Christian ethics, Athenian reason and logic, Voltairean enlightenment, needed a Nikita Khruschchev to open their eyes to hard facts and horrid realities. In Paris I counted the years before a Maurice Thorez came around to some grudging acceptance of the fact that millions (and not a few loyal Bolsheviks) had, been so needlessly sacrificed. And even Jean-Paul Sartre in those days was rather cross with Khruschchev for suddenly having induced a "crisis of faith": the masses (including Sartre himself) were not quite "ready" for it.

When, then, is a mind "ripe" for reality, ready for harsh truths? Of all the biographies of Stalin, purporting to tell the story of the October Revolution, the Building of Socialism, etc. etc., there is one which—written in the 1930s—is bound up with this whole problem of the strange timetable of the breaking of illusions. I refer to Boris Souvarine's *Staline*, and it has just been republished by "Editions du Champ libre" with revisions and additions by the author. Souvarine, now eighty, was one of the founders of the French Communist Party and the Communist International, and had, as a young man, dealings with Lenin himself. If history is full of tricks and cunning passages, what in any man's life can match the publication of this book at a moment when the "*nouveau philosophes*," a group of bright and earnest young Paris intellectuals, suddenly discover the real meaning of Stalin and Lenin which had been so bitterly and memorably recorded forty years before in his own book?

What ironies there are in the current reception! The new edition is hailed by Pierre Daix who in the 1940s had instituted legal proceedings against David Rousset...for having claimed that there were concentration camps in the USSR! *Le Monde*, too, where Souvarine for decades was referred to only polemically and contemptuously, is full of praise. All at once a prophet is given honor in his own land—the "embittered," "emotional," "subjective" anti-Communist is seen to be an objective scholar whose book, had they only been able to bring themselves to read it with open eyes, would have spared them so much heartache—and mental anguish.

In his new preface, Boris Souvarine recalls that the publication of his book had originally been rejected by Gallimard on the advice of none other than André Malraux! As he told a friend of the author, "You may be right, Souvarine, but might is not on your side...."[1]

How much, then, of ideology in our time has been a matter of power and not of persuasion? I note in Bertolt Brecht's recently published diaries that he had actually read Souvarine's biography of Stalin shortly after its first publication. He still went on in later years to write a poem about Stalin the great Farmer who was instituting a magnificent agricultural revolution. Mankind may, as the English poet said, be only able to take just a little bit of reality; the ideologists of the Left of our age—how many famous names are numbered among them!—were often unable to take any reality at all. It is good that Boris Souvarine is still alive to remind us all of that grotesque spectacle of intellectual self-deception.

"Gambizzazione"

I never fail to be astonished by the dark vitality of the Italian political vocabulary. As *Encounter* readers know from my previous fascination with the new semantic variations—"Strumentalizzazione," "Egemonizzazione," "Caotizzanione" (see "European Notebook," November 1975), one always runs across new words that are ingeniously expressive and quite unenviable. A man called Publio Fiore, who was a Christian Democrat in the local Rome authority, was the fortieth victim of the "Red Brigades" whose terrorist program (at least up till then) was to shoot their political enemies in the legs. There is now a new word for just that *"gambizzazione."* In this way they have crippled journalists, local officials of the governmental party, and persons in the Catholic movement (which, to be sure, didn't stop them from adding insult to injury by wrecking headquarters and meeting places). I was interested to note today that even one of the Communist Senators, who happened to be the Party's specialist for police affairs, conceded that the terror from the Left (i.e., from the *"autonomi"*) had now exceeded that which had come from the Fascist Right. Whoever had suspected that had, in the past, been always denounced as a "reactionary."

Consequently, the whole attitude of only yesterday to the "Repressive State" in Italy is changing. Now there is serious concern on the Left, among Socialists and Communists, about the police not being efficient enough in tracking down the extremists in their lairs.

I am struck here by the difference between the Italian and the German extremists. The West German gangs go after "leading personalities" in an attempt to "smash" the "corridors of power." In Italy the tactic of the *brigatisti* was to "execute" (as they prefer to put it, in their "non-repressive" vocabulary) figures in the middle levels of government and administration, to "mete out justice" to those "little men" who don't command special police protection. There is method in the murderous madness; for it does in its chaotic way make for a systematic paralysis of the administration and the economy. Needless to say, none of the victims are in any way persons about whom the Working Class has been agitated. The terrorist gangs speak ideologically in the name of the Proletariat, but they have never taken the trouble to find out what the men and women in the factories actually feel and think. The boys (and girls) with their itchy fingers on the triggers in Italy come, of course, mostly from the middle class of students. The Italian high schools and universities have—the trend is roughly the same everywhere in the West—taken on a third more students than they could ever possibly deal with. Even the best of marks and degrees do not guarantee a job. The usual grades, inflated and meaningless, are quite ignored, as the "academic lumpenproletariat" grows.

I am surprised that so many of my friends among the foreign correspondents in Italy take so calm and cool a view of the raging violence in Italy. I note that Peter Nichols of the (London) *Times* finds much that is remarkable in the Italian situation: tolerance, flexibility, a capacity for adjustment. Even the piece from Rome in the *Financial Times* today sounds positively jolly: "It should not be forgotten that Italy has a long tradition of absorbing traumatic shocks and adapting itself to changes and conditions, without losing either its basic humanity or its many other national characteristics in the process...."

This kind of attitude does not impress many Italians I meet here, for example Rosario Romeo, the well-known historian. Not the "humanism" of the national tradition preoccupies him, but rather the habits of violence—doing it, and accepting it—mark the present period, as it did in the past those Southern regions where the Mafia held sway. As a professor he feels very acutely the disappearance of the "little" democratic liberties that foreigners tend to overlook, as if forests were not made of individual trees. Professors have been already driven so far that they must now submit their writings to special Student Committees who function as—naturally, it's all "non-repressive"—boards of censors. I did not find among writers and intellectuals and academics here that light-spirited attitude toward Italian affairs that European (and American) publications take so easily. I found fear, and anxiety about violence, and concern about beastly everyday illiberal pressures; and that too—for all the confidence in the survival-qualities of the old vaunted Italian character—should be recorded.

"Execution" in Turin

I wrote too soon. The sharpshooters of the Red Brigades, noteworthy in the recent period for their *"gambzzazione,"* have now been aiming higher. The death today here in Turin of the deputy editor of *La Stampa* is a murderously cruel new turn. They obviously shot to kill. He was hit by four bullets in the head, and the Red Brigade communiqué prided itself on having executed (*giustiziato*) a "slave of the State." But for some two weeks there was some hope that the sixty-one-year-old Piedmontese journalist, who had had such a sturdy career in the mountains as an anti-Fascist member of the Resistance, could be saved. He died after thirteen days of agony.

What had been happening only yesterday was still a kind of limited war; this is the new phase of the terror. It had already been announced in an earlier series of warnings when the armed terrorists fired only at their victim's legs: "If this doesn't have any effect, we'll be aiming higher...." Perhaps this wasn't taken seriously enough. One is no longer surprised at the plots from the Right; and I note this week the death of a young Communist at the hands of the neo-Fascists. But murder on the Left has a peculiar aura about it. Many do not want to believe it, register it, or face up to it. Normal police power, exercised in almost every other Western country (except, possibly, the similarly complex-ridden Bonn Republic), are denounced here as "revivals of the Police State." One hears the argument here (as in Western Germany) that "this is exactly what the terrorists want...they want us to become Law & Order characters...we shouldn't give them the satisfaction...."

The editor in chief of *La Stampa* issued an appeal here the other day to Italy's intellectuals to draw the line clearly against terrorism of every stripe; but there was a protesting dissent from the well-known novelist, Leonardo Sciascia (also writing in *La Stampa*), who argued to the effect that there were simply no such "intellectuals" for surely intellectuals are by definition persons who want to understand and to serve only the truth....

I could not help recalling the words of yet another Italian writer—Ignazio Silone—made at a meeting some thirty years ago of the International P.E.N. in Basel who pointed out, with the simple dryness that is his style, that intellectuals have never been seen to have either a higher morality or a firmer character than any other social group, and that he rejected the notion of some special "collective patriotism" of the literary class.

The impression should not, of course, be left that Carlo Casalegno was the first to be "executed" (read: murdered). The seventy-year-old president of the Turin Bar association, Fulvio Croce, as well as the Genoa public prosecutor, Francesco Coco, has also been assassinated. If one is analyzing tactics one can, I suppose, point out that these two had something to do with the "Red Brigades," having been involved in various trials of captured terrorists. Casalegno was a journalist. As it happened his involvement with the Red

Brigades extended to the bitter fact that his own son was a member of the extreme Left! After the attack on Casalegno the extreme-Left paper *Lotta continua* published a long interview with Casalegno's son. He made the point that although his father was indeed a "reactionary," the old man was a decent person and had an honest character, and it was quite barbarous not to see human beings in a human perspective. One could only wonder whether the young man on the occasion of the other "executions"—other people's fathers—also managed a "human perspective."

I have looked up Carlo Casalegno's last article in *La Stampa* which he wrote on 30 September. "Our Italian experience has taught us that for all the criminality of terrorism it has a limited political impact so long as public opinion doesn't give in to panic or authoritarian temptations...." Yet the fact remains that the terrorists, with some additional bases among the Turin factory workers and facing only a weak badly-paid and ill-trained police force, are having rather a free run of things. The Italian editorials I have seen are courageous and have a noble ring about them—"some of us will fall, and other democrats will take their place..."—but can strength of personal character make up for the weakness of the basic institutions? Even the strongest of men are helpless where the state is ineffective.

On the French Left

It is now more than a half a century since the camp of the French Left split into two. The date was 29 December 1920, and from that time on the ranks of the militants have been confused and divided by raging polemics between Socialists and Communists, not without a certain satisfaction to the moderate and conservative forces of the nation.

Jean Jaurès, the Socialist leader of the prewar period, had been murdered in 1914 (and one recalls that it was his widow who had to bear the costs of the trial which had acquitted his rightwing extremist assassin). And from that time onward— to the bourgeois figure of François Mitterrand who, in five recent years, managed to forge out of tiny factions a Socialist Party which is the largest force in France—there was only one outstanding personality in the Socialist leadership: Léon Blum. I have just been reading in the new Blum biography by Jean Lacouture the account of that historic split in Tours. Moscow had set out some twenty-one conditions in order to give the new Third International a Bolshevik party line, and it was Blum who rejected them with the words:

> The quarrel is not between a reformist and a revolutionary interpretation, but between two very different views of revolution. There is a fundamental difference between Socialism and what the emerging Communism will be. Some of you will want to go along with this new party with the notion that it will later be amenable to change. This is an illusion. We are being confronted with a power that is too strong, too coherent, and too stable to allow for modifications....

His conclusion of 1920 was pessimistic:

As of tomorrow we will be divided. But will we thereafter be denouncing each other, before the eyes of the bourgeoisie, as traitors, renegades and madmen? Or will we be capable at least of conceding a certain amount of good will to each other?

Thirty years later Léon Blum was dead, and what did we find in his obituary as printed in the Communist Party's *L'Humanité*? That Blum, who had after all been the father in 1936 of France's modern social legislation, was nothing but "an accomplice of the bourgeoisie and of imperialism." The anecdote is told by the historian, Professor Annie Kriegel, that a Paris trolley-car conductor could not conceal his joy at the news of Blum's death and kept ringing his bell as he drove through the avenues and boulevards.

In Tours, in 1920, some three-quarters of the delegates voted for the Bolshevik line. Only a minority decided to stay in the "old house." It was only in the period after 1934 that the two historic parties of the French Left found their way to a political alliance. Then too the Socialists were the stronger, and the platform was also called the *"Programme commun."* Still, the Communists rejected the offer to participate in the new Government. As Maurice Thorez put it, the Party would only take over the "Ministry of the Masses." The tactic was clear: the Communists would take credit for all the achievements, and blame the government of Leon Blum for all the shortcomings.

The recent expectation of a victory of the Left has once again pushed the Socialists forward into the strongest position. If the vote is no longer to be a mere radical protest but an installment of new political forces, then the Socialists appear to be the more plausible candidates. More and more the Communists found themselves in crisis and seemed to be the "losers" in the coming victory of the Left. France is not Italy. It is one thing for the "Party of the Proletariat" to come to historic compromises with the "Party of the Bourgeoisie." It is quite another to appear to be losing one's working-class legitimacy to another Party of the Left. Berlinguer can make it, where Marchais simply loses too much face to the Social Democracy.

I must underline that it was not exactly "Social Democracy" that François Mitterrand had been preaching; he is still too much part of the old revolutionary French rhetoric which even trapped so civilized a statesman as Leon Blum. But this is the direction into which Mitterrand has been propelled, as he points to a Swedish model of "social progress in freedom." Has he, then, become what he has always refused to acknowledge—a Social Democrat? For the Communists at least he has now taken over the mantle of the hated Blum. In any case, it is an historic change, which in the perspective of a half-century of the French political Left, is, I think, of great importance.

February 1978

Note

1. The book had been recommended for publication by Brice Parain and Georges Bataille, to whom Malraux said, "Je pense que vous ares raison, vous, Souvarirte et vos amis, mats je serai aver vous quand vous serez le plus forts."

    It was the regrettable intervention of the late Bernard Groethuysen, a famous historian, whom I often saw in Paris in the 1940s, that stopped the project.

Prize Winners

"There is no collective in the city or the country, no far-away team of geological prospectors in the Taiga, no merchant ship on the seas or isolated village in the mountains where the books of Leonid Brezhnev, *Little Land* and *The Reconstruction* are not read and re-read and studied again, as inexhaustible sources of thoughts and ideas...."

So wrote *Pravda* about the Lenin Prize-winning author (one imagines the award was unanimous and that there was no other candidate). Like Stalin in his time, he embodies certain unique qualities of political infallibility and literary genius, at least so long as he lives and holds supreme command. Has any author's works—not surely since Mao Tse-tung's *Little Red Book*—been so systematically praised and distributed for the hundreds of millions? Possibly with this difference—that they do not, in these more enlightened days, need necessarily to be actually read, or recited out loud or waved in the air, for it is quite enough that they be available everywhere as a kind of documentation of the omnipresence of the great and powerful man.

In point of fact the material involved consists only of two thirty-page-long articles that originally were published in the Moscow journal, *Novy Mir*. As Victor Nekrassov has pointed out (and he himself is also a Lenin Prize winner), it was in the same *Novy Mir* that, after Khrushchev gave his official permission, Solzhenitsyn's first novel, *A Day in the Life of Ivan Denisovich*, had appeared. The wind blew differently in those days, but also with storm-like intensity. Poor unfortunate Pierre Daix in Paris, still worried about the feelings of old Stalinists like Maurice Thorez, had to submit to pressure from the Soviet ambassador to complete his translation of *Denisovich* with more dispatch!

The liberal posture then reinforced the new anti-Chinese line—for surely all the "European cultures" had something in common with each other that was foreign to the "barbarian," "totalitarian" China—what a strange and revolting cult was this adoration of the work of Mao! And now comes a new cult, at least for the time being, of the literary works of yet another Marxist-Leninist genius. If the vaunted "Dialectic" of historical materialism has still any intellectual uses, then it might explain away such contradictions and perhaps "transcend" them.

Am I, in worrying about such facets of East-West literary life, succumbing to "Cold War" prejudices? Why isn't it possible for a powerful politician, even a dictator, to be a good writer and a genuinely popular author? Remember Marcus Aurelius, think of some of the Indian Moghuls; yes, indeed, rulers and despots have been masters of prose. Why not Leonid Ilyich? But in the prose is the answer. The prose is the man, and the man is not a sovereign force above and beyond the State bureaucracy but is only a part of that vast gray apparatus, and reflects its style, ambitions, and utter grayness. The members of the Lenin Jury, which awarded the prize, needed no long-sessions to discuss and evaluate. They knew only too well the vanities of the new ruling class and its elite figures, their literary longings, their penchant for prizes, their dreams of longevity and ubiquity.

It is a kind of Byzantism, but it hardly pervades all of the literary sector; quite the contrary. The poet Andrei Voznesensky has also been given prizes and distinctions, enjoys special privileges, and may well be read in the Taiga by wandering geologists. Yet there is a deep difference between politicians in literature, and litterateurs in politics. The game is played differently. In the struggle over the recent anthology, *Metropol*, prose and poetry pieces collected by a number of leading Soviet writers on non-political but still critical themes in everyday Russian life, the power-political scene takes on unusual colors. Here members of the elite are not out to acquire more medals but are willing to take chances and put their privileges at risk. Some of the *Metropol* authors, like Voznesensky, and Aksyonov, and Iksander, have had their books and plays and films postponed, their royalties suspended, their trips abroad cancelled. They in turn have threatened resignation from the Writers Union—meaning virtual unemployment—if some of the younger and unknown writers are punished for daring to write as they pleased. The boss of the Moscow Writers' Union has called the *Metropol* anthology nothing less than "*pissoir*-literature," and now no Soviet ambassador is pressing anybody abroad to hurry up with their translations for the greater glory of a "European" (i.e., non-Chinese) Russian literary spirit. Still, the anthology is being translated at the moment into a number of foreign languages, as if to document another kind of omnipresence, the non-conformist spirit seeking a voice of its own.

Powerful governments and powerless writers make a curious combination. Ambitious politicians intrude on the literary scene; ambitious writers step on political toes. Once, when he was locked up in a prison he knew not where, after a trial he couldn't remember, Lukács (it was just after the Hungarian Revolt of 1956) changed his mind and remarked that "Kafka is, after all, a socialist realist! ..." Brezhnev as a Great Writer suggests that novels like *The Trial* should be written only by prosecuting attorneys and *The Castle* only by those who actually live in regal dachas behind high walls. Kafkas are unpersons.

August 1979

Between Frost and Thaw

Two leading Soviet ideologists, Comrades Ponomaryov and Sagladin, were present in St-Ouen at the Twenty-Third Congress of the French Communist Party, and this appeared symptomatic for the newly established harmony between Marchais and Moscow. Relations between French Communists and their big brothers in the USSR had been slightly strained, but in no way comparable to the cool distance and even icy critical exchanges between the Soviet party and the Italian party, which under Enrico Berlinguer, has been talking for years about "openings" and "revision" and "European unity" and even "pluralistic democracy."

Under the leadership of Maurice Thorez the French party was markedly more Stalinist than the Italian; and when it made its break—the French rather military term for it is *"Détachement"*—the Italian post-Stalinist period was quite different from the uncompromising Gallo-Communist nationalism of the French comrades. True, in his five-hour conference speech Georges Marchais made a point of not pronouncing "Euro-Communism" to be dead; still, the major emphasis was on the renewed accord with the Soviet bloc of Communist states.

So can one now conclude that Moscow has reestablished its control or "leading influence" on a powerful West European movement? And is it true, as the dissident ideologist Jean Elleinstein put it, that "an ice age" has replaced "the thaw"? (These metaphors irritated the leadership so much that innumerable references were made to them in St-Ouen and in *L'Humanité*).

Against the onset of a new "frost" there had been the warnings of several hundred intellectuals, in old Party magazines, in newly-established reviews, even in the bourgeois media; but there was little left of this "contestation" when the well-oiled machinery of the Party got into gear. What could a few unhappy French writers on the Left do against the stalwart and confident forces of some "70,000 professional activists and 12,000 loyal intellectuals," to whom Marchais proudly referred? None of the heretics was expelled; they were all simply overwhelmed.

Still, the new "iciness" is not of Russian or Siberian provenance, but French; and indeed the rapprochement with the Moscow Central Committee was possibly not even the essence of it. What was it then? Let us remember that when

Georges Marchais took over the leadership of the party— Roland Leroy was a strong hopeful in those days, and he is now no longer on the secretariat of the Central Committee—the Communists were everywhere stronger than the Socialists on the French Left. After Marchais' policy of a "Common Program," after his strong unconditional support of François Mitterrand in the presidential elections, traditional popular support for the CP waned, and the SP grew. The Communists were no longer in the forefront. The stronger the general Left became, the weaker its particular Communist sector.

Marchais was quick and energetic to draw the consequences, and with such élan that he was able to maintain his personal leadership, despite the obvious failures, and indeed even to strengthen it. No small political achievement! Working against him was (in the slangy phrase) "Comrade Frust"— the frustration and disappointment widespread on the Left—and also "Comrade Frost," the old ice-cold dogmatists who, with Leroy, had been against any kind of innovation or renewal. Marchais manoeuvred brilliantly; and even Professor Pierre Juquin, who had publicly supported the various dissidents, has now been included in the top leadership. All in all, in my view, what has happened is not so much a submission to Moscow as a reconsolidation of a battered movement, which can now continue its old tactic of watchful waiting.

August 1979

Terror Targets

That old slogan of Mussolini's *"Vivere pericolosamente!"* (Live Dangerously!) still has relevance for many sectors of Italian life, and perhaps none more so than in Padua academic community. Early in the spring there were the elections to the student assembly, and the participation—some 6,000 out of 60,000—is considered fairly high. Taken together, the liberal and the Catholic elements had about half of the vote, with the Left running behind at 34 percent. Then all hell broke loose. Dons and professors who had emphasized the importance of standing up and being counted were set up to be knocked down. It is not un-dangerous to take a clear position against the preachers of "Terror" and the excesses of the *"Autonomi."*

The automobile of a psychology don was set on fire, followed by more arson against the vehicles of a professor of agriculture and a philosopher. On 14 March a bomb went off in the flat of yet another faculty member. The "pressure" proceeded apace, and even escalated: Professor Guido Petto was given a savage beating with iron rods; and it was with wooden clubs that the dean of the literary faculty, Ottone Longo, while waiting for a bus, was knocked to the ground by two masked attackers who left him with a broken arm and serious head wounds.

This kind of terror is no longer a "clandestine" activity, and the *"Autonomi"* groups are guise public. Like the solid 120-page journal *Controinformazione*, with its editorial address in Milan, the magazine *Autonomia* is available in the Padua bookshops and has a circulation of some 5,000 copies. Nor is there anything secret about the so-called "Radio Sherwood" (as if Padua was a forest teeming with Robin Hoods) run by Emilio Vesce, who has now been arrested. The polemical targets are not only in academe but also in the working-class movement, and the attacks are steady against the villainous activities of the Italian trade unions. Indeed they appear to be completely surrounded by pernicious enemies, and their advertising slogan is, " Whoever doesn't read *'Autonomia'* is either a priest or a spy!" It is almost as if a subscription would be protection against the widespread violence of the hit men—and they always justify the tactic of leg-shootings (what used to be called *"gambizzazione,"* and is now called *"azzoppamento,"* from *"zoppicare,"* to limp, for the rationale is that it is all preparing for "the period of mass action.")

After all, Marxist theory usually takes a dim view of the assassin's "petty-bourgeois individualism" and insists on the "responsible controls" of a mass movement. In this the *"Autonomi"* are rather more in the traditional revolutionary line than are the more extreme factions like the *"Brigate Rosse"* and *"Prima Linea."*

Still, the struggle is not all one-sided. Rome, still on the trail of the Aldo Moro kidnappers and .killers, has now struck in Padua with the arrest of the professor of law, Antonio Negri. He may or may not be connected with the Moro murder, but he was one of the most eloquent of the ideologists who inspired the turn to violence. With Toni Negri, who studied in Gottingen and taught at the Sorbonne, the police sought Franco Piperno who succeeded in fleeing—Piperno's wife, Flora Pirri Ardizone, is a Sicilian millionairess, a kind of southern counterpart to the rich Milan publisher, the late Giangiacomo Feltrinelli. (Precious little is heard these days about the old theory that Feltrinelli had not accidentally blown himself up with a bomb but had been murdered by Fascist right-wingers; in testimony in recent trials even the left-wingers now concede it was an "honorable accident" in the service of the movement.)

What is especially dramatic about the events in Padua is the role of the local Communist Party, which has energetically taken up the struggle against the "Autonomist." After all, two of the victims (Professors Petto and Longo) were members of the Party and had consistently argued that Terrorism in Italy, even when it paraded itself in slogans of the Left, really was a phenomenon of the Right, part of a reactionary strategy to create confrontation and tension. But any observer who hears the radio broadcasts, reads the pamphlets and magazines, and knows a little of the personal backgrounds of the terrorist ultras (so many of them are militants who split to the left from the Catholic Action or Communist Party ranks) can hardly accept this kind of semantic juggling. The Terrorist Left is what it is, and believes in what it says and does, down to "signing with the blood of the enemy."

Will Rome be able to prove the guilt of Padua? The cadres of the "armed Party" may not enjoy the support of the toiling masses, but it benefits from public apathy and the understandable fear of eyewitnesses who are reluctant to come forward with evidence and testimony. I found considerable concern everywhere here that the counter-blows against the Padua ideologists may not succeed in the courts, and thus only serve to strengthen the *"contropotere,"* the prestige of the "Anti-State" forces.

August 1979

The 1980s

European Diary

The Line of Non-Alignment

By now it seems almost to be a law governing political particles—pieces breaking off and away from larger blocs are not in themselves capable of forming a bloc. The recent breakaway examples of Iran and Nicaragua, suddenly no longer attached to the Western system of alliances, illuminate the properties of so-called Non-Alignment. Once free of East and West they appear to be perforce independent of even that third bloc which for decades now has been trying to align itself along the lines of non-alignment. Contradictions will out; and first Tito and currently Castro have been trying vainly to hold together nations and peoples that are unwilling, or incapable of toeing a line. There are some who ascribe the difficulties even to "racial" factors, as Third World solidarities crumble in the attempts of "white" leaders of classic Left Revolutions to assume ideological leadership; for, after all, what did the "spirit of Bandung" in 1955 signify if not a decisively new color consciousness?

Still, if some differences are proving intractable, other factors make for such harmonious cooperation as there is. In a world of warring ideologies—China v. Russia, Vietnam v. Cambodia—some new comradely alignments are bound to take place, as impassioned rivals seek advantage, territory, prestige, allies. The grotesque result may be that within the Bloc-Free Alliance new blocs of antagonistic allies are being formed.

Tito dominated the first summit conference of the Non-Aligned in Belgrade 1961 as Castro did in Havana in 1979. For Tito it was then not only a matter of finding friends who would support an endangered Yugoslav sovereignty, but also an ambitious attempt to take over the leadership of revolutionary-communist forces and to play, far beyond the Balkan borders, a role in world politics. Castro is now playing the same role in Caribbean repertory. (Poor Che Guevara lost himself in unimportant backwater provinces; Fidel Castro is finding his true self on the world's stages.) One feels sure that the flamboyant *Lider Maximo* does not conceive of himself as a mere satrap of the great Soviet chairman in the Kremlin, but rather as a commander of powerful and effective Expeditionary Forces (now in West Africa, now in East Africa, tomorrow anywhere) who has become a necessary and indispensable ally of an expansionist empire.

It is not new in diplomatic history, these efforts of little nations with very narrow power bases to play a large role on the broader scene. Many have been tempted; a few have tried; and no world situation is more propitious than the current one in which the balance between great blocs of alliance issues in curious zones of "weightlessness," in which small and light particles appear to move freely and to have special impact. In any case the little nations are courted by the big powers and can therefore, take themselves most seriously. Even the Maos and the Tengs get around to saying, "We art not a great power," as one bloc to the discomfort of the other picks up the big "China card" placed discreetly on the card table by the "little" Chinese.

With Tito's difficulties in Havana, has even the non-leadership of the non-aligned passed from the European theatre, It could be only that the eighty-seven-year-old Marshal is too old and slow to command swift-moving allegiances, or that the "Yugoslav model" is no longer the attractive alternative for developing Third World nations. Marxism, at any rate, is no longer enough to provide a framework o secure sovereignty. The Czechoslovaks lost their sovereignty because of their "liberal" rule, the Cambodians because of their despotism. What will be the formula when the old heartland of non-alignment should be forced to get back into line. Some new phrase will be found, some pernicious formula for "change" and "progress," some ingenious rationalization to "move the Revolution forward." Small wonder that Titoism is so word shy these days, suspicious of any slogan that seem to impugn the integrity of neutrality ant sovereignty.

The old adventurousness has given way to conservatism. One needs allies who respect the true meaning of national independence and not the dangerous rhetoric of violent overturnings. A lonely Tito may find himself standing alone, as an ever combative Fidel Castro goes on battling bravely alongside Big Brother, knocking the bloc off anybody in their way. A terrible choice stands before the new nations of the Third World—to get lost in the melee of rival blocs or to lose themselves in the new giganticism of their very own third bloc whose Orwellian credo now reads: non-alignment means following the line.

February 1980

European Diary

The Very Latest from Paris

Anyone who follows in the slightest the atmosphere of French cultural life knows that the "latest" could only refer to the emergence of a "New Right" on the crowded scene. The phenomenon has commanded pages of critical analysis in *Le Monde*, all in tones of grave concern. Meanwhile, the various working groups flourish—such as the "Club de l'Horloge," or the circle around the review *Nouvelle École*, and many others, which like the "Synarchie" of prewar times, have their connections with a few leading politicians and high officials.

The curious spark for the new fiery controversies in the Paris press was provided by *Le Figaro*—not so much the daily newspaper as its weekend color section, *Figaro Magazine*, edited by Louis Pauwels, which has become the tribune of a new self-styled reactionary philosophy. Its newness lies in the fact that it has precious little to do with the old nostalgia for a Bourbon monarchy or the decrepit sentimentalism about Marshal Pétain's regime but rather with a few lingering surreptitious sympathies for the German Nazis. It is also unusual in a political scene where all conservatives like to think they are crowding "the Center" and there is nobody on "the Right."

The owner of *Le Figaro*, the Press Lord Louis Hersant, may perhaps be a sympathizer of "the New Right," yet the curious fact of the matter is hat the daily newspaper is conspicuously more liberal than its magazine. The columns by Frossard, as well as the political commentaries by Annie Kriegel, are often in striking conflict with the weekend pieces, and not infrequently polemicize against them.

But for the most part the excitement is about details of style and manner. This has always been the case in postwar Paris where one wave of newness has always followed another. Who remembers now whether the "New Look" was a little longer or shorter, or whether the "nouvelle Vague" was really different, and if so how much difference did it make?

One thing is clear: whenever the old "newness" fades, there is room—no, there is a vacuum—in Paris cultural life. On the Left there has lately been a full and fascinating period of defections, self-criticisms, revisions, and breakthroughs. For all its excesses, it brought to a long overdue end an intellectual monopoly of *gauchisme*; and few people regret its break-up. The spotlight, if not exactly the pendulum, now swings to the other direction.

The traditional French Right was not exactly a "stupid party." From Joseph de Maistre and Balzac to Taine and Renan, not to mention Charles Maurras, the French reactionary movement had no dearth of brilliant minds. But strangely enough our "New Right," as it has emerged, is rather short on mental and political qualities, and rather strong on that ruthless bitter tone which marked some of the more dispiriting quarrels of the past. It is a movement without old virtues, but with all the new vices: it is fashionable, very chic, even when it is calling up spirits from the vast deep of ancient Indo-European or Celtic traditions, and mixing these with a bit of the latest conclusions of genetics and experimental psychology. Needless to say, the unfortunate Nietzsche—forever doomed to fall into the wrong hands—also figures in the élitarian promotion of "superman" ideas, a mystagogical mélange of a new heathenism...to combat the new religiosity which is showing itself on the Left, as in the recent book by Bernard-Henri Lévy on the virtues of monotheism. The lines cross and crisscross; and with them goes that Breton extremist, Edern-Hallier, now on the Left, now on the Right, but always in the middle of things.

No compass will help to find one's bearings. The other day, the ultra-Left daily newspaper, *Liberation*, came to the conclusion that the New Left and the New Right had so many things in common. What is true, however, is that there has been taking place a quite extraordinary "transvaluation of values" (to drag Nietzsche into the matter again). The Left has been traditionally linked with the Enlightenment and with atheism; the Right has always been tied in with French Catholicism. The "new" intellectuals may be making historic shifts in position; but is it conceivable that "the masses" of "the People" will ever follow?

Still, there is much that is familiar and unchanging. The New Right, like the Old Right, believes in small, superior, privileged elites, and wants to have done with "the superstition of Equality." It also wants to finish off certain traditions of civility, and the comments on the death (by his own hand) of the writer Jean-Louis Bory were wild and vicious. More in this acidulous style than in its intellectual conceptions is the French Right recognizable. As Raymond Aron has pointed out in *L'Express*, the old baggage of anti-Semitism has been jettisoned.[1]

Is the New Right conceivably a new and coming power in the land? I may be wrong, but I don't quite see it. It still would appear that the old Right has been dissolved by great twentieth-century events, and that the Center can yet hold.

For the time being the whole controversy appears to be a kind of "escapism," since it is so much easier in Paris to occupy oneself with the fireworks of intellectual polemics than with the far more complex and difficult problems of analyzing the crises of French and European society. Even within the ranks of the editors and writers of *Figaro* itself there is now an open tendency to put distance between themselves and the strange extremism that has obsessed its weekend color supplement. "Figaro here, Figaro there..." one inevitably hummed, as Jean d'Ormesson who was once the paper's editor in chief, writing under the sign of the quilled *F* to his readership ("between center right and center left"), tried to sound a warning against the specter of new fearful doctrinaires—it was all only "another Loch Ness monster...."

March 1980

Notes

1. But this is not to suggest that the problem is not in the air, and topicality can be ominous. General de Gaulle once remarked to a wartime group of Jewish maquis: "Today anti-Semitism is impossible; but remain vigilant, for it will come again...."
1. Alarming was the recent much discussed interview (in Madrid) with the old Pétainist, Darquier de Pettepoix, who still is pleased with the persecutions and deportations under the German occupation.
2. Dispiriting was the interview the other day with the famous Renault chief, Pierre Dreyfus, scion of an old Alsatian family (an ancestor served as doctor in the court of Louis XV) who as a boy took religious instruction from Rabbi Simon Debre (the grandfather of the Gaullist leader Michel Debre). When asked whether he could expect any help from the French in the event that Israel's very existence was endangered, he replied: "Not for a single moment...."
3. Surprising was the newly revealed role which "Jewishness" played in high French Communist policy, determining whether "too many Jews" were in top Party committees, and yet whether it wouldn't be a good idea to let the electorate in certain quarters know that the Party's candidate Comrade Fremontier's real name was "Frydmann."
4. All in all, it is very much a sign of the times that a widely-noticed new novel, *Le livre des égarés*, indicates an inward turning, a search for "roots," on the part of an author—François Debre (son of France's most strident nationalist—who is only "a quarter Jewish" and yet is searching for protective ethnic traditions.

European Diary

The Veterans

Nobody who follows ideological affairs here is surprised by the weary, elegiac tone among writers and intellectuals that has crept into even lyric poetry. Here are a few lines from Germany's leading voice:

> ...Damals dachten wir alle,/morgen wird es besser sein, und wenn nicht/morgen, dann übermorgen./Na ja—vielleicht nicht unbedingt besser,/aber doch anders, vollkommen anders/auf jeden Fall./Alles wird anders sein./Ein wunderbares Gefühl. Ich erinnere mich.

This is from the "Third Chorus" of Hans Magnus Enzensberger's *Der Untergang der Titanic, eine Komodie*.

> ...Then we all of us thought that there would be a better tomorrow... and if not tomorrow, then the day after.... Well, if not exactly better, then at least different, utterly different in any case.... Everything will be different. A wonderful feeling. I remember it well....

Enzensberger, a self-styled "revolutionary poet," was the founder of the leading intellectual review of the German Left, *Kursbuch*, in which all the ideas and emotions of "the generation of 1968" found expression. As if they were discovering for the first time Wordsworth's "bliss was it in the t dawn to be alive" and Yeats's "terrible beauty...all changed, changed utterly," they surrendered themselves to eloquence and utopian inspiration, nowhere more strikingly than in those two great street-fighting tribunes of the movement: Rudi Dutschke (who has just died at thirty-nine, ten years after the assassination wounds of a decade ago in Berlin), and the German-born Sorbonne spokesman, Daniel Cohn-Bendit.

Some ten years on found both Rudi and Dany no longer storming barricades but patiently involved in the ecological work of the so-called Green Movement. The far-away revolutions of Castro and Ho Chi Minh had proved disappointing; and perhaps now they could make a few small desirable changes closer to home. A phrase in the latest *Kursbuch* speaks of "*Blauäugigkeit*," of the starry-eyed quality of the old idealism: as Cohn-Bendit writes, "From all those 'real-existing' socialist countries with their 'real-embattled' Parties I expect only real-existing oppression...." The conclusion he has now arrived at is that a struggle against existing power cannot be a struggle for power: "To change social conditions calls for the disintegration of power, and at the same time a renunciation of power. This is for me what I have learned over the last ten, eleven years...."

Ten or eleven years ago young Peter Roos was a nineteen-year-old Swabian beginning to study at Tübingen University, or what passed for studies in the pamphleteering, sloganeering spirit of the day. As he recalls in his fascinating personal memoir of the period (*Spiegel*, 7 January 1980),

> The revolution would be coming, for sure. It was our turn. We read Brecht, Seghers, Marx; listened to Eisler and Biermann; looked at Grosz and Kollwitz.... Sent home unwanted books: Thomas Mann, James Fennimore Cooper, Karl May, and the like.... Our shelves featured the little blue volumes of Marx, the works of Bloch, Benjamin, Lukacs, Wilhelm Reich. Above hung the obligatory Che Guevara poster. And Brecht and Brecht and Brecht....

He looks back in some anger and bewilderment (but one wonders why all those Marx-obsessed characters never looked for the "cash-nexus" and inquired occasionally who was making money out of all those books and posters and records that kept a whole generation generously supplied with its ideological paraphernalia).

> We were all marching in a kind of phraseological goose-step.... We wrote theses and manifestos in which there wasn't a single sentence of our own. I wrote about "Language and Class Realities." Whatever individual personality we may have had, we put out like the light-switch on our desks....
>
> And why did we never clean up? Not on Fridays, not any day. Today we wonder about getting some daily in several times a week, and we even consider buying a washing machine. But then we were against all "division of labor," all "exploitation," all "master-servant" relationships, all "consumerist technology".... So it was that we devoted all our time to help free the oppressed peoples of Indochina, and we left whoever it was that had the job of cleaning our student digs—Swabian, Greek, and Turkish peasant women—to scrub our filthy kitchens, and sweep up our leaflet-littered rooms....
>
> That's the way we were, the generation born in 1950. Our youth is gone, and we have become hateful adults, as neurotic as they come, impatient, individualistic, sentimental, and spoiled....

And now what lies ahead for them? Should they go in for nostalgia, or perhaps for mourning?

> Could it be that it was all simply that old familiar swing of the pendulum? Is the new generation passive because we were active? Are they quiet because we were so loud? Do they think only of themselves because we always thought of the others? Were we Left because our fathers were Right? Does red follow brown and brown red?...
>
> I suppose I'll try and get away from it all by going out to the countryside. Pleasant greenery, on the bicycle. Nice to relax a little.

Something old has passed away, something new is a'coming. A young doctor also writes in *Kursbuch* about the arguments of the "old men of '68" and he repudiates the whole ideology of all those embattled APO militants of yesteryear. Boring stuff, nobody under thirty wants to listen any more....

To be sure there is still a brave persistent handful who are hoping to "march through the institutions," and in one mole-like way or another there is here and there some notable headway (in the left wings of the social-democratic parties, in the progressive press, in TV public-affairs programmer). But what they all have had to survive is a terrible triple challenge—first, from their elders, the "know-it-alls" who always "knew better" (and in fact did, especially about reform v. revolution); second, from the next generation of youth who crowded the noisy militants off the stage; and third, from the vacuum created by the failure of their own romantic devotion to Paradise Now. The years go on but they still like to fancy themselves as the Youth (in German there is a special telling adjective which derives from the Youth Movement, *jugendbewegt*, and it can fit even starry-eyed seventy-year-olds). The new Youth is not really deserving of the name, with their old-fashioned return to greater quietness, personal ambition, eclectically critical attitudes. The Veterans of '68 still think they embody true youthful ideals. Small wonder that the new generation in *Kursbuch* and elsewhere have been counter-attacking the "superciliousness," the persistent know-it-all *Besserwisserei* which had in fact outraged the earlier generation in the pre-'68 world.

Evidently this new *Jugend* is busy developing new virtues of their own, and they include an attractive penchant for self-criticism. "Unlike the militants we are neither so hard on others nor ourselves...."

And yet, if one follows the reports from West Berlin's Frei Universität and from the Abendgymnasium in Frankfurt-am-Main, one knows that no such generalizations can be entirely acceptable, for there are still cadres around and in sufficient quantity to cause academic trouble. Perhaps the difficulty lies simply in the idea that one can talk about "a generation," that a portrait or a psychograph is possible and plausible.

But that bit about revolting against dogmatic omniscience is surely an accurate sign of the times. Rudi Dutschke was buried last month in West Berlin, add Professor Jürgen Habermas praised his socialist idealism and Dr. Hellmut Gollwitzer paid tribute to his Christian ethics— but there are still a few who remember his "worst hour," that absurd trip he took to Prague during the "Dubcek spring" to warn the Czech revisionists and reformers about going "too far" (i.e., in the direction of "bourgeois liberties"), flinging warnings and grave lessons around with a raised German-schoolmaster's *Zeigefinger*.

In any case the inheritance of the '68 generation is full of ambivalences and contradictions—leading, at one end, to the élitarian conspiratorial groups preaching (and practicing) terror; and, at the other end, to the proliferation of local and not un-useful committees of civic action known here as

Burgerinitiativen. But the largest social contradiction of that entire period remains: the unbridgeable chasm between middleclass students and working-class workers, between an elite and a mass, between the people and self-appointed leaders (those who have always cried "*All power to the people!*" when they really only meant "*All power to the people who cry all power to the people!*").

Or as Enzensberger puts it in his *Titanic* allegory:

Sie verstanden wohl, was er sagte,
aber sie verstanden ihn nicht.
Sein Worte waren nicht ihre Worte.

(They quite understood what he was saying,
but they did not comprehend him.
His words were not their words.)

April 1980

European Diary

How to Relax in the Cold War

The phrases, in all their sloganizing fury, come from the East, but they have been finding their echo in the West—"*a relapse into the Cold War!*," "*enemies of Detente and Peace!*" President Carter and the Americans have been the main targets of the new Moscow ideological offensive since the U.S. was unprepared simply to accept without protest the Soviet Army's military intervention across the Afghanistan frontier. But why should the Kremlin have been surprised at the Americans' surprise?—and surprised they appeared to be, as upset and even bewildered as Imre Nagy had been in Hungary and Alexander Dubcek in Prague. All had been tempted to believe in the peaceful and "defensive" role of the Red Army, illusions regularly confirmed by firm handshakes and close embraces and even, as once in May, by a Presidential kiss.

Historians record that moment of hilarity some fifty years ago which broke out in the conference hall of the old Comintern in Moscow—an English Communist had tried to register an objection to a Kremlin resolution, remarking "But we can't say that—it simply isn't true!..." It could be that Carter's consternation over the bitter disappointment of discovering that Chairman Brezhnev had not quite been telling him the truth also proved a source of merriment in Moscow. But in this case the bit of fibbing is having more formidable consequences. As one Italian writer put it (in the *Giornale Nuovo*), "Carter has been forced to shut the Book of Psalms and open up the World Atlas...."

I wonder whether the rhetorical propaganda against that *ol'debbil* "Cold War" is as effective as it used to be. Whatever the clumsiness and even primitivism of the Bolsheviks on the home front, forever shaky from permanently planned economic failures, they do have a skillful way with words and special talents for exporting them to the ideological markets of the West. Even in the days of their military weakness their verbal cannonades were more powerful than the West's. In the 1950s thousands of important Europeans (Sartre among them) rushed to sign the "Stockholm Appeal," once the formula by which the struggle against the Bomb and for Peace was dramatized. It had its uses, although it has been long dropped, long since forgotten.

"Cold War" itself may well have been of Western origin, and the phrase has been attributed to Walter Lippmann (though some say he had it from Bernard Baruch on his park bench). At that time it was intended to contrast a cold from a hot war (recently ended), and only now is it the antonym of détente; it was a short form to denote a limited amount of postwar tension among competing national powers. What it meant was that we had our differences, our conflicts and confrontations, but these would in time produce a certain number of conventions and understandings, as we agreed about signals (and how to give them) and united in removing certain "contained" areas of difficulty from direct or overt conflict—all in the hope that the cold war would not become hot. There was also a "cold war" of ideas, and it remains difficult for me to see why this intellectual clash was ever felt to be something negative or evil. Still, the phrase "cold warrior"—or, along that Central European line in Germany which separates East and West, *"der kalte Krieger"*—became an ugly epithet of the day, even with its ungrammatical twist. (For if a person who is engaged in the Cold War becomes a cold warrior, does he when he has his hot lunch become a hot luncher?) But the phrase wormed its way into the vocabulary of the day, and no amount of semantics will get it out.

Yet it seems to be able to work both ways, though seldom in our own press and publications are there references to Comrades Suslov or Ponomarenko, after a particularly sharp and aggressive Politburo speech, as "cold warriors." All these warriors, in East and West, appear to have sinister designs on the peace of the world. It is hard to formulate it exactly, but one can see what is meant when it is said that they want to "hot up" the Cold War, although perhaps "refrigerating" it (or "deeper-freezing" it) might come closer to an accurate reading of the temperature of world politics.

But, to be sure, there are temperate or well-tempered souls amongst us, a few far-sighted politicians, a handful of wise statesmen—men (as Giscard d'Estaing reminded us the other day, and one wonders whom he had in mind) "on whose calm and insight world peace depends"—militants against militarism joined with progressives against a relapse, all relaxed chaps who know how to gird their loins to defend the hard-won relaxation.

Is the semantic confusion beginning to become troublesome? Some think of it as a kind of capitulation in the terminological war. For, after all, "Cold War" and "Détente" are not simple opposites like cold and hot war. They represent the way in which we see the two great continuing periods of the postwar era; and as Dr. Kissinger has just reminded us in Davos, the former was not all bad, the latter not all good. Both periods had much in common, not least the paradoxes of diplomacy and deployment. The most warmhearted (if that is the word for such cardiac-cold characters) Soviet-American summit took place in Moscow in 1972, shortly after President Richard Nixon had presented Chairman Brezhnev with the news of the mining of the North Vietnamese harbors. The most dramatic episode of Washington-Moscow relations took place in 1948-49—the confrontation over the Berlin Blockade was icy, the welcome relaxation after the victory of the Air Lift enabled West Berlin to go about its normal business peacefully. As the Germans knew, *Spannung* and *Entspannung* lie very close together; and history is full of such twists and turns of cooperation and confrontation. The "cold war" did not exclude agreements, settlements; understandings; the much oversold era of Détente included wars, military interventions, revolutionary coups, and armament build-ups. In any event, while the West went about its affairs "relaxed"—young John F. Kennedy's book popularized the phrase *While We Slept*—the USSR proceeded to "catch up and overtake" in many spheres of the East-West arms race.

I don't suppose I can persuade anybody to give up that messy bit of military meteorology, "Cold War," nor its useless companion term, full of foreign vagueness (and an eccentric accent which most proof-readers overlook), "Détente." But we might do well to remember how George Orwell in his studies of the language of politics (and especially in the Newspeak of *1984*) demonstrated the deviousness of linguistic penetration, the compulsive mechanism by which victims are forced to adapt a useful terminology, and how words and phrases function as the instruments of strength and subjection. For my own part I will try to hold to a definition that I once read: détente is the continuation of the Cold War by other means, and sometimes by the same.

May 1980

European Diary

The Comeback of Drieu La Rochelle

It remains a kind of odd distinction: Drieu La Rochelle was the most talented of the French writers who collaborated with the Germans during the Nazi Occupation of World War II. (that is, if we except the case of Louis-Ferdinand Céline, which was a quite different matter.) It was he who in those years continued publishing the famous Paris journal, *La Nouvelle Revue Française*. But the years and the decades go by, and in recent days the whole affair of "literary collaboration" has been reviewed and reconsidered, and Drieu La Rochelle has indeed become some thing of a "cult object." So many elements lend themselves easily to a dramatic renewal of interest: his suicide after the German defeat (in order to escape a punishment which he probably need not have feared), his posthumous works which include a "Secret Report" (his confession of moral bankruptcy) as well as the manuscript of a novel, *Dirk Raspe* (presumably about Van Gogh).

In the generation of the earlier World War Drieu was with Henri de Montherlant and Louis Aragon among the literary leaders of the socalled front veterans (Céline arrived much later). Among Drieu's friends was the young André Malraux, with whom he remained close even after political differences separated him from his other comrades on the Left; indeed he was the godfather of one of Malraux' sons (of the relation with Josette Clotis Malraux), and in his last days, when all was lost, he even thought of joining Malraux' Brigade, in fact named him executor in his testament (which Malraux conscientiously fulfilled).

A biography was recently published by Dominique Desanti, who used to be something of a Communist philosopher and became well known through an earlier book of memoirs about her Stalinist years. She thought of it as a study of "a seducer betrayed." Now a second book about Drieu has been issued by Hachette and is receiving widespread notice: one of the authors (Pierre Andreu) belonged to the semi-fascist party of the ex-Communist Jacques Doriot and has a certain engagement; the co-author (Frederic Grover) is one of those indefatigable American researchers who, like Herbert Lottman in his *Camus* biography and Philip Kolb's *Proust Correspondence*, take endless pains with factual documentation. All taken together, including a film of one of Drieu's works made in the 1960s, has pushed the whole case into the center of attention.

Drieu was born in Paris (in 1893), but his parents had come from Brittany and Normandy; as a young literary aspirant he traveled frequently across the Channel and English indeed became his second language. (He later turned out to be the confidant of Herr Otto Abetz, Hitler's man in Paris, but he hardly knew a word of German.) Each of the biographical details has a curiously ironic twist. He studied political science, but failed his examination. He first married a Jewish doctor, Colette Jeramec, and later a Polish beauty named Alexandra Sienkiewiscz, who was supposed to be "the ideal wife," but among his various liaisons, escapades and adventures (often with prostitutes), there was his long passionate affair with "Beloukia," the wife of the French automobile king, Louis Renault.

His experiences at Verdun and in the Dardanelles led to his first stories, and his collection *The Comedy of Charleroi* is still very readable. Politically he was for some form of "united Europe," flirted on the left with Communist tendencies, but moved rightwards towards sympathies for Fascism, out of a bitterness over French weakness and indecisiveness and his supranational hopes. To be sure he would have much preferred a French rather than a German, a Nazi, Europe; but rather the latter than none at all. Drieu was not the only French intellectual who did not simply "go along with the victors" but lost his way in a desperate search for "larger forces."

There is an analysis of Drieu's quest in Paul Nizan's book about "Fascist Socialism" (Nizan had been a Communist, who broke after the Hitler-Stalin pact and was killed in World War II). "There are qualities here," Nizan wrote, "which cause one to regret the loss of such a man. And yet he was not alone in being the victim of a struggle which led to cooperation with hangmen...." At the time Drieu was a guest at the Nuremberg Party Rally (after which, typically, he went on to Moscow).

His latest biographers pay rather more attention to his sexual drives than the interested reader is likely to sustain (how impotent he was, why he was so attractive to women, what kind of love ruled his life), especially when so little is clarified. Unclarified, too, are the complex sources of his turbulent anti-Semitism, even though we now also have a reprint available of the magazine *The Last Days*, which he edited with Emanuel Berl, a Jewish friend. It was a strange obsession, and evidently it was taken seriously by almost nobody. He could write mean and nasty pamphlets, and yet provoke surprisingly little personal hatred. Neither Colette Jeramec nor his many Jewish friends appear to have held it against him. No doubt about it, there was a certain magical charm to his personality, to his youthfulness; his adolescent immaturity, his disarming impulsiveness.

For a generation which considered itself "lost" or "desperate" he succeeded in capturing the mood both in his novels and in his personal life. There was also abroad in the land a love for the provocative (and it took Aragon from surrealism to Stalinism). In Drieu it exemplified itself in a weariness with life, a disgust with ideas, which could not lead to convictions and passions. There was no end to his naive disappointments. When he was editing the *Nouvelle Revue Française* he was turned down by both André Gide and François Mauriac. Why should he ever have thought of asking them? His predecessor, Jean Paulhan, fought in the Resistance; and Drieu wrote badly of him. The inexplicable complexities mount:' Drieu saved Paulhan from arrest and worse; and was duly thanked in a letter. He also went out of his way to help Malraux and Berl and others during this period of the Occupation and, the Underground. All *collaborateurs* had their reasons and excuses, but very few actually used their position to "prevent the worst." In the end he put a simple end to the intricacies of his emotional turmoils: the self-destructiveness, adumbrated in so many of his writings, culminated in his suicide in 1945.

The life and death has, obviously, its dramatic interest; the books, I think, even more so. Beyond the conventional efforts of sympathetic biographers and critics, the paradox and irony of Drieu La Rochelle challenges. I suspect that the new fascination with Fascism and even Hitlerism is not an altogether "negative" attraction, as the recent grotesque Paris cults of figures like Leni Riefenstahl and Arno Breker would suggest. Can it be a genuine nostalgia for such dark journeys "to the end of the night"?

In his own work—see his writings of 1927-28, The Young European (*La Jeune Europe*) and Geneva or Moscow (*Geneve ou Moscou*)—he liked to present his own views as symptoms and signals, rather than as directions; and he declined to fulfill the normal expectations of the French intellectual reader for lessons, morals, rules, myths. He had lost his sense for the nation; all the nations were exhausted, useless; the provinces might still barely survive, in which case a greater Europe might well emerge. "There are too many fatherlands, and they no longer exist...."

He found something "clownish" in the attempts of the local or the provincial to assert itself; and perhaps the nostalgic impulse of readers today is driven by the present confusions between exhausted old forces and pregnant European ideas powerless to be born. He had no fears for the "idea of France" from the Second or the Third International; for him the real dangers of a spiritual disorientation lay in the vapid village historians and their distracting local color. In the last analysis, readers may be turning again to Drieu as a prophet of disorientation. In another amoral era of foul compromises an enigmatic spectacle of desperation takes on a certain pertinence.

June 1980

European Diary

Of Passing Scandals

Usually the sensational melodramatic questions of the day are confined to the boulevard press. But these days even the most sober and serious papers are putting breathtaking possibilities before the French reader. Did President Valéry Giscard d'Estaing receive those valuable diamonds from ex-King Bokassa, and how did he dispose of them? Did Georges Marchais, chief of the French Communist Party, lie about his movements and whereabouts during the years of the Nazi Occupation?

The Central African scandal, a story which the satirical weekly, *Le Canard Enchaîné*, humorlessly pursued, is now to be taken up in the law courts as writs of libel fly furiously from the outraged members of Giscard's family. The mystery of Marchais' activities during the time when the Communist mythology had every good man and true fighting in the Resistance was lifted by the publication in *L'Express* (edited by Jean-François Revel and Raymond Aron, and published by Sir James Goldsmith, wearing his French hat) of several wartime documents which disclosed that Marchais had stayed on longer in Nazi Germany than he had previously disclosed...and as a volunteer worker.

Against such lurid happenings what do the other affairs amount to? How much time is left over to pore over the scandal that followed Cabinet Minister Robert Boulin's suicide, and his last letter accusing certain colleagues (members of the Chirac *Rassemblement*) of having organized a damaging whispering campaign against him? Here, too, the law is taking its course, with journalists lined up in a scrimmage against politicians.

I wonder how much such scoops, scandals, revelations, and trials will actually change the Paris political scene. Interestingly enough, none of the political parties appears to want to make any political capital out of any part of the exposés. The Socialists have been severely reprimanded by *L'Humanité* for deigning to show interest in such matters, although they and the governmental parties have really been very reserved in their reactions to the Marchais case. Indeed, Jean-François Revel actually suspects that all the leading French radio commentators received special guidelines to "play it down." As for Comrade Marchais himself, he has shrewdly offered to cooperate in any investigation of his life and letters, with only one condition—namely, that all the other leading politicians submit themselves to an inquiry looking into their wartime records and their peacetime bank accounts.

Who knows but this rage for counter-investigation may lead to an inquiry as to whether journalists are themselves above moral scrutiny? (Documents are now circulating about the royal presents King Bokassa handed out to the visiting press.) I was reminded of the current Milanese ploy where charges against the terrorists, the *brigate rosse*, alternate with accusations of corruption against the judges and the economic leaders, the *brigate grasse*.

Almost by definition, "the latest scandal" doesn't last very long; each gives way to the next. Who still remembers (it was only three years ago) the assurance from Minister Poniatowski that the puzzle surrounding the mysterious murder of Prince Jean de Broglie (ex-minister and businessman) had been solved and the guilty persons detained. Far from it; the police are still busy making their inquiries.

I suspect that when the storms on Left and Right die down we will still see, in the dawn's early light, the solid figures of the President and the General Secretary in their respective places. Valéry Giscard d'Estaing has the unshakable self-confidence, the *désinvolture*, which goes with his protected life and brilliant career. His "aristocratic" family tree may be of more recent dating than he likes to pretend, but he does have something of a nobleman's traditional contempt for what are considered to be bourgeois prejudices, and questions are not answered nor charges denied. Never apologizing and never explaining can be a sovereign posture that impresses.

In the face of charges that he had no legitimate militant background in the anti-Fascist Resistance, Marchais almost broke into tears. Petty-bourgeois sentimentality, perhaps, for there is no reason to believe that he would lose any working-class votes in the Party's proletarian strongholds simply because he wasn't, long ago, deported to Germany but stayed on, for one reason or another, as a factory worker. The younger generation in France doesn't find the old quarrel about spotless records in the underground resistance very relevant any longer; and, more than that, any outside attack from the bourgeois camp has an automatic effect of "solidarization." After all, the great old leader of the Communists was actually a deserter in 1939 (after the Hitler-Stalin pact nullified the Party's support for a just anti-Nazi war), and that never proved an obstacle to Maurice Thorez's subsequent return from Moscow, with General de Gaulle's permission, and to his service with honors in the first Gaullist cabinet.

Scandal is, to be sure, a weapon in politics; but political interests often dictate an anomalous puristic or puritanical attitude on the part of the leading politicians concerned. If all are somehow involved, then all like to appear loftily above the battle. At the moment neither the Conservative Right nor the Communist Left wants to help the Socialists in any way, and it is the forces of Mitterrand and Rocard who would benefit from any public dismay or outrage. If Marchais were to become a candidate for the Presidency, the defeat of the Left would be certain, a happy prospect for the Government's well wishers. So at the moment as the mud flies thick and fast, there appears to be an objective Giscard-Marchais alliance, denied with all the proper ideological indignation on both sides, but scandalous circumstances in Paris have always had an odd way of making strange bedfellows.

Once upon a time, as in the affair over Queen Marie Antoinette's diamond necklace, scandals may have been premonitory signs of a revolution to come. Nowadays they are only passing episodes, harbingers of nothing.

October 1980

of progressive political change that the very suggestion of a comparison with the *ancien régime* must raise hackles on decent liberal spirits? Or, again (for there is the old third hypothesis), is there a continuity between old and new?

Solzhenitsyn, the great witness to Russian agonies and the thunderer against Western decadence (which includes much of our democratic ways and press liberties), is a man of polarization. He demands—and gets—an all-or-nothing reaction. His faithful believers, and not a few among his millions of readers, follow him totally; and for recent critical remarks of my own one reader reminded me sharply, "Solzhenitsyn has always been right...." Others are irritated to outbursts of hostile analysis of "the egocentric manipulation of his fame and unique literary energies." One psychiatrist remarked to me recently, "Can't you see that the man is sanctimonious."

What one can see is the conventional difficulty in accepting the honesty and integrity of extraordinary men who throw strange and disagreeable ideas at us. Solzhenitsyn is a very special phenomenon of our time, and apart from one book on the subject—George Nivat's recent study, published in Paris (Editions du Seuil)—I wouldn't know what to advise readers to turn to in order to get behind the superficialities of much of the discussion. Somewhere in his book called *The Yawning Heights*, Alexander Zinoviev (who in his satirical coolness, without pathos or fury, is poles away from Solzhenitsyn's spirit) writes, "One should not judge him too strictly. He grew in loneliness. Criticism and adoration are just too partisan...."

For Solzhenitsyn, the rise of Bolshevism was from the very outset an "Invasion." It came from elsewhere, from the outside, was imposed. But Zinoviev, on the other hand, remembers how his grandmother used to keep a picture of Stalin in the pages of her old Bible....

A century ago the Slavophiles despised everything that came from the West as unholy imports, as corrupting elements of the authentic Russian spirit. In the raging discussions of that day one liberal named Chicherin (not to be confused with Lenin's associate) protested energetically against the belief in a noble peasant folk.

> They want to convince me that the peasants, among whom I live and whom I have known since my childhood, represent the highest human ideals. This seems to me to be utter nonsense. The man of Russian Enlightenment, Peter, is presented now as a corrupter of popular integrity and against him the feeble-minded Fedor Ivanovich becomes an ideal Czar who never missed a church service and actually rang out the bells himself....

There can be no doubt that there were genuine successes which the spirit of Russian Liberalism was able to register in Russia; old institutions were reformed, new social and economic arrangement introduced; from Count Witte onwards there was even a kind of "great leap forward." But once the violent Revolution came out of the ruins of World War I, nothing remained of the

European Diary

"Russian" (Good), "Soviet" (Bad)...

No, the passage is not from an Intourist visitor:
One is given a welcome in this counter, but the politeness is so burdensome that the observer is quite unable to get about to look at anything by himself. Never bind alone to examine and ponder makes it difficult to come to any independent judgments, and that is what one is after. The Russians are convinced of the efficiency of the lie. Not that their spirit is lacking in sensitivity or insight, but in a country where not even the rulers have any feeling for the virtues of freedom, not even for themselves, there the governed must needs keep aloof from the obvious dangers of candor.... The profession of "foreign mystification" is a very Russian one.

To be sure, it could have been a useful text for all those naive Olympic tourists; but actually the context was Marquis de Custine's Czarist Russia of the early nineteenth century. Has nothing changed since 1839? His description of the far-reaching controls over all aspects of lifer of the suspicion and secrecy concerning the slightest social details, of the utter absence of what in the West could be thought of as public political life; the whole of Custine's book has been a treasuretrove of quotations for a long time now, all apparently suggesting the unshakeable historical continuity between the Old and the New Russia.

One can hardly avoid thinking of de Custine when Solzhenitsyn, in his latest article in *Foreign Affairs*, posits an absolute opposition between all that is quintessentially Russian and the whole spirit and structure of the Soviet Union, indeed writing that the present holders of power over an honest, noble, deeply Christian and kindly native population are really a kind of foreign Occupation power.

He argues that it has become a life-and-death matter for the West to learn to comprehend the difference between an enslaved but slowly awakening people and this imposed coercive system from without...with which no coexistence is at all possible.

This as I say, an old argument, taking on new forms in our own day. Is the Soviet regime more backward, less capable of forward development than the old tsarist Russia, which had liberal tendencies ever since Catherine the Great? Or, put another way, is this regime so identified with the banal modern notion liberal heritage. For Solzhenitsyn, there is only one (and a very simple one at that) way of reading history; and he goes to great and angry lengths to polemicize against the American historian Richard Pipes for having discerned traditional Russian traits within the Soviet system.[1]

The paradox is, obviously, that the Soviet rulers, despite changes of party line and dialectical vocabulary, always insist on the one and true version of the past; and now even from the stony Yankee hills of Vermont comes a call for an authentic dogma of historical interpretation.

Nor is he alone. The editor of *Kontinent*, the exiled Soviet novelist Vladimir Maximov, refers to Western democracy and totalitarianism as "two dead-end streets," and in his own projected constitution (*Kontinent*, no. 14) he forbids trade unions to have any kind of "central organization." Whether old or new, illiberalism doesn't change very much.

At any rate, the bitter and heated debates all round these themes have been with us before, and perhaps here too we can make out the element of "Russian continuity." Like de Custine we are still on the outside looking in, puzzling, pondering, worried whether we will have a free quiet moment to make up our own minds. Meanwhile, we keep on taking our battering: what must be done, why we have done it all wrong, where we absolutely have to take our stand, if the most somber of destinies is to be avoided. It is probably all for the best that we listen patiently to the great Russian debate, and follow it feelingly. The dialectical hair-splitting of the various Marxist groups, which used to dominate the arid arguments over the "Russian Question," turned out to have dramatic historic implications, even beyond the deaths of Mao and Tito. Ideas have consequences.

October 1980

Note

1. See, in *Encounter*, Richard Pipes' critique of Solzhenitsyn (June 1979); and the whole debate on this subject between Pipes and a young Soviet historian. W. G. Krasnow (*Encounter*, April 1980).

Mauriac, between Province and Paris

François Mauriac called himself "a Catholic novelist," then later "a Catholic and novelist"—an important distinction. When he died ten years ago at the age of eighty-five, he had achieved every kind of honor and success: elected to the French Academy when relatively young, and at the end a Nobel Prize winner. The only thing lacking was his inclusion in the de luxe edition of the Pleiade classics, and his novels were recently accorded this honor. So Mauriac was at long last published by Gallimard—he had never become one of their authors despite his friendship with other writers on their list (André Gide, Paul Claudel, Marcel Proust).

The new biography of Francois Mauriac (published by Editions du Seuil in large format, over 600 pp. long) is by Jean Lacouture, himself from Bordeaux, like the novelist. Lacouture is well known as a reporter, but he is also the author of two excellent biographies devoted to André Malraux and Léon Blum.

In comparison with Blum the politician and Malraux the author and man of action, François Mauriac is not an overtly "rewarding" subject. At least, not in the years of his earlier success when he led a fashionable life in Paris. But the themes change once he takes a stance on the war in Abyssinia, having been a conservative in keeping with family tradition, and then supports the Spanish Republic in the Civil War. He was no longer acceptable to the right wing newspaper *Echo de Paris*; and even readers of *Le Figaro* (the newspaper to which he contributed most regularly) came to regard him as a "renegade." François Mauriac became an embattled chronicler of the Fourth Republic: he supported the "decolonizer" Pierre Mendès-France, and then Charles de Gaulle: it was an eventful period, rich in anecdotes.

Lacoutre also presents a revealing portrait of the childhood and youth of the author, who was born in 1885 and went to Paris in 1907. These early years constitute the relatively less well-known part of the novelist's life. His father died very young so Mauriac grew up "fatherless" like Sartre, like Camus. The family was well to do, and the social milieu drew him towards the Right, as it did his dearly loved brother Jean, who remained an arch-conservative to the day he died. When François Mauriac later wrote against colonialism and Fascism, he was confronted with previous articles of his that sounded quite a different tone—after all, when he traveled to Rome with Prime Minister Pierre Laval he had been favorably impressed by Mussolini; and at the beginning of the Spanish Civil War he had leaned towards Franco.

Even before this political *volte-face*, Mauriac had alienated the conservative milieu from which he sprang—by means of his novels. These were dominated by themes of sex, greed, brutality, materialism, sin, and an absence of divine mercy. The outwardly imposing Christian family is here "a knot of vipers," and readers were warned against Mauriac's novels by the religious authorities. His admiration for Baudelaire, Rimbaud, and Claudel was shocking enough. He himself was shocked when he championed Paul Claudel in the Academic Française without success—some naval officer who wrote quite enjoyable adventure novels was preferred.

Mauriac once wrote that the truth about an author's life is not to be found in memoirs and confessions, but in his novels. As a young man he had come into contact with the socially progressive Catholic movement Le Sillon (The Furrow) and its founder Marc Sangnier, of whom the novelist wrote a cryptic and gently ironic portrait. Stronger at first was the influence of the aesthete and nationalist Maurice Barrès; he wrote a review praising Mauriac's first volume of poems and it immediately paved the way for the young author.

His biographer goes into few details about the novels themselves—he does not claim to be a literary critic. Yet the fact of the matter is that for almost thirty years novel-writing was Mauriac's real life, and any reader of the biography would wish for some additional material to aid his reflections on what it was about these novels that had such a controversial effect—and what gives them lasting value.

Lacouture adopts a different tack with the journalist, polemicist, moralist, and autobiographer. One cannot help concluding—and this is confirmed by a remark of Mauriac's—that it is principally this "late Mauriac" who will endure in the field of literature and in the history of the French intelligentsia. Unlike Jean-Paul Sartre, Mauriac never formulated a theory of political commitment. He became *engagé* almost unawares, as a result of things that angered or offended him—and his own indignation provoked his indignant readers, which made it all the more effective. The editor of *Le Figaro*, Pierre Brisson, kept faith with him for a long time. Not until the conflicts over the North African liberation movements was Mauriac obliged to cross the Champs Elysees to join *L'Express* further up the avenue, and there he published his weekly "*Notes Bloc*."[1]

It may be that Mauriac was less important as a novelist than that other Catholic defector from Right to Left, Georges Bernanos—both of them, incidentally, motivated by an aversion to "respectability" and not by any sudden conversion to liberal-left convictions. But as a journalist Mauriac had a wider range—a subtle irony, which was foreign to the blustering Bernanos, a sly humor with suggestive malice, which ensured that he always had the laugh on his side. (When a Dominican took him to task for underrating the Surrealists, Mauriac retorted: "If this Father preaches Lautréamont to me, I'll take the liberty of preaching Jesus Christ to him.")

A controversy with Albert Camus in 1945 is still memorable. Camus, who had been active in the Resistance and was unable to get over the execution of some of his closest friends and fellow combatants, took a hard line during the early postwar "purges" (in *Combat*, the newspaper he edited at the time). One argument concerned the writer Robert Brasillach, who had worked for the Paris collaboration newspaper *Je suis partout*, which specialized in denunciations. Mauriac, among others, had pleaded—unsuccessfully—that the death sentence should be commuted. Albert Camus later came to the conclusion that his own hard vindictive line had not been justified; he publicly declared that Mauriac had been in the right on that occasion. This self-criticism was also voiced in Camus' last novel, *La Chute*. Camus had had the vision of "a France purged clean" and had later seen this to be an illusion. It may be attributable to Mauriac's Catholic upbringing and mentality that he never believed in a "new-born" society in this sense; on the other hand, the kind of self-criticism practiced by Camus is hardly conceivable in Mauriac.

The Mauriac of the novels and of the chronicles is one and the same—yet they seem two separate writers. The world of the novels is based on themes that Mauriac absorbed in his childhood; the articles and notes are based on an alert awareness of contemporary realities. The novels refer to a provincial milieu, the journalism to Paris.

At one point Mauriac had a falling-out with the Editor of *L'Express*, Jean-Jacques Servan-Schreiber, who compared de Gaulle to Mussolini, to Hitler, to Franco, and even called him *canaille*. In turn, Mauriac labeled the ambitious journalist and politician a "Kenedillon," a little would-be Kennedy; and this label stuck.

One of Mauriac's last books glorified De Gaulle. Indeed the General also thought highly of Mauriac, but in a ceremonious rather than an intimate fashion. At their first meeting after France was liberated—during the Occupation Mauriac had managed to write a book under a pseudonym for an underground publishing house—De Gaulle chatted with him only about André Gide and how to get the old master elected to the *Académie Française*—by no means Mauriac's most urgent concern.

His last novel, *Un adolescent d'autrefois, A Youth of Long Ago*, was written at the age of eighty-three, and remains one of his most powerful, with an animal sensuality and joy of the chase reminiscent of Maupassant.

Jean Lacouture records that a. trenchant review of Sartre's which appeared before the War—to the effect that Mauriac was not a real novelist since he didn't allow his characters room to breathe and simply manipulated them—hurt the novelist deeply and also influenced him profoundly. (Sartre later judged this criticism to be too harsh.) Wounding, too, was what André Gide once wrote, not without some spite: "I annoyed a lot of people when I said that noble sentiments make for bad literature. Your literature, my dear Mauriac, is first-rate. But if I was a better Christian—I would have difficulty in following it...."

One of Mauriac's strengths was the openness with which he upheld bourgeois or middle-class values, property, tradition. When Sartre turned down the Nobel Prize, Mauriac confessed that he had difficulty in understanding the decision. "In my own case, the money was just what I needed at Malagar [the family property] for installing a new bathroom...." (At least one reader regrets that Lacouture did not quote this revealing remark.)

In an ugly attack, Roger Peyrefitte—the writer of scandalizing novels, not to be confused with his cousin, the minister—branded Mauriac a secret homosexual. In all matters relating to the erotic in the life of Mauriac, model husband and family man, Lacouture maintains a discreet reserve (Mauriac's widow and sons helped him while he was collecting material). The temptation of homosexuality is cautiously implied; there are allusions to various "leanings."

Indeed, this is the problem with the biography of a novelist which doesn't delve too deeply into either the works or the "private sphere," but sticks to the public data of a life and times. The reserve is commendable. But surely there is still scope for investigation into why this pious Catholic, with an apparently happy childhood, created a fictional world utterly lacking in divine mercy. In the non-fictional world of engaged views and committed convictions, what private experience was responsible for the honesty and acuteness that transcended all the usual narrow restrictions of ideology?

November 1980

Note

1. See J. G. Weightman's remarks on Mauriac in his *Encounter* piece (January 1959), reprinted in *The Concept of the Avant-Garde* (Alcove Press 1969).

European Diary

Milosz, the Unknown

The news of the new Nobel Prize-winner for literature came through on the Thursday morning and, as these things happen, I had just been informing the editor of *Encounter* that my essay on Czeslaw Milosz, which had been promised for this number, could well be postponed for a while. My last-minute suspicions were that the Swedish Academy would be turning to somebody like Graham Greene or V. S. Naipaul whose work was so easily accessible. And so there I was with a winner, but with no bets placed.

Milosz's German publisher was even worse off, for he had no books at all in print; and only the paperback reprints of *The Captive Mind* (1951) and of a small volume of decent translations of the Polish poems could claim the honors of the day. A long queue of publishers and literary agents of a dozen different languages began to form outside Stand T908 in Halle 5 of this gigantic Book Fair to try to pick up copies of Milosz's *oeuvre*; but even the Niezalezna Oficyna Wydawnicza soon ran out of their samizdat copies. At the official Polish stand there were, of course, none; but the Warsaw authorities seemed to be pleased at the choice of a Pole (although born in Lithuanian Vilna, then as now Russian-controlled) and soon a large blow-up of a passport photo was patriotically adorning their national exhibit.

The local literary journalists, usually among the best-informed cosmopolitan spirits in Europe, were not exactly faced with an embarrassment of riches. On the basis of a slim book of political essays and an even thinner book of verse they had to fill columns in the ambitious literary supplements which every October flood the kiosks of the Frankfurt Book Fair. Small wonder that so many commentators tried to make brisk capital out of ignorance by turning the whole affair into a political *cause célèbre*. According to the Frankfurter Rundschau, the strike at Gdansk cast the deciding vote for a Polish prizewinner. Would perhaps some political victory in Rome have tipped the scale in favor of Alberto Moravia? In any case, the winner in a season of "Papal chic" just had to be a Pole.... Not having read any of the books, the critics could perhaps be forgiven for assuming that simply being a very good writer had nothing to do with the matter at all.

At one of those elegant and excited literary luncheons at the de luxe Hessische Hof hotel I listened to one of the great professionals among the

Book Fair elite: "What's his name again? Milos? Milosch? Never heard of him. But obviously, after Wojtyla and Walesa, it was time for a Pole, and Stockholm has a nose for these things. All a matter of politics, no doubt about it...."

What was really in no doubt was the embarrassment of having some quarter-of-a-million books exhibited at the Fair, and none by the "obscure" poet who takes the Nobel Prize. The English were prepared with shelves of Greene and Naipaul, and the Italians were even hedging their Moravia bets with Leonardo Sciascia. But Czeslaw Milosz? With the exception of a few university *Slawisten*, one or two exiled Polish men-of-letters (our friend Tadeusz Nowakovski disappeared from circulation for a day to dictate six different articles for German *feuilleton* pages), and your very own *Encounter* correspondent, delinquent though he was, few had ever heard of him and hence took the award as a kind of Scandinavian provocation, and in some sense a blow against the book business. How much, after all, are the verses of a Polish poet worth when balanced against the millions of copies of popular world-famous novelists?

What I found painful was the gap between the affluent publishing world and simple cultural information (no, not literary appreciation or aesthetic insight, but simple information), and with what distressing arrogance the vacuum of ignorance gets quickly filled. The newspapers—a factual report in the *Times* (based on valuable notices culled from the *TLS*), a thoughtful evaluation in *Le Monde*— tried to make good and do their reportorial duty. But surely no reader was really taken in: this fellow (what was his name again? Milosch?) could just not have been given the prize for being a good writer....

I happen to have known Czeslaw Milosz for almost thirty years, value everything he's ever written (except perhaps that which I cannot judge, such as his much-praised translations of Shakespeare, John Milton, and T. S. Eliot into the Polish) and I trust what I am now reporting is not a caricature of the Book Fair scene. In the copy of the *Corriere della Sera* which I bought at a Frankfurt kiosk I found a story from Stockholm to the effect that Polish authors like Isaac Bashevis Singer and Milosz are represented in Sweden by a charming and beautiful publisher (naturally of Polish origin), and that accounts for the Nobel successes. And what Milan knows, Turin knows even better: in *La Stampa* there was the news that the Swedish committee just could not make a choice between the greatness of Borges and Moravia and finally awarded the prize to a man so unknown that nobody could muster polemical arguments against him. This kind of thing—ignorance camouflaged by gossip—I found especially depressing in Italian journals that pride themselves so much on their cultural "*aggiornamento*," their knowledgeability.

An unknown scribbler? Two years ago an international jury awarded him one of the best American prizes, and *World Literature Today* devoted a special issue to his work. His name has appeared in many of the best-known journals, indeed only last month in the *New York Review of Books*. But America is evidently a land and a literature which is far away and about which we know little. Milosz departed our shores (after having lived in Paris when he "chose freedom" from postwar Stalinist Poland) a long time ago. California is indeed distant; a curious French critic was recently told by Milosz's French publisher that, alas, his whereabouts these days was quite unknown. Still, he has been turning out a remarkable series of books, from *Zdobycie wladzy* (a novel published by Faber as *The Usurpers* in 1955) to his sensitive memoirs of his East European childhood and a volume of criticism entitled *Emperor of the Earth: Modes of Eccentric Vision* (University of California Press, 1977). But I will leave this to another time; at the moment I want only to record the strange happening.

One should mention the little scandal of last summer when even I (no insider by a long shot) got wind of Milosz's candidacy for the Nobel Prize. A Stockholm newspaper reported some confidential exchanges within the Swedish Academy which indicated that contact had been made with the official Writers Union in Warsaw with the result that they had been assured that Polish writers did indeed recognize the man, forgotten or far away as one of their greatest national literary figures. This was especially noteworthy since Milosz was only available in Poland in *samizdat* editions "outside the censorship." It is obviously a matter of some European cultural significance if the Poles, unlike the Russians in the case of Solzhenitsyn and of Pasternak, could coolly register the honor, even welcome it, and not explode ideologically at the "provocation." In any event, the man's name was being mentioned for years in informed circles in America and in France[1] as a candidate: that is to say, before there was a Polish Pope and a Polish freedom-fighter of Gdansk to establish any kind of pattern for a hat-trick.

But enough of finger-wagging; annoying the Book Fair elite with imputations of ignorance only brings the counter of what is disdained here as *Besserwisserei*. Who, after all, reads a Polish poem? Let the good European publishers get their best translators busy.

January 1981

Note

1. His great uncle, Oscar de Milosz, was a distinguished French poet, and in 1931, welcoming to Paris his young and gifted nephew, predicted (in an interview) that he would one day be the glory of the family....

J-J S-S Rides Again

The moral challenge of a soldier's wartime conscience, which Jean-Jacques Servan-Schreiber described in his first book, *Lieutenant in Algeria*, was as nothing compared to the appeals and demands of his best-selling book on *The American Challenge* and the great global cry in his new book, simultaneously launched in fifteen countries. All the spiritual stimulation and scientific solutions taken together surely give us something to be getting on with—the ethical fiber of his native land, the well-being of modern post-industrial society, the very survival of the great globe itself. No wonder most critics in most countries have found it a bit of a muchness: I have just been reading the most devastating of critiques in *La Quinzaine litteraire* by Bernard and Jerome Cazes who know something about the subject.

The reaction to the book suggests, if the matter needed any underlining, the vast turning away in the West from uncritical Third World posturing which began slowly in the early days of President Truman's "Point Four" program to the organized chorus of voices dinning in the halls of the UN. Honest observers simply do not accept that there is a real historic Bloc out there, and certainly do not accept the Servan-Schreiber thesis of some kind of unity which binds together oil-rich Arabs with the abject poor. But even the smallest of details, once so carefully formulated by the old editor of *L'Express* and the erstwhile commentator of *Le Monde*, now slip away in a mess of pop pap. Feisal is a leader with "an eagle's countenance, a fearful ineluctable look...." The Arab world—all of it presumably, and singular in united will—"is as open now to what the future will bring as it was bound in the past to everything that was great and worthy...." Armand Hammer, the American oil billionaire (whose feeling for the refineries of life includes the MSS. of Leonardo da Vinci), is "a tiger" of a man "who even fifty years ago was of help to Lenin...." His attorney and East-West tradesman in Paris, M. Samuel Pisar, is also a far-sighted fellow. (In a recent TV program Pisar actually predicted that Western help for Soviet car production would create a new motorized consumer class, and with the millions of automobiles would come tens of thousands of miles of new highways, and on all those highways would bloom a whole new world of snackbars and motels!)

Person and events are seen with the same "fearful" look. We are told that Israel knew exactly when Sadat was to launch his Yom Kippur war, but under the instructions of Dr. Kissinger only pretended to be surprised. The book is crowded with the unprovable in support of the irrelevant; and when at one point the author suggests that his long book may be just a bit too long, for once how right he is! "Inside dopesters" is what David Riesman once called the self-appointed cognoscenti who seem not only to have all the sources, but to be at the very source itself. Here the author knows what Tito and Indira Gandhi and all the other powers-that-be said to each other, and is also in a position to quote them verbatim.

Still, there may be something to be said for the whole enterprise. Who does not share the sense of urgency about alarming the whole apathetic world to looming dangers? And who has not been tempted to break out or the confines of small, intellectual audiences and reach millions of possible readers? There is a vaulting vision here, and an historic victory to be won: the reconciliation of the West and the South (there is nothing here about the Communist East), thus saving peace, prosperity, human hope.

No mean task for an ambitious publicist, but the realities may just not be so. What if there is no such thing as "the South": or *le tiers monde*, or the Third World? Perhaps what we have to deal with is something much less dramatic, more mundane; a plurality of different peoples and economic crises often caught less in a problem of "development" than (as in Uganda, Tanzania, etc.) in a misery of "backwards-developing" societies? And what if the probability is dismally high that all that marvelous new technology, which is supposed to help the poor peoples make a great Utopian leap forward, will be distorted and exploited by a hundred ruling elites for their own power purposes? Strange to see in Paris, of all places, the political factor being so utterly overlooked.

I simply do not as a reader know what to make of an argument which constantly tells me that "the Third World wants..." and "the Third World feels..." It does not become any, more meaningful when, since the Brandt Report, it becomes the wishes, aspirations and demands of "the South." True, in some international conference of diplomats something called "the Group of 77" presents some urgent resolution or other to be passed; but then Cuba begins to roar a dissent in the name of "the socialist bloc": and fissiparous tendencies reassert themselves. When the simple fact of the matter is that the Palestinian question has not proved strong enough to unite the Arab world which now has its eyes fixed on an intra-Moslem war between Iraq and Iran—or does this also have to do with "Western greed" and the South's need to "attack poverty"?—then the cosmic notion of a Unity which links Latin America with Africa and Asia (including the Indian sub-continent. and the micro-insular world of the Pacific: Oceans must be seen for the fantasy it is. No amount of facts and figures about the technology of electronics and computers will make a "world-processor" out of this. Realities have to be programmed in before there is any hope of reality coming out.

Not that Servan-Schreiber doesn't come up here end there with something interesting and dramatic; he is, after, all, a man of many qualities who has often been courageous as well as unconventional. But form here just triumphs over content. All the popularizers from Vance Packard to Alvin Toffler seem to be learning more from each other than from the actual shape of developing things. We are simply being totally over-challenged. The sensational argumentation belongs to a new literary genre—works of the eco-imagination, or social-science fiction.

February-March 1981

European Diary

Incident in Vitry; "Terza Pagina"; Exit This Way

Incident in Vitry

The happening took place shortly before Christmas, and it involved some 300 or so Mohammedan workers from Mali, all emigrants from the same village and similarly dressed in their traditional *boubou* and *gandoura*. They had been living in a town not far from Paris, Vitry-sur-Seine in the Val-de-Marne department, since their *poste* in the neighboring commune of St Maur had been medically condemned and was to be reconstructed.

The mayor of Vitry, Paul Mercieca, happens to be a Communist, and the mayor of St Maur, Jean-Louis Beaumont, turns out to be a friend of President Giscard; and this double piquancy no doubt gave a special sharpness to the nationwide notoriety that both local politicians suddenly enjoyed.

Moving from St Maur to Vitry, the men from Mali—all workers who had left their families behind in "French Africa"—found themselves new and not unattractive living quarters, with the help of subsidies which the French government gives to foreign "guest-labor." In a matter of days (I am sorry, but it was Christmas Eve) the mayor made an official call in the company of senators and other local dignitaries, members of his Party and of the CGT-trade unions, and also a squad of sturdy law-and-order specialists. The concierge was arrested and handcuffed, and the hundreds of keys in his possession confiscated; gas and electricity were cut off; the boilers were put out of action; some damage to doors and windows symbolically testified to the new status of a "homeless community." Mayor Mercieca simply informed the representative of the Mali workers: "Back to St Maur—there's nothing here for you!"

The Malis wanted to stay where they were, and did, repairing as much as could be fixed and put into function again, and found themselves in the middle of yet another great French scandal Against the "commando action" of the Communist Party the entire Left rallied to protest. But one began to wonder: the protest was mainly against the "methods" but hardly against the essence of the operation. The socialists of Vitry, for example, were full of indignation mixed with pertinent housing advice on the availability of quarters...in St Maur. Well, it finally came up to the level of Georges Marchais, general-secretary of the Communist Party of France, to whom the imam of the mosque in Paris had written to ask for the disavowal of his local Party enthusiast. But Marchais only had loyal solidarity with his Vitry comrade, and he reiterated his warning that the Party disapproved of the creation of "ghettos" of foreign workers in the Paris outskirts. This raised a few eyebrows, for when other labor and liberal groups had expressed concern about such concentrations they had been charged by none other than Marchais' CPF with the most evil "racism."[1]

Why, in fact, was there a Foyer with hundreds of available beds in Vitry? The previous tenants were North Africans and Portuguese, and after a series of disagreeable protests over rent they had been forcibly removed by the CRS Police, all on the ground that Mayor Mercieca needed the places for young French proletarians. In any case, the problems were becoming "difficult," especially in the local schools where there were "too many foreign pupils." (Nobody found the argument credible, since schoolchildren were not involved here, only the billeting of male workers.)

The doubletalk soon spread, as Communist controlled communes elsewhere also raised the xenophobic hue and cry about "aliens" and "foreigners." A few intellectuals might have been outraged at this betrayal of the great enlightened traditions of Party and Revolution, but most political observers sensed the shrewd, perhaps even cynical, stratagem to win new votes. In some of the suburban communities of Paris the total of foreign workers amounts to some 13 to 17 percent, and "Internationalism" is just not on. The local cry is: "Enough is enough!" and in such an atmosphere of resentment and hostility the French Communist Party can only gain, not lose, from its "racist" turn. In and around Paris live (mostly from Africa and Portugal) more than a third of all the *ouvriers immigrés* in France. The stormy argument turns on whether they are actually taking away jobs—in automobile factories, construction sites, road-building—from Frenchmen, who are after all citizens...and voters.

Someone has suggested a liberal way out, namely by giving the vote to those foreign workers who have established residence after a certain number of years. This may not solve the underlying social problem, but no one doubts that there might be a resurgence of enlightened internationalism in the ranks of comrades Marchais and Mercieca— for workers who are also voters (at least in Western Europe) they have a deep respect.

"Terza Pagina"

No doubt about it journalism here has a special style and distinction, and no one, for example, can fail to be impressed by the major role of writers and poets in the columns of the Italian daily press. In France and Germany a few, Britain and the USA hardly any; but in Italy all the major literary voices have their platforms in the various newspapers of Rome, Milan, and Turin. On the one side, it could be that the *literati* and the intelligentsia here feel more strongly the crisis of values, of institutions and social behavior, and have accordingly been driven to engagement and commitment. On the other hand, it could be that the politicians and statesmen of postwar Italy were so utterly incapable of clear and incisive expression that the Italian writers had to take over the function of civic communication. This is the point that Italo Calvino makes in his recent book *Una pietra sopra* (Einaudi), thus explaining how he and all his colleagues came to be performing as a kind of billboard for the nation.

Then, too, there is the tradition in the Italian newspapers of the "*Terza Pagina*"; and once established as a feature the third page has to be filled with essays, fiction, poems, think pieces which the reader has come to expect. The first two columns are the so-called *Elzeviro*, often a short story, and if you have ever wondered why so many Italian writers produce so many short stories, remember this special little marketable corner. I myself have just been catching up with some of these in Bompiani's new collection by Luigi Malerba, *Dopo il pescecane* (After the Shark).

They are keen to supply the demand, but this has its dangers as well as its advantages. The writers are free to say anything, and they go on saying, chatting, musing and surmising, no matter what. This was the embarrassing case after the murder by the terrorists of Aldo Moro. In the *Corrière della Sera* the late Pier Paolo Pasolini had his guaranteed place to write as he pleased, even when it pleased him to call summarily for a "People's Trial" against the Christian Democrats; for, after all, he was an accredited revolutionary, a recognized moralist, a licensed prophet. As such he smote friends and foes alike.

I have often found in other European capitals, not to mention New York City, a certain envy and admiration for the Italian connection between highbrow writers and daily journalism. Does Saul Bellow write for the *Washington Post*? Did T. S. Eliot offer his verse to the *Times*? Grass and Böll wouldn't be found in the *Frankfurter Allgemeine Zeitung*. It could be that the postwar post-Fascist Italian press had a special need for prestige, for unlike in the rest of Europe the average citizen here reads less; fewer papers are sold; and journalism necessarily takes on an elitist character. Again, to give the other and shinier side of the coin, it might well be (as the writers themselves like to believe) that intellectuals sense more acutely the crisis of society and respond more urgently than the man-in-the-street to the call to duty and action. In any event, nowhere else that I know do the famous writers of a nation jump so rapidly into print whenever some public issue presents itself.

Calvino complains that the weekly and monthly magazines, which once used to play an important role in helping to mould public opinion, no longer do so. Still, for my own part, I feel a certain weariness as I receive yet another collection of ageing, yellowing clippings in the form of a new book of essays, editorials, comments, and general pronouncements. Alberto Moravia, until very recently, was unchallengeable as the fastest editorial gun in the West. Alas, one recalls as the years go by so very few of his pieces. Leonardo Sciascia is another whose *belles lettres* are more memorable than his newspaper columns. I feel no more cheered by the latest of the collections, a new book called *Un paese senza* (A country without), published by Garzanti for the fifty-year-old Alberto Arbasino, who explains that it is "an adieu to the 1970s, a farewell to a little-loved decade."

A country without what? Arbasino writes: "A country without memory, with a loss of general knowledge, without an awareness of its own anthropology, a land of dreamers with no roots in reality, of day-trippers into the imaginary, a land that has turned its back on itself, a land of provincialism which ignores all opinions but its own, and is prepared to assert itself even while being unclear about all essentials and repressing even the smallest details." In this spirit Arbasino, in the great tradition of Italian critics and prophets, accuses, attacks, satirizes, warns. The examples of Manzoni and Leopardi are detectable here, and indeed in the work of someone like Italo Calvino one senses that old Manzoni is being dragged into relevance. Arbasino, for all his thundering as a happy warrior, is still unhappy about the general literary situation: "Our Italian literature amounts to less, say, than the Austrian literature without German readers, or perhaps English literature without an American readership."

My worry is not that the Italian journalist-critic doesn't know what he is talking about, but rather that he is so totally over-informed. He reads everybody's novels, the histories from everywhere, and is up-to-the-minute about trends, modes, styles, and fashions. The references in his writings are so many and wide, the suggestive asides so innumerable, that in the end we are quite convinced that if his native land is thoroughly, completely, and hopelessly provincial it is fortunate at least in having in him a seer with a world horizon. I am afraid that the knowing winks of a know-it-all are themselves the signs and symptoms of a provincial. His point of departure is always that anything of importance is inevitably happening somewhere else. In Paris, as in New York, one constantly encounters the certainty that what's important is taking place now among them, and anything else—that is, before they begin to pay attention to it—simply doesn't exist. Arbasino is characteristic of that spirit in Italian writing today which suspects that greatness of spirit is not among them, is actually elsewhere. The charm and the error consist, of course, in not knowing how "typically Italian" all that is.

The note is registered in various scales by Luigi Malerba; and in one of his stories, "Mafioso," his protagonist is so impressed by the power of the *onorata società* (as the Mafia likes to think of itself) that he tries everywhere to "only connect," going even as far as the top man in the Ministry of Culture, to try to make contact, to join, to belong at long last, and of course he gets nowhere fast.

If the highbrows are a shade too bitter, some of the middlebrows save the day with a decent, modest tone of irony. Mondadori has just published the last collection of newspaper pieces I will mention, Luca Goldoni's *Dipende* (It all depends...). It is good to get a moralist sometimes who is less engaged and funnier than the all-too-earnest Moravias and Arbasinos. As Goldoni writes, "We are not a people of 57 million—but of 56 million, 999 thousand, 999, plus one. This one is every one of us—when he gets around to talking about all the others."

Exit This Way

If there is one conspicuous example of efficiency in the East German set up, it is the Exit Visa department. You don't even have to apply to get out. The latest "emigrants" are two more writers, and it is almost as if Lenin liked the Platonic idea of banning men of art from the ideal republic. Frank-Wolf Mathies, aged thirty, and the twenty-nine-year-old Lutz Rathenow have now joined a long line of East German writers in the West who never even asked to leave. Some, like Wolf Biermann, get the bittersweet news while doing their stint abroad; others are simply "transported."

For young Germans, born and bred in the postwar East German Communist Republic, it is always a difficult fate to comprehend, this cruel expatriation from "the only thing we know," the DDR. But in a society where everything is nationalized and is the property of the State, anybody can be expropriated and subject to export. The East German minister of culture once announced in Leipzig that "Unsere Literatur gehort uns (Our literature belongs to us!)...." What he meant was that it didn't belong to you, or to some "common national culture of two separate states" (which the DDR's constitution still mentions), certainly not to the shared language or the outside world. In Germany the phrase for chattel slaves or indentured servants was *Leibeigenen*, for the bodies belonged to their owners; now we have the new concept of *Geisteigene*, for minds and spirits are also part of the new social property-relations. When a bureaucracy considers itself to be the owner of literature, then it has the absolute personal right not only to cultivate its own garden but also to remove ruthlessly such weeds as it deems harmful.

In this light why treat young writing as a bloom of new flowers? Rowohlt in Hamburg was the Western publisher who brought out a collection of the stories of Frank-Wolf Mathies, and in one of the tales he writes of Elisabeth G.'s "panic every time she switched on to the television station of the land she lived in and felt herself paralyzed by the voices and words addressed to her..." As for the green automobile which she saw parked on the street opposite her house, inside were three men "who did nothing but sit inside, unmistakably self-confident, unmistakably bored...." Weeds, nothing but poisonous weeds.

Ullstein (in West Berlin) is the publisher of Lutz Rathenow's work, and the one I have been reading is called *Mit dem Schlimmsten wurde schon gerechnet* (One has already reckoned with the worst). In it there is a "*Protokoll*" against two unfortunate characters, with an enormous dossier of testimony, legal petitions, evidence from workers' collectives, and whatnot. The investigation has to do with the disappearance of a little piece of electrical apparatus, actually a minor switch to install electric lighting in a factory toilet, in order to make the proletariat happier. It is all so humdrum and harmless, but the atmosphere conveyed is dark and uncanny. Not something we would want in our garden.... We don't need the spurious sensitivity that registers "a significant loss in the collective discipline," even if the reference is only to declining team spirit during a Saturday afternoon football match.

Like so many other talented older East German writers, they could only publish their new work in the West. But this fact alone—quite apart from whatever was written, or its explication by literary critics—is a culpable act nowadays because it has been legislated into illegality on the grounds of "foreign-currency impropriety." If only that were the sum total of the matter! Why, then, the confiscation of manuscripts and the inquisition of novelists and poets' Well; the minister of culture (who, of course, owns it all), says that writers who get published elsewhere should go elsewhere. Even then he is not altogether consistent, and leaves a dialectical exception for authors like Stefan Heym who still live in the East and go on publishing in the West...at the moment.

The problem of a split culture has been with the Germans now for decades, and a long time ago when Uwe Johnson chose to move his books and writing table from East to West across a still-open frontier he explained that he was merely transplanting himself from one currency area to another. He said nothing then of censorship or political pressures; but even the mere "financial" stratagem has taken on the character of a cultural crime. Try as they might, German writers are finding it well nigh impossible to keep on improvising "bridges" across the two cultures. Günter Grass has spent years advocating an all-German Cultural Foundation that might support a bridge between the two Germanys, otherwise so hopelessly divided politically and economically. But the peremptory expulsion of the literati, young and old, indicates that the break is nowhere sharper than here. When they hear the word culture, they reach for your passport.

April 1981

Note

1. As I write, a Paris correspondent reports: "The French Communist party yesterday denied that M. Georges Marchais, its leader and presidential candidate, had warned Parisians of the danger that Asian immigration could turn parts of Paris into a 'Hong Kong on Seine.'

"However the sense of the Communist leader's warning, continuing an obvious attempt to win white votes in areas heavily inhabited by immigrants, appeared to be the same, if less colorfully expressed:

"'The situation created by the Government and by M. Chirac, Mayor of Paris, in the Place d'Italie area where thousands of South East Asian refugees are now concentrated, leads me to emphasize that we Communists are opposed to the formation of ghettos of any kind with all the problems of cohabitation, schooling and social burdens which they create."

The area in question is thickly populated with Vietnamese, Cambodians, and Laotians who have fled from the Communist takeover in Indo-China.
(*Daily Telegraph*, 16 February)

European Diary

French Ideology

At least in this the French remain unique: no other people can take a book so seriously. Here, at the moment, is an ideological pamphlet that deals with a few ideas out of the nineteenth century, reconsiders life and letters under the Vichy régime, and debunks a few schoolboy notions—and it has been for months now at the centre of a national controversy. Indeed on the front page of *Le Monde* both the chief editor and the foreign editor have felt compelled to clarify their own views on the whole provocative subject.

To be sure, pamphlets have always played such a role in French politics, at least ever since the great explosion caused by Abbé Sieyes' screed, *Qu'est-ce que le Tiers État?*. They need not be narrowly political, for literature, philosophy, and even anthropology have been known to fuse furious argumentation on a national scale. One thinks in recent years of the writings of Jean-Paul Sartre and Albert Camus, and of the disputes over the nature of Soviet Russia in little Left Bank magazines. And only the other season the young men of the so-called *"Nouveaux Philosophes"* movement became best-selling authors because their books became what are known as "media-events." It seems so strange and surprising for a new generation to come along and attack the grand old tradition of *gauchisme* that everybody felt obliged to sit up and take notice.

After all, "Anti-Communism" is still taken to be a kind of "visceral" phenomenon, having essentially to do with the "gut reaction" of a bourgeoisie worried about its private property. Could there actually be anti-Communists who attack Marxist-Leninist repression because they believe in freedom and an open society? What a shock to have to acknowledge figures out of the militant '68 generation as tribunes against totalitarianism of the Left! And they didn't even have guilt-complexes about getting "applause from the false side."

An intellectual scandal, but more than that—for; where a presidential election is decided by so few votes (last time by not more than a few hundred thousand), then such currents and counter-currents on the cultural scene have to be taken in earnest. The counter-offensive on the part of the "New Philosophers" against the Nouvelle Droite was no less notable. Leading these outriders of the wild West is Bernard-Henri Lévy, busy not only with his own books but as an editor and publisher of a whole series of other titles from other authors.[1]

His third book, *L'ideologie française* (Grasses) has caused a greater stir than the others. He smites friend and foe on both Left and Right, and perhaps most of all the "Myth" of France, the mythology of its democratic universalism, its *"rayonnement,"* its presence of a radiating enlightenment. The debunking argument is based in part around Gobineau, whose notorious *Essay on the Inequality of Human Races* established a disastrous form of European racism; and in part around the true correlation of forces in the affair of the Dreyfus case, with Church and Army and even a section of the French Left stooping to anti-Semitic abuse as the good Captain gets condemned as a spy and sent off to Devil's Island. And, in part, it is about Marshal Pétain who was responsible for a Vichy law about the Jews which pre-empted Nazi occupation policy and even went beyond what Hitler had in mind at the time. As for the so-called Left opposition, it has to be recalled that the French C.P. was for a while pro-Vichy and helped to denounce its Popular Front allies when Léon Blum and Edouard Daladier came up for Pétainist assault.

All traditions go; little remains, and there are no excuses allowed. Lévy has little patience with the rationalizations that would blame the influence of party bosses in Moscow or the power of the Nazis in Berlin. France herself is the source of the fascist, anti-democratic potential in the nation.

As a piece of intellectual and cultural history the book has obvious weaknesses. There was another tradition which criticized Gobineau, defended Dreyfus, resisted Pétain; but it is not one which interests the author at the moment when bombs destroy synagogues, police round up foreign workers, and official censorship stealthily increases. Can one distortion ever serve to rectify another distortion? In any event, once again a book is in the news, provoking the citizenry, and keeping the French penchant for polemics at the boil.

May 1981

Note

1. See my previous comments on Levy's ideas in *Encounter*: "The Very Latest from Paris" (March 1980), "God's Own Testament" (September 1979) and "A Year of the 'New Philosophers'" (November 1978).

European Diary

Sartre, a Year Later

Perhaps Sartre was a better prophet than even he pretended: he has been dead a year now, but some thirty-five years earlier, just as he was beginning his postwar fame in 1945, he said: "C'est terrible...tout vivant un monument!" (how awful to be a living monument....). Another remark came to mind as I looked at the hundreds of articles which were published to mark his death and now its first anniversary: in an interview with *Le Nouvel Observateur* in 1975 he revealed: "I admire nobody, and I don't like it when people admire me. We are not here to be admired." But a moment later he qualified this to say: "*Admirer*, this is a feeling which is based on the sense of being inferior to the admired one. *Estimer*, this is an authentic attitude which one can have to another."

Something less than admiration or esteem accompanied the official feelings, expressed un-memorably at the time by President Giscard d'Estaing and Prime Minister Raymond Barre; but *Le Figaro*, in which paper Sartre had once published his dispatches from America, wanted to give vent to the Right's ideological feelings in no uncertain way and went so far as to offer a rather tasteless (and untranslatable) venereal pun: *Un chantre mou*.... So it was that on this occasion, even those critics of his zigzag intellectual course, with its political reversals and moral contradictions, felt a certain solidarity with the man and his life. There is a special low level in French polemics that contrives only to honor its victims.

Still, this can only be expected when figures of the intellectual elite spin away from the esoteric world and become Cult Figures. Sartre's name became a credential and his signature a label as he rushed valiantly to assume a "publisher's" responsibility for papers or magazines that might otherwise have been repressed. All this, and the petitions he signed and the international "courts of inquiry" he blessed, is almost forgotten and is no longer weighed in the balance when currently Sartre is given the "estimate" he expected, the "judgment of posterity." The anger and resentment appears to be gone from even the sharpest criticism, which I find nowadays quite free from yesterday's hateful pettiness. What is notable is the cool distance that time can give, for a year is indeed a long time in the posthumous history of a "total intellectual."

I have just been reading two new books published here which have put Sartre back into the French discussion, and they are worth noting. Olivier Todd, before he became a columnist for the rather right-of-center *L'Express*, was a regular writer for the left-wing *Le Nouvel Observateur* and was closely connected with Sartre's monthly review, *Les Temps Modernes*. His volume of memoirs, *Un fits rebelle* (Grasset), is at once a view of Sartre in those years and a self-portrait. In an almost literal way Todd is attempting to bring Sartre back to life and he quotes him to this effect: "I am used to armed attacks. One assaults me, robs me of purse and honor, and runs away. I rise and come back again. The bullet or the knife have left no marks."

These words are from the year 1956, and it was a time when much in Sartre changed, withered, revived. In the spring Sartre had revealed himself as a late-Stalinist and defended against all critics the record of the French Communist Party and the Soviet Union. His attitude towards the Bolshevik leadership can only be called admiration. Moscow's course was wise and sound, indubitably progressive and in tune with history. He traveled in Russia and in his reports he seemed to come across an intellectual and cultural freedom that existed nowhere else in the world. Then in the autumn came the events in Budapest, and after the Hungarian Revolution a surprised and shocked Sartre confessed that he now could feel only a total rejection of the Soviet system. Nevertheless he composed himself enough to remark that much of the fault was due to Nikita Khrushchev's error: namely, making public the whole record of Stalin's crimes, which the people (given their economic backwardness) were not yet mature enough to comprehend and master.

The years between 1953 and 1956 were embattled ones, and as he himself admitted certain inner disasters were camouflaged by a public aggressiveness. No matter; little harm could come to a philosopher of such fame and distinction, enjoying a curious protection of both invincibility and power which, indeed, Sartre (in his autobiography *Les Mots*) strictly rejected for literary intellectuals, but which he nevertheless exploited to advantage.

Although the political critique is not new, Olivier Todd documents Sartre's career from the writing tables of the Café Flore to the battlefields of Vietnam with many striking personal details. It is not an account without ambiguities, perhaps inevitably so, for the author is at once a confidant, a critic, and a chronicler pleased with the cultural importance of the whole moving subject. Here is a snapshot of a harassed and angry Sartre, dismissing out of hand all the critical reviewers, but admitting that he had not read a word of them, had only "heard about them from friends."

More of the man can also be found in the pages of Bernard Frank's *Solde* (Flammarion), a lively book with many colorful sketches and anecdotes, all related with much humor and no vanity. It has been less of a success than Todd's book possibly because the author is taken less seriously, since Frank as a companion of Françoise Sagan and the "frivolous" Saint-Germain des

Pres set is all too lightly dismissed for his charm and wit. Here, in contrast, is the "respectlessness" which Sartre himself preached and which does the subject good. I found many details unforgettable: Sartre and Simone de Beauvoir on a bicycle tour to search for a Maquis and returning to Paris empty-handed; Sartre meeting André Malraux, talking through a long and delicious meal, while Simone waits quietly, patiently in a nearby cafe. Nothing is meanly told, and the points all relevant: "One wonders whether Sartre ever asked himself how it was that his cutting conclusions always conveniently connected themselves with a special inquiry commission as in a short-circuit." It used to be said that when Sartre raised his flag over a building, one could be sure that it would soon be blown to bits.

Frank is interesting too on that great torso of Sartre's *Flaubert* study, now taken to be such a standard classic in many parts of the Continent (Germany, for example) but not in France or the Anglo-Saxon world. He is properly skeptical and wonders why Sartre thought his thousand pages of Flaubert were such an illumination of contemporary literary dilemmas. Once again, Sartre sets us all at some dramatic crossroads where we can only expect the worst. In any case Sartre never finished the work, and it remains a kind of cliffhanger of literary criticism, leaving us in eternal suspense as to whether *Madame Bovary* was to be an authentic masterpiece, or indeed whether it would, in the next thousand pages, ever have got written at all.

Let me note too the memoirs of a priest which were recently published, for they report on the days which he shared in the same German Stalag when Sartre wrote a "mystery play" at Christmas for the benefit of the camp inmates. Thereafter the friendship between the theologian and the atheist remained untroubled.

As for the Sartrean relationship to the arts, there is a special number of the review *Obliques* which deals with the sculptor Giacometti, the German "Kafkaesque" painter Wols (who died in Paris in 1951 and had illustrated works by Sartre, Artaud et al.), and many others whose talents he recognized early on. Here also is the unfinished Tintoretto, fragment, of which only an excerpt had been published in *Les Temps Modernes*. The earlier special issue of *Obliques* had printed for the first time pages from Sartre's *Ethics*; and the expectation is strong that we will be getting many surprising items in the collection of posthumous writings.

All in all, my impression is that the French attitude towards Sartre has become, with distance, easier, more complex, subtler: even aloof. I note that in Vincent Descombes' recent history of French philosophy, *The Self and the Other: 1933-1978*, Sartre is only given some seven pages (and in an appendix!), and that not a word is given to *L'Etre et le Neant*; on the other hand, his old friend and colleague, Maurice Merleau-Ponty, who later went his own philosophical (and political) way, is awarded a whole chapter. This is, I am told, not untypical, for the influence of Merleau-Ponty is showing itself far stronger in France, and elsewhere. The non-philosophers, strongly drawn to Sartre as a writer, persist in seeing in the old star an incomparable man of thought. To be sure, a reputation's changes of fortune constantly move up, down, and around; and these views will also be revised. A great spirit has more than one afterlife.

The current turn of the wheel is for Sartreans rather unfavorable. We are too close to have new perspectives and yet too distant to be affected in the old overwhelming way. I recall that a year after the death of Albert Camus an article appeared in the newspaper which he had helped to establish (Robert Kanters in *Combat*) with the headline: CAMUS S'ÉLOIGNE. He may have been "moving away" then, but these days he is being read as never before.

If the tone of last year's obituaries is nowhere to be found today, one can always say that Sartre never strove for an unquestioning esteem. Only in the German intellectual reviews is he still getting an uncritical reception for his views and judgments, and even his scattered views on *Madame Bovary* have been collected to give testimony, or shed light', or whatever. In any event I find the French relationship to Sartre decidedly more appropriate than the one I encounter in Germany, the critical spirit more independent, the commentaries more detached.

As for the Anglo-Americans, let me add a last word, for this is something which the French characteristically ignore and the systematic Germans overlook: for in recent years, I am convinced, the most interesting and important studies of Sartre have been appearing in English. In this respect it is we Continentals who have proved ourselves to be "insular." Among many I mention only two: the recent American study of *Heidegger and Sartre* by Joseph P. Fell (Columbia University Press, 1979), and the older, much neglected little book by the English novelist and former Oxford philosophy don, Iris Murdoch, which strikes me as still being superior to the French and German monographs on the subject.[1]

There is a special kind of attention being paid here, at once critical and creative, which goes quite beyond the bounds of anecdotal memoirs and the confines of admiration (or esteem) and debunking. To follow too closely Sartre's by-ways in literary circles is to miss the philosophical dimension of the thinker who was fixated on Hegel, Husserl, Heidegger. Strange that this cross-Rhine culture I connection should be more illuminated by the "Anglo-Saxons" than by the French and Germans themselves. In any case, it does seem to me the "thinking about Sartre" without the contributions of the Anglo-Americans remains, like those characters in *Huis Clos*, narrowly confined in "closed rooms."

July 1981

Note

1. I should also mention here Peter Caws' excellent study *Sartre* (Routledge, 1979).

European Diary

A Dividend for Marchais; Italian Miracle

A Dividend for Marchais

I suppose that one must now, in the light of what 1 has just happened, take a backward glance at the phenomenon of "Euro-Communism" (about which I and George Urban and others have written so much in these columns). There were the Big Three: Berlinguer, Carrillo, Marchais; and all of them in varying degrees seemed to be wrestling with similar ideological problems. These included: a new critical distance to the USSR and Kremlin foreign policy; a doctrinal abandonment of the theorems of "the Dictatorship of the Proletariat" and a One-Party regime; a readiness to make long-term alliances with Socialists and Social Democrats and indeed with bourgeois-liberal parties; and a perspective of extending the social achievements of "bourgeois democracy" without abandoning civil liberties (no longer taken to be mere "illusions" and "formal" freedoms).

All of us, amateur and professional birdwatchers of the Party Line, came to two conclusions when faced with the question of why the Spanish, Italian, and French Communist Parties were whirling about so unusually, and chirping such strange songs.

1. In the first place, it appeared to be a strategy to move closer to the levers of state power. There seemed to be a recognition of what had to be avoided: namely, their long-range exclusion from all important governmental decisions as a "permanent opposition," as well as a sharpening of the struggle into civil-war proportions which could only lead to some reactionary-authoritarian regime coming to power. Berlinguer dramatized the point by referring to the end of President Allende in Chile when he explained to the Italian comrades the importance of an "historic compromise" with Christian Democrats.

2. At the same time it all had to do with the historic troubles which have long afflicted the Soviet claim to ultimate leadership of all the parties in their Communist International. It was, after all, Palmiro Togliatti, the late leader of the Italian Communists, who first announced "Polycentrism." It was also part of the growing mental inability to defend "the Soviet model" of a New Society, and even more to apologist for such "progressive" interventions as the "brotherly" invasion of Hungary and Czechoslovakia.

It was, no doubt, Carrillo who went further than the others in his critique of the USSR (once the "workers' paradise"), in his acknowledgment of the merits of "pluralistic democracy" (once a mere capitalistic sham). By contrast Marchais seemed only to be paying reluctant lip service to the new ideological notions; his formulations sounded rough and opportunistic. It was hardly out of character when just before the Parliamentary elections in France in 1978 he instigated the break-up of the Left Coalition and subsequently acceded to Brezhnev's demands for "solidarity" with the Soviet move into Afghanistan. During the recent campaign Marchais was in fine old form, defending "the French proletariat" as his local mayoralty candidates took brutal measures against foreign workers in the Paris suburbs; and not least, castigating the socialist campaign of François Mitterrand.

And yet the party found itself in a position to be able to snatch an historic victory from the jaws of an electoral defeat wherein a fourth of its traditional voters went elsewhere. The price of having four ministers in the new cabinet may have been humiliating, but it was quickly paid. To what extent this will further weaken the Party or enable it to rally its followers remains to be seen. But who was there in the 1970s who would have predicted that, after turning its back on "Euro-Communism" and breaking with a Socialist movement that grew to command an absolute nation-wide majority, the Party would be rewarded with just those prizes that seemed to have been finally lost?

And what of the brave new world of Euro-Communist ideals in Spain and Italy? Here all the hopes of the "democratized" strategy and tactics turned out to be chimerical. Nothing paid off. In Spain the Catalans revolted against Carrillo, and there were serious intellectual defections as the contrast between a liberalized ideology and the old authoritarian Party structure became glaring. In Italy the Communists appear to be as far from having a share of governmental power as ever before. Their electoral support has been dwindling from old-time highs, and Signor Craxi's Socialist Party has been renewing itself and growing.

Politics has its paradoxes. As in the dealings of the Bourse, dividends are often paid out not to those who have invested but to those who have sold short.

Italian Miracle

There are very few observers who have taken on the challenge of trying to explain "the Italian miracle" namely the wondrous survival of this land wracked by more troubles than most ordinary nations could live through. Encounter readers will recall the ingenious interpretations in these pages by Domenico Bartoli, one of the most keen-witted of Italian journalists (a former Editor of *Il resto del Carlino* and *La Nazione*). After an earlier book on the "Italian No-Man's Land" he has now taken another look at the roots of the

Italian malaise in a book entitled *The Years of the Storm* (*Gli anni delta tempesta: Alle radici dei malessare Italiano*, Editoriale Nuova, Milano).

No one can fail to be astonished by the relative stability of Italian life, despite the Terror from an "Armed Party" which is still powerful and despite corruption scandals that proliferate sinisterly, even beyond the range of the traditional Mafia and the "*sottogoverno*." The way the Italians order these things nowadays has miraculous qualities, though quite different ones from the "Italian Miracle" which characterized the dynamic burst of economic energies in the first two decades after the end of Mussolini's regime.

The puzzle is everyday: how can so much private initiative still develop in a society which combines a maximum of bureaucratic inefficiency with a minimum of governmental authority and decisiveness? How can the great nationalized industries actually keep going when managers never have time to go in for business management but need all their time and know how to manoeuvre in the political jungle? How can things add up when no amount of un-profitability and deficit ever leads to a bankruptcy? And how can the taxpayer (who rarely pays taxes) pay for everything in an increasingly devalued currency?

Bartoli's point of departure is the "third disaster." For him the first disaster was the collapse of Liberal Italy between 1922 and 1925; and the second catastrophe was the collapse of Fascism in a senseless war. The economic and political "decay" since 1970 is the third disaster in a time-span of only 60 years. Bartoli has an historical sense, and Fascism for him remains a piece of Italian history and not (as it is often presented) the story of an adventurous demagogic *condottiere*. Only in recent years, especially after the recognition in many Italian circles of the emptiness of the old tag "anti-Fascist," have there been real attempts to make hard sense of the past.

One cannot help, therefore, being struck by certain Italian patterns of adjustment to and compromise with strong political power that have a disconcertingly topicality. How easy it has apparently been for well-known Fascists to make the transition to the Catholic forces or to the Communist Party, simply by substituting one rhetorical style for another. The examples Bartoli offers are embarrassingly numerous; but then there is also the opposite movement, and he recalls one Mussolini "true believer" (even in the lunacies of a Nazi-style *Rassenpolitik*) who turned, changed, and finally died in one of Hitler's concentration camps.

After 1945, failing the active presence of national traditions, the country seemed to be turning to a kind of "Church-State" form. But if there was an Alcide de Gasperi who defended principled positions (his "Austrian" background?), there was also the flexible opportunism of an Andreotti who could move easily from extreme clericalism to an alliance with the Communists.

Still, these may only be the wrigglings on the agitated political surface. Deep down there are other factors such as the decline of marriage and the fall in the population, rising unemployment and the mounting numbers of foreign (African) workers trying to improve themselves in a "modern economy" where certain jobs will just find no native takers. The firmly cemented position of the trade unions in an industrial society—sometimes taking "dogmatic" decisions, sometimes (as in England) being merely "bloody-minded"—has also played a role in paralyzing some of the newly found dynamism. Still, Italians will not be put down. I note that in Turin recently, the workers, faced with an arbitrary call to down tools and go out on strike, took to the streets to demonstrate their unwillingness.

It is a thesis full of ironies that Bartoli is offering us—on the one hand a dedication to extremist activities, and on the other a devotion to entitlements for jobs and pensions. In Italy we can see "revolutionification" and "bureaucratization" going hand in hand, as Post-Industrial Man demands at one and the same time his rights and privileges and all other appurtenances from a despised State which he steadily wants to weaken, and if possible see disappear. If this is Bartoli's "Italian Paradox," then it would be foolish to expect any kind of better future, only a hardening of the well-known Italian difficulties. But Italy has never been short of ingenuity, and it seems constantly to be able to find new uses for old abuses.

September 1981

European Diary

On the Death of a Friend: Romain Gary

A few months ago my friend Romain Gary killed himself. He left behind a last note, written in his almost childish handwriting which, as I know from the days when we were classmates in the same French *lycée*, had scarcely changed over the long years: the same tiny script in which he wrote, never altering a stroke, his fifteen or twenty books, of which the best were not the most successful, and the easiest became best-sellers and famous films, all (with possibly one exception) unfailingly less than good. In one film, which he himself had produced and directed, the leading role was played by a Hollywood star who happened to be his wife. A few months before his own suicide she was found dead in a car, parked in a Paris side street to which, in view of the pills and drugs she had taken, she could not have driven alone. For my own part, I do not believe that Jean Seberg's death, or the macabre circumstances accompanying the police inquiry and the autopsy, provides any kind of key to Romain Gary's final decision. He himself put the point vigorously in his last letter. They had long been separated. "I used to be her husband, then I became her father..." he said of the tragic American girl who was some twenty-five years his junior. Naturally the boulevard press in a half-dozen European capitals, not to mention the gossip columnists in Manhattan, all had special versions of their own.

Romain Gary was not only an enthralling storyteller, marked by the humor of his Slavic-Jewish background (which the French found so agreeably alien), but a man of adventure, spectacular as a fighter-pilot or diplomat or roving reporter; and he would hardly have been surprised at the fictional publicity.

In Bern, as I remember, when he was a French attaché, he was living with his first wife, the English novelist Lesley Blanch, who was somewhat older than he. She taught him to write in English, in a rather elegant prose-style of his own, and a number of these novels (such as *Lady L.*) he later translated into French. I know at least two thrillers of his that he penned under a pseudonym, and I suspect there were others. Who knows what a full bibliography of his writings would look like? He had a weakness for literary hoaxes, and in one case actually republished an early novel under a new title. Only last summer in Zurich he dug out for me a sheaf of notices, and not a single reviewer had spotted the "revival." Had he simply fooled his readers, or was the novel that forgettable? We were friends and I repressed the question.

For me, Romain Gary was so fascinating an entertainer that I always felt it irrelevant or out of place to venture the critical question about literary quality. Some of his novels are obviously very close to his own personal adventures; others take place in German-occupied Poland among partisans and refugees, or in Vichy France among youth gangs; and although he was at the time either in London or in Africa, these were among his strongest pieces of fiction.

The day after his death had been reported in the newspapers came a telephone call from a popular illustrated Paris weekly. As an old friend I was supposed to explain, to tell the whole story, to reveal it all. How could I? A reporter flew down to see me anyway, stayed overnight, and grumbled only when he left, "Didn't get much out of you, you know...." They expected more since one of his books, a kind of autobiographical novel, consists of a dialogue between the two of us. But this too was a joke, a trick, a hoax if you will. The manuscript of the book was quite complete when he gave it to me and suggested only that I insert some questions and remarks of my own in order to fill it out. (Perhaps he had been inspired by a story I once told him of how that fine writer, Witold Gombrowicz, had composed an autobiography and pretended that it was a French interview, although he had written it in Polish and in the English version the interviewer simply disappeared.) Original texts are not always reliable primary sources.

I once asked him for a short story, and I published it in the Paris monthly review I was editing at the time. Called "Sunshine," it was the tale of a German Jew whose business manager had taken over his company ("Aryanized" it, as it was termed) and in whose cellar he remained hidden from the police. In the hopeless darkness he thought of Goethe and Schiller and whether old German humanist values could ever be saved. Years went by. His loyal protector came down and told him, every now and then, how the war was progressing. All sense of time is lost, and the reader soon suspects that peace had long since broken out but that the man in the cellar didn't know it, would never know it.

Romain had something of the passion and persistence of a tribal bard, and he once compared himself to a gypsy violinist. I have known a few others, with Eastern talents married to Western experience: Gregor von Rezzori, for example, who also moves from heights to depths and, when he rises again, flies better than most would give him credit for. But they win only notoriety and have only themselves to blame.

Romain Gary was one of that type of man who, as they age, like to put on different faces, showing themselves with beard, and then only mustachios, and finally clean-shaven again. He was obsessed with himself. I once accompanied him in Zurich when he went shopping for an expensive fountain pen; he must have tried his hand at a dozen, testing them all, writing his own name again and again. He was an observer of sharpness and exactitude, felt things intuitively, worried about his friends and couldn't simply stand by when they were ill or troubled. One of our former schoolmates became despondent after a divorce, and Romain set about finding him another wife, arranging for their marriage in Geneva where they were presumably to live happily ever after.

Every once in a while he would call me up, and suddenly ask, without preamble or explanation, "Did you ever really understand? ..."

"No," I would answer, "I didn't either..." Whereupon he would hang up, apparently satisfied.

This, I take it, was his aching sense of the meaninglessness of things, of floating in unreality, and it must in the end have overpowered him. He had just taken a holiday with his son in Greece; friends reported they had seen him, the night before, in Saint-Germain-des-Prés. With what insight I know not but his son said that he "understood" his father's suicide, talking to that curious reporter to whom I could find nothing to say. I never found out what that understanding was. My friendship and my incomprehension belonged together for most of a lifetime.

Strange that his readers should have been so demonstrably moved to hope, to take up dedicated causes, to side so sympathetically with the author. I still get an occasional call from one of his oldest and most loyal fans. She never met him but remains convinced that they somehow shared a love, that she could have mothered him, that she might have been the only woman in his life, that he was the one man she would have given anything to know. Taken together, her confidences to me, as an "old friend," tell the whole story of her life, marriage, affairs, career. I doubt whether I really know more about anybody than this character straight out of a Romain Gary story. The last time she phoned she was sobbing and couldn't go on.

That was the moment when I at least understood one thing: why he was constantly changing his address or his telephone number, and why it seemed such a privilege to know where he lived and how he could be reached. It took me out of my benumbed sadness and raised the query how an author could so dominate a reader, and not necessarily by means of the finest literary techniques. What novels, after all, did Emma Bovary read? I mused over the kind of tale Romain Gary might have been inspired to write about this posthumous incident, and was even tempted to put pen to paper myself. Then I happened to recall that in one of his novels he tried to renew the old legend of "the Dybbuk": a tale of how a Jewish victim creeps into the soul of a German policeman.... My old friend must not become my own Dybbuk.

The man was something of a hero, a fabulist, a high-flyer, a showman. He thought of himself as "a lyrical clown," or sometimes as "a terrorist of humor." He tried to combine slapstick with sentiment, to mix a vision of real horrors with comic grotesqueries. Am I, with these feeble attempts at characterization, only trying to protect my soul from his persistent influence? It could be that I am yet again failing to understand, to comprehend what it was in the mind of my oldest friend that led him to lie down on his sofa and fire a bullet into his forehead.

In its obituary columns (4 December 1980), the *Times* wrote: "M. Romain Gary, who took his life on Dec. 2, at his Paris flat, was one of the revivers of the romantic novel in the Russian tradition. He was 66. In the words of M. Maurice Schumann of the French Academy, he was a hero after the manner of Dostoevsky and Joseph Kessel...He used to say of himself: 'I have not a drop of French blood, but France runs in my veins.' He was one of the first to join General de Gaulle in London: 'My relations with him were very difficult, and of my dozen meetings with him he threw me out of his office four or five times. He rather liked my cheek.'... His best known novels included *Les Racines du Ciel* which won him the Goncourt Prize in 1956 and was later filmed. The highly successful *Lady L* was also adapted for the screen, by Peter Ustinov, with Sophia Loren in the title role."

August 1981

A Man and His Double

It is rare indeed that a literary obituary need to compete with fast-moving cultural events, but in the case of my memoir of the life and death of Romain Gary (277-280) no sooner was it in print than the newspapers here were carrying revelations which called for a bit of curious updating.

I had noted my suspicions that Romain Gary's penchant for pseudonyms would one day cause the bibliography of his various works to be revised. But now with all the drama of a Pirandello character switch the whole case of "Emile Ajar" has been added to the Gary story.

It was in 1973 that a young and unknown French author suddenly was acclaimed as the author of a masterpiece entitled *Gros-câlin*. No one knew the name, Emile Ajar, but he soon followed with another novel which also became a best-seller (and later was made into a film with Simone Signoret). Nobody had yet seen the now famous author, and when he rejected literary prizes (including the Goncourt), journalists became even more eager to snap a photo and catch him for a quick interview. Finally, in Copenhagen, the mask apparently fell—and a nephew of Romain Gary, Paul Pavlowitch, stepped into the limelight. The game was up, and he went on to become the literary editor of Mercure de France, his publisher. No one thought of Uncle, who had appeared as a figure of some fun in Ajar's novel *Pseudo*.

But alas, when Romain Gary committed suicide last December, with him also died "the young hope" of French literature, whose four books had been so enthusiastically praised by so many Paris critics who never had a kind word for Gary's own books penned under his own name. Among his papers there was a full report: on the Life and Death of Emile Ajar. Ironically enough, the nephew now emerged from behind the shadow of the uncle, as Paul Pavlowitch rushed into print with a confession of his own, *L'homme que l'on croyait Ajar* (just published by Fayard). On the dust cover the name AJAR is printed in gigantic letters, as if this were yet another book from the hidden hand of the mysterious author. But it was only the effort of a would-be ghostwriter to cast a small shadow of his own.

Pavlowitch has also just appeared on Bernard Pivot's popular TV show, *Apostrophe*, telling his story sympathetically; and the final Pirandello turn was provided by the novelist Michel Tournier, who did a piece of impressive literary detection by locating the "Ajar style" in an early piece of fiction by Romain Gary. As for the Paris critics who condemned Gary as "an entertainer" and praised Emile Ajar as "a creative artist," they haven't been heard from yet. They will just have to accept the fact that the mercurial Romain Gary made two names for himself as a writer. (He was the only author to be awarded two Goncourt prizes, since no one writer can, according to the by-laws, win twice.) I suspect that he himself found the double game deeply upsetting when the growing reputation of his playful creature began to overshadow his own. Two souls dwelled, Faust-like, in his breast; and he put an end to one before finally putting an end to the other.

October 1981

European Diary

Where is Prussia?; In the Vienna Woods

Where is Prussia?

One could over the years see bits of "Prussian feeling" accumulating, and now the gigantic West Berlin exhibition has tried to "draw a balance" of the splendors and miseries of the Prussian past. A Socialist mayor took the initiative, a Conservative mayor opened it; but little was heard from the "legitimate successors" of the powers-that-used-to-be in Mark Brandenburg. Neither President Carstens nor Chancellor Schmidt made the trip from Bonn, and I detected no trace of any minister. If these still be "Prussians," neither punctuality nor the old sense of duty sways them. To be sure, old Dr. Adenauer wouldn't have turned up either, not merely because "*der Alte*" didn't care much for Berlin—like Churchill he was firmly convinced that Prussia was the root of all German evils.

And with that we are already deep into the controversy of the Prussian Exhibition. There must be a hundred books and at least a thousand important articles published on the subject pro et contra, over this past year. Even the Exhibition itself is hard to get hold of, spreading as it does over some thirty-three different shows. One can easily go astray, and no wonder that important themes seem to have been lost—foreign critics have been wondering whatever happened to Hegel, and where did Bismarck disappear to, and can it be true that Kant's old city of Konigsberg is now Kaliningrad?

I listened to a half-dozen lectures and roundtable discussions, and the one word which was repeated most often was "*Ambivalenz*." The American historian of Prussia, Gordon Craig, seemed to be especially amused by this most un-Prussian notion. But surely this is the key concept, for Prussian history, soberly presented and analyzed, exhibits both tolerance and drill, militarism and cultural vitality, imperialism and the rule of law, class- and caste-feelings and popular Social Democratic breakthroughs, cosmopolitan academic centers and narrow-minded censors. You clicks your heels and takes your choice: high stylistic power, or low brutality.

When did it really end? Some say with the establishment of the all-German Reich in 1871, others with the Kaiser's defeat in 1918, still others with the dismissal of that Prussian Social-Democrat Braun in 1932; and a few insist that it all really crashed only when the Allies formally abrogated the word, the name, the state, the geographical area after World War II. But what does remain indisputable is that in 1981 Prussia is "in."

Thirty years ago, to the West and the East the Cold War competition was only over who was really and truly more "anti-Prussian," the DDR or the BRD. If in the West all the Bismarck statues disappeared, in the East a whole magnificent Prussian Palace, the Königschloss, was blown to pieces. Times change. In the DDR there is a bestselling life of Frederick the Great by Ingrid Mittenzweig, and there were some who thought that this Marxist voice should have been added to the Berlin discussions. Still, there was controversy enough as evening after evening old ex-Prussians and non-would-be Prussians, plus a few Swabians, Gauls, Latins, Celts, and Yankees, sat around conference tables in endless open-forum conversations. The audiences were large, patient, intensely interested. I couldn't help feeling that they couldn't be there simply out of curiosity. For a people plagued by an "identity crisis," here clearly was longing, genuine *Nostalgie*.

But where indeed was the Prussia being longed for or sentimentally mourned? The Potsdam of the Hohenzollerns lies out of reach of the half-Berlin of today. It lies in a new Communist half-German State, which may pride itself on "tradition" (its Army goose-steps elegantly), but when they get around to putting up the statue of Frederick the Great on Unter den Linden again, *der alte Fritz* would not be looking out at his prized *Refugium* for harassed writers (after all, he gave Voltaire political asylum). A few vital lifelines to the past have been broken. And yet, as the East German poet, Günther Kunert (now in the West), tried to argue the other evening, "it is all so very Prussian...." The adjective is real, but where is the old place, the sandy Mark, with all its splendors, miseries, and ambivalence? On show, in thirty-three different exhibitions, until next April.

In the Vienna Woods

It was not quite the old-time "Four in a Jeep," but we all sat together, Easterners and Westerners, for several days under the camera-eye of Austrian television and within shouting distance of its microphones, trying to make believe we had some kind of "togetherness" in common. But then came one foreign correspondent with a long tale of woe of how for frustrating months in the Soviet Union he couldn't get in to film a Russian hospital or a Siberian school. At which point a *Pravda* editor recounted how he couldn't get very far out of Washington or New York when he was there as a reporter. Things (as a neutral Austrian observer remarked) are tough all over. Or, as a witty Hungarian journalist cracked (at midnight, discreetly, in a Grinzing *Weinstube*), "We'll stop telling lies about you, if you'll stop telling the truth about us."

This is the way it usually runs at East-West conferences of journalists and intellectuals. By day: stiff, formal, un-decisive chess games, as white moves against black, and vice versa. By night: some more honest sense of the realities underneath. One wonders if anybody, even the Party-line delegates themselves, believes the routine formalities of their ideological presentations. Editors from the official Government and Party newspapers of Poland, Hungary, and East Germany were unanimous in their outrage at the Western press, manipulated by the bourgeoisie, meekly following every signal and instruction from the American Pentagon. What impression can it possibly make when newspapermen from *Le Monde* and from the *Frankfurter Allgemeine Zeitung* to insist that they never ever had an order to distort, that they always wrote as their conscience (and their professionalism) dictated?

One was grateful for the occasional breakthrough of the more neutral Austrian atmosphere: a scintillating two-hour press conference with Chancellor Bruno Kreisky, full of subtleties and surprises, almost as if the Metternichean tradition had not died; and every now and then an intervention from an Austrian diplomat or indeed from Dr. Gerd Bacher, the Viennese television host, which cut across the conventions and the clichés. For the rest I came away only with a number of current ironies and paradoxes. How could it be otherwise when I found myself sitting between two Hungarian colleagues—both had been prominent editors in Budapest in 1956, both participated in the Revolution on the side of Imre Nagy; one remained and became a Party ideologue for Kadar, the other fled to Vienna and became the leading Austrian expert on repressive East European regimes.

Massive was the attack from the East on the West's "anti-Communist" reporting. But to no avail, for in the first place there isn't really so much of it around in the West any more; and in the second place that wasn't the real cause of their anger and discomfort. Actually what upset them most grievously is the enthusiastic attention being paid these days to certain new Eastern developments, the positive efforts to report what is going on in Poland and to give a picture of the dissident tendencies in Russian, Czech, and East German culture. The very facts are subversive. The intellectual inquiry—why were things so much more obviously liberal in the Budapest and Warsaw of today than in Sofia, East Berlin, or Moscow?— is even more "counter-revolutionary." One needs no prejudice or instructions or ideology to be able to note the difference between the official treatments of Russian Nobel-Prize-winners Pasternak and Solzhenitsyn, and the honors recently awarded to the Polish Nobel laureate, Czeslaw Milosz, when he returned from the USA to visit the land of his mother tongue. No signal is needed to be impressed by the social (and cultural) divergences of Hungary and Romania. Privately, not a few like to boast of the differences; publicly, they protest at "imperialist efforts" to "divide and rule." Not that they protest too much; only that they never were really prepared to concede in argument what they were really mad about: not what we think, but what their own people think.

The second paradox was that inside every East-West debate there is actually a West-West discussion struggling to get out. One half of the West European and American press corps is "Defensist," eager and proud to contrast their liberties with totalitarian censorship. The other half couldn't care less, and they busied themselves with their continuing struggle against their own Establishment, investigating it, exposing it come what may. One editor from London waxed almost lyrical about his freedom to edit and to write as he pleased. One correspondent from the *New York Times* saw only the dangers at home, the bureaucratic enemies of a free unfettered press littering the banks of the Potomac—like some sheriff bringing a new law and order to a wild frontier, he announced his credo as being, "Walk down the street and fire at all sides...." A gentle BBC broadcaster demurred, "I hope you're not shooting real people...."

What are real people? As I say, by day we all shot at each other, and only in the Viennese evening were there moments when the firing had to stop.

February 1982

European Diary

Ceremonial Farewell; The Lowenthal Paper

"To die is to become the prey of the living"
—*Jean-Paul Sartre*, L'Être et le Néant

They were for more than half-a-century Europe's most legendary "intellectual pair," together in the cafes of the Paris Left Bank, uninterruptedly exchanging ideas and gossip, "engaging themselves almost as one in the causes and crusades of the day. There was over the years an extraordinary constancy, even when on occasion they separated and took to themselves other companions along other routes, and even indeed (as she has recorded in the volumes of her memoirs) when there was on this or that point of philosophy, literature, or politics a measure of sharp disagreement and open conflict.

Yet one can't help noticing that it was not Simone de Beauvoir whom Jean-Paul Sartre appointed to be his heir and executor, and it was not to her that he turned but to "Victor," the young militant Benny Levy who provoked him to a deep revision of many views (on Jews, on violence), for his "political testament" (and it surprised so many of his intimate circles, not least Mme. de Beauvoir).

"I have been, I am no more...." Now that he is dead, is it time only for "prey" and "booty"? Of the 560 pages of Simone de Beauvoir's "ceremonial farewell, " (*La cérémonie des adieux, suivi des Entretiens avec Jean-Paul Sartre*, Gallimard) 160 are a detailed chronicle of the miseries of the philosopher's last years, the rest a record of conversations, or rather, interviews, which she conducted with him in Rome in the summer of 1974. Taken together they are at once a biographical document and a personal obituary, a mournful farewell and a pious act of possession against other freebooters, as if she would always be the first to pray and to...prey. For the clear message emerges, "He was, after all, mine...." Even though as she writes, in final resignation, "His death separates us, death will not unite us...."

But her record of the dying years of Sartre's sufferings, his illness and blindness, his collapse into physical and spiritual helplessness, has no sentimentalism about it, only a literary rigor and even ruthlessness which has already given pain to their friends and embarrassment to French critics and readers. Or is this, too, part of the "continuing debate and polemic" which Sartre always knew would follow and from which he would now forever be excluded? Once again there are the charges and countercharges that the philosopher was being "used and abused," that both the essence of his ideas and the meaning of his life were being misunderstood and misinterpreted. Who is guilty here? Perhaps no one is innocent.

Indeed there is in his *L'Être et le Néant* (1943) a section called "My Death" in which Sartre reflects on a philosopher's capacity for infinite self-interpretation; in the last analysis, when he is "no more," he is an easy victim for commentators yet to come, since it is history which would always have the last word on meanings and truths. When death comes one argument ends, another discussion begins, and the philosopher who is "no more" remains forever defenseless.

The title *La cérémonie des adieux*, appears to be a phrase of Sartre's own, which he would use to her at one of their separations. Now she writes, "Here is the first of my books—the only one—which you have not read before it was printed and published. It is entirely for you and yet touches you not. When we were young, at the end of every discussion the victor would say, "And now you are caught in your little box...." Well, now you are in your little box, never to come out again. Even if I were to be buried next to you there would be no access...." (I should note that in the French the form is always here "*vous*" and not "*tu*," and it should not be mistaken for coolness or formal distance: the *tu* between Sartre and, say, the young militants of 1968 is far less intimate than this *vous*.)

If her description of her mother's mortal illness was that of "a gentle death" (but there was irony in that title), this account of Sartre's dying miseries is a chronicle of horrors in which no miserable detail is considered too unimportant to be registered; and although I can understand (and indeed even sympathize with) the howls of the embarrassed Paris critics, I wonder whether Sartre himself would have much objected. Revolted by the onset of his own mortality, he may have hated the nauseating *Ding-an-sich*, but never its literary representation. Eyes go dark, and he falls and hurts himself like a stumbling baby; bladder and intestines lose control, and he is repeatedly found in his own wetness and dirt; alcoholism is a desperate refuge (little whisky bottles, hidden away), and he sleeps through the night on the apartment floor. The little fellow had always been fairly robust, but the combination of Scotch and innumerable *Corydran* pep-up pills only reduced his resistance and self-control. At one point, when Simone de Beauvoir calls his attention to the increasing incontinence, he cracks, "At my age one must be modest...." Quite immodestly she records the stains and odors and, endlessly, all the other signs of general physical disintegration. Once he put to her the fearful question, "Will I never be able to see again?" and she replied, "No, I'm afraid." She reports: "This was so heartbreaking that he wept through the night. It was awful to be present at the agony of a hope...."

In these last years when he was almost blind he knew only what was read to him (among other things, Joachim Fest's *Hitler*). Although he himself would say that it made no real difference, one is saddened that the final volume of his *Flaubert* remained a vague, futile project. In some moments of energy he breaks out into Sartrean "*engagements*" and hurls warnings against the Bonn Bundesrepublik (for the Germans want to dominate Europe again), and even against the dangers of Italian "repressiveness" (although he might have been told how weak and helpless the Italian state really was). Occasionally he would be read newspaper reports from *Libération*, which he had helped to establish and which has become a useful journal. And it is in *Libération* that one aspect of the "continuing polemic" has been raging as Sartre's adopted daughter (and heir) has defended herself against Simone de Beauvoir whose views have been represented in *Le Canard Enchaîné*: there we are told, among other things, that Sartre's young favorite and companion always enjoyed his great generosity but never took the trouble to take care of an unpaid telephone bill.

It is all reminiscent of the goings-on in one of the blackest of Balzac's novels. One old friend visited Sartre in the hospital and recorded his last words as: "And the next whisky will be on me...." Simone takes the trouble to correct him, and to give the authentic deathbed version: Sartre closed his eyes, touched her hand, and said that he loved her very much.... Such gestures, she hastens to record, were very unusual for him.

The various conversations, of which so little notice has yet been taken, make up the bulk of the book. I was very much struck by the revelation that at least one of Sartre's famous political articles— the one that praised the "great freedom" he found in the USSR—was not written by him at all, but came from the pen of his "secretary" at the time, M. Jean Cau. But now that he "is no more," how can one put it to him that this does not quite square with his vaunted theory of Engaged Writing, the unconditional existential personal responsibility of the Committed Intellectual? Was, then, his devotion to freedom as he understood it so absolute that he could afford to take liberties with it? Still, I prefer the image of his erratic spontaneity to the ceremonial solemnity of the Sartreans, young and old. Logic and inconsistency were harmonious parts of his irascible intellectuality, and he often appeased his ideological friends out of politeness or weariness or sheer talkativeness. "All right," he says (pressed on by Simone), "let's discuss it, if you wish...."

In the end I wonder if any reader new to Sartre (and to his *compagne*), could come away from these pages of a "ceremonial farewell" with a notion that Sartre was a figure of importance. For my own part I needed to reassure myself by turning to *L'Être et le Néant* and to the pages of his extraordinary novel *La Nausée*. It only served to remind one that even for an Existentialist philosopher it is the works that remain that need to engage us, and not the last melancholy ruins of his personal existence.

The Lowenthal Paper

I don't suppose I need to underline for readers of *Encounter* the importance of the role that Richard Lowenthal has been playing in the whole postwar period towards the clarification of international (and, especially, ideological) problems, whether in the early Cold War period or the late détente phase. Several dozen sharp and argumentative articles have appeared in these pages. When he was a leader-writer on the *Observer* in London (in the great days when David Astor was publisher and distinguished writers like Andrew Shonfield and Sebastian Haffner were influential), the diplomatic line was incisive, vigorous, and persuasive.

But there was another side to Lowenthal's importance, and it may (in the slight confusion when his byline takes on an umlauted ö) have been lost on his Anglo-American followers. The current explosion in German leftwing politics over a memorandum which he recently wrote on the future of the Social Democracy under Helmut Schmidt and Willy Brandt calls for a little personal history. For, long before his emigration to England as a refugee from Hitler (and his subsequent academic work at Columbia and California), he was active in German left-wing politics, first as a Marxist leader of the student youth, then as an independent socialist. When the war ended he published—only in German, and under the pseudonym "Paul Sering"—a small, powerful book called *Jenseits des Kapitalismus*—it played an extraordinary role in the clarification of Left-wing politics, then dominated by such figures in the SPD as Dr. Kurt Schumacher and Mayor Ernst Reuter. After he took up Willy Brandt's invitation to return to Berlin as a Free University professor of politics, Lowenthal found himself at the centre of the student turmoil of the 1960s. He never faltered in his critique of Marxist-Leninist totalitarianism and in his support for the forces of reason and moderation which triumphed in the Bad Godesberg program of 1959, in no small way a victory for "Paul Sering."

Now again, not for the first time, or the last, the Left seems to have lost its way. The bromidic phrase, here and in Britain (not to mention France, Scandinavia, and Italy), is: "What do Social Democrats stand for?" Should they turn to the Left, as with Tony Benn and Papandreou and Erhard Eppler, and renew themselves at the sources of "pure socialism"? Or should they continue to face the new social and political issues of the day with a less outdated ideology than ever before, with open-minded skepticism and gradualist many-sidedness (as do Helmut Schmidt, Roy Jenkins, Michel Rocard)?

The "Lowenthal Paper," as the German newspaper headlines daily refer to it, was originally written for the Social Democratic Party's magazine, and only became a *cause célèbre* when leading figures like Herbert Wehner and Anne-Marie Renger began to Xerox copies and send it around—as if it were a bomb-shell against Willy Brandt and for Helmut Schmidt in the tense, skirmishing of Left-Right forces before the all important SPD Conference in

Munich this April. The Munich *Parteitag* is likely to be, as *Der Spiegel* reports (14 December 1981), "the toughest battle over fundamentals since Godesberg in 1959."

This wasn't, apparently (and he has since confirmed it to me), Rix Lowenthal's intention, although he did send Willy Brandt a copy of the manuscript, accompanied by a letter which noted that they had "grown somewhat apart in recent years...." For him, as readers of *Encounter* well know, politics is not a matter of personality wrangles and faction-fights. The theoretical suppositions were important, and he wanted to get the principles and the concepts right. Brandt had been obviously looking to the left, to the "integration" of all the groups and grouplets that had first emerged in the 1968 militancy, and should now return from their isolation in ecological-pacifistic-anti-parliamentarian romanticism to the mainstream of socialist politics. Chancellor Schmidt had been warning against the influence of the "dropouts" (die *Aussteiger*) which would alienate the real heart of the socialist movement, namely, the broad masses of the working people who were realistically concerned with jobs, growth, security in the real present-day society, not in a green utopia of Maypole dancers.

Rix Lowenthal took a clear position on behalf of the realists, although it was not easy, personally, to seem to be opting against Willy Brandt, with whom he had once collaborated on a biography of Ernst Reuter, Berlin's great "Cold War Mayor." When the Festschrift for Brandt's sixty-fifth birthday was published, he was the editor. But, as the Germans say, es scheiden sich die Geister, there comes a parting of the ways. When signatures began to be appended to the "Lowenthal Papier," the lines drew taut and it suddenly was: "*Rix oder Willy?*"

It is, to be sure, in some ways an uneven contest. Brandt still has great power within the Party apparatus (not to mention the Socialist International of which he is chairman), and there are forces on the German Left who have even been hoping for his return to the chancellorship. On the other side a "theoretician," a mere intellectual—but surely it would not be for the first time in the history of the liberal-Left that the vigor of polemical clarity could win the day. Yet when I asked him the other day whether the debate was really about "theory," he said no, it was about "strategy." The Party must simply know what it wants and where it is going. To turn its back on "Industrial Society" in order to pick up some marginal anarcho-alternative votes in the wilder precincts of the "homeless Left" would be sheer folly—and electoral disaster.[1] Ecology can help correct some of the excesses of contemporary technological civilization, but the protection of the environment is not a full-time program for a prospering modern economy. Who will be there to spare two million workers the miseries of unemployment if we are all to be tender-hearted woodmen busy sparing the trees? And indeed, the riotous excitement about cutting down a piece of a forest adjacent to the Frankfurt Airport occupies more attention on the far Left than the Bundesrepublik's failing finances or Poland under martial law.

On this issue, as on many others, two extreme and mindless ideologies are ranged against each other. One has been supporting growth at any price, as if any expansion of industrial society (at no matter what cost to the plundered environment) contributes unfailingly to social well-being. The other has been opposing economic expansion, making with its fetish of "zero growth" an absolute commitment to "ecology" and "the environment," and agitating as if expanding industry and innovative science were themselves evil.

Here Rix Lowenthal, reasonable as always, takes a strong moderating position against both extremes. In a sharp comment on an official SPD document on the subject (written by Volker Hauff), he points out that ...it is not a simpleminded matter of either ecology or growth, of either quantity or quality, for even a selective growth—paying attention to environmental considerations (and sometimes deciding hard priorities one way rather than another)—would have ultimately to be quantified for its social and political-democratic justification.... Modern society cannot live with an absolute priority to prevent all ecological damage. It is foolish and stultifying to be constantly melodramatizing the "imminent exhaustion" of all our natural resources.... The "friends of the earth" have themselves been poisoning our political environment by setting up a "Green" or an "Alternative" ideology which opposes all industrial growth, all forms of modern economic development, and indeed seeks to subvert democratic-majority decisions, based on an assessment of the general public interest, in the name of "local victims" and their veto right of absolute self-determination....[2]

The opposition to Lowenthal is not confined to the "drop-outs" of '68, frenetically trying to find an Ersatz exhausted revolutionism by battling with the West Berlin police to defend the squatters occupying tenements, or marching against nuclear power plants, or demonstrating for "peace without weapons," but reaches into the higher responsible circles of Schmidt's government and party. Men like Minister Volker Hauff and general-secretary Peter Glotz think of themselves as youthfully "future-oriented," but it is almost as if they were trying to build the future in one country, and appear insensitive to the economic pressures of an inventive Japan or to the political pressures of a totalitarian East which is, as in Poland, ready every day to move whole police regiments and army divisions to stave off (only fifty miles away)! "liberalization" and "dangerous ideas." Lowenthal would have wished that his old friend Willy try to "integrate" not the ragamuffin mob of neo-romantic *Aussteiger*, disorienting a society against its own best interests, but a troubled electorate alarmed by new economic and diplomatic uncertainties. Neither on the issue of "Peace" nor of Poland has Nobel-Prize-winner Brandt been in tune with the major thrust of social democratic opinion in the West. Troubles in El Salvador and Namibia drive him to angry militant protest; tragedy in

Warsaw stirs in him only caution, worry about strong words, and a sudden eagerness to leave other people's internal troubles alone.

But, even as I write, Brandt's newfound prudence in the face of wholesale violations of human rights has also become Chancellor Schmidt's remarkably neutral attitude towards the establishment of a military *Junta* in a "neighboring land" where German friendship and finance were supposed to be "relaxing tension." In today's newspaper (*Frankfurter Allgemeine Zeitung*, 31 December, p. 4), I note that Richard Lowenthal's name is among the signatories calling for a more vigorous critique of the shameful events in Poland than either Brandt or Schmidt have been able to bring past their lips. It could be that soon the coming battle will not merely be about a sounder political strategy, or a more coherent social theory, but about those quintessential European values in whose defense Rix Lowenthal has never faltered.

March 1982

Notes

1. Such considerations are often taken to be a conflict of principle versus expediency. This is not so. It should be a principle of a serious political party to want to come to power and to exercise governmental influence on behalf of its ideals. The comfort of a dogmatic purity is the expediency of narrow ideological spirits.

    A *Guardian* editorial recently pointed up the problem in the British context (*International Herald Tribune*, 30 December):

    "The choice before Labor is clear. Either it settles for being a narrow, committed ideological party, taking perhaps 20% of the vote election by election, but never very much more—which is what Benn is offering—or it seeks to recreate, even at the expense of compromise, a broader, left of center coalition which carries with it some prospect of power."

2. "Hauff contra Lowenthal?" in *Die Zeit* (Hamburg), 18 December 1981, p.11.

Thinking about Flaubert

"For him the important thing was to incorporate passionate, turbulent emotions in trivial occurrences. The most solemn and decisive truths emerge from the mouths of fools. This book demonstrates that themes are good or bad depending on how they are presented—and the best themes are often the most ordinary...."

Gustave Flaubert was as surprised as he was delighted by Baudelaire's, review of *Madame Bovary* from which this quotation is taken. He had suddenly discovered someone else whose mind was Flaubertian. And yet thirteen years later in *L'Éducation sentimentale.* "ordinariness" was still being mistaken for lack of plot. The book repelled contemporary and later readers alike. Jules Barbey d'Aurevilly, a writer not entirely forgotten today, tore both these novels to pieces, although for us they are the cornerstones on which Flaubert's reputation rests. "In our opinion there are already enough ordinary minds and commonplace things in the world without adding to them," he grumbled, and supposed that some piece of steel machinery produced in Manchester could turn out books just like M. Flaubert's. As for *Madame Bovary,* this was the sort of novel that everyone carries around with them in the baggage of life, but fortunately never writes down.

Even Léon Daudet, an extreme rightwing polemicist and often a perceptive judge of literature (his father, Alphonse Daudet, had been Flaubert's friend), must have been disturbed by the triviality since Marcel Proust had to explain to him: "In the last hundred years every literary innovation has been achieved in what contemporaries have regarded as a vulgar fashion.... You can condemn me as well as Flaubert. I can't imagine more noble company."

Had not Flaubert already made fun of such arguments? "How I hate these everyday heroes with their lukewarm sentiments who one meets in reality." And Leon, the solicitor's assistant, agrees with him: "It is consoling to escape from the disappointments of everyday life by thinking about more noble characters...."

When Nathalie Sarraute called Flaubert "the master of us all" in an essay which distinguished between those who celebrated him as "the master of the glance" and those who praised him as the discoverer of "psychological reality," such recognition was not so taken for granted as it was when Marcel

Proust and Franz Kafka were preoccupied with Flaubert. (Kafka, in a letter to Felice, had called himself Flaubert's inadequate pupil.)

Is it, then, psychological realism that gives Flaubert his lasting appeal? Is it the comedy of opinions, of clichés, of ideologies—the whole spectrum of the "inauthentic" which makes Flaubert so modern (especially in *Bouvard et Pécuchet,* the novel of ideas which he left behind after his death)? *Madame Bovary* has proved the power of fiction: after all, the concept of *Bovarisme* like *Don Quixoterie* has survived. Sainte-Beuve (the critic whom Flaubert most respected) complained that the cuckolded country doctor Charles Bovary was not portrayed as sympathetically as the reader might have wished. "The sculptor need only have kneaded the clay gently with his thumb and this would have been sufficient to make a noble and moving character out of the ordinary head. It would satisfy the reader, in fact he would almost have expected it. But the author continually resists the idea: he does not want it to happen...."

The last book that the Austrian writer Jean Amery published before he committed suicide in 1979 was dedicated to this character, Charles Bovary; he tried to defend him against his creator, Flaubert. This reminded me of Miguel de Unamuno's effort to rewrite the life of Don Quixote in order to protect him from Cervantes. The parallel is particularly striking because *Don Quixote* was Flaubert's model, and Emma Bovary, like Cervantes' hidalgo, found diversion from the triviality of her existence by reading novels, and embarked on adventures which themselves ended in triviality and disillusionment.

What did Flaubert think about the power of literature? The thirteen volumes of letters published by Conard—so far only a few volumes of the uncensored Pleiade edition (Gallimard) have appeared—contain conflicting evidence.

At one point Flaubert, like Emile Zola, wishes to arrogate to the novel the achievements and the methods of a "science" (and, not surprisingly, the pen of the doctor's son was often compared to a scalpel by critics and caricaturists). But elsewhere he can write: "Literature is the least mendacious of all lies," and the contemporary findings of science become the stuff of comedy in *Bouvard et Pécuchet,* as does the whole notion of progress.

Not even Flaubert can explain the mystery of how novels create myths and images which survive their own time, when of all modes of expression the novel is the most time-bound. Although it is indispensable, the aesthetic theory which appears in his letters to his friend Louise Colet and also to his literary disciple Guy de Maupassant is by no means Flaubert's final word on the subject.

When he wrote to Louise Colet (24 April 1852), "The further art goes, the more scientific it will become, just as science itself will become more artistic," he said in the same letter that to him "the imagination of a single being appears just as legitimate [as] the appetite of a million people." And we can take "imagination" to mean also the work of the writer, who does much more than record what his waking, critical, conscious mind dictates:

> In truth, I am a man in a fog. Only with great patience have I managed to divest myself of all the surplus fat that has built up over my muscles. The books I am most anxious to write are precisely the ones for which I am least equipped. In this sense then, *Bovary* has been an immense feat of strength which only I will be able to assess properly. Themes, characters, the effects I'm striving for, all these lie outside myself. I'm sure this will enable me to make great advances in the future. But at the moment I am writing this book like someone trying to play the piano with lead weights on each finger....

He was also oppressed by the idea that the novel had such a long tradition in France that it might already have exhausted itself. He was alarmed to find in Balzac themes he believed *he* had invented: "All we can do is be clever enough to tighten the strings on our guitar, on which so many tunes have already been played, and be virtuosos, because naively is an illusion in our epoch."

Part of Flaubert's aesthetic theory is the idea of creating a novel that is a total work of art, in which every word, every sentence—"read and roared aloud countless times"—sounds exactly right. But admiring Balzac as Flaubert did, he must have known the many weaknesses a novel can have yet still carry the reader along and leave a deep impression. The novel is not a sonnet in which one bad line can ruin the whole effect. But even this is not true: Baudelaire wrote unforgettable poems that contain botched images. Through its narrative quality, its tempo, its suspense, a great novel can overcome weaknesses—more like cinema than poetry, it will never be a "perfect" work of art.

Flaubert believed in *impassibilité*, in objectivity; but, still, he is more involved, more present in his novels than his aesthetic theory would have him be, and the reader is far too caught up to worry about such inconsistencies.

Marcel Proust and then a whole procession of learned "Flaubertologists" have written reams about the way in which Flaubert's stylistic innovations (his use of tenses, the way he mixes simultaneous dialogues and acoustic backgrounds, his combination of description and conversation, of objectivity and sarcasm, of verbal clichés and deep emotions) correspond to the new content of his books—and Jean-Paul Sartre's monumental work suggests in its analyses of individual texts just how much we have lost through that last unwritten volume on *Madame Bovary*.

Agreed, then: Flaubert—among whose disciples we may reasonably number Heinrich Mann, Maxim Gorki, James Joyce, Henry Green, Céline, Samuel Beckett—is a master who cannot be ignored, though a large proportion of his slim body of work is now scarcely readable—today, who opens *The Temptation of St Anthony* or *Salammbô*? Yet, curiously, the novel that is most the product of its epoch, *L'Éducation sentimentale*, remains strikingly relevant.

Lost illusions: this had already been the subject and the title of one of Balzac's books. But Flaubert portrays the helplessness of non-heroes who can never forge their own destinies; who suffer their own lives but never control them; victims, never masters of their fate. It is a demonstration of the psychology of the powerless and the temptation to compensate by turning to ideologies—or perhaps of the hold of ideas and clichés over such people. All this is new content in a new form. The master of post-Romantic self-irony is drawn to epic themes, and finds himself embedded in everyday triviality. More than that: in a modern political ambivalence, George Sand contended that *L'Éducation sentimentale* proved Flaubert's: acceptance of the Revolution, and indeed he is reputed to have said as Paris burned, "This would never have happened if they had understood my *L'Éducation sentimentale!....*"

How does this remark fit in with the hermit of Croisset, who confined himself to the ivory tower and art-for-art'ssake? It is one of those contradictions between committed opinion and. creative method which separate Flaubert the aesthete from Flaubert the novelist, and which give the reader the impression not of the perfection of form, but rather the illusory, irresistible impression of life itself.

Novels are not read over and over again for their style alone—and Kafka kept rereading Flaubert. Flaubert insisted that the secrets of the workshop were irrelevant for the reader: only the end effect mattered, and he claimed one could express feelings all the more accurately the less one felt them oneself. His evocative powers must, then, have more to do with magic than with science. At any event, they strike us as equally effective in the early heavily corrected drafts as in the final versions.

When he was only thirty, Flaubert wrote to his friend Maxime du Camp that perhaps only after his death would his work be appreciated. Du Camp had been urging him to think of his literary career. Just how effective his novels are is best known above all to those writers for whom he has become a mentor, even a tyrant from whom they have had to free themselves. Some forerunners are difficult to equal or surpass.

April 1982

European Diary

Mosques in the Factory; "1983"; News of the Day; Wajda's *Danton*

Mosques in the Factory

Paris

It was only a matter of some 165 Moroccan workers on strike and of a shutdown involving a thousand, but the popular press phrase has it that "Never have so few strikers reduced so many eager workers to complete inactivity." That may indeed be the way many in France would like to see the latest outbreak of so-called "industrial action" at the Renault Works. For almost a year now there has been trouble in Flins, and in the nearby factories; as a result of the difficulties with the *immigrés* the loss of production has amounted to 150,000 automobiles. During the long-running conflict at Citroen the government intervened and criticized, rightly, the role of management. This was not quite on when it came to related recalcitrance at the government-owned Renault establishments. After all, the most powerful man here—and easily more powerful than the four cabinet ministers that his Party has placed in the Mitterrand cabinet—is Henri Krasucki, the Communist president of the CGT trade union. He rejected out of hand the proposal to appoint a mediator, or arbitrator, on the grounds of rather special French logic, namely, the government couldn't appoint anybody to be above the government. *L'État* in France is always something of a monolithic force.

In any event, the CGT has played a leading role in the other strikes: Citroen, Peugeot, Talbot. In Renault it was overtaken on the left by a rival trade union group, the CFDT. But it is not the "jurisdictional competitiveness" that has been prolonging the industrial action, but the so-called "basis," the "masses" themselves, in person. And this caused the Socialist prime minister, Pierre Mauroy—after all, the elected representative of the masses—to flare up. These immigrants, he exploded, have simply no "feeling for French social reality.." They were being incited by extreme religious groups. Gaston Deferre, the minister of the interior, spoke of "integralists," even of "Shiites," although the Muslims involved, from North Africa, Mali, and Senegal, were Sunnis. Have the Ayatollahs, then, taken over the workers and are exercising real proletarian power in the factories?

The Moroccans involved—and they are far fewer than the Algerians—did not emigrate from the urban centers but from the *"bleds"* in the South which have been relatively free from Westernizing influences. It was often the case that large families came to France, with whole hierarchies being part of the emigration, inclusive of imams. Small wonder that a constant demand in the plants has been for places for prayer, a mosque in every factory. The *immigrés* were trained to attend to the assembly line in about three weeks' time, and very few indeed (unlike their French colleagues) ever rise to more qualified jobs. Where, then, should the special insight into "French social reality" come from? Had somebody like Giscard made the crack, it would have been put down to his usual arrogance and cynicism.

We have heard much about the West German problems with the four millions or so of *Gastarbeiter* (mainly from Turkey), but France in relation to its population actually has more foreign workers. The European among them—mostly Portuguese, but also Italians, Spaniards, and Yugoslavs—are considerably easier to "assimilate" than the Muslims out of Africa and Turkey. Nevertheless, it must be recorded that from all we know about popular feelings as registered in public opinion polling, most of the strangers in the land do not say that they have been subjected to what the Germans call *Fremdenhass,* "hatred of the foreigner." All the more reason why even the most populistic of politicians need not go in for "racialistic" overtones. The Communist Party tried it a few years ago, and in the notorious case of "People's Justice" against an alleged Moroccan drug dealer lost much face and worker support; the Party line was quickly changed. After all, it is not a "handful" that one is dealing with: roughly 80 percent of the unqualified workers in and around Paris are Africans. There are 7,000 in Billancourt and in Flins, 4,000 in Aulnoy. And it can be said that on their shoulders the French workers were able to step up into the better-paid areas of more specialized employment. As for the Moroccans who are at work down the French mines, there appears to be very little envy indeed even among the two million French unemployed. True, one can hear mumbling and grumbling, and one Paris lady told me that "all the troubles of France are due to the Arabs in the country." But my impression is that these are only small, unrepresentative voices.

Still, the unrest goes on and on; and I suspect that even the most "primitive" workers in France know the technological score, namely that automation is still on the march everywhere, and soon the robots will be in place, making their work on the assembly lines totally superfluous. There is a fear of imminent redundancy which has made the pressure for becoming "more qualified" a desperate industrial factor. What is at work here is not an alleged ignorance of "French social realities," but on the contrary a sensitive alertness to what is happening in an increasingly high-tech economy. One doesn't really even have to genuflect five times a day to Mecca to understand that.

"1983"

Zurich

Ever since the onset of the New Year we have been going through some kind of special numerological break-through in so-called "cultural consciousness." There is nothing obviously peculiar or magical about "1983," but it has provided us with no end of centenaries, bicentenaries, and other jubilees. The Protestants are immersed in Luther (b. 1483), and music lovers in Wagner (d. 1883); the French are honoring Stendhal (b. 1783) and Colbert (d. 1683); the Left everywhere is busy with the memory of Marx (d. 1883); and there are a few other celebrations of giants: Schumpeter (b. 1883), Keynes (b. 1883), Kafka (b. 1883).

Uncanny as ever, it would seem to be Kafka who is the most topical or relevant, for there is something grotesquely mysterious about Europe's wholesale wallowing in the bygone relationships of "yesterday's men" and the crises and madnesses which have since overtaken the contemporary world. Hitler came to power just fifty years ago in the Berlin *Reichstag*. Did Wagner imply Auschwitz? How radical or how conservative was the great Protestant reformer who broke up the unity of the Catholic Church, now seeking to piece itself together? Orwell's "1984" may be throwing its shadows in advance, but why should there be an international conference on Franz Kafka in (of all places) Caracas?

I am surely not alone in hoping for a little light comic relief, perhaps a Moliére jubilee or a Nestroy anniversary, or some reason to celebrate Rabelais who after all left us with the wisdom that "rire est le propre de l'homme." But there is little to laugh about in the year in which the great tyrants of modern dictatorship are being remembered. Not long after the fiftieth anniversary of Hitler's *Machtergreifung* in 1933 comes the hundredth birthday of Benito Mussolini which one Italian publisher is marking with a new edition of his; *La Mia Vita,* first published in 1910.

Alas, but there is much that is grievous to think about here, reflecting upon the nature of one-man rule and one-party domination in our time. Or can't they be so easily subsumed? What despotic elements belong together, which fundamental "systemic" differences have to be underlined? No doubt about it, Lenin created a one-party state and Stalin consolidated it; but should the Bolshevik-based concept of "Totalitarianism" embrace also the German and the Italian dictatorships? The Nazi rule was not quite so "total" and far more devoted to the mindless cult of war and violence. The Italian Fascists—and they alone earned the name, which shouldn't be a catch-call propagandistic epithet—were neither total nor murderous (except for the Abyssinian adventure and the occasional isolated political hit job).

Wading through the hundreds of "special articles" on the subject which have been flooding all the newspapers and magazines, I have the feeling that the European intelligentsia has come to grips with the phenomenon of Fascism more effectively than with that of the Third Reich. I am re-minded of the incisive literature from Ignazio Silone's *School for Dictators,* written during the war in his Zurich exile, to Denis Mack Smith's recent Mussolini biography (published in Milan by Rizzoli who are also bringing out Mussolini's *My Autobiography, 1926,* which has never before been published in Italy!). The central historical point is surely that it was possible, within the authoritarian framework of the national institutions, to get rid of *il Duce,* and to end his regime; not unlike the demise of Franco's regime in Spain. Nothing like it is conceivable in the totalitarian cases of Bolshevik Russia or Nazi Germany. The campaign against Italy's Jews which was initiated in the last phase of Mussolini's fascism was a result of *Il Duce*'s being a vassal of *der Führer;* it was not a product of some homegrown anti-Semitic fanaticism as in Germany, which doesn't of course excuse it but suggests an important historical distinction.

But are such distinctions only the concern of historians and scholars? One wonders whether in all the anniversary effusions the European mind in general is confronting its tragic past and, conceivably, drawing appropriate political lessons. I note that in France two great trials will be taking place—of Klaus Barbie, the recaptured Gestapo chief of Lyon, and another of a Vichy prefect, a man who later became a minister, was involved in deportations, but also subsequently rendered services to the French resistance. One has already been condemned to death, although in the mean-time capital punishment has been abolished. But such complications are as nothing compared to the complex issues—and the still unhealed wounds—which are about to be ripped open when all the details of the Nazi occupation of France and Marshal Pétain's Vichy government, of the immorality of collaboration and inconsistencies of resistance, descend on a battered public opinion. It is, to be sure, all unavoidable; inevitable, in fact. But, on the one hand, it is the routine mechanisms of legality and justice which are at work; and on the other hand some vague, if deep, feeling that it might all be serving some higher purpose of enlightenment, of "mastering the past," of burning some vital lessons of politics and sociology into our hearts and minds. One wonders about this whole cycle of crime and punishment. The criminals will be put away, but not really out of society's fear that it needs to be "protected" against them (which of the surviving villains of those days were likely to become "repeaters"?)— nor out of an impassioned ethical aware-ness that all political murderers need to be given their ultimate "just deserts," in the spiritual expectation of some atonement or expiation.

The memories, in any case, are all too topical. Whatever lessons are drawn from the past tend to be narrowly purposeful, tied closely to some current political crisis or psychological impasse, as in the West Germany of today where one tends to remember only that which it is "useful" to know to keep a post-Hitler democratic half-nation on an even keel. Whole chunks of history are neglected, and quick superficial analogies run wild. After a nasty West German demonstration recently there were police raids and a number of quick arrests in Nuremberg, following which there hysterical editorials about new "Dreyfus Affairs." The knowledge of a little history can be put to very silly uses; the past may be "prelude." but not necessarily to profundity. I can't help thinking that an historical awareness that becomes a function of instrumental manipulation is worse than none at all. "1983" is not yet in a sinister league with "1984," but the increasingly total conscription and mobilization of "all our yesterdays" is neither instructive nor helpful.

News of the Day

Milan

Not unlike London, or Paris, or New York, one finds journalists and editors here mourning the passing of the great newspapers of yester-day. One sometimes wonders whether all those distinguished "thunderers" in Fleet Street, or in Manhattan, or on the Seine, were ever what they are now, in obvious nostalgia, held to have been. Nevertheless, Italian tradition has it that the *Corrière della Sera* was, until only recently, the formidable national newspaper which had to be quoted, for it was the journal that formed opinions. Little catastrophes like world wars some-times make a difference, and such institutions get dented, get bent, but somehow in one form or another live on to fight another day.

In France *Le Temps,* sadly compromised under the Vichy regime, emerged as *Le Monde,* with Hubert Beuve-Mery giving it a new lease of life on the left of center. In Germany, out of the no less compromised *Frankfurter Zeitung,* once the pride of Weimar culture, came the new *Frankfurter Allgemeine* as the stalwart of enlightened conservatism in the Bonn Republic. As for the *Corrière,* the Italian penchant for nonconformist conformity somehow contrived the steady continuation of the famous daily from fascism to post-fascism under its old name, and indeed under Mario Borso to campaign in the new scene for old liberal values; there wasn't even a change of ownership.

One Milanese aspect is unusual. In contrast to the dailies for "top people" elsewhere, the prestigious *Corrière* was at the same time the largest-circulation paper in the country. The explanation is that in Italy there are proportionally fewer readers of newspapers than in other Western democracies, and there is something very "élitarian" about newspaper reading.

Still, the sad story I want to relate could be easily read on the faces of *Corriere* subscribers as well as editors and journalists, and I have run into its far--flung correspondents in recent years on several continents, all with worried looks about the course and the future of the paper. A certain traditional pride has disappeared and almost definitively so since the exposure of some of the *Corriere*'s links to the mafia-like freemasonry known as "P2." So much has been exposed that all that remains to be known is who will take over from the Rizzoli publishing house and move in what conceivable direction.

The serious difficulties are not really new, and have roots in the confusions of the 1960s. I have been reminded of this by reading the new book by Enzo Bettiza, *Via Solferino,* which is subtitled *La Vita del' Corrière della Sera' dal 1964 al 1974,* and is rich in anecdotal memoirs and perceptive analyses. Bettiza, along with Indro Montanelli, led a major defection from the *Corrière* after secret pre-parations to start another and rival paper: which they did, *Il Giornale Nuovo.* It has proved to be, somewhat to the right of center, a formidable and impressive rival to the *Corriere;* and, on the left-of-center in Rome, the new *Repubblica* also gained ground. It appears to me, as I buy my Italian papers at the local kiosk, that these two journals are the Italian papers with the sharpest profile, with figures like Raymond Aron writing a column in the former and Alberto Ronchey transferring his commentaries from the *Corriere* to the latter. I would say that the *Repubblica is* these days, due to its literary and cultural features, rather stronger in *the feuilleton,* while the Montanelli-Bettiza *Giornale is* more cosmopolitan in its worldwide political reporting.

I note that the crisis has become serious enough for the *Corrière* to close down its evening edition, and the shadows over the morning daily grow longer. My friends here tell me that the *Corrière*'s difficulties lay in a "double bind." Above, on an ownership level, there was a compromising irresponsibility, as the proprietor moved from flirtation to flirtation with almost all the trends on the radical left; she was a very impressionable hostess in her famous "salon," and thought of the newspaper as its chic daily extension. From below there were the grievous pressures arising out of the so-called "Syndicalization," which on one level interfered to censor news and comment and on another inflated the paper's hired staff beyond all manageable budgetary proportions.

It is something in the nature of a "novel" that Bettiza has written, not because he has made up anything but because he wanted to tell the story so well. He happens to be the author of two real novels; and as a Dalmatian, who knows many Eastern and Western languages, he also has a special distance from the Italian scene which only sharpens his perceptions. I would not want to give the impression that his book is utterly objective, nor that it is the "last word" on the life and possible death of one of Europe's great newspapers. It is rather the "first word," and other historians will have to carry on from there.

Wajda's *Danton*

Paris

I found even the early afternoon performances in the five cinemas crowded and quite sold out. For weeks and months now *Danton* has been packing them in, some finding in it a work of art, others a manifesto, with a few critics underlining its allegorical or scandalous political intentions, and more than one its heterodox approach to orthodox history.

One almost senses that we are already living in the shadow of the bicentennial of the French Revolution; and for all the dutiful devotion President Mitterrand is showing in the preparations for 1989, it is probable that it will be another who will be making the grand opening. The shadows gather—every criticism, according to the last works of Albert Soboul, of the so-called "Terror" is reactionary and impermissible "antinational." And I found that even among those who are fans of Andrzej Wajda, and especially his latest film, there is the lurking worry: "It may well help the enemies of the Revolution" (who also seem to be lurking, somewhere, ever since 1789). In France the past is always too much with us, late and soon.

Historical "costume films," to be sure, are obviously more difficult to make, whether *Ben Hur* or *Danton;* on celluloid more realism is required than on the stage. Unlike in his Walesan *Man of Iron,* Wajda does not lose himself in the movement of the masses, but keeps the people at a distance, standing in queues before bakeries, listening, visibly moved, to the accused Danton's eloquent words, watching the execution. The action is mostly in the Convention, that self-purging parliament, and in the committees zealously devoted to "the public," its happiness and its security.

This, I should say, is not Georg Büchner's text, but a play that Wajda had produced on the stage some seven years ago. At the time, Stanislawa Przybyszewkaj's drama seemed to be somewhat "Robespierrean." And in the film, which doesn't quite take Danton's side, there is a focus on victims and executioners alike, especially when they are embodied (and later disembodied) in one person, heroes and monsters at once. Wajda had his scenario, written by Jean-Claude Carrière, ready three years ago, and waited happily for Gerard Depardieu to be able to play the leading role. Danton is here understated, his power and natural strength subdued, and his famous voice almost hoarse and inaudible when we most expect the stentorian Girondin outbursts. He is not at the center of the tension, no star. On the other hand the Robespierre figure (played by Woyciech Pszoniak) has rather more vitality than we have been used to. A skilful Parliamentary manoeuverer, he even wants to save Danton and, especially, his friend Camille Desmoulins. (The latter is played by Patrice Chereau, of Bayreuth Wagner production fame, and the prosecutor FouquierTinville by the director Roger Planchon, two very subtle performances that almost suggest they helped Wajda create his masterpiece.)

Desmoulins, on the verge of collapse, doesn't allow (in a foolhardy rather than courageous gesture) "the Incorruptible" into his room; Danton gets drunk during his talk with Robespierre and begins to snore. Even if one is impressed by his self--discipline and indeed his superiority, Robespierre remains the despot—and when a revolutionary has fallen from grace he orders the painter David to paint the unfortunate citizen out of the picture (Stalin would have liked that). Perhaps not quite a total despot, since he is also a man of some personal skepticism and self-doubt, and he senses that it will be only a matter of time, a few months possibly, hardly more, before the executioner follows his victims to the scaffold. This bit I found to be no more than a contrived element of retrospective wisdom, and I also regretted the traditional famous "last words" ("Show the people my head—it's worth it....") when we really know that he spoke at the end only of his newly wed wife.

Still, this Danton wants to be heard by "the People," and not by the court of the Revolution, which he helped to establish in power and whose violence he now would want to end. One is reminded a little of the Russian intensity and eloquence of Leon Trotsky who, on the verge of being pushed aside, declined to fight for power. Danton resigns from the Committee of Public Safety. He knew too well the toll of the guillotine, which he first sees in the mist as a black-draped "widow." In the end it would also be his blood that flowed. Indeed it is almost as if the leading figure in the film was Dr G's insatiable instrument of revolutionary bloodthirstiness. A small child appears to give a small recital before Robespierre; the text is taken from the Declaration of the Rights of Man; the words are mumbled and murmured meaninglessly. How could we help wondering whether the violent course of events had negated the text, or whether the words when one day spoken clearly would again recover clarity. For the time being, the truth is simply that the rulers have all power, and between the conception and the reality have fallen dark shadows. One has become sick unto death of virtue and terror.

Wajda's colors are pale, for all the redness of the killings. Street scenes are not invariably convincing, and the women come only as masks, and anecdotes. The whole of this revolutionary world has become a stage—the convention, the club, the eighteenth-century Paris houses, the tumbrils, the prisons, the gallows. I suspect that only Danton was intended to be real, with his tragic fate pointing to the real ironies of other times, other places.

I found unforgettable the scene in which the printing presses are destroyed—and Desmoulins wrote in his *Cordelier* (which the Revolution censored and then burned): "Give Moscow the freedom of the press, and tomorrow Russia is a republic!" One doesn't have to guess very hard about the thoughts of the cinema public in Warsaw to which Wajda recently exhibited his *Danton*.

June 1983

European Diary

Boomerangs?; The Trial Begins; Germans Among Themselves; Latin Learners

Boomerangs?

Zurich

In its strict usage and proper employment, the "boomerang" is a very accurate and purposeful weapon indeed, a missile "thrown so as to hit an object in a different direction from that of projection, or so as to return to or behind the starting point...." But the *Oxford Dictionary* goes on to cite "Holmes" (Oliver Wendell, not Sherlock, I suspect) to the effect: *"Like the strange missile which the Australian throws, your verbal boomerang slaps you on the nose."* In that stumbling, bumbling sense I want to record the boomerangs of Helsinki and Moscow, of East and West Berlin. What objects have been hit, what noses slapped?

The so-called "Final Act" of Helsinki had no real finality about it at all, and the diplomats went on trying to finalize further in Geneva and Belgrade and now Madrid, all in the interests of "European Peace and Security." East and West, neutrals and unaligned among them, have been at it for ten years now. For the USSR the military and diplomatic aspects were clearly the major interest, while the Western democracies paid rather more attention to "Basket Three" into which the more humane issues were bundled. The Russians had taken the initiative, and the Western powers went along with it only after much skepticism and hesitation. That the negotiations took place at all, thus tacitly recognizing Soviet gains in the post 1945 frontiers, was already registered as a victory for Moscow. Soon the West, in turn, was to claim its triumphs in the promises and commitments to further "human contacts" and advance "human rights."

Thus there was an exchange of missiles in opposite directions—how stands the balance of hits and misses? What happened first in the Eastern bloc of nations was the emergence of a whole host of independent "Helsinki committees," watchdog groups, which began to direct systematic attention (it called for much courage) to the violations and misdemeanors in each of the Soviet-influenced "satellites." Such civic groups on behalf of civil liberties or cultural freedom are, of course, routine matters of democratic protest; but there is, in the diplomatic phrase of the day, no "symmetry" here. Neither in old or new Russia is criticism and dissent a self-evident thing. When the Tsar was moved to abolish the slavery of the serfs he went on to exile the students who were enthused enough to congratulate him—for, after all, subjects are not supposed to have opinions of their own, and certainly not to express them in public. In the national struggle between autocracy and liberalism, the tradition of the autocrat whose police officials do not tolerate unauthorized view-points was the Russian force that triumphed.

For a brief moment in both Prague and Moscow there was the feeling that "Basket Three" of Helsinki was providing a kind of new Magna Carta. The "Carta" movement was soon silenced. One sometimes can feel bitter enough in the face of the horrendous repression to suspect that due to the illusions of Helsinki more individuals were persecuted than would otherwise have been the case. Nevertheless, the promises and guarantees and commitments that had been agreed continued to be a source of real embarrassment to the ideological bosses of the police censorship. Solemn, if not binding, the "Final Act" was supposed to be; and the underlining of affixed signatures in Helsinki makes the Polish Martial Law look even worse than it is.

Obviously the contradictions were built in from the beginning—on the one hand an international agreement, duly underwritten by all sides; on the other hand, the safety clause of "nonintervention in internal affairs." The leaders in the Kremlin felt certain they couldn't be touched, couldn't be hurt; they have grown accustomed for a very long time now to embarrassment in the face of charges of hypocrisy. Still, I wonder whether they think it today such a brilliant idea as when they cajoled the Americans and their allies to make the journey to the Helsinki station. "Boomerang" may be an unoriginal aboriginal analogy; but given the verbal missiles that U.S. Ambassador Max Kampelman, for one, has been hurling in Madrid at the keepers of the Gulag, some noses have surely been slapped.

Shortly before last Christmas, the authorities in East Berlin gave the poet Stephan Hermlin a nice present, and it was (as he said) "the fulfillment of a lifetime's dream." They enabled him to hold an All-German conference for peace, and to invite all the leading writers of Western Germany to join him in solemn and binding prayers for an endangered world. A whole host of writers responded to what he dreamingly called his "private invita-tion." True, every one was allowed to speak his piece as he pleased even if Günter Grass began to grumble at the news from Poland on that week-end of 13 December, and Robert Jungk objected to not being able to get out of the lift in the Academy of Arts building to mix and mingle peacefully with the young artists on other floors. Still, everybody in East Berlin and the DDR could follow what was going on—by watching the filmed proceedings on West Berlin television (the East TV thought the affair so "private" that it broadcast nothing).

Now I see that the entire protocol of Hermlin's All-German Writers Congress has been published in West Berlin by Günter Grass's publisher, the Luchterhand Verlag. In the foreword the statement can be found that it will also shortly be published by the Academy of Arts (*"in ungekuerzter Form"*) in the DDR "simultaneously." Evidently the clocks run on different time over there, for the book ("unshortened") is not yet out; and indeed it might even be lengthened, for one hears that an additional text from the famous literary pen of Erich Honecker, the Communist leader of East Germany, is holding up the publication date. When it finally appears it might turn out to be only an "internal document" for academicians, or a protocol for "internal use only," or possibly one of those rare books sold "under the counter." Something has to be printed soon if Stephan Hermlin's dream is to have its proper documentation. How nightmarish it would be to have the record of this almost unique All-German get-together smuggled over the Berlin Wall from tainted Western sources.

Once again, as in the years of the Stockholm Appeal illustrated with Picasso's famous dove, the campaign for peace comes like light from the East. But the whole machinery of total control has become increasingly difficult when TV cameras are allowed to focus on all the little dark corners. More than that. Some East German pastors took the religious call for peace most seriously, and even called for peace demonstrations amongst their own people. Stefan Heym suggested that there was enough "militarism" (at least in the school textbooks) for the East Germans to be getting on with. A few spokesmen were venturesome enough to ask about the absence of that eminent fighter for peace, Robert Havemann (under house arrest in East Berlin until his death in April). These are notes and tones not often heard in the DDR. Cacophony of this kind would almost be enough to make a nightmare of Hermlin's dream.

Whether it will turn out to be a boomerang or not, all this surely belongs to the "Paradox of Helsinki" as the "Final Act" becomes more tentative every day.

The Trial Begins

Rome

The diffusion of disbelief here is very curious. The evidence is massive, the trial has begun—but that the terrorists of the Red Brigade who kidnapped Aldo Moro four years ago, killed his bodyguard, and then murdered him after fifty-five days of "interrogation," are really and truly the culprits is somehow not very convincing for many Italians. The president of the Republic, Pertini, suspects that terrorism is manipulated from the East; the celebrated novelist Leonardo Sciascia writes darkly of the real men in the background who will probably never be apprehended; Moro's widow herself has called attention to mysterious American wirepullers....

To be sure, the terrorist groups were never exclusively national affairs. The Italian terrorists certainly had connections (through the late Giangiacomo Feltrinelli) with the German Baader-Meinhof "underground" as well as in the Middle East with the Palestinian guerrillas. But all the mutterings about some hidden "Central" or "Mr. Big" who held the strings to all these "puppets," the *burattini,* has never led to the presentation of any real evidence at all. One can understand the national psychology that doesn't truly want to get at the native roots of this horrendous phenomenon. Still, that doesn't change the nature of the various twists and turns of the complicated conspiracy theories—Italian alibis. For almost a decade the young men of political violence openly presented themselves on the national scene as ideologues of the extreme Left, dedicated to the use of force to gain their revolutionary ends. The governments, the parliamentary parties, the influential newspapers, all pooh-poohed them. They were unimportant, not to be taken seriously, a passing excrescence. After all there was only terrorism of the neofascist Right, and sometimes it camouflaged itself in leftist garb. One knows of important reports prepared by local prefects that went into alarming detail about the rising power of the Red Brigades; they landed in the file-and-forget files. In the year 1977 there were sensational murders and bombings; but only in the following year, with the kidnapping of Aldo Moro, did the political establishment wake up, come to its senses, move to practical self-defense efforts. So many had tried, in vain, to tell them all about the nature and diversity of terrorist ideology—the connections between legal and illegal groups, between *"Autonomia"* which offered itself' as a representative of the revolutionary proletariat, and groups like *"Prima Linea"* all of which had journals and pamphlets which could be read and studied. But you'll never know if you don't want to know. Even newspaper editors were full of ironies and little satires, pleasant jokes and harmless feature stories...until they themselves were targeted and shot, bombed, and eliminated; and then, at last, they began to take the threat seriously, even if their attentions were refocused on "secret foreign forces...overseas agencies...big shots abroad...."

The man in the Roman "Arena" who dominates all the forty-three other accused is Mario Moretti, and no one who has taken in the scene has any doubt that here is no *burattino* but quite evidently a powerful gang leader who has full authority over the others. Their fanaticism cannot be denied; they were "propagandists of the deed," violent men of passionate conviction; and they were tools of nobody. Even the so called *pentiti,* the handful who confessed in remorse and to some extent changed their views (and who hoping as they do for a lighter sentence thus have no reason to hold anything back), do not for a moment suggest a "foreign plot." What we know is clear: as clear as the fact that the genuine conspiracy was ignored for years, and almost a decade of democratic self-defense neglected in fanciful flights into imaginary melodramas. It was all marked by that special kind of blindness that pretends to some deeper and clearer sight.

The kidnappers of Aldo Moro had one main objective: to dramatize and demonstrate the powerlessness of the State; that bullets were more important than ballots, more decisive, obviously more deadly; and that an ideological group which could not win a percentage of the parliamentary vote could move forcefully into the center of the political stage. (There is, as for so much of the terrorist dramaturgy, a new Italian word for it, building on the slow increasing recognition of the PLO—*"olpizzazione."*) By calculated violence they would make it, too.

The operation failed. The "armed party" can still inflict much damage in society, but the curtain has come down on this particular phase of the drama. The Roman trial has begun, and will after a while even manage to become boring. The Italian public will soon, after not too long, as the witnesses drone on and the theatrical incidents repeat themselves, find the spectacle less instructive than it is at the moment. But a great lesson is there for all to see—how a democracy, plagued by severe social and economic troubles of all kinds, pulled itself together to face the threat of internal civil war and to defeat it.

Germans Among Themselves

The Hague

The phrase that has been picked up here from East Berlin is *"deutsch-deutsch,"* that new and neutral diplomatic coinage which avoids he old implications of hostility which still mark usages of "East Germany." The old usages remind one of the "Cold War," when East-West distinctions between freedom and un-freedom, between liberal democracy and one-party dictatorships were felt to be of some importance. The illusions of *détente* helped to bury all that. Even words and ideas had built-in "tensions" which had to be "relaxed." So it came to pass that Communist countries in Eastern Europe which had for decades liquidated all- socialist parties, and for whom social democrats were still a species of "social fascists," came to be referred to in all the media as . . . "the socialist countries"! The old conventional designation of "the so-called *Deutsche Demokratische Republik*" (which, it used to be said, was neither German nor democratic nor a republic) disappeared almost everywhere. Only Axel Springer's newspapers in Bonn still put it in quotation marks; for the rest it is simply and quietly the DDR (although a few old timers are still to be heard saying *"die Zone"*).

"German-German" has thus come to be the adjective that characterizes the relations between the two independent sovereign states which emerged from the Allied and Soviet division of the defeated Third Reich. It is a quiet word of discreet camouflage, disguising all the differences, and merging all the contrasting colors into an environmental blur. It has now also been conscripted into service for the Peace Movement, uniting all Germans on both sides of the "East-West" frontier, as if both were being mortally endangered by the NATO defense establishment. I have already written, above, on the historic conference of writers and intellectuals which was held last winter in East Berlin—a "private initiative" of the East Berlin poet, Stephan Hermlin—to launch the new all-German peace campaign. And now in Scheveningen there has been a second round of fraternal talks, mixed with a little agitprop and a few additional boomerangs. Once again the West German media have given the affair full coverage, as contrasted with the selective censorship of the East German controlled organs; nevertheless, what goes out on Western TV is also seen in the East, and what the Soviet-German strategists gain on the straightaway they have been losing on the roundabouts.

One could catch up here on what took place earlier by either reading the full protocol of the East Berlin conference as published in the West or by locating the shorter limited edition published by the DDR Akademie. Who could be surprised by the obvious fact that the DDR wants the German-German peace talks to have the widest possible publicity in the West but the least possible exposure in the East? Very obvious; but it is one of those little disagreeable truths of political life that are rarely taken up in these roundtable discussions. The words delude; there is no symmetry here; a free and balanced exchange is missing. There may be a certain thrill to the *samizdat* aspect of unorthodox remarks and texts "getting through," but it is only a substitute for what a self-respecting, genuinely Open Forum should insist upon: equal time, reciprocity.

Given this distortion, most of what is said and done at these affairs appears to be blurred around all the edges. Thus, all the West German writers from the Bundesrepublik (and from West Berlin, as well as from a few other West-European lands) get up and hold forth as if they were demonstrating some rare kind of civic courage against old-style arrogant princely authorities, as if they were exercising their rights of free speech in some repressive, highly endangered context. Actually they are as free as birds, and can sing without hindrance. So they should; but some one should remind them from time to time that this is the advantage, not enjoyed by all their brethren, of living under the rule of law and human rights. I happen to like the idea of nonconformity, even when it is practiced without risks and dangers; but it should not be put on dramatic show as an exercise in pseudo-heroics. Nobody is stopping anybody around here for speaking his piece on this, or indeed any other subject.

The Germans may often talk as if they invented the word peace; yet they do have a special point about being on the line of the military frontier between the two armed camps and therefore becoming the most likely opening battlefield in the event of a European conflict. Consequently, when the talk ranges from art and culture to literature, at bottom the theme is really one of a shared national anxiety. This is clear, but less clear, is what the Germans by themselves are supposed to be able to do about this, given their dependence on rival East-West security systems. Reunify and constitute a new neutral belt? Break out of NATO and the EEC, COMECON, and the Warsaw Pact, and become a no man's land in the heart of Europe? Many in the West are willing to open discussions on anything, if there seems to be a real hope of avoiding war; nobody (except a handful) in the East can speak quite freely on such loaded security matters without a signal from Moscow.

In the old days, a decade or two ago, the Germans recognized the connections between *Frieden* and *Freiheit* and held out singlemindedly for peace with liberty. But, again, in the new blur of recent political astigmatism the one (the former) has become for the *Friedenskaimpfer* all sufficient; "better Red than dead," indeed better Red than living on in the frightful shadow of the new weapons which the Americans and all the NATO powers (including Helmut Schmidt's government) are asking for their defense against a relentlessly rearming USSR. As a matter of fact the very idea of "peaceful coexistence" called for a kind of decoupling of the ideals of a peaceful world and a free world. Not that this necessarily calls for a Woodrow Wilsonian "war to make the world safe for democracy" or an Eisenhoweresque "crusade for freedom." The explodable fissionable planet may well have to reconcile itself to an uneasy truce, with raging political conflicts and even limited military engagements, in a time of "Neither War nor Peace."

But there is surely no need to have to reconcile oneself to a new kind of Orwellian *newspeak* where nothing in international affairs ever gets to be called by its right name. In meetings like the ones in East Berlin and in Scheveningen, there would appear to be a self-denying ordinance, a secret index o f"hard words." Everybody knows them, understands what they mean; but they could, if spoken openly, upset the arranged harmony.

Thus, when Günter Grass enters a protest against repression in Poland he feels obliged to connect it immediately with a protest against the Turkish military regime. Well and good. But then that main spokesman of the DDR, Hermann Kant, rises to reject the comparison, to defend the peaceful objectives of Poland's progressive martial law, to insist on the exclusive dangers to peace from "the Right," from the fascists, from the enemies of the Soviet Union's camp of peace. Grass is not exactly silent on any public issue that comes up, but here one does not find him reacting with the same fiery and polemical temperament to which he has accustomed us. Evidently peace among even the most warring conceptions of Peace must be maintained. Coexistence.

My impression is that the German writers and poets and artists are getting into deeper waters than they know. Some have in the past shown some expertise in practical political matters, and even proposed concrete measures for the Willy Brandt era of reforms and *Ostpolitik.* But in this stormy ocean of weapons and throw-loads and defense technology they are obviously all at sea. What remains is rhetorical attempts to express Utopian sentiments: which, when well put, may have some literary merits, as utopians often have, but in the present very ideologized crisis seem either irrelevant or serviceable only to those who want to encourage a dark, romantic spirit of *Angst* in Europe.

Still, the German-Germans want to go on, meeting soon again in Cologne and/or Sofia, and one wonders how long the traveling caravan can hold up in their carefully cultivated togetherness. As is by now rather well known, the churchmen in the East have a rather different conception of peace from the Party ideologues, and there disagreeable differences are emerging. When DDR writers like Stefan Heym and Gunter de Bruyn begin to take the struggle for peace so seriously as to criticize "the militarization of youth" in their own Communist society, which denies any scope ford homegrown pacifist sentiments, then one begins to see (as the dialecticians say) "the deeper contradictions."

This certainly was not the original conception of Stephan Hermlin, and of those in the official Party establishment who allowed him to take his unprecedented "private initiative" last year. Perhaps they still are willing to accept these as tolerable side effects. But there is drama to the dissidence; and they have been here before.

As for the GermanGerman intellectuals and men of letters who have been announcing their love of peace, they have by now convinced all and sundry. As they say, one needs peace to write books, paint pictures, rhyme verses. One suspected as much before one came to East Berlin and Scheveningen, and surely no one needs any further persuasion. Peace, brethren, is better than war. If only we could agree on any other thing: any other honestly spoken, clearly worded, mutually acceptable thing!

Latin Learners

West Berlin

This place is, of course, an "island" and it has needed no special persuasion in these days that "we are all Falklanders now...." Still, its current preoccupation with Latin America has nothing to do with the altercation in the South Atlantic.

Having no power itself the old German capital and half-city has always looked for "spiritual" connections; and sometimes its timing has been a little oddly off. I remember some thirty years ago coming here for a cultural conference, and on that weekend the Korean War broke out. Now the Berliners have been planning for years a Latin American festival, and when it finally takes place the minds of everybody are preoccupied with Argentinian juntas and Peruvian diplomatic initiatives.

And yet, hasn't this always been the trouble with "Latin America," this European projection of the Iberian and Lusitanian New World? An awareness of the aboriginal America was long ago repressed, and with it most of what followed. We probably can't help seeing it only with our own eyes. Columbus glimpsed the green mountains and the mighty rivers and thought he had located the Biblical Paradise. How many searched here for El Dorado (as in V. S. Naipaul's chronicle of the adventure)? Thomas More was supposed to have read about the Inca state before his inspiration of King Utopus's utopian isle. Some European intellectuals still look for their ideal Revolution north of the Sierra Maestre or west of the Andes.

No doubt about it, this ethnocentric focus has deeply upset the Latin American cultures, never evaluated for themselves in their own terms, always echoes of echoes. Their question, as these days of the Berlin "Latin American" festival have again underlined, is: Who, then, are we? Or: how do we find ourselves?

The long weekend was dominated by the presence of that distinguished Mexican poet and essayist, Octavio Paz, who is evidently as much translated here into German as in France and the English-reading world. On one fine sunny day I found the Berlin Stadtbibliothek crowded with some eight hundred young people, listening all afternoon and evening to readings and roundtable discussions. A touching occasion, especially when one considers how recondite some of the biographical and topical illusions are. More accessible, no doubt, is the social radicalism of Mario Vargas Llosa's vision, with novels about revolts and other Brazilian millenarian longings. Still, he was able to charm and instruct with talks about Gustave Flaubert and William Faulkner, and for a moment one could think that the long-awaited "cultural bridge" had been constructed or, perhaps, that there was some reality in the notion of "world literature."

How popular are they in their own native lands? Not very. They may be respected, admired, honored; but not more. Either they are "too revolutionary" and literary critics attack them for being so political; or they are not revolutionary enough, for somehow in all their writings there emerges a critical picture of the compulsive narrowness of Latin political passions. I have been looking through the numbers of *Vuelta*, the monthly which Octavio Paz has been editing in Mexico for the last five years or so. For all its opposition to the Somoza tyranny, it is clear that the developing events in Nicaragua under the Sandinista regime leave something to be desired— what can writers say when new censors replace the old, when the poor still have no say in running their own lives, when Indian settlements are violently uprooted, when the bitterly disappointed; begin to take refuge in Costa Rica, Honduras, Panama, and Mexico? One only hopes that it is not merely presented as an "old European story"; their tragedies must come to be seen as their own.

I wonder whether the Brazilian writer Darsy Ribeiro, a figure of many talents, can for very much longer hold fast to his "happy dream" that all of Latin America should become a kind of greater Cuba. Here in Europe he is at least being told that not only is there in and out of Castro's infamous prisons a representative cross-section of some of the best emigré writers who had escaped from reactionary rightwing dictatorships, but the best of the Cubans themselves, e.g., Armando Valladares, Reinaldo Arenas. But to judge from the recent Latin books on South American politics available here during Festival week, the ideological blinkers about the new repressiveness remain formidable. Even the most Left-oriented of the local German literati—say, the editors of journals like *Kursbuch* and *Transatlantik* (both inspired by Hans Magnus Enzensberger) have long since given up being frustrated by such taboos.

If the Berlin Festival had a lesson, it was in my view that the literary encounter is easier and more successful than the political engagement. In an article in *Vuelta* the novelist Ernesto Sabato takes up the problem of the Argentine population's European roots, and its persistent difficulties with democracy and representative institutions. As he remarks, "Peron, for example, is incomprehensible to the European and American sociologists; he defies analysis, remains a closed book...." Part of the problem is surely that those fateful ideological categories of "Left" and "Right" which mean so little and confound so much in the Western world have been exported everywhere; and when they come back to us from Buenos Aires and Santiago, murky and misleading, shedding no light and many ambiguities, it only serves us right.

August 1983

European Diary

More Sartriana; Kisielewski and Warsaw; Genet's Comeback; Bettino Craxi

More Sartriana

Paris

His adopted daughter and heiress, Arlette Elkaim-Sartre, has published a volume of notes, *Carnets*—as many as could be found—written by Jean-Paul Sartre during the five months of the "phoney war," from November 1939 to March 1940. The publisher (Gallimard) has also brought out the fragment of the *Ethics* that Sartre an pounced at the end of *Being and Nothingness* (part of this had already appeared in a special number of the magazine *Obliques*). Sartre knew why he had not completed and published the *Ethics:* after the enormous impact of *Being and Nothingness,* this much more conventional work—which drew upon Hegel more than upon Husserl and Heidegger—could only be a disappointment.

In his paradoxical way Sartre was always a moralist, but he was no ethical philosopher. He never got beyond the statement that ethics are on the one hand inescapable and on the other hand defy fulfillment in our time. Since then, two volumes of letters—mainly to Simone de Beauvoir—have appeared (*Lettres au Castor,* Gallimard); further "Sartriana" can be expected. Meanwhile items appear in *Les Temps modernes,* once the magazine that Sartre wished to see "devoted wholly to the present day" and which more and more is concerned with all Sartre's yesterdays, in fact taking on an increasingly commemorative character.

In places I found the *Carnets* to be disappointingly unspontaneous and didactic in tone—something one associates more with Simone de Beauvoir than with Sartre. He writes of his novel *Nausea* in terms of having "proved" this or that theory in it. In conversations with soldiers in his regiment he injects, among some lively observations, philosophical discourses that sound a very schoolmasterly note. Nevertheless, for anyone interested in Sartre these *Carnets* are indispensable, besides providing a record of those months during which France held its breath. Like many Frenchmen, Sartre thought at the time that this *drôle de guerre,* this war of waiting, interrupted by minor skirmishes, was typical of "the new character of war" and not (as it really was) merely the calm before the storm. Had the book an index of names, Martin Heidegger's would be the one with the most page references. Even in political terms Sartre finds his thought important, but he also notes—and this is surprising—similarities between Heidegger's and Descartes's methods:

> The method of Heidegger and those who may follow him is basically the same as that of Descartes: examining human nature with methods appropriate to the mind itself, knowing that human nature is already defined by the questions it asks about itself....

But another remark, at the very beginning, reveals the incompatibility of Sartre's philosophy with the natural sciences:

> The error of idealism is to posit mind first. The error of materialism and of all naturalisms is to make of man a natural being. The religion of man, seen as a natural species: the error of 1848, the worst error, the humanitarian error. Against that establish the reality of the human condition, man's being-in-the-world and his being-in-situation. The concept of the human race has wrought incredible havoc; for Castor herself [Simone de Beauvoir] became aware in conversation one day that she has two fixed points of reference in the infinite series of time: the appearance of the human race, in the past—and, in the future, the disappearance of the human race. My embarrassment, faced with the great scientific anticipations of fiction: the extinction of the sun, a collision between the earth and a comet, etc. For me it all has no meaning and is a bore.

Sartre rejected what he called a "racism of the human species" rejected even the idea of evolution in so far as it encouraged a deification of mankind—this time not as "being" but as "becoming."

The sincerity and modesty of many of his reflections are moving:

> I have a clear inferiority complex with respect to Gauguin, Van Gogh, and Rimbaud because they succeeded in losing themselves.... I am coming more and more to think that, if one is to achieve authenticity, something's got to crack.... But I have protected myself from cracking. Even during wartime I am always thinking that I have first to write what I see and feel. I am bound to my desire to write.... This intactness is something that rightly irritates others.

Anyone who has waded through the massive *Critique of Dialectical Reason*—another book Sartre never finished—will be astonished to read the analysis of the oath ("*le serment*") given in the earlier *Carnets*. In the *Critique* the oath is seen as the crucial revolutionary act; it creates the group that directs its power against each individual member and exercises it with his sworn consent. The oath creates solidarity through terror, with terror regarded here as something positive (see, for example, p. 448 of the French edition).

To the thirty-four-year-old Sartre of the *Carnets,* however, the oath appeared as a logical contradiction and an absurdity:

> The oath to oneself, the prototype of all oaths, is an empty incantation by means of which man seeks to charm his future freedom. Moreover he only swears when he feels strongly that there are risks in his failing to abide by his oath. An oath is an avowal of distress.... I cannot will my subsequent willing.

A clever dialectician can resolve such a contradiction "at a higher level"; but it seems that on this point the Sartre of 1939 was thinking philosophically, the Sartre of 1960 ideologically.

Sartre who mentions everything he is reading, quotes frequently from Arthur Koestler's *Spanish Testament,* which had just been published. Reading Emil Ludwig's biography of Wilhelm II prompts him to reflect at length on the significance of the Hohenzollern Kaiser's stunted arm.

Returning to the question of his authenticity, Sartre says:

> It's true, I am not authentic. Everything I feel, even before I feel it I know that I am feeling it. And then I only half feel it, being so busy defining it and thinking it. My greatest passions are no more than nerve impulses.... Everything that men feel I can read, explain, put down in black and white. But not feel. I pretend; I give an impression of sensitivity and am a desert *(J'ai fair d'un sensible et je suis an desert).*

Something similar was said by the novelist from Rouen to whom Sartre devoted his last great work (and it too was left incomplete): Gustave Flaubert. It is an honest, perhaps even exaggerated confession, and other observations, too, possess the same pitiless candor.

Towards the end—the German *Blitzkrieg is* still a month -and-a-half away— Sartre talks about a second reading of André Malraux's *La Condition humaine:*

> Started to reread *La Condition humaine.* Irritated by a fraternal resemblance between Malraux's literary processes and my own.... I have never been influenced by him but we did come under certain common influences—influences that were not literary ones.... I sense ... how much I am of a period with Malraux *(même intellectualisme).* I have to say that nothing is carried to perfection with him. The syntax is sloppy, the words often ugly and ambiguous. It feels like reading over my first draft....

Sartre often expresses self-dislike; but he is taking self-criticism rather far when he writes:

> I was not made for friendship. I have disappointed all my friends, not through any disloyalty, forgetfulness, or want of consideration but through a profound lack of warmth. I have always behaved, as far as that goes, with consideration towards everyone, never missing an appointment, never being neglectful. But there was a diligent quality about it all that must have come out without my wishing it....

It is such remarks as these that make the *Carnets* incomparably more engaging and indeed more interesting than the many dictated reminiscences and other utterances of later years. One special item that merits attention. After reading Leo Ferrero's play *Angelica*, Sartre comments disparagingly:

> Feeble. Ridiculous plot: it's Orlando's fault if he fails in his work of liberation. The first duty of a revolutionary who has brought about a revolution is to seize power. Even when the purpose of that revolution was to restore a people's freedom. To free a nation from a tyrant and then, having deprived it of its leader without having instructed it in the use of its freedom, to refuse the responsibilities of power is to leave that nation a ready prey for a fresh tyrant. There is no such thing as revolution without dictatorship....

But isn't that exactly what does happen in Sartre's wartime play *The Flies*, first performed under the German occupation and subsequently seen as a testimony to the *Resistance?* No one, as Sartre said of Kierkegaard many years later, is a writer of any importance without being contradictory. But perhaps some-one ought to look into the hitherto unsuspected influence of *Angelica* on *The Flies,* on the shadow that falls between the idea and the deed....

Out of Warsaw

Zurich

We were supposed to have met in Vienna, but the Polish authorities at the last minute refused to let him have his promised visa (it was just on the eve of the Pope's visit). But the conference organizers in Vienna proved to be very resourceful; with new Austrian cleverness and speed they dispatched a TV cameraman to Warsaw who video recorded at his home the speech Stefan Kisielewski intended to make in person, and there in the Viennese conference hall, surrounded by twenty large television screens, we saw and heard one of the last open and public voices of dissidence in General Jaruzelski's Poland.

This time they let him out. Kisielewski had a hearty welcome in Zurich, was given an important (and remunerative) prize, and was listened to closely; for he is one of the few who have a large conception for the desirable future of his troubled country (essentially, an accommodation with the Soviet power but on the basis of a new "Finlandized" Poland, pluralistic and semi-independent). He is an eloquent man, and of many distinctions. He is the most popular publicist in the land, but beyond the journalism he is also a novelist and a composer. Until "martial law" he wrote a regular column for the Catholic weekly in Cracow, *Tygodnik Powszechny,* and even his *nom de plume,* "Kisiel" (which is evidently a sweet-sour Polish dessert), reveals his undisguised openness and courage: these pieces have appeared for years in the Paris Polish review, *Kultura*. surely one of the formative influences on the Solidarity movement. Taken together, his work and personality form another of the strange "Polish exceptions," displaying an effective unity between the diaspora and the homeland that few exiles have ever managed to achieve.

The prize he has just been given in Zurich was the Award of Freedom, and although he has been enjoying less and less of it in Warsaw (his articles appear nowadays mostly in the non-legal periodical press put out by the underground) his itinerary includes most of the West European capitals. This is doubtless facilitated by his "Catholic connections"; Kisielewski is a Catholic writer who belonged to the liberal tendency in the Church from old prewar days, and was until recently a member of the parliamentary group Znak in the Sejm.

A certain amount of "free space" has been carved out of the totalitarian society, and until very recently Kisielewski was expounding his general views rather openly not only in print but also in his lectures (twenty-five in the last year, with thousands in the audience participating in discussions). He put it to me that the sharpness of views occurred mostly over issues of liberty and not of the economy; and this was especially so among the Polish youth.

As for the new effort to reestablish state-controlled trade unions, his travels in Poznan, Gdansk, and Wroclaw convinced him that "the toiling masses" were not being rallied by the weak and discredited Party.

What of the gamble which the General's regime took by allowing the Pope to return home for a second time? He thinks the risk was well taken, on both sides. For the Government there has been some advance in containing the persistent Solidarity spirit, which is now hardly felt outside the factories. On the other side the underground circulation of ideas remains vigorous; and his own latest book is a collection of a hundred columns, with the jacket cover illustrating him battering his head against a stone wall a hundred times. Naturally he continues to believe in the power of the word.

Not that he has any illusions about the wordless power of a brutal authority; he was once beaten up outside his home by policemen in mufti. I could see that he was embarrassed by the references to his courage, and he often tries to cover up his modesty with sly wit and outlandish humor (which doesn't always go down well). He told the assassination story he had heard on his return from Australia (he immediately headed for Warsaw when the General declared martial law). The story was about Colonel Gaddafi who had a fit after the Vatican Square shooting, and went into one of his temper tantrums: "I told that bloody Turk to go to the Holy City and rid me of that Pole! The stupid fellow understood nothing—I didn't mean Wojtyla in Rome but Begin in Jerusalem."

I asked about Adam Schaff, once the official exponent of orthodox Marxism-Leninism in Poland, in a later phase of slightly less doctrinaire ideas. Evidently he has transferred his *existent* from Warsaw. He now works in Vienna for an inter-national organization as the official Polish representative. Schaff and Kisielewski have been debating in the pages of the Austrian *Europaische Rundschau*. For Kisielewski, Schaff remains "the kind of Marxist who believes in the ultimate victory of Communism but meanwhile wants to live in another century. He likes to live in the West, and at least enjoy the last days of dying capitalism...."

Genet's Comeback

Paris

Suddenly he's back again: his plays have been put on by Patrice Chereau in Paris and by Peter Stein in Berlin; his *Querelle* was made into a film by Fassbinder; and his books are being reissued. Contrary to all expectation, Genet appears to be at the peak of his fame.

I found Jean Genet, at seventy-three, living near the Place des Ternes, in one room. There was a mattress on the floor (but this is how he sleeps in luxury hotels too). Large ashtrays were full to the brim, unemptied for days on end. "Let's go to the *Brasserie Lorraine*," he suggested. "I liked sitting there during the Occupation, looking at the handsome German soldiers."

What of German visitors today? They're more numerous now since his "renaissance," and all come to express their admiration. "That's just German sentimentality," he says; "it doesn't appeal to me." As he said in Berlin, "The Germans used to be strong.... Now you're just gross!" After touring the city for two hours he is *au courant*: "A completely Americanized city! At least it might have occurred to them to put a glass dome over the stump of the *Gedachmiskirche*."

When Director Hans Neuenfels wanted to know how he enjoyed his newfound fame in Germany—the productions, the films—Genet replied, "To be famous in Germany is not to be all that famous." When I tried to get a recordable conversation going, I asked about the meaning of the unseen trial of a traitor in *The Blacks*. Could it be that at the back of his mind was Sartre's somewhat elliptical remark, in his book *Saint Genet,* about the Moscow Show Trials and about the unmasking of traitors as a stock ingredient of revolutions—could that have inspired him? "Whether you understand it or not," Genet replies, "doesn't really interest me." After seeing Patrice Chereau's production of *The Screens* he says, "That's the first production of *Les Paravents* since my death." In another conversation he says, "I don't know whether I've brought a new form of expression into the French language. I don't know whether I've created a new kind of writing. But if I have succeeded in doing anything of the sort it's not because I love the French language—it's because I hate it!"

Jean Genet's latest work, *Four Hours in Shatila,* appeared in the *Revue d'études palestiniennes* (Winter 1983); and it is not easy to believe that this little old man (he speaks fluent Arabic) sneaked into the camp after it had been devastated and saw the dead only hours after the massacre. One remembers that years before he had traveled to New York to live with the Black Panthers, and to be present at their trial.

In his early days Genet got around the city streets a good deal as a thief and a male prostitute. Now he can afford to fly, thanks to his royalties, and he is still on the go, traveling light, careless about his health. He does not own a house or an apartment, but he has bought himself a grave in Morocco.

Over the past twenty years or so Jean Genet has written a few important essays; but no poems, novels, or plays. Of the earlier time of his "literary activity" he speaks in the past tense, as he does of the time when he "had a sex life." Having grown up as an orphan in his village and been shunted between reformatories and prisons, he finally—as he puts it himself—"wrote his ticket" with his astonishing books and had his cause embraced by France's leading writers from Cocteau to Sartre. This remarkable destiny may partly explain the fascination the t surrounds him even today.

Has he remained, then, the epitome of all that is "beyond the pale," of the "downright unspeakable?" This self-taught writer still commands a force of language and imagery to burst prison walls, yet even today he is unfamiliar with many things educated people talk about. "What do you mean by Chekhov? Who's Chekhov?" But what he does know—Ronsard, Dostoevsky, Proust—he knows intimately, almost I felt as if he had written their works himself. He has spent months reading and pondering the few books he regards as essential, sometimes devoting a whole day to just a few lines.

Genet is an outsider who has found his way to the centre of things. He is a self-indulgent devotee of his own *abjection,* of utter degradation. Amid the stench of "sweat, sperm and excrement" he writes lean, clean, and well-formed periods worthy of the devout Bossuet, Louis XIV's court preacher. There was a time when refined aesthetes had a taste for dirt—*le gout de la boue*—and regarded it as the ultimate in refinement. Here we have a man who actually comes from the dirt, yet manages to surpass the aesthete in the regal sublimity of his language.

The fact that Genet has now recovered his fame does not mean that he is better understood and reintegrated. It is rather a function of the insoluble enigma he presents, the contradictions that manifest themselves in his various conversations and elsewhere. A few familiar phrases recur, but otherwise he keeps shifting his ground.

Does Genet want victory for "the oppressed"? Does he still share their cause if they themselves resort to injustice and terror? Or does he think that if they were to win he would find them as alien as he finds all victors?

Is he—as André Malraux said in the Assemblée Nationale to justify the performance of *Les Paravents* at the National Theatre against protesting Gaullists—"the poet of death, who sees everything living from this viewpoint"? Genet is all *"existence,"* and at the same time appears to be a total man of letters. In his novels he reminds us that the reader should always be waiting for what comes next, which might well clear up some of the obscurities; and in his plays he reminds us that the action is taking place in a theatre, with stage conventions, and nowhere else. In this way he destroys the illusion of realism; what he offers is fascination, not a message.

In *Les Bonnes* he wished the maids might be played by very young men. The reverse is the case with *Les Nègres,* where he believed the actors should all be black—an attitude he has modified for Peter Stein, with whom he has spent hours talking about Africa. If this conversation had been taken down like the one between Genet, Sartre, and Giacometti it would only prove that he claims the right to contradict himself. Sartre said it: there was no good writer who did not contradict himself. He meant Kierkegaard, but perhaps hinted at Genet (and himself).

Is it possible to give a "valid interpretation" of Genet? The three plays he wrote after recovering from the shock of Sartre's *Saint Genet* analysis—he says the recovery took six years— lend themselves to the most varied explications. One thing the performances, in Genet's sense, have in common: exaggeration; ritual; the wheel coming full circle; the mirror-effect. One of the best books so far written about Genet—by the Englishman Richard Coe—begins with a detailed account of the 1947 ballet *Adame Miroir,* in which all the basic motifs are wordlessly presented. Another extensive interpretation is also given in English, by Philip Thody. I doubt whether Genet's new French and German admirers have such good guides.

Both the keen-witted analyst and the poet come across characteristically in the little volume *Lettres a Roger Blin.* Speaking of the tightrope walker, Genet says: "Being outwardly damned allows him the freedom to indulge in the most daring feats, since he is no longer troubled by being observed.... What he has to express is a necessity which is not demanded by life, but demanded—and commanded—by death."

To Roger Blin he writes about the first French performance of *Les Paravents* (the world premiere took place in West Berlin during the Algerian war): "Every scene in every set must be prepared and played with all the rigor of a self contained play, with no visible joins. And there must be no hint that another scene or another set is to follow...."

The ritual and ceremonial of funerals take up far more space than homosexuality, which Jean Genet (unlike André Gide) associates with betrayal and theft, not with "naturalness"—yet Genet refuses to accept Sartre's interpretation of homo-sexuality as something imposed on the "thief" by others. These, he maintains, are feelings he has always had, and what else was there in the reformatory? By contrast with the highfalutin' interpretations of others, Genet insists on his sobriety and straightforwardness. He does not want to destroy the norms of bourgeois society; he simply confronts them provocatively as one who is different. The learned dissertations written about him by criminologists and sexologists only lead us away from the works: what matters is literature. Still, evidently he is not afraid of kitsch: "I want to write a book that is full of flowers, snow-white petticoats and blue ribbons..."—and he gets away with it. To him, as to Baudelaire, evil is "the distinguished thing," special, sacred. In Hitler's Germany, which was a " Robber state," he would not have wanted to be a thief. There is nothing more foreign to him than the "banality of evil."

A curious fate: the outcast, through his writing, joins the ranks of the chosen. He sees writing not as activity, but as atrophy. A pose? With the plays he entered a new world of expression: we must "feel events as we feel something burning us." No, Genet is not cut out to be a cult figure; he has no slogan that would go on a banner. In his writings and his life both liberty and license are things he takes for granted. If this is immoderate, it is because immoderation is the essence of the man.

Bettino Craxi

Rome

No matter that his father is of Sicilian origin, Italy's first socialist prime minister is taken to be a typical Milanese, indeed of that robust, decisive Northern character which marks one as *il tedesco*—a "German." It was only seven years ago that he took over the leadership of the Socialist Party, vowed to reform it, revitalize it, and overcome at long last the postwar polarization of Italian politics between the Christian Democrats and the Communists. What are the prospects for this new, unprecedented coalition of non-Communist forces under a young and vigorous Social Democratic leader?

In the first place we—and he—have to face the fact that the majority of his cabinet ministers were not selected by him but by the general secretary of the *democristiani*, Signor Ciriaco De Mita, as agreed by the various *correnti* of his own conflicting factions. The basic formula remains the same as before, the *"pentapartito,"* the coalition of five parties. In a sense it is an ingathering of the defeated, although only the Christian Democrats booked important losses and the small "laicistic" parties gathered a little extra popular support. Even Bettino Craxi did not emerge as a victor, despite his singular tactical triumph. In the earlier regional elections the Socialists were able to increase their share of the votes to some 15 percent, and it seemed to presage the long-hopedfor breakthrough. Craxi then forced Prime Minister Fanfani into new elections to the Parliament, but he reached only 11 percent. The five wound up with fewer deputies; at the same time Almirante's rightwing "neo-fascist" party (which isn't acceptable to any coalition per-mutation or combination) registered an advance.

Italian politics seemed to be, in Indro Montanelli's phrase, in the shadow of the "white and black ballots"—i.e., the unmarked ballots (those who did not vote for any party) and the fascist ballots (those who voted for Almirante). Popular feeling grew stronger against the Communist Party, which after all only wants a chance to get in on the governing coalition. Is it Bettino Craxi's illusion that he has an opportunity to introduce a "new politics" on to the Italian scene?

Party politics and their traditional organizations are declining in force, and decline has long set in in both the public and private sectors of Italian industry, now showing even larger deficits than ever before. The only item that isn't sinking is the rate of inflation. The bitter joke was: Who says Italy hasn't gone red? Not the color of politics but of bankruptcy.

The *democrisdani* may still be convinced that Providence has ordained them to be the party of the State, although they are now having difficulty with the "accident" which would explain losing both the presidency and the prime ministership of the country. It could be that difficulties will be made for a Craxi government, bringing on old familiar "crises" and yet another fall of a makeshift cabinet in Rome. In that event one thing is surely clear: the elections to come would register a compounding of the mistrust, disaffection and even anger at and with the leading five political parties and, perhaps even more, against democratic institutions themselves. The "white" and the "black" ballots would increase, and democracy would be increasingly unable to cope with the problems which all the politicians, in articles and speeches, have long committed themselves to "confront realistically."

One must recall that only sixty years ago Italy proved to be the weakest link in the chain of European democracies. But the moment can come when the issue which in the past appeared to be "democracy vs. dictatorship" is nowadays rather paralysis vs. capacity to act. In the first years of his reign Benito Mussolini did have a number of economic successes because he could make decisions and put them through. When the active democrats in the populace feel themselves depressed and indeed oppressed by weak leadership, by lack of decisive leaders, they will be turning away in droves from the established forces which will be left with little bands of opportunistic clients. Nor does this necessarily mean that the rejection of the "weak State" will imply a turn to a "strong State," red or black; it can also lead to slow but very real decay. From its new status as one of the great European industrial nations, developed, advanced, inventive, Italy could sink further and further into an apathetic backwardness, as a Continental enclave of the Third World.

With such weakness in the foundations, how much can personal energy achieve? Craxi is, no doubt about it, a ball of fire on the current scene, and he has already made out of a declining, decaying political party a functioning entity. Can he write this large on the Italian State and society? Even among his own comrades there are divided counsels and infighting—basically on the issue of Italian participation in the new NATO rearmament program. Craxi's clarity and decisiveness on this question may stand him in good stead. Still, to take over and reorganize a party, the largest among the small ones, and to take over and reorganize a governmental apparatus: these are two separate and profoundly different things.

"*Grinta*" *is* the word they use about Craxi here, some positively, others negatively; at the moment it sounds as if it were the "in" word of Italy's political vocabulary. And it certainly suits Craxi *il tedesco,* for it is also of Germanic origins, connected with "*grimm*" but also with *grimace:* it can suggest hardness and toughness, as well as a shade of brazen arrogance, and a grimace, *"faccia feroce"* or mask of energy. Whatever he does or does not do, one or the other shades of meaning will be flung Craxi's way. Emilio Colombo (serious, respected head of the Foreign Office) is out; Giulio Andreotti (a manoeuverer) is in in his place—is this *grinta?* And how tough, how resilient is the decision to absorb some hundred thousand extra unexamined applicants into the already bloated administration?...

Optimists here plead that compromises have to be taken into consideration if in certain other matters—the life-and-death questions of the economy and the law-and-order struggle against the Mafia and the terrorists—there is to be hope for coordination and effective action. One feels much cheered by the impression that Bettino Craxi has no intention of being a five-month Premier before the old tune for musical chairs sounds again; he has his eyes set on some "historic turning-point." He may well have the *grinta;* he now needs *fortuna.*

December 1983

Manès Sperber

His last interview appeared in the in the pages of *Encounter* in the month of his death here in Paris at the age of seventy-eight. It showed him even at the end at his thoughtful, polemical best. It was as if he were trying to get across the final messages of his generation of friends and indeed comrades: Aron, Koestler, Silone, Malraux. In Frankfurt at the Paulskirche he had been awarded the esteemed "Peace Prize" of the International Book Fair, and he used the platform (although he was already too ill to read the speech himself) for a fiery critique of the Peace Movement which stunned the German audience, used to rather more tentative and guilt-ridden arguments on this subject. A nationwide controversy broke out, and his name became familiar to a vast audience who had only vaguely heard of his novels, essays, memoirs.

Still, it was a peculiar turn of fate that the East European emigré who lived for some forty years in Paris as an *homme de lettres* should have found postwar Germany the most fruitful ground for his impassioned views. Even as a militant anti-Communist, in the way that perhaps only an axCommunist could be, he maintained an extraordinary rapport with young leftwing Germans. They may have hated other "cold warriors" but they found in Sperber an Adlerian psychologist who understood something of individual "lifestyles" and thus possibly saw in him a sympathetic friend for the lost '68 generation whose slogans, trends, and indeed "gods" had all failed. The visitors to Sperber's flat in the Champs de Mars included Wolf Biermann, and Danny Cohn-Bendit, among others seeking, hesitantly, some new ideological path.

No, he was really a living refutation of the notion—once launched by Isaac Deutscher—that the Communist who breaks with the Party becomes a "renegade" and betrays in his style and temperament all the narrow fanatical qualities of his previous ideological career. Silone was another luminous spirit who moved, not from one "party line" to another, but from extremism to moderation and balance, from intolerance to a generous open-mindedness, from a tense radical combativeness to a caring humane gentleness. Even in the field of abstract ideas there was little propagandistic one-sidedness; and, in the case of Sperber, an undogmatic attitude to Marx's work and the uses (if limited) of Marxism.

He was as a speaker a man of a certain pathos, mixed with an earnest eloquence; but as a writer, especially in the three volumes of his autobiography, his person took on wit and comedy as he sketched the adventures of a frail Galician ghetto boy, wearing a funny little crooked cap, in the disintegrating world -of the Habsburg Empire. Later on, to be sure, we are dealing with quite another milieu, the "rootless cosmopolitans" of an emigré-crowded Left Bank, making contacts with the likes of André Malraux and André Gide. The sense of the grotesque was still there, as the ill-fed Sperber, sipping a fine cognac as a guest in the Rue Vaneau, falls asleep curing a conversation with Gide. And from those long nights in Moscow, arguing about Bolshevism and the coming revolution (his trilogy has been called "the saga of the Comintern"), he still remembers the "accompanying music" to the chitchat of the comrades: the desperate scratching of bad matches against useless matchboxes in order to light up a lousy *machorka* cigarette.... The charm and popularity of his various books of essays owed something to this same quality: peppering theses of intellectual abstraction with vignettes sketched by a novelist's pen. It was, if you will, a "Habsburgian" quality that marked the work of many a famous Austrian writer, and Sperber could talk at length about the profound depths of a Robert Musil in contrast to the inventive narrative genius of a Joseph Roth.

The "Parisian" influences, even after half -a lifetime on the Seine, were less conspicuous, if present or discernible at all. He could be as engaged and as public spirited as the most committed of Left Bank avant-gardistes, but he felt somewhat estranged by a certain element of Gallic vanity and playfulness. We remember his impatience with some of the "nouveaux philosopher" who, as he remarked, could not speak of missiles and masses without quoting Racine and Marcel Proust. In his political mode, usually in the cause of "human rights" (especially, imprisoned writers), he was always single-minded, for the message was . . . the message: straightforward and unadorned. That quality of direct simplicity still remains attached to the draft of "The Manifesto Freedom" (1950) which Koestler asked him to write and then reworked a bit (for the text see the reprint in *Encounter*, July-August 1983).

It gave him, and not only during the last decade of his life when he became a kind of silver-haired guru for many, a special aura of sincerity or of "goodwill" which enabled errant young ideologues, with whom he might ordinarily have lost his temper, to find in him a patient, trusting soul.

If he remained a militant moralist and a political educator, it still caught the essence of the man when the "Frankfurter's" obituary (a moving piece by Marcel Reich-Ranicki) was headlined: "*Der poetische Lehrmeister*" or "the poetical mentor. "

As in his book on Adler's psychology, and indeed in his epic novels and in his critique of totalitarianism, he was obsessed with the idea (and reality) of "the individual." Few of that idea fixed European generation of ideologues and theoreticians could interrupt and divert a heavy intellectual session, as he so often did, with a series of pointed questions about wives, children, lovers, "the individual person in himself."

So it was that in the final conflict—Sperber versus the cant of the peace-fighters, whom he accused of being blind to the foreign- policy dangers of the 1980s as they once were in the 1930s—he had a kind of extraordinary immunity on the Left. Anybody else would have been excommunicated from the ranks of the decent, forward-looking, progressive intelligentsia. But, although they obviously disagreed with him, Heinrich Böll and Günter Grass rallied to his side in a rare burst of solidarity with "*Andersdenkende.*" with those who think differently. He had a memorable capacity, here and on many other occasions, of being able to suspend the "*Freund-Feind*" syndrome: to bring together, even if only for a brief tense moment, friends and enemies. There was, for him, an inviolable ethics of intellectual decency; and in his integrity he communicated it infectiously to others. He not only believed in dialogue, he exemplified it; and in recent months on German television there were at least a dozen rebroadcasts of several long conversations between Sperber and his friend, the novelist Siegfried Lenz. Something more than brilliant exchanges, earnest warnings, and flashing ripostes made for a great and lingering impression. It was (at the risk of using a much-abused concept) "authenticity."

Here was the last of a great European generation of witnesses.

June 1984

European Diary

Words, Phrases, Conceits; Of the Once and Future Leader; German Illusions; Remembering Wroclaw

Words, Phrases, Conceits

Zurich

If in the beginning was the word, then we have known from time immemorial that words can confuse and deceive, that language can enlighten but also darken meanings. Words are there to carry ideas, but only in small part: they also serve to bear the burden of needs, moods, purposes, tactics. Orwell's famous essay dealt only with the political confusions of the English language; all the other European tongues similarly tend to lose themselves in a Babel of false formulas and pseudo-concepts. My notebook is crowded with examples, but here are only three: the first one is obvious, but the other two are controversial and arguable although the phrasemongers, as is their wont, are rarely self-conscious about the semantic difficulties.

Consider "People's Democracy...Neoconservative...Late capitalist...or (in Marxianized German) '*pät-bürgerlich*'...."

The other day in the liberalleft Hamburg weekly, *Die Zeit,* I was astonished to read that Michelangelo Buonarroti, no less, wished for nothing more for the fine city of Florence than that it should become a *"Volksdemokratie."* Letters to the Editor poured in, and I suspect that common sense prevailed in the end. But even the critics did not seem to be quite aware that *"Volksdemokratie,"* or People's Democracy, is a postwar, post-1945 formulation; and that it suggests really not more democracy but less; in fact the verbal non sense is calculated to disguise the absence of democracy altogether. Whatever Michelangelo's politics might have been, he was certainly not oblivious to the meanings and nonmeanings of words. Our well-wisher for old Florence from new Hamburg was surely aware that *"demos"* means people, and that a People's Democracy is something akin to, say, a "pacifistic peace movement." Perhaps there is here an ideological lesson somewhere.

In those Cold War years of Stalin's political offensive, "People's Democracy" was the name given to those systems in which an East European Communist Party, running badly behind in the last free elections, claimed hegemony and seized total governmental power (although a few other "bourgeois" or "peasant" parties were allowed to function as a facade). This is the story of the theory and practice of the term, and to take it in any other sense—much less put it into the mouth of Renaissance Italians—is grotesque. It is the kind of anachronism that Hollywood studios used to go in for when they had a worried Caesar using his Zippo to light up a cigarette and steady his nerves for the Ides of March.

Words, needless to repeat, have always been used as weapons, and in the battles over the emergence of the "Neo-Conservative movement" there have been noisy clashes of verbal swordplay. Essentially it should refer to the group of American intellectuals who have so identified themselves. The designation, on the part of both proponents and opponents, is usually fairly precise. One can be for them or against them, but the important thing is to know what (and whom) we're talking about, for what they have been up to is argument and criticism, and not some form of mystical hocus-pocus which seeks to destroy Reason in the name of Higher Values. There are sentimental Americans who want, for example, to put the "Creationism" of Genesis at the center of science education in U.S. schools—and they are traditional conservatives, or religious reactionaries, or old-fashioned members of the "New Right"...but they are not "neoconservative."

When such semantical matters cross the Atlantic, chaos has come again. I have just been reading a short five-page article in that estimable Munich review, *Merkur,* and in Professor Hans Mommsen's text a curious thing has happened on the way to the political forum. For him "neoconservative" (he uses it ten times) is the term for certain German tendencies that in the Weimar Republic prepared the way for Adolf Hitler (even if he was not personally liked in such circles). I very much doubt whether, for instance, Oswald Spengler ever thought of himself as a neoconservative, and the whole stylistic misdemeanor is really a most unfortunate attempt to write history in a way that becomes more "relevant" or "meaningful," and that means crowding every page with such modish vocabulary. What a futile exercise! Anachronisms are not always accidental or thoughtless but sometimes are earnest, if mistaken, attempts to "get it right." I remember reading in some popular English translations of the ancient classics of how Greeks would "turn tail" in the face of the enemy, and Roman conspirators would be "ratting" on Caesar. Ideological slang is no better.

As for *"spätbürgerlich,"* it is heard everywhere in German-language areas today, ever since Dr. Marcuse in his late-late show of neo-Marxism popularized the dramatic idea of a dying "late capitalism." It is, in my view, something of a joke, but not enough people are laughing. Still, what comical figures these neo-Marxist prophets cut as they pretend to be able to judge our own era from some sovereign standpoint in the revealed new future! There is a slick bit of legerdemain at work here, not unlike that in one of Victor Hugo's dramas when he refers to himself as "a medieval knight," *nous autres chevaliers du Moyen Age.* The phrase about being "late bourgeois," or a dying, disappearing element of a doomed capitalist world, depends on the presumed certainty of being in tune with the logic of history, with the shape of things to come, with the inevitabilities of revolutionary social change. I wonder if Solzhenitsyn was ever tempted to call Brezhnev or Andropov or Chernenko the last of the "lateSoviet" leadership. Probably not, for the very phraseological turn would seem to have come from Lenin. His book on imperialism was called *The Last Stage of Capitalism,* and for some ideological movements it still remains the basic prophetic text. If you are convinced you have the key to the melodrama of history, all the world's a last stage.

Only the timing has gone wrong, and the curtain hasn't fallen. Empires may have been lost and colonies abandoned, but the *bourgeois* and his ill-starred class, the *bourgeoisie,* are still very much around, and mostly thriving. The finality of the "last act" has been a little late in coming. The stern teachers of our day will give history a demerit for being so tardy.

Of the Once and Future Leader

Vienna

Nothing fails like success, as the recent succession cases m the Kremlin indicate. No sooner is the problem of a paralyzed leadership, due to age, illness, and absence of the all-powerful Chairman, resolved than the same situation recurs: as Mar might have said, the first time as tragico-farce, and the second time as tragico-farce. The grisly joke in Moscow has it that tickets to the official mausoleum are falling off; mourners in black are waiting to get season passes....

For all the vaunted triumphs of Western Kremlinology (and the late Franz Borkenau uncannily "predicted" Stalin's death a week before it was officially announced), it rarely reckoned with the geriatric laws of biology. Party doctrine was microscopically examined, the relationships between political factions and social structures were X-rayed. Recondite expertise flourished; but when the old leader died the shape of things to come remained shrouded in darkness. Perhaps only one thing was sure: if the new man ever succeeded in speaking a foreign language (preferably English)...in the event that he ever read a Western book (a novel, or better still a detective story)...or, of a weary evening in his *dacha* he ever put on a bit of lively jazz (swing? a musical?) ...then we could be sure that the European and American press would breathe long and loud sighs of relief—*détente* was coming again, agreements would soon be signed, peace was on the march.

If this is the best that our investigative journalism can come up with, then perhaps we should turn to these profounder students of "succession crises," those specialized historians who have studied the deaths of medieval kings and Renaissance popes. For one thing that has struck me about the Soviet "monarchical" line of "infallible" successors is that they do not succeed to each other but only to the great thaumaturgical founder, to Lenin. And, in turn, what is striking about the relationship to Lenin is the peculiar pseudo-religious complex the Russian Bolsheviks have about political mortality. Death remains a puzzlement. Marxian philosophers have tried to cope with "existentialist accidents," Chairman Mao devised a notion of "revolutionary immortality." In any case (as I learn from Nina Tumarkin's Harvard study of "the Lenin Cult"), a special Party Commission tried to deal with Vladimir Illich's "mortal defection" with special rules and regulations of the embalming process and, subsequently, the public exhibition of the body (in living color). The point of it was, as the Commission explained, that "our consciousness must slowly accustom itself to the fact that Lenin is no longer among us." A real living defector was Lenin's widow, Krupskaya, who was outraged by the fetishism of the corpse, and is supposed never to have visited the mausoleum.

Stalin, to be sure, had a "cult" of his own, but it always seemed to stand neck to neck and nose to nose with Lenin's— as both figured on plaques, posters, and pictures with the originals, Marx and Engels. Stalin may have been fourth in the line, but then (as his henchmen let it be known, especially to gullible Western visitors) he was a most modest man.

Between Malenkov and Khrushchev fell a shadow, and in the darkness not only Malenkov but also Stalin disappeared, putting Nikita in the direct line of succession and descent. No better or more precise word for it has been found than "non-Stalinism"; and the so-called era of liberalization was introduced very discreetly (except for the indiscretion of the CIA's getting hold of the "Secret Speech" of the Twentieth Congress). Nobody dared to move forward to something new, but then nobody risked going back to the old ways. No new show trials took place, and there was no purge or liquidation of old comrades who had somehow gone astray. Nor would there ever be another Stalin again, he who had destroyed so many of his loyal friends and comrades. No, the *Nomenklatura* would look after its own most protectively.

But, then, how do you get from one leader to another if the principle of the *Chistka* is no longer orthodox and the heresy of death persists in intervening? Perhaps the problem could be solved by seeing to it that each new leader is older than the one before. One runs up against biological limits and complications here; but nothing would seem to haunt autocrats with a neurosis about age and mortality more than the specter of youth. A younger generation has to be sedulously excluded.

A certain political price has to be paid for this, of course; and so it was that when younger men emerged out of the Party ranks of the educated, scientists and soldiers and writers among them (like Solzhenitsyn and Sakharov, Sinyavsky and Grigorenko, Lyubimov, and Aksyonov), they were not dealt with as in the past. In the first place, they happened to be genuine dissenters and regime critics (and not "innocents" forced to recant or "confess"); and, in the second place, they were not killed or condemned to die in Siberia, but at worst "treated" in a "psychiatric" ward, and at best sent to suffer the fleshpots of Western exile.

Through all of this a new, imperious party rule survived and it is reminiscent of the practices of the late Roman Empire, which knew in its august political worship only the "living gods. " Lenin, obviously, remains the one exception. Malenkov continues as an unmentionable. Khrushchev has still not re-won his biographical entry in the official Soviet *Encyclopaedia*: once his every word filled millions of pages, hundreds of books; today not fifty column lines can be spared for the man who was deviant enough to die quietly.

It could be that Brezhnev's biggest mistake of his life was to continue the cult of Lenin's death. Like Khrushchev he never summoned up the spirit of Stalin, but on the occasion of Lenin's hundredth birthday (some forty-six years after he "no longer was amongst us") there were flamboyant exercises in the new fetishism, under the million-bannered slogan that "*Lenin is more alive than many who still live...!*" Nobody proved to be more dead than Brezhnev when he was no longer amongst his comrades. After his burial his name, too, went to ground. The ubiquitous bits of wisdom from the Leader were no longer his but Andropov's. Nothing, surely, is as short-lived as a Soviet dictionary of quotations.

Now, again (as in those farcical repetitions which so amused Karl Marx as he contemplated Napoleonic successions and monarchical electors), Chernenko is the single source of quotable eloquence. Lenin has found yet another direct descendant. Every reign becomes for the successor an interregnum, peopled obscurely by unmentionable regents, with no names worth remembering. Between the embalmed founder of all good things and the true fulfillment of his succession falls a shadow, a nothingness.

History, then, becomes empty and without meaning; and it is only natural that some of the dissidents (Roy Medvedev, for example, and Solzhenitsyn above all) have been hoping to find some sources of renewal in efforts to salvage the past. Witnesses who can give testimony are to become the great healers of revolutionary amnesia. The specter which has been haunting Europe is the specter of the memory hole. The trouble with so-called historical materialism is that it has nothing to do with history: "historic" is only the one-and-only founder, and the one-and-only current living leader.

All the rest are unhistorical unpersons. Orwell would have been amused.

German Illusions

Hamburg

The former West German ambassador to East Germany (he was called merely "the Permanent Representative") returned to the scene of the Bonn Republic to write a bestselling book. Ambassador Gaus' solutions to the "National Problem," which he vigorously re-raises are less convincing than his analysis of the German ambiguities and uncertainties hidden within the current acceptance of a divided nation. He senses change and movement, feeling as he does that things cannot (i.e., should not) go on as they have been going. As Günter Gaus puts it, "*Es gibt heute nichts Selbstver-standliches in Deutschland*," nothing can be taken as self-evident or as a matter of course any more.... Another new book that I have been reading offers fifteen experts on the subject of "the Identity of the Germans," and there are exactly fifteen different little portraits.

The old big picture used to include a vision of a great and traditional German *Vaterland*, with expansive frontiers ("*von der Maas bis an die Memel*"). That era, and its ancient Teutonic longings, is long since gone. The new big picture was one of "*Europa*," and that seems also to be receding into an historical background or being put off to a later time of Continental unities. Diagnosticians have been busy but there seems to be no therapy in sight. Nor is the medical image accidental, for I have been looking at my bookshelf of German political books of the last decade and they seem to me mainly concerned with the German "illness," with weaknesses and shortcomings and painful troubles. Ullstein published a book about *Die Deutsche Neurose*, Mohn's alarm was a "Warning about Germany"; Egon Bahr's cry was "What Will Become of the Germans?"

The "Germany" in all these books seems to be some pathetic creature, a dog constantly snapping at its own tail. If there were space I would try and compare the current crop of books and pamphlets on "the German Question" with those of, say, thirty years ago. The bylines and titles are different, but I wonder whether many of the realities have really changed, objectively speaking. I think of the speech that Raymond Aron made to German students in Frankfurt in 1950 (I mentioned it recently in my memorial article in the February *Encounter*). To read again his remarks is surely to be struck by how apposite they still are. Aron was one of the first of the French-German "bridge-builders," and even during the war warned against yet another "vindictive" peace that would foreclose any future for the German nation. Nevertheless, he told those Frankfurt students—and today they would all be between fifty and sixty—that they could not reckon, no matter how painful the recognition might be, on a reunited German state. Divided Germany was part of the division of Europe, and one would last as long as the other. The diplomacy of Soviet propaganda was not to be taken seriously, and was not so intended:

The Soviet power has installed itself, politically and militarily, throughout Eastern and Central Europe, and there is no sign that it is supposed to be temporary. Reunification of Germany assumes "free elections" in those areas where People's Democracies have been established. Who could imagine that the Soviet leaders would run the risk of losing elections which, in their totalitarian style, they have always managed to win with 99% and better? The German hope and wish for unity is legitimate, and, more than that, natural. We cannot accept the present status of Europe, but at the same time we cannot change it....

That status quo was accepted, if slowly. One recalls all the furor in Germany that was caused by Professor Karl Jaspers' book which called for the acceptance and recognition of two German states, *die Zweistaatlichkeit*. The ethnic or national sense of anomaly remains, but it is not very much relieved by the pious sentiment that, surely. one fine day there will be one Germany again.

There is, of course, a school of utopian nationalists who, looking back, contend there were postwar diplomatic opportunities that were missed. This might-have-been argument is dismissed in great critical detail by Professor Herman Graml in a study published in the scholarly German historical journal, *Vierteljahrschrifte für Zeitgeschichte*. I doubt whether all the convincing documentation and footnotes will help much. Hard evidence rarely holds out against the onslaught of invincible hope, bitter outrage, or deep illusions. Somehow it all *should* have happened, and can *still* come to pass.

Günter Grass now is to be found in the ranks of the born-again German national hopefuls. In a recently published conversation with Fritz J. Raddatz, Grass is quoted as saying: "I don't believe that for Western Germany there was quite the prospect of an 'Austrian solution,' but something like that would have been possible...."

The vagueness of that "something like that" is so vast, who would want to be polemical and pin it down? But that, after more than thirty years, nothing more precise than that can be formulated is proof of Raymond Aron's melancholy prescience all those years ago. For Grass and his friends nothing is more irresistible than an illusion whose time has come. The *Bundesrepublik is* evidently living an existential lie, *eine Existenzlüge,* if it considers itself an independent state rather than a partial, unfinished *Teilstaat*. Nobody really believes that the West German state is "provisional," but will thinking make it so? "Provisional" for decade after decade? With a new and different history of its own, special "national" memories and functioning governmental institutions? Even Günter Grass finds the West German Constitution an excellent document, and he even goes on to consider himself a protector of the constitutional law, *ein Verfassungsschützer.* The German mind becomes curiouser and curiouser—how does a society continue to live under a good and defensible Constitution when its very existence was a mistake and its continuance is a "lie"? I am not sure what ails Germany today, or what precisely pains its intellectuals; but to put one's finger on its *"neurose" is* to touch the point where very strong convictions are joined to very weak logic.

Remembering Wroclaw

Paris

For one reason or another I have been prompted to think about that great and notorious "cultural conference" which I attended in Breslau in late August of 1948. I suppose that Wroclaw can, after so many years, be referred to by its old, still familiar German name (after all, the German language is still allowed to call Warsaw *Warschau* and not *Warszawa*). At any rate, some historians of the 'Peace Movement" have been looking back to those discussions, as if to find additional pacifistical "roots" in the 1940s.

Yet, as an attempt to rally "the peace-loving" forces of a war-torn Europe, that Breslau conference was a distinct failure. No worldwide inspiration came from the assembly (the subsequent "Stockholm Appeal was another abortive attempt); and the various international figures—to the extent that they were not already members of the "apparatus"—were very reluctant to get themselves conscripted into an obvious propaganda campaign. More than that, it was early days yet for the Kremlin's "satellite system," and certain differences came to the fore that separated the East Europeans from the down-the-line sloganeering of the Soviet delegates. Then there were the heretical Yugoslavs, and nobody east of Tito's frontiers would fraternize with them; nor indeed with the bourgeois Westerners. I have been looking through the published edition of Max Frisch's Diaries (the volume on 1946-49), and there in his entries was recaptured the whole oppressive atmosphere of the day. There is also a documentary report by Dominique Desanti which, from the Communist side, records the failure on "the cultural front" of Moscow's "peace offensive" to win friends and influence people.

I was also reminded of those days in Breslau at the recent meeting here, a Sorbonne conference on "Science and Peace," at which the Nobel Prizewinning Polish writer, Czeslaw Milosz, reminisced. Milosz was at the time an official embassy person in Washington, and he was approached by the Breslau conference organizer, one K—Z—, to obtain a message of greeting from Albert Einstein. Einstein obliged. In it he warned against the growing dangers from the Superpowers, of their militarization, and he pressed for an international agreement on atomic controls. He also added a brief polite note to the conference assembly.

As Milosz recalled, the message from Einstein was not quite militant or orthodox enough for Stalin's agitprop ... and as a result its contents were kept secret. The perfunctory words of greeting were, however, read out proudly by Julian Huxley, who must have believed that this was all there was. It was typical of those days in Breslau when censorship went hand in glove with defamation. A. J. P. Taylor was provoked into loudly defending himself and, indeed, "the West." T. S. Eliot and Jean-Paul Sartre (then not yet a "peacefighter" or a fellowtraveler) were both called by the Soviet writer Alexander Fadeyev "hyenas of the typewriter."

Nowadays Moscow has proved itself to be rather more skilful in its Western approaches; and, as we have seen in the recent period, Soviet approval has been dispensed to every kind of "pacifist" movement wherever and whenever it raises its head—to strike a blow against its own native "war machine." A shrewd measure of ideological tolerance, or coexistence, currently informs their antiwar propaganda, as they welcome liberals, disenchanted cold warriors, churchmen, hippies. In the old Wroclaw days the line was hard and unyielding. Doubtless the Poles in early 1948 were calculating to establish some broad "unity," but when in June the Titoist defection took place there was too much danger in cultivating ambiguities. I remember a few sympathetic West European writers and painters who would happily have gone along with peace, progress, and people's democracy; but they happened to work as artists in a style which was far removed from "Socialist Realism"; and they were, accordingly, treated like enemies.

I recall too an outburst from the late Elio Vittorini, at that time one of the leading figures in the new postwar Italian literature and the editor of a fairly open-minded cultural magazine, *Politecnico* (supported by Togliatti's Communist Party). He listened impatiently as one official speaker after another attacked the USA, concentrating their fire on "American racism" and the exploited, oppressed, black masses in the Deep South. "One simply has to say it," Vittorini remarked: "'Culture' is the 'Negro Question' of the Soviet Union." Writers and artists who had been censored and imprisoned, or if you will "exploited and oppressed," knew what he meant. The officials, ultra-sensitive to the slightest ideological deviation in those days, were shocked. I can still see those stony, unsmiling faces before me.

Meanwhile, back in Rome, Togliatti was moving towards canceling the Party's support for *Politecnico,* and the magazine folded. Today Berlinguer's party might well want to have an intellectual review of that caliber, but the Vittorinis are long since gone.

Not only publications fall by the wayside when there is an abrupt, or unexpected, change of Party line. There may well have been a time when light jokes could have been made on the zigzag manipulations of the Comintern; and sometime fellow travelers in New York have occasionally hummed for me, with a bit of ideological nostalgia, the refrain of an old song called *Our Line's Been Changed Again...!* Things, most of the time, were more earnest than that. At a recent meeting on the Rhine I ran into a young man who happened to be the son of the Polish organizer of that Wroclaw/Breslau conference all those years ago. He told me that the conference, as an "opening to the West," had been thoroughly prepared—but how was his father to know that the Iron Curtain would suddenly descend on his show, that the line would be changed yet again?

The erring comrade was dealt with severely, and cast into disgrace; he died not long after. One could be grateful, the young man said, that his father had not been subjected, as were neighboring Czechs and Hungarians, to the fate of monstrous show trials and hangings. Still, "rehabilitation" would be a kind of decency or a form of compensation. But the Party never forgives others for the injustices it does unto them. Something of the spirit of Wroclaw/Breslau still lives.

June 1984

Sherlock Holmes and Socialist Realism

Sherlock Holmes was always involved hi shady matters of good and evil, and his most recent career—newly presented, as he has been, by novelists and film directors. as a hopeless drug addict or an un-controllable neurotic— has updated his relevance to sharp-eyed observers of the contemporary scene including. especially, the censors. Blue pencils have become sharper as various government offices where well-instructed officials have arrogated to themselves the power to keep language pure and metaphorical reference safe and sound.

In Russia, to be sure, the translations have a traditional reliability and have for generations been favorite and bestselling reading matter. Keeping up with the popularity of the Conan Doyle hero, the Soviet television establishment has recently made a film of "The Memoirs of Sherlock Holmes." But the censors heard a dangerous barking in the dark of the night, and pronounced the film "ideologically harmful." The clue was not hard to find. It lay in the remark made by Holmes to Dr Watson (who, then, was not yet his friend and chronicler): "How are you? You have been in Afghanistan, I perceive." Watson is surprised, even astonished (and not for the last time). But Holmes has spotted the tell-tale evidence: the stiff, injured arm of an army donor bearing a tropical tan—where else could the injury have been sustained, if nor Afghanistan!

The subject is evidently a very sensitive matter in Moscow; the TV producers were reprimanded, and the passage was censored. It became: "You have been in a country in the Orient, I perceive." A bit vague for a bloodhound of Holmes's ultra-sensitive nose—but there are obviously dangers in making geographical references too precise—enough to suggest "here be monsters."

Where the Russians lead, the Czechs can't be far behind. The Prague writer Josef Skvorecky tells the story of the new translation of Sir Arthur Conan Doyle's "The Sign of Four." At one point Holmes is giving melodramatic chase to a smugglers' boat on the Thames, and exclaims: "Ah, there is the 'Aurora'! And going like the devil!" But the new translation has the detective noting: "Ah, there is the 'Naiad'! And going like the devil!" What had happened—why was the vessel rechristened in mid-flight? Well, the "Aurora" happened to be the great and unforgettable battlecruiser whose guns signaled the Bolshevik Revolution of 1917. As Skvorecky notes, "It goes without saying that a boat used for criminal purposes must not bear that sacred name." In any event, whatever she was called, Holmes would spot her, trail her, follow her evil crew to the end.

If, after all, Conan Doyle couldn't really have known better, more modern authors—and film directors—have to be looked at with even greater vigilance. Take Bohumil Hrabal, one of the best-known Czech writers, whose story was the basis for the Oscar-winning film, *Closely Watched Trains*, made by Jiri Menzel. Hrabal did not quite get back into good standing after the events of 1968 and accordingly his short novel *The Village Where Time Has Stopped* became available only in "samizdat," in an emigé edition. Subsequently he rewrote it, eliminating what might get him into renewed trouble. In most cases it is not very hard to know how the mind of even the most sensitive censor works.

Thus, in the original edition there is a scene in which a sacked manager sentimentally requests that he may take two old office lamps with green shades as souvenirs of his twenty-five years of service. But the Party liners are hard men and not to be moved: "the working-class manager, waiting for his opportunity, threw both lamps out of the window and on to a junk heap where the green shades splintered, and [Francin] pressed his palms to his temples, for something cracked in his head as if his brain had been shattered, and the working-class director said: 'A new era is beginning!'" Years passed; Hrabal recanted, and was readmitted to the Prague Writers Union and a new edition of his old novella was released under the title "Harlequin's Millions." The new director is no longer a rude and ruthless fellow, but a kindly character, and he feels sorry for the old manager. He finally turns to his factory committee members and asks: "Well, what do you think, comrades? Shall we not be magnanimous? Take the lamps as souvenirs of old times which were good to you."

The difference is between realism and "socialist realism." Curiously enough the author had seen the transition coming, and indeed with Holmes-like acumen had spotted the danger and the tragedy.

In a book published in 1969, and then seized and banned by the censors, Bohumil Hrabal predicted his own fate. In "The Buds" this scene is described: "A cab driver drove me this year from the Barrandov studios, and suddenly he asked me, laughing: 'You're Mr. Hrabal?' I said: 'Well, I am.' And he said: 'Heh, heh, so they've outsmarted you, haven't they? You wanted to be a 'poète maudit,' and they've turned you into a socialist realist. That's what I call an achievement!'"

Holmes would have spotted the difference, and Watson might have told the tale of "Closely Watched Authors," or why the censor barked al midnight.

April 1985

Note

1. See Vladimir Voinovich, "Sidelights on Censorship," *Survey*, Autumn 1984; and Josef Skvorecky, "A Cabaret of Censorship, *Index on Censorship*, October 1984.

Kultura's Achievement

There is, alas, only one exception to the general rule about magazines and journals that are produced by exiles and emigrés in the West; for they are almost all invariably inward looking, self-indulgent, fractious, cut off from a faraway homeland. The one great exception is the famous Polish review, *Kultura*, edited in Maisons-Laffitte just outside Paris throughout the postwar period, and with the most astonishing success, both among its readers in the West and in the "cultural underground" of Communist Poland.

It is not easy to explain when one realizes that its leading spirit, Jerzy Giedroyc, came from a Lithuanian aristocratic background, and Russian remains his only other language for conversation. More than that, he was no popular figure in the first waves of refugees from Poland to the West, for he was very far from being a strong nationalist in the old sense, and indeed in his old prewar magazine *Polytika* he had shown his international spirit. It was something of the same atmosphere that prevailed in the pages of his *Kultura*, and over the years it was here that the writing of such "cosmopolitans" (subsequently to enjoy world fame) as Czeslaw Milosz and Witold Gombrowicz appeared. One should, I suppose, always be skeptical when so-called "insiders" call others "outsiders." And indeed I can remember the excitement in Paris when both insiders and outsiders seemed to merge: manuscripts began to come out of Warsaw, even from leading Communist writers and Marxist thinkers, which began to indicate that there might be a common spirit when all began to abandon (or even to "revise") the dictates of received ideas. Suddenly it was no longer an "emigré" journal. When the first period of so-called "Thaw" came there was a bridge available between inlanders and outlanders. Even noms de plume were abandoned, as in the case of Stefan Kisielewski, the gifted Warsaw Catholic writer, about whom I have written before (see *Encounter*, December 1981).

I remember that euphoric moment in the autumn of 1956 when Gomulka came out of the shadows to become party secretary; and *Kultura* joined the enthusiasm. Support also came at the time from Jan Novak, the first director of the Polish section of Radio Free Europe in Munich. How long ago all this is! Today RFE and Radio Liberty, both in the same building in Munich's "Englische Garten," are the main target of Party propagandists in Warsaw; the present director of the Polish section, Zdzislaw Najder, has even been sentenced to death in absentia. And the Germans in Munich, once so pleased by hopeful *Ostpolitik* news from the East, now grumble about the "problematical propaganda" coming out of Bavarian broadcasting houses to "the Iron Curtain satellites." Certain truths, and indeed even plain news bulletins, can have a "subversive" effect inside the Soviet Empire nowadays; and this runs against the German nostalgia for "détente" and its fetish of "relaxing tensions." Without tensing a few muscles a human being can't even manage to stand upright.

I wonder whether this hasn't something to do with the strange fact that when Jan Novak's recent book was published—a fascinating Polish story of the wartime connections between the Warsaw underground and the Allies in London (for whom Novak was an intrepid courier)—it was widely praised in America and England, and was immediately translated into French and other languages; but no German publisher was interested. Nor is Zdzislaw Najder at all known among German writers and critics, although his several literary studies of Joseph Conrad have won him an international reputation. A curious place, this Munich: home of illusions, myopia, self-imposed blinkers.

I bring the Germans into the matter because *Kultura* has to its credit several important attempts to bridge the grievous misunderstandings which have made a barbaric battleground of Eastern European cultural conflicts. The Poles have tried to build bridges not merely among themselves, but with special numbers in Russian and Czech, and a program of publishing leading Eastern European writers and poets. Once again, I suspect that this was not the easy and popular path. I know how pleased Poles are when they are seen and taken to be "Westerners," for only a "geographical accident" consigned them to the East; so why trouble oneself with the sticky problems of strange, faraway Slavs and other neighbors?

Still the Germans are on the frontier, and in the latest special issue of *Kultura* Adam Michnik takes up the borderlines of Silesia and other controversial issues. For unreasonableness in the West on such matters can only tie Polish interests to the Russians, and in this case surely maintain such "tensions" as to make a future German reunification even more unlikely. In the Bonn republic there are still active "emigrés" and "refugees" from areas that are now Poland (and, in the case of East Prussia, part of the USSR). What bridges are they trying to build? As Najder writes in *Kultura*: "The coexistence of peoples who have long suffered at each other's hands can scarcely be served by the repetition of hoary old legalistic formulas, and their endless repetition in German or in Polish. What is deeply necessary is the aware-ness that such neighbors are bound not only by frontiers but by a common destiny" This note comes through very strongly in the Polish writings, as if the signs of this new awareness were more keenly present among the Poles than among the Germans. Adam Michnik, a historian with political imagination, proposes that the Polish government, at long last, publish a documentary white paper on the thorny issue of the "expulsion of the Germans" (the "ethnic" farmers, workers, professionals who were summarily driven out after the war was over). He understands what this means, and only asks in return that understanding Germans would not be so concerned with the feelings of official Poland, the regime of General Jaruzelski, to whom so many in the West wish a stable and orderly future since the instability and disorder promised by a "Solidarity" resurgence might be just too upsetting.

All in all, one can only wish that *Kultura* has the impact in Central Europe that it has enjoyed in Eastern Europe, where it has been a consistent creative force in culture and politics. We have much to learn from the Poles.

June 1985

The Crown Jurist: The Death of Carl Schmitt

They all had something in common, these great figures of European fame and Teutonic notoriety—Martin Heidegger, C. G. Jung, Gottfried Benn, and the recently deceased (at the age of ninety-seven) Carl Schmitt. The Philosopher, the Psychologist, the Poet, and the Jurist: each of them had a flawed relation-ship to the dramatic breakthrough of Hitlerism in their time. None of them showed any special sympathy for National-Socialism up until the year of the *Machtergreifung,* the Nazi "taking of power"; none was in his work, or personally, any kind of herald, or comrade, or fellow-traveller of the Movement; none "joined up" in the time of the struggle, the Führer's own *Kampf,* but only when the final political victory was already won.

Then, not unlike many others (perhaps even the millions), the moment for enlistment and engagement had come. Carl Schmitt, for one, entered the NSDAP as a party member in May 1933. Soon thereafter he became the leading figure in the Nazis' Association of Academic Lawyers, and in the next year took over the direction of the of ficial jurists' journal, the *Deutschen Juristen Zeitung.*

In that first year of Hitler's thousand-year *Reich* Martin Heidegger accepted the appointment as head of Freiburg University and delivered his muchdisputed *Rektoratsrede.* I often listened in Paris in the postwar years to the attempts of the French Heideggerians to make philosophical, and even metaphysical, distinctions between what he said on that unfortunate occasion and the ruling ideology in faraway Berlin; they persuaded nobody but themselves. Even general intellectual admirers of Heidegger like George Steiner (see his Fontana paperback study) concede that the political kowtow was indefensible. But, for the moment, Mephisto had won yet another Faustian soul.

Still, it was only for a moment, for what our four souls also had in common was that they could never quite fit, no matter what the shape of the times, into any established order. They surely tried, but were soon frustrated, or weary, or disappointed, or involved in conflict. The poet Benn (who was also a medical doctor) served in the *Wehrmacht*; he referred to this time as his "internal emigration"...and indeed went on, alone of our four, to make a full and candid reckoning with the political past, in his book *Doppelleben (Double*

Life). After the war, C. G. Jung wrote a very "Jungian" gloss on the deep psychological meaning of his earlier, prewar, essay on the rise of "Wotan" in an aroused Germany. As for Carl Schmitt's memoir, Ex *captivitate sales,* written in 1950, one historian called it "a tame and unconvincing apologia."[2]

Were the groves of academe especially vulnerable? Hitler no doubt had won over most of the German student body, if somewhat fewer of the professors and dons. Nevertheless, many of the "big names" remained aloof although foreign critics were always likely to classify them as "forerunners"—I refer to Oswald Spengler, Stefan George, and others among so-called "predecessors." They were different; and they had their differences, as had Ernst Jünger who—he published a cliché-ridden anti-Semitic essay in 1930—after 1933 demonstrated his constant independence. Schmitt had justified the Nuremberg race laws as "the constitution of freedom," but as a Catholic who had many Jewish and liberal friends he came under fire (in 1936) from the SS organ *Das Schwarze Korps.*

The ignoble spectacle of compromise with the evil empire of the Third *Reich* is often taken to be especially disheartening to men who had faith in liberal Enlightenment ideals. But after all Diderot had remarked that if the Plague were to become King it would have no difficulty in assembling a glittering court. Power has its fasciations, and they become overwhelming when they are perceived as coming *en masse* from the people. In some cases the critics who reread the books of the "predecessors" became convinced that they could detect where the rot had first set in, and how the ideas or sentiments or (as in Heidegger's case) the very vocabulary were to issue in an Hitlerian *Weltanschaunng.* But most of the time there was a real change, a sharp break, and we are often faced with an element of character shock and cultural surprise. Was there anything in the brilliant books by Friedrich Sieburg before 1933 that could have hinted that later, in Paris, he would turn out to be a "sturdy National-Socialist," even trying to explain to the French that Heinrich Heine was not really a *German* poet? There was often an almost inexplicable factor of "contagion," or imitation, involved here; and I sometimes think Eugene Ionesco understood the process best of all when he portrayed the absurdity—in his grotesque play about the only man who could not be a rhinoceros—of confounding breaks with continuities.

This is, I think, especially so in the case of Carl Schmitt, who was not alone in exposing analytically the historic weaknesses of the Weimar Republic, but did not go so far as to point the way towards a Nazi solution; rather he saw a possible way out in an "emergency dictatorship," possibly General Schleicher's which would have prohibited the Nazi Party and militia.

When the moment of compromise came it went rather further in Carl Schmitt's case than, say, in the Heidegger incident in Freiburg. The Philosopher evidently kept some of his Jewish students whereas the Jurist published learned exercises in anti-Semitism which stood in crass contrast to the sentiments and attitudes he had earlier exhibited.

In general, his powers of formulation were put to good use by the leaders of the Reich who were only too pleased to be able to exploit theories of identity between *Führer* and *volk*; to echo his thesis that robust legitimacy took priority over pale and empty legality; and to accept the Friend/Foe (*Freund/Feind*) political dichotomy which sent them off on a "total" search for "total enemies." At the outset, Schmitt was thinking of Hobbes, not Hitler. Later he made it eerily clear that this central principle of his "Political Theology" joined concepts to reality in the dramatic possibility of *"physische Totung* (physical death)."

Whose death? Who were the enemies, and wherein lay friendship?

In 1934, after the bloody Rohm purge, the scholarly professor published an article in his official law journal which proclaimed that "the Leader was protecting the Law (*Der Führer schutzt das Recht*)." But this could hardly be what he really meant or truly believed. It was not for nothing that Schmitt's German critics (mostly then in exile abroad) saw in the development of his jurisprudence a kind of "philosophy for warrior barbarians," and called his method "dialectical-diabolical." His was a mind that was always drawn to problems of power and decision. He was a theoretician of breakup and breakdown, and he welcomed what he called "the bankruptcy of *idees générales,"* by which he meant the collapse of the old liberal values and norms.

No, justice was not what he was after, not old-fashioned justice with its finicky and never quite certain approaches to moral standards. His motto, taken from Hobbes, was: *auctoritas non veritas facit legem*: and for him it was always a matter of power which determined law. It shouldn't be surprising that Carl Schmitt not only influenced the German Right; intellectuals on the Left, too, picked up ideas and images in order to strengthen their recent onslaught on the liberal-democratic state, as in the Marcuse school of critics of "pluralism."[3]

The trouble with opportunism is that the opportunities for ambitious outsiders do not usually last very long. The true believers, and especially the longtime Party faithful, are addicted to trusting only their very own (and not even them). The outsiders are always suspect, soon distrusted, quickly isolated, in the end rudely dropped. I think again of Ionesco's hapless Bérenger who so much wanted to be a rhinoceros like the others, but wanting it didn't make it so.

There were some who longed to see Carl Schmitt among the accused on trial in Nuremberg. But he was set free in 1947 and lived quietly in Westphalia, sharing his thoughts with the intellectual pilgrims who came to Plettenberg and who didn't really believe, or allow themselves to be disturbed by, the indictment (as Günter Maschke noted in his obituary in the *Frankfurter Allgemeine Zeitung*) that he was a genuine collaborator with Nazi ideas; that he had any real responsibility for the death of the Weimar Republic[4]; that he had turned his back on the traditional ideals of law and justice as exemplified in liberal and humane social orders. One such pilgrim conceded this much: "Schmitt's answers to the great problems were in vain. But which political philosopher has fared any better? What always remains are the questions...." Pretty tentative stuff with which to memorialize a man who loved total confrontations and total solutions.

There is a passage in the *Mémoires* of Raymond Aron which recalls his curiously impassioned defense of Carl Schmitt. Aron was generous enough to plead that "at no time did Schmitt ever belong to the National-Socialist Party" and "as a man of high culture he couldn't be a devotee of Hitler and, in fact, wasn't...." With all due respect to our late friend, Aron was in error on the first point. And as for the second, Carl Schmitt certainly gave, over a period of some three years, a very good imitation of being a devotee. I am afraid there was more than a touch of naivety in the notion that a man of "high culture" (*homme de haute culture* or, as the Germans say, *hohe Bildung*) could never bring himself to give personal support to a beastly and bloody despotism.

Culture and character have never been interchangeable.

September-October 1985

Notes

1. Although Steiner's conclusion (p.150) is that "Heidegger has postulated the unity ...of thought, of poetry, and of that highest act of mortal pride and celebration which is to give thanks," he, nevertheless, can write (p.116) on the philosopher's politics: "Is there anywhere in Heidegger's work a repudiation of Nazism, is there anywhere, from 1945 to his death, a single syllable on the realities, on the philosophic implications of the world of Auschwitz? These are the questions that count. And the answer would have to be, No."
2. C. G. Jung, *Essays on Contemporary Events* (1947), ch. 1, "Wotan" (March 1936) and ch. 4, "After the Catastrophe" (June 1945). For a critical view see Paul J. Stern, *C. G. Jung: The Haunted Prophet* (1976), ch. 15, "The Flirt with the Devil," pp. 22121; Robert Wistrich, *Who's Who in Nazi Germany* (1982), pp. 27577.
3. One could note that Walter Benjamin corresponded with him and wrote an essay about his theories before 1933. So did Hugo Ball, the cofounder of Dadaism. After the war the left-liberal critic Rolf Schroers wrote a book, *Der Partisan,* inspired by Schmitt. One most interesting recent publication, edited by Jacob Taubes, is *Der Fürst dieser Welt: Carl Schmitt und die Folgen* (Paderborn. 1983).
4. "If," Schmitt's quoted remark on this subject runs: "If I were the gravedigger, then the Republic must have already died, or someone else must have done her in...." Something less, surely, than a "total" clarification of the issue.

Raymond Aron

"Neither the Right nor the Left laid claim to him and everybody was suspicious of him."
—Raymond Aron on Tocqueville

"He was a prolific author and, as is sometimes the case with sociologists, he alternated between writing articles for the daily newspapers and writing thick books, and since he wrote a lot he did not always say the same thing on the same subject."—Raymond Aron on Marx

"He is a solitary man, and the older I get the closer I feel to these 'outcast writers (auteurs maudits).'"—Raymond Aron on Pareto

Cold indifference, melancholy, lack of enthusiasm, icy clarity, dryness, pessimism, skepticism, callousness—these were just some of the faults for which the philosopher, sociologist, political scientist, historian of ideas, essay-ist, and journalist Raymond Aron has been reproached. This was so even on the part of those who had a high opinion of him and not just those who reviled him as a "cold warrior," "an instinctive (visceral) anti-Communist," as being "unworthy to teach" (in the words of Sartre in 1968), and even as a "neo-fascist." In the same way, he was branded by the Gaullists (in whose *Rassemblement* he had participated in 1947) at the opposite extreme. For them, between 1956 and 1961, Aron was a defeatist, a capitulator, and a traitor to the integrity of French territory because he predicted and advocated Algerian independence in two eloquent pamphlets. This did not stop those politicians who later recognized this same Algerian independence at de Gaulle's behest from blaming Aron for his "premature" insight.

With a few moving exceptions, particularly in the book *De Gaulle, Israel and the Jews* (which is even of a confessional nature), Aron stuck mostly to an objectivity in which his own feelings and emotions were expressed as impersonally as possible. As Simone de Beauvoir recalls in her memoirs, he was regarded as endowed with a perfect intellectual apparatus; and he could get on the nerves of his partners in any discussion, with his remorseless alternatives: *"De deux choses l'une"* (either...or). This reproach to the effect that he was a well-oiled mental machine, perfect in every respect, hurt Aron so much that he defended himself against the charge both in newspaper articles and in books.

Is it a question of literary brilliance? After the war there was the fascination of Sartre and Camus, and later of course also of Levi-Strauss, Lacan, and Foucault. For a long time Raymond Aron was not linked in the same way with an arresting new idea or trend. The historian François Furet (author of a much--acclaimed work, *Considering the French Revolution),* wrote at the time in a much quoted essay on Structuralism (in my own Paris magazine *Preuves)* that after the crisis of Marxism, which in retrospect proved Aron's judgment correct, the hour of the sober empirical thinker was still not at hand, but rather that of a new general theory, "as if in France even the theory embracing the 'end of ideologies' needed its doctrinaire exponents...." Aron once wrote of himself that he had been influenced by Marx and other German philosophers and sociologists, but that his mental style had more and more in common with English and American social science.

Among the major themes with which the name of Raymond Aron was linked in the 1950s and 1960s were the contemporary peculiarities of "Industrial Society" (three volumes in the paperback series *Idées,* sold in large numbers) and "The End of Ideologies." Both groups of themes were popular and were also widely misunderstood. A curious and defective theory of "convergence" between Capitalism and Communism, between East and West was derived from the characteristics of Industrial Society, and it was just the opposite of Aron's interpretation, since Aron never believed in the possibility of ascribing political systems directly to technological and economic factors. The notion of "The End of Ideologies," which besides Aron was chiefly developed by Americans like Edward Shils and popularized by Daniel Bell, was overtaken by the ideological resonance of a New Left and by the brief triumphant appearance of the ideologue Dr. Herbert Marcuse. Perhaps nobody quite understood Aron's notion of ideas and ideals as the link between state power and secular faith (Fascism, Stalinism). In any event, ideologies were not at an end, neither in the East nor in the West, now in the 1960s on the eve of a new ideological fervor or a "Romantic relapse" (as Richard Lowenthal called it).

Two important Catholic thinkers, the historian Henri Marrou and the Jesuit Gaston Fessard, have related how Raymond Aron's two dissertations for a state doctorate were received in March 1938. The *Revue de Métaphysique et de Morale* had devoted a full length report to this public "disputation" at the time. Marrou could write later that Raymond Aron's studies in Germany had become a "major point in French intellectual history" and had been instrumental in overcoming the prevailing positivistic orthodoxies of the time. The presentation of German philosophers of history from Dilthey through

Rickert and Simmel to Max Weber, and the *Introduction to the Philosophy of History* imported ideas and methods into France (not only directly but also in a synthesis of his own) that were largely unknown. Young Aron did this in a way that was censured at the public "disputation" of his "theses" by famous teachers like Celestin Bougle and Leon Brunschvieg. Father Fessard, whose last book was devoted to Aron's work, gave a detailed account of this in the two-volume *Festschrift* in honor of Aron's sixty-fifth birthday. One of the examiners shouted at the candidate: "Are you being devilish or only desperate? (*satanique ou déséspere?*)." Bougle charged: "You discussed your own problems instead of taking up the problems of your authors."

Aron, who later criticized "the pathos" of that dissertation, conceded that he was spurred on by a certain personal necessity, and that he considered it justifiable to examine the truthful viability of the ideas of various authors without going into each and every aspect of all the works concerned. Through these two dissertations as well as through discussions, Aron had drawn Jean-Paul Sartre's attention to German phenomenology, and to Husserl in particular. Aron claimed little credit as the "godfather" of French Existentialism, and although he stressed that his approach at the time was comparable to that of the author of *L'Être et Le Néant* he liked to acknowledge that Sartre alone could have moved forward "with genius."

This debate took place two weeks after Hitler's "annexation" of Austria. That is to say, in an atmosphere of political disaster, which Aron perceived more dramatically than most Frenchmen because he had experienced at first hand the significance of Hitler's National-Socialist victory. Beset by topical political and polemical problems, Aron never wrote that other philosophical work which he had in mind, and there remains a gap in his later work. The treatise on world politics (*Peace and War*) and the two-volume *Clausewitz*, and his numerous critical works on Marx and Marxists, are no substi-tute for that great book on Karl Marx that Aron never wrote, although "thirty-five years of reading and rereading Marx" predestined him to do so.

Anyone who knew Raymond Aron as a commentator on world politics, a polemicist against "progressives" (*Opium of the Intellectuals*), a professor at the Sorbonne and then at the Collège de France, whose lectures combined the most extensive information and methodological acumen—in short, knowledge and understanding—and anyone who further recalls his special attachment to Montesquieu, to Tocqueville, and to Max Weber may be surprised to learn that Aron not only read Marx much earlier but with far greater fascination than those thinkers of whom he calls himself "a late straggler." And it may also surprise them to learn that he always remained conscious of this lasting attraction even in his most radical and devastating critiques. So it is not a question of *coquetterie* but of necessary elaboration when Aron declares in his essays and his books, in the face of the newfangled Parisian "existential Marxists" and "structural Marxists," that he had made a thorough study of both Marx and the political economy of his own times, and neither in Sartre nor in Althusser and the others had he found the slightest trace of knowledge about the mechanisms of the market and of planning, but always just the same abstract reasoning which Karl Marx had scoffed at in the fanatical Young Hegelians in his book *Die Heilige Familie*. (That is why Aron called one of his polemical works *The Holy Families of Marxism*.)

Aron was never a Marxist—even when he called himself a socialist—but always a student of Marxism. He even reproached the fastidious German Marxists of the lofty Frankfurt School with a real lack of seriousness, although he had contributed to the famed *Journal for Social Research*. In *Liberals and Libertarianism* (1969), Aron wrote:

> My age grants me the privilege of recalling a period in the past, the 1930s and the Frankfurt Marxists. They were already mixing up Marx and Freud. They tirelessly denounced the weak and endangered Weimer Republic, which in their eyes did not deserve to survive. When Hitler came to power, even though they condemned Western capitalism much more strongly than Soviet communism, they did not hesitate. Ever faithful to the Marxism of their youth, they continued their remorseless criticism of the liberal society not in Moscow or Leningrad but in New York and California.

He warned against irresponsibly extreme criticism of frail liberal regimes that are dependent on a general consensus, and he polemicized against intellectuals who apply stricter standards to faulty democracies than they do to the cruelest tyrannies—these distinctions remained constant factors in Aron's political commitment for fifty years.

In the 1950s it was not so much the Communists as the pro-Communist and *"progressiste"* Parisian ideologues that Raymond Aron was attacking. I often heard him say that he did so with a sense of a mutual set of assumptions and values which were being betrayed; whereas he did not feel a similar fraternity or solidarity with those on the Right. He wrote sharply that the French academics and the Paris intellectuals who were following the tide and would not stand for any criticism of Stalinism

> have no desire whatsoever to change present-day France, nor do they feel any real longing for revolution. They wish neither to "change the world" nor to "interpret the world" itself. They merely wish to accuse it. Theirs is a dissidence which contents and exhausts itself with carping and thus quite calmly puts up with a situation which is in any case far from intolerable.

Although some of Aron's treatises, which mostly arose out of lectures, are a bit diffuse and stylistically inconcise on account of their origin, all those argumentative books and broadsides are, in my view, well worth reading. They remain fascinating both in their liveliness and in their combination of nuance and firmness. In fact I am convinced that, even in respect of intellectual profundity, Aron often gave of his best in his polemical pamphlets and occasional writings, which suited his unusual gift for dialogue. Here we find such memorable formulations as: "Contrary to the frequently heard reproach, the Fourth Republic was not incapable of holding on to Algeria but of getting rid of it." Or (March 1964):

> For twenty years I have been fighting fanatics who claim to be optimists but who are prepared to tolerate and even to justify all sorts of crimes as long as they are committed in the name of the right ideas and of the party to which they have signed away their souls. Today I fear more strongly than ten years ago the dangers of conformism and of indifference, which the exhaustion of all-embracing syntheses leaves in its wake.

In many essays and several books Raymond Aron took issue with Jean-Paul Sartre, his former "*p'tit camarade*" at the Ecole Normale Supérieure. Especially after the publication of the *Critique of Dialectical Reason,* Aron produced several lectures and a book on *The Philosophy of Violence.* Previously, when Sartre kept on identifying Stalin's reign of terror with the interests of the Western European proletariat, Aron had reacted quickly and sharply. (See his collections of essays.) This time he was intent on precise analysis, pointing out certain illogical "phenomenological" shifts of thought and historical distortions. Aron demonstrated that Sartre only seemingly harmonized with his Marxism the Existentialism he never abandoned, and merely achieved a fictitious synthesis. The inherent contradiction in the gigantic torso of Sartre's later work *Flaubert is* already apparent here.

In the summer of 1979—for the first time in half a lifetime— Aron had a friendly talk with Sartre once again. The two of them visited President Valéry Giscard d'Estaing along with André Glucksmann (once a student at Aron's lectures on Clausewitz) in order to press for a generous intake of Vietnamese refugees. Up till then the dialogue had been one- sided, as Aron had noted:

> My friends are amazed that I still carry on a dialogue with a partner who declines to take part in it. The abuse to which he treats me from time to time certainly ignores that mutual give and take which he himself in his *Critique* acknowledges to be the highest ethical principle.... That doesn't discourage me. I have retained my youthful admiration for the extraordinary fertility of his mind . . . while remaining fully alive to his arrogant indifference towards careful verification and towards the proper use of reason. His outbursts of rage are far too excessive to affect me in any way. I accept him as he is, with his cult of violence and his extravagance.... The truth is that our starting points, our systems of reference, our mentors and our problems are to a large extent the same. Sartre presumably won't read my comments and won't try to understand them. So what? I have derived keen pleasure from the discourse with a partner who is at once both present and absent.

The polemical tradition which remains irrepressible in France—and partly consists in thinking that you haven't disposed of ideas until you have destroyed those who hold them—stretches from Joseph de Maistre to latter day successors on both Right and Left (recently mostly on the Right again). Sartre paid homage to it, without ever really taking his own outbursts completely seriously, for here the playwright (and man of the theatre) came always to the fore.

This tradition was utterly foreign to Aron. In addition, he wanted those same people on the Left to listen to him; he wanted to convince them. In recent years, now that certain ideological battles have become a thing of the past, Aron's long-term influence has been making itself felt again. The "New Philosophers" were, most of them, Maoists in 1968. They branded Marx as a repressive thinker and his doctrine as "opium for intellectuals" (where did they get this idea from?). They referred back to Aron even if they didn't quote him. But in his last period even Sartre paid tribute to Russian dissidents, whom he had earlier declared to be a slanderous invention of the Western gutter press (in his comedy *Nekrassov*).

Aron wanted to teach, to instruct, to persuade, but he never sacrificed a nuance of his thought in order to gain approval. When Maurice Merleau-Ponty broke away from Sartre and the whole circle surrounding *Les Temps Modernes* and also revised his own Marxism of "humanism and terror" (in *Les Aventures de la dialectique),* Aron criticized this book in *Preuves* and entitled his essay *"Les Mésaventures de la dialectique."* Merleau-Ponty had sought to establish a connecting link between Sartre's philosophy and his political aberrations, and Aron found these nonexistent.

I am writing these pages to mark Aron's death on 17 October. But even an extensive, more carefully considered essay could only be one testimony among others. His work is too varied. It alternates between intellectual stocktaking and academic methodology, between measured reflection and thoughts of the moment, between philosophical objectivity and political commitment. One glance at the bibliography in the two-volume *Festschrift* in honour of Aron, or the convenient appendix to his recently published *Mémoires, is* enough to demonstrate that. A critical survey would itself have to be of book length and would presuppose universal discernment. It may be best to stick to selected examples.

It struck me again and again—whether it was in two-page articles in *L'Express,* in twovolume works like *Clausewitz,* or in essays for the new periodical *Commentaire* founded by Aron himself—that here was an author who was never content merely to pass on his opinions but who tirelessly compiled and incorporated the widest and latest information. This scrupulous curiosity is a trait that distinguished Raymond Aron from other committed intellectuals of his generation (and also from occasionally more brilliant later writers, from Michel Foucault to the *"nouveaux philosophes"*). Aron puts forward theses but would never sacrifice the slightest detail to them, let alone overlook a counterargument. He was indeed an ever-alert "spectator," eager to discern and dissect how we live and think now.

This is not to say that Raymond Aron wrote nothing but excellent books and farsighted editorials. Neither he nor his friends would ever want to claim that. Like everyone who writes a lot for the moment, particularly in *Le Figaro* (which at that time, however, had no room for Aron's heretical views on Algeria), he has occasionally been wrong in his prognoses. Too often he heralded the imminent end of the Fifth Republic. Still, a study of Aron's journalism would be highly rewarding.

From the wealth of themes and fruitful suggestions I feel moved to mention especially Raymond Aron's commitment after 1945 to the complete reintegration of Germany into the international democratic community. His was a realistic appraisal of the facts, and he stood practically alone.

Aron's doubts about "reason in history"—he only concedes such a rationale to individuals, and among them only to those reasonable activists in politics—were finally confirmed by his experiences in Germany in 1933. His doubts about progress as a moral category were likewise confirmed by the peculiar "rationality" of the extermination of millions of people belonging to "inferior races," which was carried out with the highest industrial efficiency. But even before this Aron had refused to regard history as an agent of truth. Historical results incorporated neither a logic nor a law nor a moral value. Un-Teutonic as this surely was, Aron never overlooked the extent to which his own education and intellectual development was indebted to German thinkers (though it should be added that no debt was ever repaid more fruitfully). After 1945 Aron, both politically and personally, viewed the German nation, stateless as it was at the time, in a light that was by no means obvious just then.

Aron's essay "For a European Germany" appeared in June 1949 in the first issue of *Der Monat*, in which he wrote: "The attitude of the victors was not calculated to inspire immediate respect in the losers.... Hitler took it upon himself to conjure up the age of great invasions and of barbarism once again. One must at least admit that this age did not come to an end with the defeat of Hitler." It should be the most important task of the Occupation authorities to open the borders and to reestablish human relations between individuals and between nations. "Let them tear down the prison walls, those built by Hitler and the one which sustains the memory of Hitler's crimes. For far too many years every nation has indulged in a bitter monologue. It is time for a dialogue to begin."

On 30 June 1950, Aron spoke before a group of students in Frankfurt. On that occasion he said: "I can't stick to the limited theme of 'Franco-German relations.' The entire situation of Europe as it emerged out of the Second World War is involved here." A "national unification of Germany," even through neutrality, might be deemed worthy of approval, but the sharp-eyed observer didn't think that such offers were meant seriously.

> The Russian authorities are firmly installed in East Germany both militarily and politically, and it seems as though they have no intention of leaving. Reunification presupposes free elections in those regions which are at present called People's Democracies. Do you imagine that the Soviet authorities will run the risk of losing elections, 99% of which they have won already thanks to their tyrannical methods? ...The German call for unity is legitimate, and it is also quite natural. But that is only part of the truth. We cannot accept the current division of Europe, but neither can we change it, at least for the moment.

The solution could take decades, and we are *now* looking back over more than thirty years.

> You Germans are obviously distressed by the partition of your country. But the fundamental fact is not the partition of Germany; it is the partition of Europe. Eighteen million Germans are victims of the Stalinist system, but the Poles, the Czechs, and the Rumanians are not suffering any less just because they all ended up together on the wrong side of the Iron Curtain. The question ought really to be put like this: Is it possible to end the partition of Germany without putting an end to the partition of Europe? My answer is: Unfortunately this is not likely.

Towards the end of this speech, Aron made an observation that became depressingly topical again:

> Anyone who has the sad duty of reading the press of both countries will be aware how easily emotions are aroused and how great the distance between their national outlooks remains. I belong to a generation which saw its task after the First World War as the soothing of feelings of hatred and the reconstruction of Europe. We carry within us the bitterness of our failure. We were not able to prevent the catastrophe....

And Aron called on his audience not to lose patience when faced with the trivialities of everyday life: no evanescent emotion and no vague idea ought ever to be the mainspring of our actions.

Aron always warned against illusions, against utopian wishful thinking. "Shaped by French university teachers"—he once wrote—"at the age of twenty I imagined the world other than it was, and then I discovered the reality of the Germany of 1933.... What cripples utopia is not our ignorance of the future, but our knowledge of the present."

February 1984

Index

Abasino, Alberto, 261
Abetz, Otto, 240
Achard, Marcel, 95
Acheson, Dean, 31
Adenauer, Konrad, 31
Akhmatova, Anna, 193
Aksyonov, Vasili, 333
Alberti, Rafael, 22
Algren, Nelson, 69, 76
Alleman, F.R., 32
Allende, Salvator, 271
Althusser, Louis, 352
Amalrik, Andrei, 187-189, 193-194
Amendola, Giorgio, 159, 161
Amery, Jean, 293
Andreu, Pierre, 239
Andropov, Yuri, 331
Anouilh, Jean, 95
Aragon, Louis, 144, 162, 164-166, 239, 240
Ardagh, John, 103
Ardizone, Flora, 224
Arenas, Reinaldo, 314
Arenguren, J.L., 23
Aron, Raymond, xiii, 143, 182, 183, 326, 334, 335, 348, 349-356
Artajo, Martin, 19, 23
Artaud, Antonin, 269
Astor, David, 288
Autant-Lara, Claude, 53
Aymé, Marcel, 95
Azaña, Manuel, 22

Babel, Isaac, 59
Bacher, Gerd, 283
Bahr, Egon, 334
Baldwin, James, 136, 148
Balzac, Honoré de, 9, 93, 230, 295
Banti, Anna, 131
Barbey d'Auurevilly, Jules, 292
Barbie, Klaus, 299

Barlach, Ernst, 61
Baroja, Pio, 16-17
Barre, Raymond, 267
Barrès, Maurice, 119
Barthes, Roland, 176, 177
Bartoli, Domenico, 272-274
Baruch, Bernard, 237
Bataille, Georges, 52, 218
Baudelaire, Charles, 93, 249, 323
Beaumont, Jean-Louis, 258
Beauvoir, Simone de, 68-76, 140, 176, 177, 285-287, 315, 316, 349
Beckett, Samuel, 64, 144, 294
Bell, Daniel, 350
Bellow, Saul, xii
Ben Bella, Ahmed, 136
Ben Gurion, David, 40
Benes, Eduard, 80-81, 82
Benn, Gottfried, 345
Benn, Tony, 288
Berlanga, Luis, 167
Berlin, Isaiah, 203
Berlinguer, Enrico, 154, 155, 156, 216, 271, 337
Bernanos, Georges, 95
Bernstein, Leonard, 148
Berteaux, Pierre, 187
Bertolucci, Bernardo, 131
Bettiza, Enzo, 195-98, 301
Beuve-Méry, Hubert, 178, 179, 300
Biermann, Wolf, 326
Billoux, Francois, 107
Bismarck, Otto von, 281
Blanch, Lesley, 275
Blin, Roger, 322
Bloch, Ernst, 61
Bloch-Michel, Jean, 72
Blum, Léon, 105, 106, 216-217, 248, 266
Bo, Carlo, 130
Bokassa, Jean Bedel, 243
Böll, Heinrich, xiii, 64, 182, 183, 328

357

Bonnard, Abel, 98
Borges, Jorge Luis, 253
Borkenau, Franz, 331
Borso, Mario, 300
Bory, Jean-Louis, 230
Bossuet, Jacques Bénigne, 321
Bougle, Celestin, 351
Boulin, Robert, 242
Boumedienne, Houari, 136
Bourdet, Claude, 109
Brandt, Willy, 288, 289, 291
Brecht, Bertolt, 44, 61, 62, 174, 192, 213
Breker, Arno, 241
Breton, André, 164
Brezhnev, Leonid, 219-220, 236, 237, 331
Brien, Alan, 145
Brunschweig, Leon, 351
Buber, Martin, 35
Büchner, Georg, 302
Bukharin, Nikolai, 72
Burachatra, Prem, 7
Busch, Ernst, 62
Buzzati, Dino, 131
Byron, George Gordon, Lord, 70

Cadignola, Tristano, 180-181
Callois, Roger, 203
Calvino, Italo, 131, 175, 260, 261
Camus, Albert, ix, xiii, 7, 69, 72, 74, 248, 250, 265, 270
Èapek, Joseph, 80
Èapek, Karel, 79-80
Carlyle, Thomas, 203
Carmichael, Stokely, 138, 149
Carrière, Jean-Claude, 302
Carter, Jimmy, 191, 198-199, 236
Casalegno, Carlo, 215-216
Castro, Fidel, 75, 227-228, 232, 314
Cau, Jean, 287
Caws, Peter, 270
Cazes, Jerome, 255
Celan, Paul, 40, 187
Céline, Louis-Ferdinand, 294
Cervantes, Miguel de, 293
Cesairé, Aimé, 134, 136
Chagall, Marc, x
Chamfort, Nicolas, 100
Chateaubriand, François René, 94
Chereau, Patrice, 302, 320
Chernenko, Konstantin, 331 333
Chiaromonte, Nicola, 180, 183

Chirac, Jacques, 200, 264
Churchill, Winston, 281
Cioran, E.M., 144
Clair, René, 95
Clark, Ramsay, 150
Claudel, Paul, 93, 248, 249
Cleaver, Eldredge, 138, 149
Clementis, Vlado, 84
Coco, Francesco, 215
Cocteau, Jean, 95-96, 100
Coe, Richard, 322
Cohn-Bendit, Daniel, 232-233, 326
Colbert, Jean Baptiste, 298
Colet, Louise, 116, 293
Colombo, Emilio, 325
Conan-Doyle, Arthur, 339-340
Connolly, Cyril, xi, xii
Conrad, Joseph, 341
Corneille, Pierre, 97-98
Craig, Gordon, 281
Craipeau, Marie, 71
Craxi, Bettino, 272, 321-325
Croce, Benedetto, ix, xi, 157, 161
Croce, Fulvio, 215
Cunhal, Alvaro, 154, 155, 179

d'Alembert, Jean le Rond, 94
D'Annunzio, Gabriele, 119-125
Dahrendorf, Ralf, 159
Daix, Pierre, 164, 166, 219
Daladier, Edouard, 266
Daniel, Jean, 109
Danton, Georges Jacques, 302-303
Darwin, Charles, 204
Daudet, Alphonse, 100, 292
Daudet, Léon, 292
Davis, Angela, 149
Debray, Regis, 135, 167-172
Debre, Francois, 231
Debre, Michel, 51, 231
Debre, Simon, 231
de Broglie, Jean, 210-211
de Broglie, Louis, 95
de Bruyn, Gunter, 312
de Custine, Marquis, 245, 247
de Felice, Renzo, 157-161
Deferre, Gaston, 104, 105, 296
de Gaulle, Charles, 51, 73, 98-99, 105, 106, 108, 109, 141, 164, 231, 243, 248, 250
Deleuze, Gilles, 186
de Maistre, Joseph, 230, 354

de Mendelssohn, Peter, 120
de Mita, Ciriaco, 321
Depardieu, Gerard, 302
Dery, Tibor, 4, 64, 201-202
Desanti, Dominique, 239, 336
Descartes, René, 316
Descombes, Vincent, 269
Desmoulins, Camille, 302, 303
Dewey, John, 8
Diderot, Denis, 346
Dilthey, Wilhelm, 350
Domenach, Jean-Marie, 179
d'Ormesson, Wladimir, 94
Dostoevsky, Fyodor, 66, 118
Dreyfus, Alfred, 266
Drieu La Rochelle, Pierre, 239-241
Du Camp, Maxime, 295
Dubcek, Alexander, 236
Duclos, Jacques, 107
Duerrenmatt, Friedrich, 65
Dulles, John Foster, xii, 30
Dumont, René, 138
Dutschke, Rudi, 232, 234

Eden, Anthony, xii
Eichmann, Adolf, 35-43
Einstein, Albert, x, 336
Eisler, Hanns, 62
Eliot, T.S., xi, xii, 7, 337
Elkaim-Sartre, Arlette, 315
Elleinstein, Jean, 221
Emmanuel, Pierre, 102
Engel, Erich, 62
Entralgo, Pedro Lain, 14
Enzensberger, Hans Magnus, 232, 235, 314
Eppler, Erhard, 288

Fabre-Luce, Albert, 51
Fadyeyev, Alexander, 337
Fanon, Frantz, 134-140
Farrère, Claude, 94
Faulkner, William, 57, 313
Fauvet, Jacques, 178, 179
Fell, Joseph P., 270
Feltrinelli, Giangiacomo, 171, 224, 307
Ferdinand VII, 21
Fermi, Enrico, x
Ferrat, André, 163
Ferrero, Luc, 318
Fessard, Gaston, 350, 351
Fest, Joachim, 287

Fischer, Ernst, 56, 202
Flaubert, Gustave, 52, 93, 113-118, 142, 143, 269, 292-295, 313, 317
Forcella, Enzo, 169, 196
Foucault, Michel, 95, 186, 349, 354
Fourastie, Jean, 203
France, Anatole, 96
Franco, Francisco, 13, 16, 18, 19, 21, 25, 249, 250
Frank, Bernard, 268
Frederick II, 282
Fried, Eugen, 163
Frisch, Max, 336
Furet, François, 350

Gadaffi, Muommar, 319
Gaitskell, Hugh, 26
Gallardo y Gomez, Manuela, 23
Garaudy, Roger, 165
Garçon, Maurice, 52, 96
Gardella, Ignazio, 130
Garibaldi, Giuseppe, 161
Gary, Romain (Émile Ajar), 275-280
Gatto, Alfonso, 132
Gaus, Günter, 334
Gavi, Phillipe, 141
Gaxotte, Pierre, 94
Gendzier, Irene, 140
Genet, Jean, 11, 97, 113, 115, 167, 320-323
George, Stefan, 346
Gérard, André, 53
Gerstein, Kurt, 46, 47
Giacometti, Alberto, 269, 322
Gide, André, 7, 241, 248, 250, 322, 327
Giedroyc, Jerzy, 342
Giereck, Bronislaw, 192
Ginzburg, Natalia, 131, 175
Girnus, Wilhelm, 61, 63
Girodias, Maurice, 52
Giroud, Françoise, 168
Giscard d'Estaing, Valéry, 127, 167, 200, 242, 243, 244, 258, 267, 297, 353
Glotz, Peter, 290
Glucksmann, André, 353
Gobineau, Joseph Arthur, 266
Godard, Jean-Luc, 53
Goethe, Johann Wolfgang, von, 61, 198, 199
Goldoni, Luca, 262
Goldsmith, James, 242
Goldstücker, Eduard, 55, 88

Gollwitzer, Hellmut, 234
Gombrowicz, Witold, xi, 276, 342
Gomulka, Wladislaw, 80
Goncourt, Edmond, 116
Goncourt, Jules, 116
Goodwin, Doris Kearns, 190-191
Gorki, Maxim, 294
Gottwald, Klement, 80, 83
Graham, Billy, 198
Graml, Hermann, 335
Granin, Daniel, 67
Grass, Günter, xi, xiii, 242, 243, 244, 263, 305, 306, 312, 328, 335
Green, Henry, 294
Greene, Graham, 252
Groethuysen, Bernard, 218
Gros, Brigitte, 127
Grover, Frederic, 239
Guevera, Che, 135, 170, 171, 227
Guttuso, Renato, 131

Habermas, Jürgen, 160, 234
Haffner, Sebastian, 288
Halevi, Benjamin, 43
Hammer, Armand, 255
Hamsun, Knut, 75
Hauff, Volker, 289
Hausner, Gideon, 41-42
Havel, Vaælav, 79
Havemann, Robert, 307
Hay, Julius, 3-4
Healy, Denis, 26, 28
Hegel, G. F. W., 314
Heidegger, Martin, ix, 186-187, 313, 316, 345, 346
Heine, Heinrich, 100
Hermlin, Stephan 306, 307, 312
Hersant, Louis, 229
Heym, Stefan, 263, 312
Himmler, Heinrich, 36
Hitler, Adolf, 27, 36, 250, 298, 330, 347, 351, 355
Ho Chi Minh, 232
Hobbes, Thomas, 347
Hochhuth, Rolf, 44-49
Hoffer, Frederic, 9-12
Honecker, Erich, 307
Höss, Rudolf, 38
Hrabal, Bohumil, 340
Huchel, Peter, 61, 62
Hugo, Victor, 93, 94, 331
Husak, Gustav, 84, 85

Husserl, Edmund, 315, 351
Huxley, Julian, 336

Ionesco, Eugene, 64, 346, 347
Iskander, Fazil, 220
Ivinskaya, Olga, 71

Jaruzelski, Wojciech, 318, 342
Jaspers, Karl, ix, xii, xiii, 335
Jaurès, Jean, 106
Javits, Jacob, 150
Jeanson, Francis, 134, 141
Jenkins, Roy, 288
Jeramec, Colette, 240
John Paul II (Karol Wojtyla), 317, 318
Johnson, Lyndon B. 190-191
Jouve, Pierre-Jean, 96
Joyce, James, 57, 67, 144, 294
Jung, Carl Gustav, 345, 346, 348
Jungk, Robert, 305
Jurnaek, Pavel, 78

Kádár, János, 283
Kafka, Franz, 55-58, 65, 66, 67, 78, 88, 220, 293, 298
Kampelman, Max, 306
Kant, Hermann, 311
Kanters, Robert, 270
Kennan, George, 26-32
Kennedy, John F. 190, 191, 238, 250
Kerr, Clark, 148
Kessel, Joseph, 278
Keynes, John Maynard, 298
Khrushchev, Nikita, 212, 268, 332, 333
Kierkegaard, Sören, 318, 322
Kimche, Jon, 39
Kindler, Eugen, 90
Kisch, Egon Erwin, 88
Kisielewski, Stefan, 318-320, 342
Kissinger, Henry, 237, 256
Klima, Ivan, 79, 81
Koestler, Arthur, 22, 69, 72, 73, 317, 326, 327
Kolb, Philip, 239
Kolbe, Maximilian, 46
Komatsu, Kyo, 6
Konetzke, Richard, 204
Kramer-Badoni, Rudolf, 48
Krasucki, Henri, 296
Krauss, Karl, 36
Kreisky, Bruno, 283
Kriegel, Annie, 110, 229

Index   361

Krim, Belkacem, 138
Kristol, Irving, x, xiii
Krupskaya, Nadezhda, 332
Kunert, Günter, 67, 282
Kurella, Alfred, 56, 60-61
Kuron, Jacek, 192

Lacan, Jacques, 205, 350
Lacoste, Robert, 105, 135
Lacouture, Jean, 248, 250
Landau, Moshe, 43
Landolfi, Tommaso, 131
Langer, Frantisek, 80
Lanzmann, Jacques, 70
Laval, Pierre, 249
Lawrence, D. H., 167
Leavis, F.R., 203
Lecanuet, Jean, 128
Legris, Michel, 178
Lenin, Vladimir, 58, 59, 180, 191, 332, 333
Lenz, Siegfried, 328
Leopardi, Giacomo, 261
Leroux, Gaston, 100
Lévi-Strauss, Claude, 350
Lévy, Benny, 285
Lévy, Bernard-Henri, 230, 265, 266
Lichtenberg, Dean, 46
Lindon, Jerome, 50, 51
Lippmann, Walter, 237
Littré, Maximilien Paul Èmile, 101
Loebl, Eugen, 87, 90, 92
Lomgo, Ottone, 223
Loren, Sophia, 278
Lottman, Herbert, 239
Louis XIV, 321
Lowenstein, Karl zu, 48
Lowenthal, Richard, 182, 183, 288-291, 350
Ludwig, Emil, 317
Lukács, Georg, 57, 64, 66, 202, 220
Lumumba, Patrice, 135
Luther, Martin, 298
Lyubimov, Yuri, 333

Mailer, Norman, 175
Malcolm X, 149
Malenkov, Georgi, 332
Malerba, Luigi, 131, 261
Mallarmé, Stephane, 96
Malraux, André, 141, 170, 171, 213, 218, 248, 269, 317, 326, 327
Malraux, Clara, 170
Malraux, Josette, 239
Mandelstam, Osip, 59
Mann, Heinrich, 295
Mann, Thomas, x, 57
Manzoni, Alessandro, 261
Mao Tse-tung, 219
Marchais, Georges, 154, 216, 222, 242, 243, 244, 259, 271-272
Marcuse, Herbert, 186, 330, 350
Marias Julian, 13, 23
Marquez, Gabriel Garcia, xi
Marrou, Henri, 350
Martin de Gard, Roger, 95
Martinet, Gilles, 127
Martinez Barrios, 22
Marx, Karl, 58-59, 66, 104, 298, 326, 333, 350, 351, 352
Masaryk, Jan, 88
Masaryk, Thomas, 80, 82-83
Maschke, Gunter, 347
Masson, André, x
Mathies, Frank-Wolf, 262
Maupassant, Guy de, 53, 250
Mauriac, François, 95, 98, 241, 248-251
Mauroy, Pierre, 106
Maurras, Charles, 98, 230
Maximov, Vladimir, 247
Mayakovsky, Vladimir, 165
Mayer, Hans, 55-67
Mazas, Miguel Sanchez, 19
Mazas, Rafael Sanchez, 19
McLuhan, Marshall, 132
Medvedev, Roy, 188, 333
Memmi, Albert, 135, 140
Mendès-France, Pierre, 105, 106, 109, 248
Menzel, Jiøi, 340
Mercieca, Paul, 258, 259
Merleau-Ponty, Maurice, 72, 74, 186, 269, 354
Meyerhold, Vsevolod, 59
Michelangelo (Buonarroti), 329
Michnik, Adam, 343-344
Midgely, John, 26
Miguela, Ramon, 17
Miller, Henry, 167
Milosz, Czeslaw, 252-254, 283, 336, 342
Milosz, Oskar de, 254
Minder, Robert 187
Mittenzweig, Ingrid, 282
Mitterrand, François, 105, 108, 154, 170, 216, 217, 243, 272

Mnaeko, Ladislav, 87
Moliére, Jean Baptiste Poquelin, 298
Mollet, Guy, 104, 105, 106-107, 108, 109
Molotov, Vyacheslav, xii,
Mommsen, Hans, 330
Monnet, Jean, 103, 109
Montale, Eugenio, 129, 131
Montanelli, Indro, 195, 324
Montesquieu, Charles Louis de Secondal, 351
Montherlant, Henry de, 239
Moody, Dwight, 198
Morand, Paul, 98
Moravia, Alberto, xii,131, 174, 175, 252, 253, 260-261
More, Thomas, 313
Moretti, Mario 308
Moro, Aldo, 224, 260, 307-309
Moutet, Marius, 105
Mrozek, Slawomir, 64
Muller, Heirich, 37, 41
Musil, Robert, 327
Musset, Alfred de, 94
Mussolini, Benito, 119-125, 157-161, 250, 299, 324

Nadeau, Maurice, 115, 117, 171
Nagy, Imre, 3, 202
Naipaul, V.S., 252, 253
Najder, Zdzislaw, 343
Napoleon I, 99
Negri, Antonio, 224
Neizvestny, Ernst, 187
Nekrassov, Viktor, 67
Neruda, Pablo, 22
Nestroy, Johann Nepomuk, 298
Neuenfels, Hans, 320
Nicholas II, 191
Nichols, Peter, 213
Nichols, William, 203
Nivat, George, 246
Nixon, Richard M., 191, 237
Nizan, Paul, 240
Nolte, Ernst, 158
Novak, Jan, 342
Novotny, 84, 85

Ortega y Gasset, José, 16, 17, 22-23
Orwell, George, xiii, 238, 298, 329, 333

Packard, Vance, 257
Pagnol, Marcel, 95

Palezzeschi, Aldo, 131
Panova, Vera, 67
Papandreou, George, 288
Parain, Brice, 218
Parise, Goffredo, 132
Pasolini, Pier Paolo, 131, 173-177, 260
Pasternak, Boris, 71, 193, 254, 283
Paulhan, Jean, 96, 100, 167, 241
Pauvert, Jean, 52
Pavlowitch, Paul, 279
Paz, Octavio, 312
Perse, St.-John, 96
Pétain, Henri Philippe, 266, 299
Petto, Guido, 223
Peyrefitte, Alain, 209-210
Peyrefitte, Roger, 251
Philip, André, 106
Picasso, Pablo, 165
Piccoli, Michel, 167
Pilnyak, Boris, 59
Piperno, Franco, 224
Pipes, Richard, 247
Pisar, Samuel, 255
Piscator, Erwin, 44
Pius XII, 44-48
Pivot, Bernard, 279
Planchon, Roger, 302
Pompidou, Georges, 104
Primo de Rivera, Jose Antonio, 24
Proust, Marcel, 248, 292-293, 294
Przybyszewkaj, Stanislawa, 302

Rabelais, François, 298
Raddatz, Fritz J., 335
Ramadier, Paul, 107
Rasch, Yitzhak, 43
Rathenow, Lutz, 262, 263
Réage, Pauline, 167
Reich-Ranicki, Marcel, 327
Renan, Ernest, 17, 230
Renault, Louis, 240
Renger, Anne-Marie, 288
Resnais, Alain, 53
Reuter, Ernst, 288, 289
Revai, Josef, 60
Revel, Jean-François, 116, 242
Rezzori, Gregor von, 276
Ribiero, Darsy, 314
Richelieu, Armand Jean du Plessis, 94, 97-98
Richter, Helmut, 55
Rickert, Heinrich, 351

Riefenstahl, Leni, 241
Riesman, David, 256
Rimbaud, Arthur, 93, 97, 249
Robespierre, Maximilian, 303
Robrieux, Philippe, 162, 163
Rocard, Michel, 288, 344
Roland, Francis, 73
Romeo, Rosario, 159, 213
Ronchey, Alberto, 301
Roos, Peter, 233
Roosevelt, Franklin D., 190
Rostand, Edmond, 95, 102
Rostand, Jean, 95, 97
Roth, Joseph, 327
Rousseau, Jean-Jacques, 137
Rousset, David, 72
Rózewicz, Tadeusz, 64
Russell, Bertrand, 8
Rychner, Max, xi

Sabato, Ernesto, 314
Sadat, Anwar, 255
Sade, Marquis de, 168, 173, 176
Sagan, Françoise, 268
Sainte-Beuve, Charles Augustin, 293
Sakharov, Andrei, 188, 333
Sand, George, 295
Sangnier, Marc, 249
Sanguinetti, Edoardo, 131
Sarraute, Nathalie, 73, 117, 204-205, 292
Sartre, Jean-Paul, ix, xiii, 7, 51, 56, 68, 69, 70, 71, 72, 73, 74, 75, 76, 113-118, 134, 136, 141-143, 144, 165, 186, 205, 212, 248, 249, 250, 265, 267-270, 285-287, 322, 337, 350, 351, 352, 353, 354
Savary, Alain, 106, 107
Schaff, Adam, 319-320
Schmidt, Helmut, 281, 288, 289, 291, 311
Schmitt, Carl, 345-348
Schumacher, Kurt, 288
Schuman, Robert, 27, 109
Schumann, Maurice, 278
Schumpeter, Joseph, 298
Schwan, Alexander, 186
Sciascia, Leonardo, 131, 253, 261, 307
Seberg, Jean, 275
Seghers, Anna, 66
Senghor, Leopold, 135
Servan-Schreiber, Jacques, 250, 255-257
Servatius, 36

Settembrini, Domenico, 180
Shattuck, Roger, 117
Shils, Edward, 350
Shonfield, Andrew, 288
Sieburg, Friedrich, 101, 346
Sieyes, Abbé, 265
Sik, Ota, 89
Silone, Ignazio, x, 131, 153, 181, 195, 299, 326
Simmel, Georg, 351
Simon, Claude, 170
Singer, Isaac, Bashevis, 253
Sinyavsky, Andrei, 168-170, 180, 196, 333
Siroky, Vilem, 84, 85
Skvorecky, Joseph, 339
Smith, Denis Mack, 299
Snow, C.P., 202
Soboul, Albert, 302
Solzhenitsyn, Alexander, 144, 181-182, 188, 193, 245, 246, 247, 254, 283, 333
Sorel, Georges, 136, 137
Souvarine, Boris, 162, 212-213
Spaak, Paul Henri, 29
Spender, Stephen, xi, xiii
Spengler, Oswald, 330, 346
Sperber, Manès, 72, 326-328
Spitzer, Juraj, 86
Stalin, Joseph, 59, 65, 78, 80, 81, 165, 298, 353
Starkie, Enid, 117
Steevek, Pavol, 86
Stein, Peter, 319, 322
Steiner, George, 345, 348
Stendhal, 93
Strehler, Giorgio, 130, 132
Sunday, Billy, 198
Surkov, Alexei, 72
Svitak, Ivan, 91
Swift, Jonathan, 124

Taine, Hippolyte, 230
Taylor, A.J.P., 337
Thody, Philip, 322
Thorez, Maurice, 107, 162-164, 212, 216, 219, 221, 243
Tillion, Germaine, 70-71, 77
Tiso, Msgr., 81, 83, 87
Tito (Joseph Broz), 18, 228, 336
Tocqueville, Alexis de, 199
Todd, Olivier, 268

Toffler, Alvin, 257
Togliatti, Palmiro, 130, 160, 188, 271, 337
Tournier, Michel, 279
Trabochinni, Bruno, 207-208
Trilling, Lionel, 203
Triolet, Elsa, 165
Trotsky, Leon, 162, 303
Tumarkin, Nina, 332

Ulbricht, Walter, 192
Urban, George, 271
Ustinov, Peter, 278

Vaillant, Roger, 50, 51
Valéry, Paul, 96-97
Valiani, Leo, 159, 160
Valladares, Armando, 314
Van Veld, Bram, 144
Vargas Llosa, Mario, 313
Veres, Peter, 3, 202
Verlaine, Paul, 93
Vermeersch, Jeanette, 162

Vesce, Emilio, 223
Vittorini, Elio, 130, 337
Voltaire, 94
Voznesensky, Andrei, 220

Wajda, Andrzej, 302-304
Weber, Max, 351
Wehner, Herbert, 288
Weightman, J.G., 251
Welles, Orson, 58
Wilhelm II, 317
Wilson, Woodrow, x
Witte, Sergei, 246
Wols, 269
Wright, Richard, 74, 136

Yates, Frances, 95, 102

Zinoviev, Alexander, 246
Zola, Èmile, 93, 293
Zolberg, Aristide, 140
Zophiralos, Henri, 167
Zucarro de Viscarra, 17
Zweig, Arnold, 62